*Number Eight: The Centennial Series of
the Association of Former Students
Texas A&M University*

Marvin Jones
The Public Life of an Agrarian Advocate

Marvin Jones, 1943

Marvin Jones

The Public Life of an Agrarian Advocate

By Irvin M. May, Jr.

Texas A&M University Press
COLLEGE STATION AND LONDON

Copyright © 1980 by Irvin M. May, Jr.
All rights reserved

Library of Congress Cataloging in Publication Data

May, Irvin M   1939–
  Marvin Jones, the public life of an agrarian advocate.

  (The centennial series of the Association of Former Students, Texas A & M)
    Bibliography: p.
    Includes index.
    1. Jones, Marvin, 1886–   2. Agriculture and state—United States—Biography.   3. Legislators—United States—Biography.   4. United States. Congress. House—Biography.
  5. Judges—United States—Biography.   I. Title.
II. Series: Texas. A&M University, College Station. Association of Former Students, Centennial series of the Association of Former Students, Texas A&M University; no. 8.
E748.J765M38   973.9'092'4   [B]   79–5282
ISBN 0-89096-093-3 (cloth)   ISBN 1-58544-029-9 (pbk.)

Manufactured in the United States of America
FIRST PAPERBACK EDITION

For Suzanne, Emily, and Mary,
whose love and patience
renewed my strength

Contents

Preface		xiii
CHAPTER		
1.	Origins of an Agrarian Advocate	3
2.	The Panhandle Kid	18
3.	The Formative Years, 1916–1920	29
4.	The Harding Years	46
5.	The Crusade for the Export-Debenture Plan	58
6.	The First Crisis of Jones's Leadership	79
7.	The Hundred Days	98
8.	The Expansion of the AAA	111
9.	Building the New "Farm House"	126
10.	The Climactic Year in Congress	151
11.	Congressional Sunset	171
12.	Transition Time	189
13.	The War Food Administrator	208
14.	Chief Judge, United States Court of Claims	227
15.	Property, Contracts, and Courthouse	243
16.	Bid Me Good Morning	255
Bibliography		263
Index		283

Illustrations

Marvin Jones, 1943 — *Frontispiece*
The Jones brothers, 1907 — *Following page 144*
Jones in 1916
National Grange broadcast, 1927
Jones in the 1920's
Jones and President-elect Franklin D. Roosevelt, 1933
Roosevelt and Nueces County, Texas, cotton grower
Jones family picture, 1936
Roosevelt and Texas political leaders in Amarillo, 1938
Jones taking the oath of office as war food administrator, 1943
Jones and James F. Byrnes, 1943
Delegates to International Food Conference, 1943
Jones on the cover of *United States News*, 1943
Jones on a fishing trip, 1957
Judge Jones at his desk in the Court of Claims Building, 1949
Judge Jones, 1959
United States Court of Claims, about 1961

MAPS

1. Texas Congressional Districts in 1916 — *Page 25*
2. The Texas Thirteenth Congressional District in 1916 — *Page 26*

Preface

THESE were Marvin Jones's favorite passages of Scripture:

My son, forget not my law; but let thine heart keep my commandments:
For length of days, and long life, and peace, shall they add to thee.
Let not mercy and truth forsake thee; bind them about thy neck; write them upon the table of thine heart:
So shalt thou find favour and good understanding in the sight of God and man.
Trust in the Lord with all thine heart; and lean not unto thine own understanding.

So shall thy barns be filled with plenty, and thy presses shall burst out with new wine.

Proverbs 3:1–5, 10

Marvin Jones was known as a pleasant companion, a hard-working, complex, talented, gentle man. He prized his privacy, enjoyed taking long drives out of the city to get the soot out of his nostrils, but did not own or drive a car. Marvin Jones was punctual, witty, fastidious; was not much of a drinker but was right at home in a crowd with wine or whiskey; had few material interests and was frugal with his own—and, happily, also with the money interests of that forgotten wretch the taxpayer. If he liked you as a colleague, you had almost unlimited responsibility in some areas, for Jones hated to make painful administrative decisions. Often he based decisions on personalities rather than facts.

Jones was also a talented lawyer, a lover of power, a skilled legislator, a Sunday-school teacher who frequently joined other deeply committed Christians in breakfast devotionals. He was a political moderate who identified with "Mr. Average American," but he could not eat apple pie.

Prepared with his consent, this book is the first full-length biography of the gentle Texan. Despite brief glimpses of his career from his own works (*How War Food Saved American Lives, Should Uncle Sam Pay—When and Why?* and, with Joseph M. Ray, *Marvin Jones Memoirs*), Jones remained mostly a quiet power in his work in the legislative, executive, and judicial branches of government. As far as possible, I have respected Jones's request that this book focus on his public career and omit personal details. This emphasis, and Jones's desire for offstage privacy, is indicated by the title.

One muggy morning, Marvin Jones and I were together in the Court of Claims Building in Washington, D.C. He rose from his desk and motioned me to join him at a window. He asked, "What do you see?"

"I see the White House, which represents the executive branch of government," I responded, in an admittedly stiff manner.

"Yes, the White House and Congress and government agencies mean much to me," Jones mused. "Do you see more?"

"On the streets I see people—obviously from all walks of life."

"People are very important. But what else?" Marvin Jones asked the question in the tone of a patient teacher.

Remembering his religious beliefs and his arrival in Washington during World War I, I replied, "In the distance there is the cathedral where Wilson sleeps."

Judge Jones took some time to reminisce about his boyhood in the Methodist church. Then he repeated the question: "What do you see?"

Frustrated by my futile attempts to reach the special response that the judge desired, I blurted, "I see the trees."

Jones spoke then in a tone that revealed that this was what he really wanted to hear: the trees—*the land*. He told me of his love for the land from his boyhood to that moment. The window through which we gazed had become spotted with life-giving raindrops.

Then I realized the reason for Marvin Jones's questioning; I had begun my journey into an understanding of the man. A paraphrase from the Scriptures often quoted by Jones explained his questions: "Look not on a man's countenance or on the height of his stature or on his outward appearance; look at his heart" (see 1 Samuel 16:7). By asking me what I saw through the window, Jones had looked at my heart, and I, having heard him reminisce about his love for the land, had seen into his.

This book could never have been written without the aid of many persons, but I am especially indebted to Marvin Jones himself, who opened doors to research materials and answered many questions in personal interviews and by telephone. I also enjoyed the cooperation of Jones's staff, headed by Elaine Heffley.

Inspiration and support came from Dean H. O. Kunkel, College of Agriculture, Texas A&M University; and from Dr. Jarvis Miller, then director of the Texas Agricultural Experiment Station. My appreciation goes also to Dean W. David Maxwell, College of Liberal Arts, Texas A&M; and to Dr. William Tedrick, Head, Department of Agricultural Communications, Texas A&M. Special thanks go to Elaine Burger for editing and to Elizabeth Hoffman for proofreading. The following scholars read all or parts of the manuscript: W. Eugene Hollon, J. Milton Nance, Gladys Baker, Kenneth Hendrickson, Jerome Barron, Mrs. Dorothy Gooch, and Lionel Patenaude.

I am grateful for good typists, especially for Bobbie George, who first patiently translated my handwriting, and for Christine Archer, June McLaren, Ellen Kotrla, and Denise Bailey. My thanks go to the staffs of various libraries for research assistance: Alabama State Department of Archives and History (especially Miriam Jones and Virginia Jones); Mary E. Bivens Library, Amarillo, Texas; Clemson University Library (Priscilla Sutcliffe); Library of Congress, Manuscripts Division; University of Colorado Library; Texas Tech University Library; Texas A&M University Library (John B. Smith and H. C. Yu); University of Missouri Library; Nita Stewart Haley Memorial Library (J. Evetts Haley); and the presidential libraries of Herbert Hoover, Lyndon B. Johnson, and Franklin D. Roosevelt. The aid of the United States Department of Agriculture, Agricultural History Branch, will never be forgotten; staff members Wayne Rasmussen, Gladys Baker, Vivian Wiser, and James S. Ward made special information available. At the National Archives, Helen Ulibarri and Charles Neale provided help. Other assistance came from the staff of the United States Court of Claims. Those who took time from busy days for interviews included Frank Jones, Hub Jones, Judge Wilson Cowen, and Mrs. Altravene Clark Spann.

College Station, Texas   Irvin M. May, Jr.

Marvin Jones
The Public Life of an Agrarian Advocate

1.

Origins of an Agrarian Advocate

As you know, the primary sources of food are the earth, the sea, and the sky.... But most of us spend the greater part of our lives upon the land.[1]

Wealth comes from the land; when our flesh is separated from our bones, we will go back to the soil.[2]

                 Marvin Jones

For nearly three centuries pioneer American farmers moved westward in search of land, the symbol of opportunity and economic advancement. Some hardy people prospered, but the soil yielded its blessings slowly. Most farmers endured hardships in their daily struggle for mere existence, and they depended upon cooperation from their neighbors as much as upon their own individual initiative. Crop failures, the absence of an adequate market, and a myriad of personal and technical problems forced rural Americans to reevaluate their goals constantly. Those who chose to continue to devote their lives and labors to the cultivation of the soil faced the unpleasant alternatives of remaining where they were or moving elsewhere in search of better lands. Others simply quit, abandoned their earlier dreams, and moved into newly founded cities and towns.

Most of the people who left farms never returned. But though they became skilled in other work, they retained their cultural heritage and their former ties with the land.

This describes the development of Marvin Jones, whose early

---

[1] Marvin Jones to Dr. H. O. Kunkel, May 1, 1972, Marvin Jones Papers (hereafter cited as MJP), Texas A&M Archives, College Station, Texas. Unless otherwise noted, all interviews and correspondence citing Jones refer to Marvin Jones.

[2] Jones, interview with author, March 22, 1971.

economic and spiritual communion with the soil profoundly influenced his long career as a congressman from Texas, war food administrator, and federal judge.

Jones came from Protestant, Scotch-Irish ancestors who sailed across the Atlantic Ocean to the New World. In the late 1600's the family of a paternal ancestor, William Hege, arrived at Perth Amboy, New Jersey, migrated southwestward into Delaware, then on to the Cumberland Valley of Pennsylvania, and to Opequon Creek, about three miles south of present Winchester, Virginia. There the Heges built a log cabin with clapboard siding. From daylight to dark they farmed their land until its fertility had nearly vanished.

Faced with a foreboding future, the Heges awaited an opportunity to continue their trek. The American Revolution interrupted westward migration; William's grandson, James Hege, Jr., left to serve with the Pennsylvania militia. Immediately after the war, however, the quest for better land resumed. James and his family loaded their possessions on wagons pulled by oxen and followed trails down the southern slope of the Blue Ridge Mountains into Pulaski and Wythe counties of eastern Tennessee. There James Hege, Jr., participated in the land boom of the 1820's. There, too, his great-granddaughter, Martha Eliza King, eventually married Robert Degge Jones.[3]

Robert Jones had spent his boyhood in Middleburg, Virginia, before succumbing to the lure of land in Tennessee. To supplement his income from small crops of tobacco, corn, wheat, cotton, fruits, and vegetables, he operated saddle shops in several eastern Tennessee towns: Athens, Riceville, and McMinnville. The region contained some of the nation's most beautiful scenery, but its soil soon wore thin when farmed. In time the desire for new land sent Robert to

[3] Charles A. Hanna, *The Scotch-Irish or the Scot in North Britain, North Ireland, and North America*, 2:44–48; *The Jones Family: Texas Pioneers*, p. 4; A. C. Chandler and A. B. Thames, *Colonial Virginia*, pp. 303–304; L. C. Gray, *A History of Agriculture in the Southern United States to 1860*, 1:21; Freeman H. Hart, *The Valley of Virginia in the American Revolution, 1763–1789*, pp. 5–7; Stanley J. Folmsbee, Robert E. Corlew, and Enoch L. Mitchell, *Tennessee: A Short History*, pp. 158–161; Thomas P. Abernathy, *From Frontier to Plantation in Tennessee: A Study in Frontier Democracy*, pp. 257–261; Ray Allen Billington, *Westward Expansion: A History of the American Frontier*, 2d ed., pp. 318–320; Thomas P. Abernathy, *The Formative Period in Alabama, 1815–1828*, 2d ed., pp. 34–43.

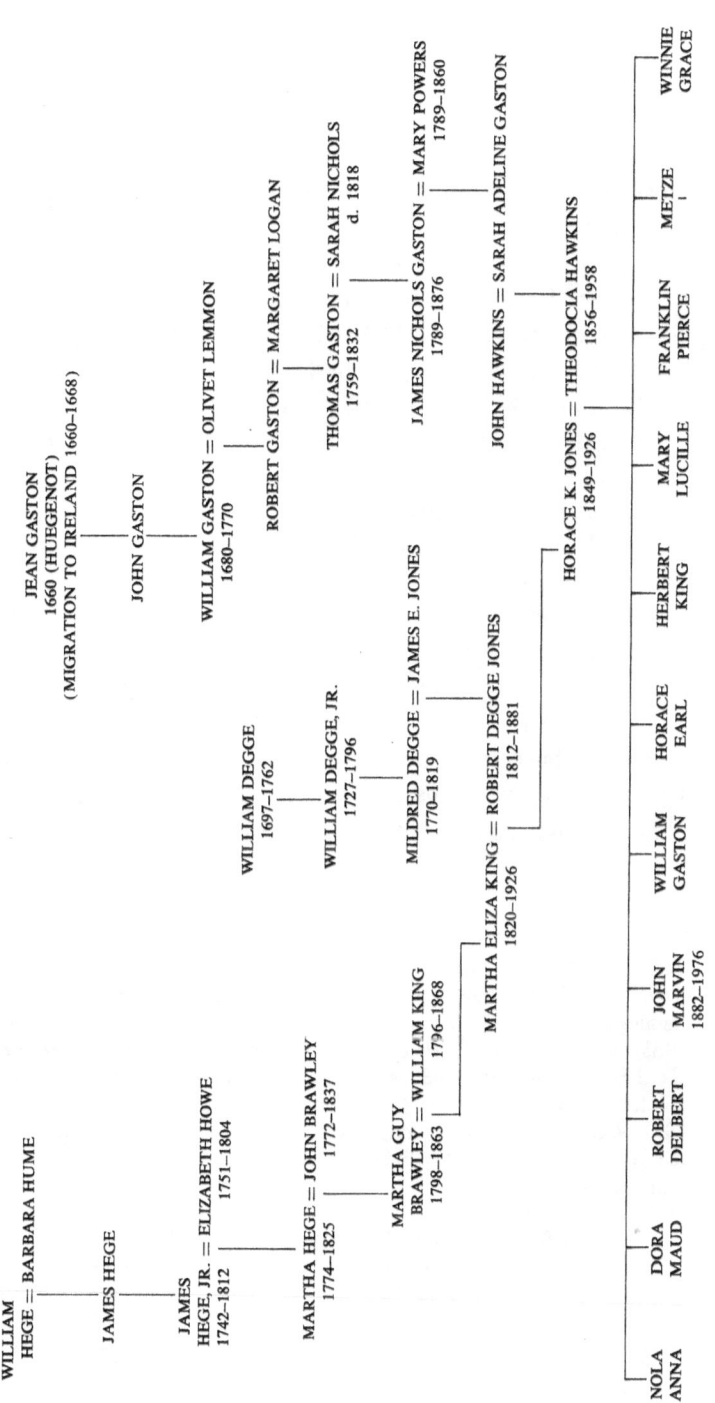

Texas. Four years after the birth of Horace, the father-to-be of Marvin Jones, the family packed its meager belongings in a covered wagon and followed a well-marked trail through Arkansas to the cross-timbers region in Cooke County, Texas, where they settled in 1853.[4]

Marvin Jones's maternal ancestors included the Gastons, who left France for Ireland and after a century or so there flung off all shackles of the Old World for land and greater religious freedom across the sea. After a nightmarish Atlantic journey they reached the Carolinas, but they found the seacoast towns there uninviting. They pressed to the Carolina frontier by way of the Great Valley Road. There the Gastons fulfilled dreams and prospered as farmers, wagonmakers, and businessmen, furnishing food and supplies to Colonel Henry Hampton's Light Dragoons and to the South Carolina militia during the American Revolution.

James and Mary Gaston, great-grandparents of Marvin Jones, were devout Presbyterians with a strong interest in education. They donated land to Reidville Male and Female colleges. They also gave a daughter to the westward movement. In 1848, Sarah Gaston married John Hawkins, who soon sought his own destiny. He moved his young family to Athens, Tennessee, where a daughter, Theodocia Hawkins, mother-to-be of Marvin Jones, was born July 6, 1856.[5]

---

[4] Marvin Jones, *Marvin Jones Memoirs*, ed. Joseph M. Ray, p. 5; Abernathy, *From Frontier to Plantation in Tennessee*, pp. 329–330; 341–343; Folmsbee, Corlew, and Mitchell, *Tennessee*, p. 293; Tommy W. Rogers, "Origin and Destination of Tennessee Migrants, 1850–1860," *Tennessee Historical Quarterly* 27 (Summer 1968):118–122; Thomas A. Scott, "The Impact of Tennessee's Migrating Sons," *Tennessee Historical Quarterly* 27 (Summer 1968):123–141; Buckley B. Paddock, ed., *History of Texas: Fort Worth and the Texas Northwest*, 4:484–485; *The Jones Family*, p. 6. Later four other children would be born in Texas; Jones, interview with author, October 15, 1971. Lathrop noted three migration patterns and concluded that nearly all the Texas settlers from Tennessee followed the middle road. Barnes F. Lathrop, *Migration into East Texas, 1835–1860: A Study from the United States Census*, pp. 50–51.

[5] Louis B. Wright, *The Cultural Life of the American Colonies, 1607–1763*, pp. 65–71; Robert L. Meriwether, *The Expansion of South Carolina, 1729–1765*, pp. 144–146; L. C. Gray, *History of Agriculture in the Southern United States to 1860*, 2:684–686; Jones, interview with author, October 15, 1971; Rubert Norval Richardson, *The Frontier of Northwest Texas, 1846–1876: Advance and Defense by the Pioneer Settlers of the Cross Timbers*, pp. 115–118. William Gaston was the grandfather of William Gaston (1778–

Not long afterward John Hawkins moved his family again: to the edge of the Texas frontier, along the Red River valley. They crammed bare essentials—clothing, food, and farm tools—into wagons and traveled by way of Fort Smith, Arkansas, across the southeastern corner of the Indian Territory, through Boggy Depot to Preston Bend, Texas, north of Sherman. The trip was a hard one. For many days they rode in the lonely wagons, peppered alternately by blowing dust and piercing rain. At night exhausted children fell asleep around campfires while curled up on blankets or beds of straw. Small wonder that many children of the uprooted grew up with a craving for land and for security and to be *somebody*.

The Hawkins and the Jones families moved many more times before settling in a community known as Custer City, ten miles northeast of Gainesville, which the *Clarksville Standard* described as being "in its virgin prime, an uncultivated agricultural Eden."[6] Robert Jones's farming could not support his growing family, however, and he supplemented his meager income with profits from a cotton gin and a corn mill. After the gin burned, he tried to recoup by moving to Duck Creek (present Garland), in Dallas County.

When the Civil War commenced, many young men left their families to fight. Robert Jones supported Lincoln and the Union, but his now-teenage son, Horace, joined three uncles who were wearing Confederate gray. When Horace Jones returned in defeat, he learned that his father's health had broken and that he himself would be expected to shoulder the family's burdens.[7]

1844), a Federalist who would serve in the United States and North Carolina congresses and on the North Carolina Supreme Court. Robert Gaston was an uncle of this North Carolina jurist. Mary Gaston Gee, *The Ancestry and Descendants of Anzi Williford Gaston II of Spartenburg County, South Carolina*, pp. 7–21.

[6] *Clarksville* (Texas) *Standard*, May 17, 1856; Jones, interview with author, October 15, 1971; Buckley B. Paddock (*History of Texas: Fort Worth and the Texas Northwest*, 4:485) notes that Hawkins went to Cooke County in 1869.

[7] Jones, interview with author, October 15, 1971; *The Jones Family*, pp. 21–22. See also Marvin Jones, "Manuscript Autobiography" (1970), MJP (five manuscripts); this is the manuscript version of *Marvin Jones Memoirs* before editing by J. M. Ray. When material appears in both sources, the published version is cited. The two sources are not identical, however, and the manuscript contains more material.

In 1875, Horace married Theodocia Hawkins. For the next six years they lived in Dallas County, striving to eke out an existence and at the same time trying to care for others in the family. Robert Jones's death in 1881 allowed Horace to move on. He acquired a 325-acre farm in Cooke County, near Valley View. The family grew to ten children. The fourth child, John Marvin Jones, arrived February 26, 1882.[8]

Like most other farmers of the rich Red River valley, Horace Jones raised wheat and cotton as cash crops. He grew varieties of corn, milo maize, sorghum cane, potatoes, cantaloupes, and peanuts for home consumption and for livestock feed. The family orchard supplied mouth-watering peaches, plums, grapes, and pecans. Stray cattle and hogs that roamed the unfenced prairies were branded and marked.

No sooner had Horace Jones harvested the wheat than came cotton-planting time. In a seemingly endless cycle the seasons passed. Work continued without slack from sunrise to sunset, even on rainy days, when odd jobs like equipment maintenance were completed. Horace Jones gave careful attention to his machinery—especially to his prized McCormick binder.

On the first Monday of every month farmers from the surrounding countryside traveled to Gainesville, the county seat of Cooke County, for Trades Day. Traveling circuses, civic affairs, and politicians drew crowds. Farmers talked with friends and swapped livestock, farm machinery, or produce. Many years later Horace Jones's son Marvin would remember those days for awakening in him an interest in the study of law and politics.

Marvin and his older brother, Delbert, looked forward to riding to Gainesville on the wagon seat with their father. In town Horace

---

[8] Mrs. Addie Martin, ed., *Valley View Centennial, 1872–1972*, p. 24; *The Jones Family*, pp. 21–22; Herbert King Jones and Franklin Pierce Jones, interview with author, May 24–25, 1973. There is controversy over the date of Marvin's birth. Birth records for Cooke County during this period are incomplete. If one accepts 1886 as his birth year and follows the traditional account of his life as revealed in the *Marvin Jones Memoirs*, p. 1–13, one must conclude that Marvin taught school for a year at Valley View during the same year he was attending Southwestern University in Georgetown. I accept the view of Jones's brothers Herbert K. and Franklin P. Jones that he was born on February 26, 1882.

Jones would drop the boys off at the courthouse. There in a county courtroom Marvin and Delbert would listen to the lawyers presenting their cases. During recesses the boys would walk into the crowded streets and markets. Their few pennies went for fruit or other edibles. Then they would stroll along looking for excitement.

The boys sometimes heard in the marketplace the fiery stump speeches of Gainesville's leading politician, Representative Joseph Weldon Bailey, during the congressman's infrequent visits home. Marvin and Delbert would sit, spellbound, on planks set across beer kegs and listen to the great orator. Often, after their father had picked them up, they would all go to Bailey's hotel room, where the adults would discuss political strategy. Marvin and Delbert Jones grew up with their father's love for Democratic politics and romantic oratory.[9]

After all that excitement Marvin could hardly wait to return home and there stand in front of his younger brothers and sisters and mimic with flashing eyes and waving hands Bailey's latest harangue. Marvin also practiced oratory and debate before his brothers and sisters, and sometimes, after his audience had fled, he conducted imaginary trials before a fence post. Often he and a friend, Fletcher Isbell, rode horseback to a night-emptied schoolhouse to practice their oratory. Marvin's brother Herbert later recalled, "I have never heard such words from such feeble lips before or since."[10]

Although the male head of this household, Horace Jones, possessed only three months of formal education, he read widely, regularly attended political conventions in the area, and actively participated in the Masons. He had little patience with dishonest people. Because of his reputation for integrity he was called on to settle many disputes in his community, Valley View. He taught his sons that the individual was important above any political mood of the time and that it was more important to do a good job and have self-respect than to seek fame.

His favorite newspaper, the *Dallas News*, conflicted occasionally with his politics, so he supplemented it with the *St. Louis Republic*. By the dim light of coal-oil lamps the elder Jones remained a student

---

[9] Jones, interview with author, June 5, 1973; Herbert King and Franklin Pierce Jones, interview with author, May 24, 1973.
[10] Ibid.

at heart during his entire life.[11] By his example he served as a model for Marvin's desire for an excellent education and for a political career.

Horace Jones also taught his son political specifics. With money tight during the depression-ridden years of the late nineteenth century, farmers went hat in hand to borrow. Walking closely behind his father, Marvin would enter a bank, peer at the teller's barred windows, observe money changing hands, and note the well-protected vault. Bankers charged interest rates of 10 percent on a sixty-to-ninety-day maximum term, even when crops could not be harvested for another six months.[12] Horace Jones explained to his son that "the financial structure of this country is geared to the needs of industry and business, and it is kept in what they call 'liquid condition'." The elder Jones said that farmers and ranchers needed a separate credit structure from that of other enterprises, since they had money coming in only once or twice a year instead of each month.[13] Marvin never forgot his father's logic.

The Joneses were devout Methodists. They worshiped by singing robust hymns and then by listening to hell-fire-and-brimstone sermons. Horace Jones insisted that his family participate in all church services. He served for more than forty years on the board of stewards of the local church and taught Sunday school.[14]

Theodocia (or "Docia") Jones shared her husband's religious convictions. Docia believed that people would be rewarded in heaven. She impressed on Marvin her conviction that one's prayers should be for spiritual growth rather than for earthly financial success. She also sought to make religion pleasant. Frequently the family would gather around the organ, which Horace played, and Docia would sing, in a clear soprano voice, old-fashioned hymns concerning spiritual progress.

> *We* are *climbing* Jacob's ladder, soldiers of the cross
> Every round goes higher, higher,
> *Sinner,* do *you* love my Jesus?

[11] Ibid.
[12] Jones, interview with author, October 15, 1971.
[13] Jones, *Marvin Jones Memoirs*, p. 5.
[14] Herbert King Jones and Franklin Pierce Jones, interview with author, May 24, 1973; Martin, *Valley View Centennial, 1872–1972*, p. 30.

> If you *love* Him, why not *serve* Him?
> Rise, shine and *give* God glory.[15]

Horace and Docia Jones continually reminded their children that as Christians and obedient servants of the Lord they were, nevertheless, also earthly sinners. As people progressed toward sanctification, they said, the Lord would gradually command of them more mature and difficult allegiance. Thus the ideas of love, service, duty, mission, and recognition of Christ came to have a very real meaning to Marvin Jones.[16]

Some frontier folk seemed to practice Christianity as well as preach it. They placed an uncommon degree of trust in their fellowmen. For example, Valley View residents seldom locked their homes. Passing strangers, therefore, were free to enter when the owners were gone and cook a meal. But these uninvited guests were expected to clean up afterward and to leave a thank-you note. Whenever visitors failed to abide by frontier customs, Docia Jones fearfully refused to let her children eat any leftovers.[17]

Usually Docia was up before dawn to supervise the preparation of breakfast. While the men fed the livestock, the smell of hot coffee would begin to cut the crisp morning air. Soon Horace and his sons would sit down to a breakfast of golden biscuits, gravy, fried potatoes, bacon, eggs, butter, and ribbon-cane syrup. Before anyone ate, however, Horace or Docia would lead the family in thanks for the Lord's help.

Dinner usually consisted of vegetables from the garden and a variety of desserts, like peach and blackberry cobblers. Sunday dinners included meat, a rare delicacy. Docia often served salt or smoked pork, especially in warm weather, since chickens were not

---

[15] Ibid; Jones, interview with author, October 15, 1971. Most versions contained five stanzas, which were usually sung in a slow semichant reflecting the dedication and the sincerity of the singer. The song began with the words: "Every round goes higher, higher, Sinner, do you love my Jesus? If you love him why not serve him? Rise, Shine, and Give God Glory," followed by "Soldier of the Cross." "He Lives, He Lives," p. 24.

[16] Jones, *Marvin Jones Memoirs*, p. 2. Unfortunately, the better account is found in Jones, "Manuscript Autobiography," pp. 6–8, MJP.

[17] Franklin Pierce Jones and Herbert King Jones, interview with author, May 24, 1973; see also Edward Everett Dale, *The Cross Timbers: Memories of a North Texas Boyhood*, pp. 35–47.

abundant and refrigeration was inadequate for fresh beef. Marvin's older sisters, Nola and Dora, helped with the cooking, washed clothes on old scrubboards, made beds, quilted, and tended to the younger children, particularly during their mother's many pregnancies. The boys helped their sisters by cutting firewood for the old oven and tending the garden.[18]

The land influenced young Marvin profoundly. Cooke County would remain with him in countless ways. The Jones farm lay in a mostly treeless region of Great Plains environment. Despite the nearness of timber on the east, Marvin Jones faced west.[19]

Despite the rigors of farm life Marvin found time to be a boy. He smoked cornsilk in a corncob pipe and discovered the bitter taste of grapevine cigarettes. He drank water from cisterns, pools, and creeks and raw milk fresh from a cow. Shedding his wrinkled clothes, he plunged into stock tanks. At other times he dug worms and wet his hook in hopes of catching a sun perch or a bass. He took pride in his shooting, and he killed rabbits, quail, doves, foxes, squirrels, opossums, and deer.[20]

Marvin loved the solitude and the dazzling beauty of the prairies, which awakened each spring to produce an array of daisies, verbenas, bluebonnets, and sweet Williams. "It was a land to love, but you had to understand its moods," the southwestern historian Rupert Richardson once observed. "There were hazards in this country too. . . . Sometimes, crops started out with promise, the rains did not sustain them."[21] When the hot winds blew, wheat, oats, and corn shriveled. Unpredictable "chances of destructive hail might not be greater than one in ten, but in a frontier region some people could ill afford odds of that measure."[22] Sometimes before a harvest insects or wild animals feasted on crops, leaving farmers very little. Droughts brought destruction to gardens and resulted in overgrazing of

---

[18] Ibid.

[19] See Walter Prescott Webb, *The Great Plains*, pp. 3–9; Jimmy Nichols, interview with author, August 11, 1973; Jones, *Marvin Jones Memoirs*, p. 1.

[20] Franklin Pierce Jones and Herbert King Jones, interview with author, May 24, 1973; Dale, *The Cross Timbers*, p. 5; James K. Greer, *Grand Prairie*, pp. 1–22.

[21] Richardson, *The Frontier of Northwest Texas*, p. 142.

[22] Ibid.

Origins of an Agrarian Advocate 13

parched pastures, and then the bony animals died when nature also sent dry, cold winters.

Marvin understood these moods of the land, and he vowed that he would never directly earn his livelihood from the stubborn and unpredictable soil.[23] He experienced a bittersweet reaction that manifested a desire to leave the land physically, to love it forever within his heart and mind, but never again to touch it with his hands.

Education seemed to hold the key to off-the-farm financial and personal success, and he began reading. Once, at the age of twelve, he read that "man came from the soil, would return to the land, and when the soil was wasted, the whole nation would decay." Later he forgot the book's author and title, but the words remained in his memory.[24]

His reading showed an early interest in human beings, not in subjects like science. He favored popular biographies and the prose of Charles Dickens, James Fenimore Cooper, Washington Irving, and Mark Twain. The works of Edgar Wilson ("Bill") Nye, a frontier humorist, sometimes provided chuckles, and occasionally Marvin read on the sly, about Dick Turpin or Frank Merriwell, although he and the other children were forbidden to waste time.[25]

Marvin acquired his fundamental reading skills at the Elm Grove School, about a mile from the Jones farm. The school had its problems. At Elm Grove there were not enough trees to make a box of matches. The tenure of teachers fluctuated widely, depending on the whims of school trustees. Family economics took precedence over formal education of children. The school year ranged from seven to nine months and was characterized by low attendance during bad weather and harvesting time and by classes of up to sixty-five noisy students at various educational levels all gathered in one room. The teacher relied heavily on textbooks. Students were ex-

---

[23] Jones to author, undated letter (March 1973), MJP; Jones, *Marvin Jones Memoirs*, pp. 2–3.

[24] Jones, *Marvin Jones Memoirs*, p. 3; Jones, "Manuscript Autobiography," pp. 16–18, MJP; Dean Albertson, interview with Jones, Columbia Oral History Project, 1952, pp. 33–34; hereafter cited as COHP-MJP. May used Jones's copy in typescript, which may or may not correspond to the final edited version.

[25] Ibid.

pected to copy and learn the exercises while the teacher went from group to group, giving as much individual attention as time and order permitted. Brisk whacks of a paddle were often administered for discipline. An exceptional teacher, Mary Carr, succeeded in inspiring many students, especially the slender Marvin Jones. Despite the irregular schooling the fundamentals of reading, writing, and arithmetic, plus some geography and history, penetrated his and other developing minds.[26]

After his education at Elm Grove was completed, Marvin Jones joined his brother Delbert in renting forty acres of blackland soil from John Davis in January 1897, and his nonfarm aspirations were sidetracked temporarily. For the next two years the brothers lived at home and tilled the leased land with their father's teams and equipment.

The work was hard. Wheat prices were low, and the cotton crop discouraged future efforts. The experience intensified Marvin's desire "to go back to the farm only when I couldn't make a living at anything else."[27]

Desperately searching for an escape, Marvin became attracted to teaching. He obtained a first-grade teaching certificate in 1899, with hopes of remaining at Elm Grove. The school administration, however, concluded that a lad of seventeen could never control his classes and rejected the application. Jones was deeply depressed for a time, but he determined to prove his leadership ability.

Again education seemed to be the answer. Delbert Jones moved west in search of it, enrolling in Clarendon College. Marvin went to Miami, Texas, fifteen miles northeast of Pampa, following a former Valley View teacher, W. S. Roberts, there. Marvin lived in a dugout behind the Miami House Hotel and attended school, worked as a handyman, milked cows, manicured the hotel garden, and greeted new arrivals at the railroad station for Mrs. Hall, the hotel proprietor.[28]

Work, study, and recreation provided a pleasant mixture. Mar-

---

[26] Jones, "Manuscript Autobiography," pp. 20–22. See M. L. Moody, "A Course of Study for Rural Schools," *Texas School Journal* 20 (September 1920):81–84.

[27] Jones to author, September 26, 1973; COHP-MJP, pp. 11–12.

[28] Jones to author, September 16, 1973.

Origins of an Agrarian Advocate

vin set aside time to play baseball for the Miami team. As a pitcher he threw a fast ball that was hard to hit, and he was sometimes a fancy fielder, at least for Miami. His club competed with teams from other towns, and Marvin made several lifelong friends who later helped him in politics—friends like Clayton Hearne and Richard and Charles Ware, from Amarillo.[29]

Near the end of his sojourn in Miami school trustees offered him a job at a meager salary, but Jones declined to remain another year.[30] He wanted a college degree, and the small salary proposed at Miami would not pay for one. Furthermore, he was homesick. The Panhandle had lost its charm. Marvin hoped for a chance to return to Cooke County, and when the Elm Grove trustees reversed their earlier decision and hired him, he left Miami.

Again he lived at the family residence—through the fall of 1902 and into the spring of 1903. In the classroom he insisted on stern respect, which seemed strange to his younger brothers. He believed that respect and formality encouraged learning. Furthermore, he feared that an unannounced visit by one of the trustees to a rowdy classroom would cost him his job. During recess, however, he joined in games with his students.[31]

When the school day ended, he would walk to a thirty-five-acre plot of land he had rented, along Spring Creek, about half a mile from Elm Grove. There several hands hired from among his older students would help him plant and harvest cotton. As a part-time farmer he earned the respect of a prominent Valley View rancher, Larry W. Lee, who arranged a loan so that Marvin could attend Southwestern University at Georgetown.[32] Delbert enrolled there, too.

After their arrival in Georgetown the brothers walked down gravel streets toward the school and soon found themselves at the rear of the campus. "We climbed through a fence and literally entered through the back," Marvin recalled later.[33]

[29] Jones, interview with David Murrah, August 1, 1972.
[30] State Certificate, June 5, 1902, 1909, obtained February 25, 1902, MJP.
[31] Herbert King Jones and Franklin Pierce Jones, interview with author, May 24 and 25, 1973.
[32] Jones, *Marvin Jones Memoirs*, 10.
[33] Ibid., p. 9.

For the next two years they dedicated themselves to acquiring an education as quickly as possible, but Marvin took time to engage in two notable extracurricular activities: debating and baseball. His batting prowess resulted in an offer to play professional baseball in the Southern League at a salary of $350 a month, and it tempted this poor country boy. When his father asked him if that was the kind of work he really wanted in life, however, he rejected the offer.

Before graduation he eliminated another possible vocation: the ministry. He felt that he was not good enough for that work. But he made a pact with his best friend at Southwestern, ministerial student Sam Black, that when death came the survivor would speak at the other's funeral. (Jones eventually eulogized Black).[34] When Marvin graduated in the class of 1905, the yearbook carried a remark that he was "a man so various that he seemed to be not one, but all mankind's epitome."[35]

During the summer following graduation Marvin roamed central and west Texas selling stereoscopes to pay off his college loan from Larry W. Lee. Later he said that from the selling work he learned more about people than he had learned in all of his university training.[36] Eventually he would put that knowledge to practical use in jury selection.

Vanderbilt University offered Marvin a scholarship for graduate study in English, but he chose instead to enroll, with Delbert, in the University of Texas School of Law. The differences between Southwestern and the University of Texas became immediately apparent. Gone were the days of cooperation and religious emphasis. Life at the University of Texas was strictly business. Marvin's years at Texas were difficult, lonely ones of personal conflict. The calculating spirit in which each student seemed to think primarily of himself disturbed him, but he determined to prove himself a good student, to excel in the art of conversation, and generally to master the system. He felt lonely, but he did cultivate a few close friends. Among them was a law student named Sam Rayburn.

[34] Ibid., pp. 10–11; Jones, "Manuscript Autobiography," pp. 13–14, MJP; Jones, COHP-MJP, pp. 42–44.
[35] *The Sou'Wester*, 2:38. The class motto was "We Are Owl Right."
[36] Jones "Manuscript Autobiography," p. 40, MJP; Jones, *Marvin Jones Memoirs*, p. 10.

Academic recognition and a sense of self-assurance came Marvin's way when he became a quizmaster and a recipient of the Ross-Rotan prize in oratory during his final year. With the honor went a monthly salary of fifty dollars. As quizmaster Jones taught classes in constitutional law and partnership. Dean Clarence Miller encouraged him to become a legal scholar, but Jones was eager to practice law on his own. He left law school after graduating in the spring of 1908.[37]

The foundation of his character had been set. Having lacked some self-confidence and a strong sense of worthiness, he had rejected the ministry and turned to law, but he had crystallized his religious beliefs after long hours of prayer. He had tempered his moralism with a quiet but intense competitive spirit borne of financial hardships. That had brought him greater self-reliance—and, perhaps as a side effect, a preference for the company of men. Throughout his life he would lack the ability to share his inner emotions with women. Although he would marry for a brief time, he never considered women as partners—only as friends or assistants. His life would be devoted entirely to politics and to the law. Defeats, when they came, would be painful despite his acquired self-reliance, but he would usually succeed in hiding his disappointments behind oratory and wit.

Marvin Jones thus emerged as a frugal, practical, and astute young man of considerable personal charm, which, tempered with modesty, enabled him to make friends easily. Abetting him was his physical appearance. He was a slender, boyish, brown-eyed man who grinned frequently.

The old interests he remembered from Valley View became his interests. In time, he would be known as an enthusiastic agrarian advocate.

---

[37] Jones "Manuscript Autobiography," pp. 44–52; Jones to Dr. Charles W. Ferguson, October 21, 1969, MJP; Jones, *Marvin Jones Memoirs*, pp. 11–13; Jones, interview with David Murrah, August 1, 1972.

2.

The Panhandle Kid

Marvin Jones pondered locations that would bring him an instantly successful legal practice. He wanted to settle in Wichita Falls, which seemed to be free from competition from well-established legal firms. On the other hand, his father urged him to go across the Red River to Oklahoma City, hub of the Sooner State boom. Finances prevented the move. Then an old family friend, Joseph Weldon Bailey, the congressman, offered to make available, rent free, his law offices and library in Gainesville. Jones declined, fearing that Gainesville had too many lawyers and that association with the controversial politician-lawyer might some day damage his own political aspirations.

Eventually Jones went on to Wichita Falls. There he learned that a former Cooke County resident, Leonidas C. Barrett, needed a young apprentice in his Amarillo law office. Jones seized the opportunity. Among the people he soon met in Amarillo were three friends from those days of baseball playing at Miami: Charles and Richard Ware, bankers now, and Clayton Hearne, an attorney.[1]

Jones rediscovered excitement in the Panhandle. It was a rapidly developing region because of the westward expansion of railroads and an accompanying flood of settlers. The Fort Worth and Denver City Railway, building toward Colorado, had brought with it the founding of a number of small towns along its route. Amarillo had been one, begun in 1887 south of the route near Wild Horse

---

[1] Marvin Jones, interview with author, August 12, 1971; Marvin Jones, *Marvin Jones Memoirs*, ed. Joseph M. Ray, p. 14; Jones, interview with David Murrah, August 1, 1972. Unless otherwise noted, all interviews and correspondence citing Jones refer to Marvin Jones.

Lake, an important watering hole for cattle drivers. Ranchers from as far away as Roswell, New Mexico, began driving their livestock to Amarillo for shipment to Kansas City and Chicago. The new town became the county seat of Potter County. By 1900, Amarillo claimed a population of 1,482. Ten years later it counted 9,957 inhabitants. Factors in this boom included the coming of other railroads and the westward expansion of farming.[2]

The Amarillo attorney for whom Jones went to work in 1908 had successfully established himself in the area. Leonidas Barrett, sixty-five years old, needed the assistance of a young man in his expanding practice, but because of unpleasant experiences with other assistants Barrett at first put Jones on probation. After one week, however, Jones's work convinced Barrett that he had found a talented, ambitious apprentice worth keeping. Barrett offered his assistant a partnership that would include 25 percent of new business. Jones wanted more immediate financial security and other benefits, so he asked for 15 percent of the new business, 5 percent of the old, and a salary of twenty-five dollars a month.

The young man had thought out his request carefully. He had estimated his monthly living expenses at less than twenty-five dollars.[3] Further, he had reasoned that the percentages of old and new business would give him valuable contacts to begin building a base of support for a political campaign.

Barrett agreed to the proposal without realizing his assistant's motives. With new enthusiasm Marvin joined the throngs of lawyers who solicited clients along unpaved Polk Street and on farms and ranches in the vicinity.

From 1908 through 1916, Jones and his Amarillo practice thrived. He won respect for his professionalism. He secured a retainer from the Turkey Trot Ranch thirteen miles away and frequently visited there. Six years after he entered into partnership with Barrett, the older man retired from most of his work, and Jones went into practice with another locally respected attorney, Ernest

[2] Della Tyler Key, *In the Cattle Country: History of Potter County, 1887–1966*, 2d ed., pp. 32–52.
[3] Jones, interview with Dean Albertson, Columbia Oral History Project, 1952, pp. 67–69; hereafter cited as COHP-MJP.

("Dusty") Miller. Jones specialized in damage suits, especially against railroads. He had begun this work while he was Barrett's partner.[4]

In most instances the courtroom oratory of Jones and other Panhandle attorneys was not preserved. An exception was *State of Texas* v. *Mrs. Edna Henson*, whom Jones defended. The case, which was tried in the Randall County Courthouse in Canyon, July 12–22, 1913, showed something about Jones's professionalism.

Mrs. Henson had been accused of violating a Texas law that required a state license of any person attempting to heal infirmities. As a practitioner of the Church of Christ, Scientist, she had received five dollars a visit from ailing individuals who had come to her for counseling, but, of course, she possessed no state license to practice medicine. Conviction would mean a mandatory jail sentence of six months and a fine of not less than one thousand dollars, even though the five-dollar fees had been left voluntarily, not in payment of any bill. The district attorney, Henry Bishop, had a strong case.[5]

Jones's defense tactics centered around a calculated appeal to the sentiments of a Protestant Panhandle. "I was a Methodist before I was born," Jones began. "I have been a Methodist ever since, and . . . I hope to stand on the sun-lit hills of glory and shout, a Methodist." Then, he reminded jurors that not all Christians belong to the same denomination, and he pleaded with them to show tolerance toward the defendant. Next he read the pertinent law and emphasized that under Texas codes the defendant, to be declared guilty, must have treated the disease.

Jones contended that Mrs. Henson did not prescribe medicine and did not treat any disease. She acted merely as God's representative in the healing process, he said. The case involved religious liberty and prayer. Jones resorted to some flamboyant oratory to appeal to local sentiment among the jurors:

> I love every foot of [Texas] soil from the hills of Oklahoma to the murmuring waters of the Gulf, and when I pass away I expect Texas breezes to waft the fragrance of Texas flowers over the last resting place of what substance there may be of this body, but I have never seen or heard of,

---

[4] Jones, *Marvin Jones Memoirs*, p. 18; Jones to author, December 31, 1973.

[5] Jones, interview with Murrah, August 1, 1972.

and I pray God I may never know of, a Texas jury sending a woman to jail for prayer.⁶

Jones then cited frontier tradition in support of Mrs. Henson's payments. Whenever neighbors pitched in to gather a sick man's crops, he said, the grateful recipient of this aid sometimes paid his friends for their services, if he could afford to. If Mrs. Henson had violated Texas law, Jones declared, then so had the salaried Methodist minister when he prayed for God to heal the sick. But neither of them, he observed, were in the same category as quacks who truly practiced medical fakery. It was those persons against whom the law was aimed, Jones contended.

The jury found in favor of Mrs. Henson. Ensuing publicity brought Jones more valuable clients.⁷ Soon he expanded his activities throughout the Panhandle and sometimes went out of state as far as Chicago.

In 1910, James N. Browning, former lieutenant governor of Texas and then judge of the Forty-seventh District Court of Texas, appointed Jones special master of the court on litigation concerning the 137,000-acre Bravo Ranch. Jones solved the dispute (between Henry B. Sanborn and O. H. Nelson) and won the respect of those two Panhandle personalities. During the same year the state created a court of appeals in Amarillo, and in the first case argued there Jones added to his reputation by securing a favorable judgment against the Santa Fe Railroad. With Jones's victory came an instantaneous reputation as an appeals lawyer, a rare specialty in the Panhandle.⁸ All the while Jones was building a backlog of favors.

In 1913 judges of the court of appeals selected Jones as chairman of their board of legal examiners. Despite his growing renown, however, Jones remained dissatisfied. At the age of thirty-four he began looking closely at political possibilities.

Representing the Thirteenth District in Congress was John Hall Stephens, a product of the Texas frontier, first elected in 1896.

---

⁶ *State of Texas vs. Mrs. Edna Henson. Address of Marvin Jones, Counsel for Defense*, Marvin Jones Papers, hereafter cited as MJP.

⁷ Jones, *Marvin Jones Memoirs*, pp. 19–20.

⁸ Ibid.; Hugh Umphres, interview with author, May 23, 1973; Jones to author, December 31, 1973; COHP-MJP, p. 72.

Nearly twenty years later he remained popular with the press and voters.[9] But trouble soon began brewing for him. Stephens served as chairman of the House Committee on Indian Affairs, and his emphasis on that subject began to be considered to be outdated. In the Panhandle and elsewhere new farms and ranches had replaced the camps of the Indians.

Marvin Jones mused over the situation. He had cultivated potential political support in conjunction with his legal practice. He had become known as a strong supporter of then-popular President Woodrow Wilson. Furthermore, Jones was young and vigorous, in contrast to aging incumbent Stephens. Finally, Stephens had lost some close political contacts because of his years in Washington and the influx of newcomers into his district. In 1915, a year before the elections, Jones announced his candidacy for Congress.[10]

At that time the Thirteenth District consisted of forty-eight counties with a combined population of 338,333. Boundaries included Oklahoma on the north and New Mexico on the west. Comprising the southern border, and included in the Thirteenth District, were Bailey, Lamb, Hale, Floyd, Dickens, Cottle, Knox, Throckmorton, Young, Jack, Wise, and Denton counties. The eastern border included Cooke and Denton counties. The district ranked second in the state in both number of counties and population.[11]

The Texas legislature was planning to divide the Thirteenth District, and this caused some potential candidates to take a wait-and-see attitude. Jones knew, however, that for him redistricting would mean a political loss, because those plans called for his home county, Cooke, to move to another district. Now would be the time for his challenge.

Several other strong candidates soon entered the race. Among them were Reuben Ellerd, a prominent Plainview attorney, and William Prescott of Paducah, who had been both attorney and judge. In early 1916 most observers believed Ellerd to be the major con-

---

[9] Walter Prescott Webb and H. Bailey Carroll, eds., *The Handbook of Texas*, 2:667.

[10] Herbert King Jones and Franklin Pierce Jones, interview with author, May 24, 1973; Jones to May, December 31, 1973.

[11] U.S., Congress, *Official Congressional Directory, 65th Congress, 1st Session*, p. 111.

tender against Stephens. Few of them took Jones's candidacy seriously, since the young attorney had never held an elective office.

Jones had strength, nevertheless. His physical appearance helped him. Here was a new personality on the plains political scene. He struck voters as a sincere, determined young man who looked a person in the eye when he talked. Because of his boyish appearance journalists Bascom Timmons and Joe Pope nicknamed him the "Panhandle Kid,"[12] but that proved to be no liability at all. Jones had already become known for his ability and knowledge.

He won the support of prominent Amarillo citizens like A. S. Stinnett, Thomas F. Turner, Ernest O. Thompson, R. E. Underwood, and Charles Ware (whom he had first met in Miami). An attorney, James O. Guleke, was put in charge of Jones's Amarillo headquarters.[13] The candidate himself campaigned throughout the district with the aid of his former law partner, Leonidas Barrett, and his brother Frank. His father and another brother, Delbert, concentrated on campaigning along the eastern edge.[14]

Because of the size of the district an effective door-to-door campaign proved impossible. Still Jones realized that personal contact with voters was essential for success. He drove a Model T Ford around the area to meet people: courthouse officials, downtown shoppers, newspaper staffs, and crowds at high-school commencements, picnics, and other events. At Matador loud music from a merry-go-round drowned out an opponent's speech, but Jones paid the operator two dollars and spoke without any noisy competition. He traveled more than twelve thousand miles, made more than 140 speeches, and at night slept on the prairie when a hotel or private residence was not available.[15]

His platform reflected two local desires: long-term loans for agricultural lands and support of President Wilson in domestic and

[12] Hugh Nugent Fitzgerald, "Pertainin' to Jones, the Panhandle Kid," undated clipping, scrapbook I, MJP. Jones's scrapbooks are numbered I and II and then 1–16.

[13] J. O. Guleke to George Thut, July 1, 1916, James O. Guleke Collection, Nita Stewart Haley Memorial Library, Midland, Texas.

[14] Horace K. Jones to James O. Guleke, May 25, 1916, Guleke Collection.

[15] Herbert K. Jones and Franklin Pierce Jones, interview with author, May 25, 1973; Jones, *Marvin Jones Memoirs*, pp. 22–30; Hugh Nugent Fitzgerald, "Pertainin' to Jones, the Panhandle Kid."

foreign policies. Jones also favored a stronger merchant marine and closer ties with Latin America.[16] Considering happenings abroad, Jones's 1916 platform as viewed more than six decades later might seem oversimplified, but it apparently did not strike his contemporaries that way. Two years earlier, in 1914, war had broken out in Europe. Germany had declared war on Russia on August 1 and on France two days later. Great Britain in turn had declared war on Germany on August 4. President Woodrow Wilson had announced at once that the United States would remain neutral, but as the months passed, neutrality had become increasingly difficult to maintain because of the German threat on oceans traveled by Americans. In May 1915 a German submarine had sunk the British steamer *Lusitania* off the Irish coast, and 128 Americans had been listed among the victims.

But when the political conventions met in the summer of 1916, the United States remained at peace. Democrats renominated President Wilson, with Vice-President Thomas R. Marshall as his running mate. Republicans chose a ticket with Supreme Court Justice Charles Evans Hughes for president and Charles W. Fairbanks of Indiana for vice-president. Democrats began campaigning for President Wilson with the slogan "He Kept Us out of War."

Jones's first effort, however, was to get himself elected. In speeches and conversations he sought consistently to use everyday language, to emphasize incumbent Stephens's age (sixty-nine years), reminding voters that the man had once said that there always comes a time when older men must step aside for younger ones, to lampoon Stephens's overriding concern for Indians (the only Indian he had seen lately, Jones said, stood woodenly in front of an Amarillo cigar store), and to criticize opponent Reuben Ellerd's "lavish" campaign expenditures.[17] He observed: "I never thought it was quite proper to offer anything of value when seeking votes. Mr. Stephens gives you garden seeds; Mr. Ellerd gives you pencils and calendars; but I'll give you a congressman if you will elect me."[18]

[16] "Marvin Jones of Amarillo, Texas for Congress," scrapbook 1, MJP.
[17] Jones, interview with author, August 12, 1971.
[18] Jones, *Marvin Jones Memoirs*, pp. 28–29; "The Hon. Marvin Jones Speaks at Albany to Small Audience;" and "Cooke County's Young Demosthenes Heard," undated clippings, scrapbook I, MJP.

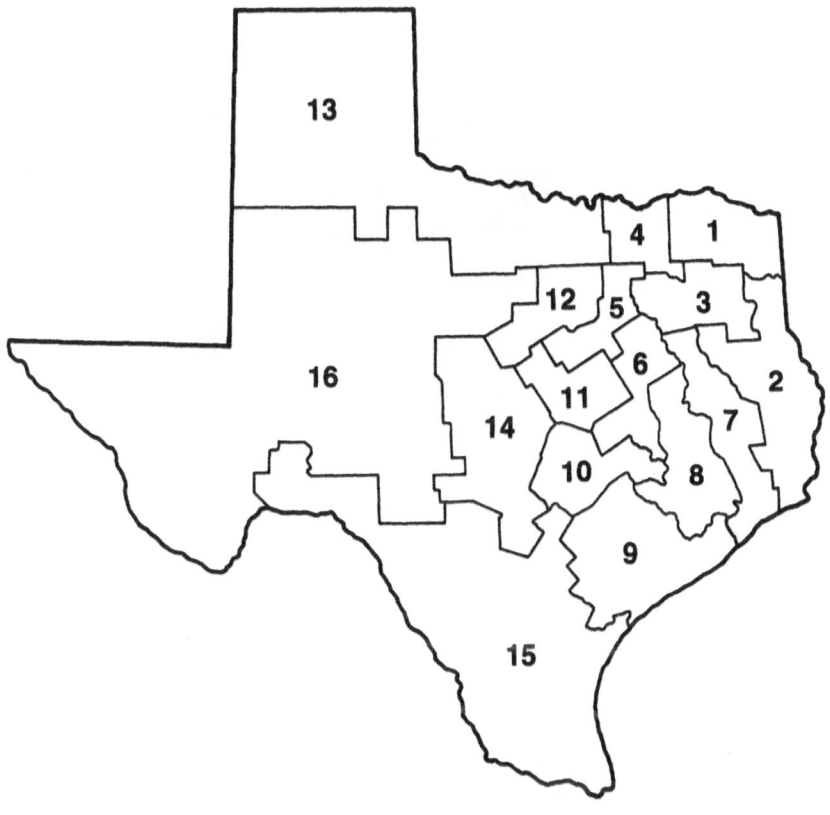

Texas Congressional Districts in 1916. Texas' senators at the time were Charles A. Culbertson and Morris Sheppard. Representatives at large were Jeff McLemore and Daniel E. Garrett. Representatives, by district, were (1) Eugene Black, (2) Martin Dies, (3) James Young, (4) Sam Rayburn, (5) Hatton Sumners, (6) Rufus Hardy, (7) Alexander W. Gregg, (8) Joe H. Eagle, (9) Joseph J. Mansfield, (10) James P. Buchanan, (11) Thomas Connally, (12) James C. Wilson, (13) Marvin Jones, (14) James L. Slayden, (15) John N. Garner, and (16) Thomas Blanton.

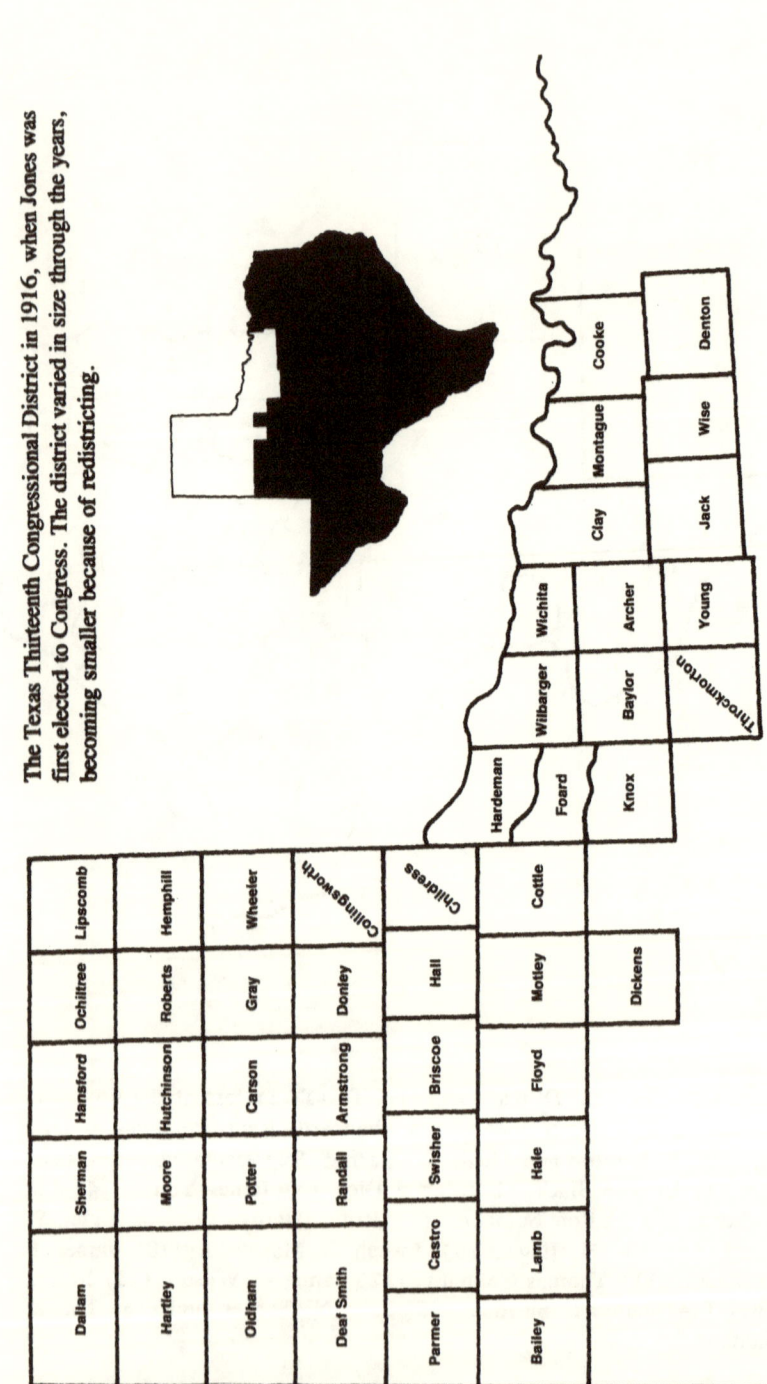

The Texas Thirteenth Congressional District in 1916, when Jones was first elected to Congress. The district varied in size through the years, becoming smaller because of redistricting.

Jones and his aides operated methodically and vigilantly. Their tools included public-opinion polls and more intensive work in locations that seemed to need it. An example is provided by a letter from Jones's campaign manager, James Guleke, to R. P. Killum of Seymour:

> We are seeking to obtain information as to the relative standing of the candidates in your county; therefore, we would appreciate a frank and candid expression from you as to what your opinion really is with respect to the strengths of each candidate. Our reports from other sections of the district are very gratifying and give us the assurance of expecting "Jones victory" in July. The "political snowball" is rolling up votes for Marvin Jones and the result will be, as we are hoping, the nomination of Jones for Congress.[19]

Workers also obtained voter lists from the various county tax offices,[20] and each of those individuals soon received a card with Jones's picture and an appeal.[21] The card read:

> Marvin Jones lived in a dugout fourteen years ago in Roberts County. He is a young man, thirty-three years of age [actually thirty-four], whose energy is virile and unwasted, who was born on the old place that his father is still running in the southern part of Cooke County, who has made his own way and who has never been a candidate for nor held public office. . . . I plead with men of all ages for an American chance for the ten thousand young men in this District. Are you going to vote to close the door of opportunity in the face of your own boy or that of your neighbor?
>
> Give the young man a chance.
>
> Sincerely,
Marvin Jones[22]

As the campaign neared its climax, Ellerd, formerly the front-running challenger, lost momentum. Veteran observers reassessed their views and wondered now whether Jones or Stephens would get more votes. Whoever captured the Democratic primary in this district of no Republican opposition would go to Washington.

---

[19] J. O. Guleke to R. P. Killum, May 19, 1916, Guleke Collection.
[20] Hugh Umphres, interview with author, May 23, 1973.
[21] J. O. Guleke to J. B. Clark, Shamrock, Texas, July 13, 1916, Guleke Collection.
[22] "Marvin Jones of Amarillo, Texas for Congress, Thirteenth District," Collection.

The answer became clear rather early on election night when a trend to Jones showed up. The final tabulation gave Jones 20,350 votes, Stephens 11,034, Ellerd 10,758, and Prescott 2,445.[23]

[23] "Jones, the Nominee," undated clipping, scrapbook I, MJP.

3.

The Formative Years, 1916–1920

THE election of 1916 would affect Marvin Jones's career permanently, turning it from private legal practice in the Texas Panhandle to Washington-based politics. Jones would have to broaden his outlook and adjust to the cosmopolitan and political climate of Washington. At the outset he realized his inexperience, but with curiosity and even confidence he eagerly anticipated his new career.

In the months following his victory in the Democratic primary, Jones was given an opportunity to commence the transition. His surprising upset of John Hall Stephens had attracted the attention of Vance McCormick of the Democratic National Campaign Committee.[1] McCormick knew that Jones would have no Republican opposition and was as good as elected, so he decided to test the young man's campaigning skills further by scheduling him to speak in behalf of President Wilson's reelection in Lawton, Oklahoma—the hometown of Scott Ferris, manager of Wilson's western campaign.

Jones's effort was impressive. The *Lawton Daily Constitution* editorialized:

> One of the most remarkable speeches of the campaign was made in Lawton last night by Hon. Marvin Jones, congressman-elect from the Panhandle . . . district in Texas. Congressman Jones is a young man, looks young and is clean cut and presents a pleasing personality. . . . Mr. Jones' speech last night was on national issues and was a masterpiece, his stories and arguments were new, and those who listened attentively pronounce it one of the greatest speeches made this year.[2]

---

[1] Jones to J. W. Crudington, June 3, 1918, scrapbook I, Marvin Jones Papers; hereafter cited as MJP. For background of the Democratic National Campaign Committee see Seward W. Livermore, *Politics Is Adjourned: Woodrow Wilson and the War Congress, 1916–1918*, pp. 11–112.

[2] *Lawton Daily Constitution*, September [?], 1916, scrapbook I, MJP.

McCormick and Ferris immediately saw Jones as a spellbinder in the mold of the frontier emotionalist. After passing his first test, Jones made three or four speeches a day in rural Oklahoma and Missouri during September 1916 for the eventually victorious Wilson-Marshall ticket (the Democrats also kept control of the House and Senate).[3] After the election Jones returned to Amarillo to wrap up last-minute business with clients before beginning his congressional career.

Some of that business took Jones to Washington, D.C., in December, along with another Amarillo man, J. R. Jackson. The two were seeking lower freight rates in a lawsuit involving the Interstate Commerce Commission. Panhandle areas lacked sufficient population and commerce to support extensive railroad development, and consequently their citizens paid higher rates than other Texans. Jones and Jackson successfully equalized Texas freight rates, but they were unsuccessful in lowering over-all rates.[4]

After the conclusion of that case Jones remained in Washington to observe the closing days of the Sixty-fourth Congress.[5] He was completely aware that he would soon be a green legislator in a city where society was vastly different.

During that December he frequented the visitors' gallery of the House of Representatives. In other moments he read everything he could about the careers of Joe Weldon Bailey, David D. DeArmond, and John H. Bankhead, Sr. His House visits allowed him to observe firsthand the tactics of Henry Cabot Lodge, Champ Clark, and members of the Texas delegation.

Jones devoted much time to cultivating friendships with the Texas members, who were a closely-knit group. Recently the Texans had lost some national prestige, but there were well-known names among them. Jones sought out two former law-school acquaintances, Sam Rayburn and Eugene Black, to make the necessary introductions, and he soon met the noted Morris Sheppard and John Nance Garner—the latter a power in the House Committee on Ways and

[3] Ibid.
[4] Marvin Jones, *Marvin Jones Memoirs*, ed. Joseph M. Ray, pp 31–32.
[5] Marvin Jones, interview with author, January 14, 1974. Unless otherwise noted, all interviews and correspondence citing Jones refer to Marvin Jones.

The Formative Years, 1916–1920   31

Means.[6] Both men welcomed Jones into discussions held during the waning days of the old Congress. As a consequence Jones became Garner's protégé and secured a room at the Congress Hall Hotel (where more than a hundred congressmen and their families resided) even before he took his oath.[7] Then on Christmas Eve, 1916, Jones left Washington to spend the holidays in Texas.

When the new Congress convened in 1917, Democratic leaders assigned Jones to the Committees on Insular Affairs, Reform in Civil Service, Industrial Arts, and Expositions and Roads.[8] These were minor committees that met infrequently, and Jones was able to attend most of the sessions. Often he sat near Missouri's Champ Clark and received valuable counsel from that veteran legislator. Clark taught Jones to write down every point of order that occurred during the sessions and look up the precedents afterward.

Jones also studied personal traits of individual congressmen with the idea of adopting some for his own use. Especially impressive to him were "doers" and those who had a detailed knowledge of Congress and its operations. Jones had little use for men who talked first and studied later. He strove constantly to avoid being guilty of that, and before long he had earned the respect of many senior congressmen.[9]

By trial and error Jones also acquired the skills of explaining a bill persuasively and clearly and of anticipating possible roadblocks. Primarily important on the House floor were sincerity, knowledge of the bill, and an ability to evaluate colleagues. Cutting remarks usually hurt the congressman who uttered them. Sympathy and compassion toward opponents combined with a simultaneous maintenance of integrity went further. Jones learned to excel in his dealings.

---

[6] Jones, interview with Dean Albertson, Columbia Oral History Project, 1952, p. 108; hereafter cited as COHP-MJP. See also Alex M. Arnett, *Claude Kitchin and the Wilson War Policies*, pp. 295–298; Bascom M. Timmons, *Garner of Texas: A Personal History*, pp. 67–88; U.S., Congress, *Official Congressional Directory*, 65th Congress, 1st Session, p. 111.

[7] Jones, interview with author, January 14, 1974.

[8] U.S., Congress, House, *Congressional Record*, 65th Cong., 1st sess., 1917, 55, p. 114.

[9] Jones, *Marvin Jones Memoirs*, p. 31; Jones, interview with Albertson, COHP-MJP, pp. 98–182. Democrat James Beauchamp ("Champ") Clark of Missouri was Speaker of the House.

According to House Parliamentarian Lewis Deschler, he became one of the best procedural strategists in the House.[10]

But most of those achievements lay in the future in that winter and early spring of 1917, when Jones commenced his congressional career. Of more immediate consequence was the possibility of United States involvement in the European war. German U-boats had continued to threaten American rights on the high seas. German saboteurs blew up a munitions dump on Black Tom Island, New Jersey, causing $22 million damage. The United States government heard of a German plot to form an alliance with Mexico in event of the United States' entry into the war and to help Mexico retake former Mexican possessions like Arizona, Texas, and New Mexico.

On February 7, 1917, President Wilson announced to Congress that the United States had broken off diplomatic relations with Germany. The Senate approved Wilson's decision. Then, on April 2, after more trouble with Germany, the president scheduled a momentous address before a joint night session of Congress. During that day, in cloakrooms and offices—wherever people gathered—many speculations were made about the president's speech. Even veteran congressmen felt intense emotion.

At 8:30 P.M. the members of Congress assembled. From his seat Jones watched the drama unfold; he would later write a description of it in his memoirs. He peered at the tightly packed gallery, where a demonstration opposing war was quickly subdued. A few moments later the president entered. Everyone stood and then sat again and heard a grim-faced Wilson ask for a declaration of war because the world must be made safe for democracy.

Wilson said that his total objective was "to vindicate the principles of peace and justice in the life of the world as against selfish and autocratic power and to set up amongst the really free and self-governed peoples of the world such as concert of purpose and of action as will henceforth ensure the observance of those principles."[11] "It is a fearful thing to lead this great peaceful people into war," he

---

[10] Lewis Deschler, parliamentarian of the U.S. House of Representatives, interview with author, October 15, 1971.

[11] U.S., Congress, House, *Congressional Record*, 65th Cong., 1st sess., 1917 55, p. 118.

continued, "... civilization itself seeming to be in the balance."[12] But, he added, the actions of Germany had left the United States little choice but to fight for "democracy, for the right of those who submit to authority to have a voice in their own governments, for the rights and liberties of small nations, for a universal dominion of right by such a concert of free peoples as shall bring peace and safety to all nations and make the world itself at last free."[13]

Jones heard the applause that frequently interrupted Wilson. He concluded, correctly, that the people supported the president, but he also believed, probably also correctly, that in their hearts "no one wanted to go to war."[14] Jones himself was not sure whether he would vote for or against the war resolution, and during the next few days he agonized over his decision. He listened to eloquent appeals from Claude Kitchin, Democratic majority leader, and Wisconsin's Henry Cooper, who contended that the nation had not taken all possible steps to stay out of the war. Jones listened also to Finus Garrett, who defended the president.[15]

For a time Jones doubted that Congress would pass the war resolution, but John Garner assured him that "when the roll is called there won't be over fifty votes against the President."[16] "Cactus Jack" then urged his young protégé to support the administration and warned that any other course would be political suicide.

But Jones continued to agonize. He discussed the matter for many hours with Sam Rayburn and Eugene Black.[17] In the end, however, Garner's influence prevailed. Jones joined the majority by voting for the war resolution, which passed the House 373 to 50, on April 6—two days after the Senate had approved it.[18]

Years later Jones would wonder whether he had voted right. He would speculate that if Germany and the Allies had fought to a draw

---

[12] Ibid., p. 119.
[13] Ibid.
[14] Jones, *Marvin Jones Memoirs*, p. 33.
[15] COHP-MJP, pp. 101–103; see Arnett, *Claude Kitchin and the Wilson War Policies*, pp. 226–238.
[16] Jones, *Marvin Jones Memoirs*, p. 33.
[17] D. B. Hardeman, interview with author, August 17, 1972.
[18] See Arthur S. Link, *Woodrow Wilson and the Progressive Era, 1910–1917*, pp. 281–282; Timmons, *Garner of Texas*, pp. 81–86.

perhaps a neutral United States could have imposed the peace it desired—a peace to make the world safe indeed for democracy.[19]

The decision to fight did not result in immediate unanimity. President Wilson asked for a draft of two million men, but quick opposition arose from key House Democrats, including Speaker Champ Clark, Majority Leader Claude Kitchin, and Chairman Hubert Dent of the Military Affairs Committee. These three men supported a volunteer program. Other congressmen, anticipating a backlash at the polls, also urged reliance first on volunteers and then, if the numbers proved insufficient, institution of the draft. The administration countered with the argument that urgency necessitated immediate conscription.[20] Opposition to a draft developed within the Texas delegation. Leaders pressed their colleagues to follow the president.[21]

The debate led to Marvin Jones's initial House speech. On April 26, 1917, he spoke on the necessity of finding a fair method of increasing the size of the army. He argued against reliance on a volunteer army, declaring that congressmen would be open to charges of placing a demand on middle and lower economic classes to fight the war. He justified a draft of men on a democratic basis, and he would later argue that, "if the volunteer system fails, it always fails in the emergency, when the cold steel of the crisis comes."[22] In his speech he said:

Under the selective draft the rich and the poor, the high and the low, the baker's son, and banker's son, . . . all must melt into a common sentiment and stand shoulder to shoulder and heart to heart. Could anything be fairer or more democratic? For once in all our glorious history let us have a war that is not a rich man's war and a poor man's fight. To this end I shall favor levying a draft upon wealth in the form of graduated income and excess profits taxes, in order that all our forces may be utilized in the prosecution of this fight and for the purpose of

---

[19] Hardeman, interview with author, August 17, 1972.

[20] For background see Livermore, *Politics Is Adjourned*, pp. 15–31.

[21] Leo R. Sack, "Texas Congressmen Take Lead in Advocacy of Conscription Plan in Debate of Army Bill," undated clipping, scrapbook I, MJP. Jones recalled Rayburn's opposition in the cloakroom in Jones, *Marvin Jones Memoirs*, p. 36.

[22] COHP-MJP, pp. 104–104a.

The Formative Years, 1916–1920 35

discouraging those who make a profit out of warfare and coin American blood and tears into money, by removing any artificial inducement of war.[23]

After much debate the draft won in the House by a large majority. As for conscription age limits, Jones believed that "men should be chosen at all ages, ranging from the average time when men enter the business world to the average time when they begin to slow up their activity." He disputed a War Department idea that the draft should be limited to the ages nineteen to twenty-five, supporting instead a twenty-one-to-forty-five range because that span would avoid depletion of any particular workforce. Congress voted for registration of men from twenty-one to thirty but in August extended registration to ages eighteen to forty-five.[24]

Many other problems urgently required solutions. The United States found itself confronted by food shortages, inflated food prices, and increased demands to provide food for European allies. The nation's wheat crops of 1916 and 1917 had failed to meet domestic needs. That, plus speculation in meat, eggs, and other commodities, brought increasing public clamor for federal food control. During the spring of 1917, however, the Wilson administration gave priority to military and fiscal legislation.

The Senate and House agriculture committees quickly forced the president's hand by calling for a farm program from the administration. Secretary of Agriculture David Houston responded by presenting a very general agricultural bill (H.R. 4961) that gave the Department of Agriculture power to control food distribution and to manage maximum and minimum prices.[25]

Hostile reaction came immediately from farm organizations in wheat- and cotton-producing states and from congressmen opposed to fixing the prices of agricultural products. The House Committee on Agriculture was divided. Chairman Asbury Lever, working for the administration bill, faced strong opposition from Texan James Young, who opposed price fixing of the cotton grown in his East

[23] U.S., Congress, House, *Congressional Record*, 65th Cong., 1st sess., 1917, 55, pp. 1200–1201.
[24] Ibid., pt. 8:248.
[25] Tom G. Hall, "Wilson and the Food Crisis: Agricultural Price Control During World War I," *Agricultural History* 47 (January 1973):25–46.

Texas district. Other congressmen from the South followed Young's lead. They contended that price controls would deny farmers some well-deserved profits while helping cotton speculators. Lever argued to exempt cotton from price controls in return for the cotton group's support of the bill.[26]

But congressmen from wheat-producing districts continued to oppose the bill, despite assurance from the administration that prices would be "managed" only. They pushed through an amendment fixing the minimum price of wheat at $2.00 a bushel, with the current market price at $2.89.[27] The bill finally became law; the Lever Food and Fuel Control Act gave President Wilson power to "stimulate" production and to control distribution of food and fuel essential to the war effort. It prohibited, for example, the use of foodstuffs in manufacturing distilled liquor. Congress also created the War Food Administration, and Wilson named Herbert Hoover its administrator.

When Lever's bill passed the House on August 3, Jones observed that many congressmen had "heaped [abuse] with perfervid eloquence and vitriolic fire upon the head of the middleman and speculator who have been pictured as fiends incarnate."[28] But he realized that speculation was only symptomatic of the fundamental issue of urbanization. All this became more frustrating for farmers because of the extreme labor required of them without appropriate financial reward. Jones hoped that Congress would help in making farm life attractive, and he believed that this could best be done by letting the farmer alone.

Thus, as a representative from a wheat-growing district, he disagreed with the Wilson administration to some extent, but he defended the Lever act on grounds of patriotism. He also believed deeply that American activities in 1917 should be confined to continental defense and protection of United States shipping on the oceans, but he yielded to other, overwhelming sentiment in Congress.[29]

Jones did, however, speak up to advocates of tight price con-

---

[26] COHP-MJP, pp. 157–158.
[27] Ibid., p. 160.
[28] U.S., Congress, House, *Congressional Record*, 65th Cong., 1st sess., 1917, 55, p. 5750.
[29] Ibid., p. 5751.

The Formative Years, 1916–1920

trols on agricultural products. If this view prevailed, he said, then Congress should also pass controls on the price of farm machinery. He wanted Congress to resolve the consumer-producer conflict and to create a marketing system that would bring producer and consumer in closer touch with each other, in order "that there may be greater publicity of prices that the consumer pays and the producer receives, and that those prices may be more nearly uniform and much nearer the same."[30] He continued:

> The tiller of the soil is the most important citizen in this country and has always been. He is the foundation and groundwork of this country's surpassing prosperity. On his primary efforts rests the magnificent commercial superstructure that has been reared in our land. If he fails, all is lost.[31]

Jones continued to support the Wilson administration, but he was not a rubber stamp. He was especially critical of Secretary of Agriculture David Houston, whom he regarded as a handsome administrator who made a good impression but had only shallow knowledge of agriculture.

Jones supported President Wilson's fiscal program, sponsored in the House by Majority Leader Claude Kitchin. Most southern congressmen with rural constituencies favored it. This program called for a conscription of industrial wealth. It increased income taxes from 2 to 4 percent and raised corporation taxes to a maximum of 60 percent. Taxes increased on liquor and tobacco and other "luxuries," but Jones joined with southerners to defeat a $2.50-a-bale tax on cotton. These congressional tax increases, combined with "liberty loans," financed the war effort.[32]

During his first congressional session Jones established a reputation as a loyal southern Democrat[33] who combined careful attendance with prompt attention to constituents' requests and research in regard to his job. He also introduced many bills and amendments that usually died in committees, but that was typical of many first-

---

[30] Ibid.

[31] Ibid.

[32] Jones, interview with Albertson, COHP-MJP, pp. 114–116, 186; Livermore, *Politics Is Adjourned*, pp. 57–61.

[33] U.S., Congress, House, *Congressional Record*, 65th Cong., 1st sess., 1917, 55, pp. 690, 1555, 1557, 1693, 1841, 4190, 7104.

term congressmen. Jones lacked political power and expertise to draft bills and to get them passed. Finally, with Garner's aid, he secured for his constituents passage of a bill granting the Gainesville Red River Bridge Company permission to span the Red River from Cooke County, Texas, to Love County, Oklahoma.[34]

Jones still found time to fish with Sam Rayburn and to golf or spend a day at the racetrack with Texas journalist Bascom Timmons. At the annual congressional baseball game "the mighty bat of Marvin Jones of Texas lifted the Democrats from the slough of despair . . . and gave them a victory over the Republicans, 22 to 21," with Wilson in attendance. Jones went to bat seven times and collected seven hits. The congressmen raised three thousand dollars for the Red Cross—and their forty-five errors left undisturbed the standing record of fifty-six.[35] Jones loved these diversions, but he usually avoided the glamorous Washington social life.

Following his first adjournment he returned to his district to visit his parents, tour the Panhandle, and make patriotic speeches that indicated a diminished isolationism in his thinking. In Gainesville he remarked:

Our great president did everything in his power to avoid the necessity of entering the strife. But the ruthless sinking of American ships, the destruction of American lives, including helpless women and children, left us no alternative. No buccaneer who ever roved the seas has been guilty of more inhuman and shameless disregard of the rights and lives of others than has the head of the Imperial German Government.[36]

He mixed humor with bluntness at Tulia:

It is said that an Englishman, a Frenchman and a German love liberty in different degrees: that an Englishman loves liberty much as he loves his wife. He buys her a home, cares for her physical needs and wants, . . . but he doesn't make much fuss about it; that a Frenchman loves liberty about like a boy loves his first girl—he is crazy about her; and that a German loves liberty about like he loves his mother-in-law. . . .

Nothing can be grander in this world than to fight the battles of liberty, nothing can be more glamorous than to fight in defense of one's country; especially when that country is America.

[34] Ibid., pp. 1069, 3147, 3545, 4501, 4983, 7243, 7445, 7462.
[35] "Ty Cobb's Only Rival," undated clipping, scrapbook I, MJP.
[36] *Gainesville Register*, August 26, 1917.

He thundered:

> I am for the United States Government, right or wrong. Aren't you? ... If I were to go out on the sidewalk here and find some man with a six shooter trying to kill my father, ... do you suppose I would stop to ask whose fault it was? ... When the American people cease to love their country as did those who served and died that this country might be free, our country will have no more history.[37]

As the war progressed, Jones strengthened his support of Wilson's war aims. In August 1917, Jones appeared before the House Foreign Relations Committee in behalf of his resolution calling for the issuance of a proclamation of American war aims and peace terms with the intention of gaining greater worldwide support for the United States. Such action, he believed, would "destroy the deception which was being practiced by the German rulers upon the German people, and through them the Russian people."[38] During that same month Pope Benedict XV appealed for peace negotiations and proposed that the war end without reparations or indemnities.

A statement issued by President Wilson on August 27 gave weight to Jones's resolution. The president said that he could not conceive that a return to the status quo would produce permanent peace. Swept up in the emotional tide of the moment, Jones called Wilson's declaration "the greatest of all the President's state papers."[39]

Jones naïvely felt that Wilson, a man who truly loved peace, could end the war and that the president, "lifting up his eyes, has caught a vision of the earth's tribes and peoples freed from the dangers of ambitious and designing monarchs." Jones asserted further that the "American people are solidly behind the greatest of all American presidents, our commander-in-chief, Woodrow Wilson."[40]

---

[37] *Tulia Herald*, November 16, 1917.

[38] Marvin Jones to Foreign Affairs Committee, House of Representatives, August 8, 1917, U.S., Congress, House, *Congressional Record*, 65th Cong., 2d sess. 1917, 56, pt. 12:120, 151.

[39] Marvin Jones, *The American War Policy: Speech of Hon. Marvin Jones of Texas in the House of Representatives September 21, 1917*, pp. 3–8. Copies of this speech were widely circulated in the Thirteenth District; see *Quanah Tribune*, October 25, 1917.

[40] Ibid.

Jones failed to foresee the tragedy that would later befall Wilson when the president's countrymen withdrew their support.

In the elections of 1918, Jones was chosen by several key Democrats to soothe agrarian discontent with administration decisions. One was a refusal to increase the minimum price of wheat to $2.50 a bushel. Republicans hoped to capitalize on this action.

Jones, in his unusual role as a Democrat from a wheat-producing district of a southern state, spoke against the Republican attacks throughout the Southwest and in Indiana. Jones's only congressional opponent of any significance, Jonathan W. Crudgington, withdrew from the race because of illness, and Jones had to do little hard campaigning of his own.[41] He won a landslide victory over the remaining contender, J. L. Lackey of Armstrong County.[42]

During 1918, as the Allies moved toward victory, Jones also advocated creation of a federal organization to supervise vocational retraining of disabled soldiers, continued previously announced support of prohibition and woman suffrage, worked for reduction of freight rates to aid agriculture, sought to have the Texas Panhandle placed in the central time zone,[43] and visited Europe (at his own expense) as a member of a congressional delegation studying military operations. Members crept to within thirty feet of German lines.[44]

The emotion caused by observing war firsthand impelled Jones to enlist in the army. He was assigned to Company A, 308th Battalion, of the Tank Corps, stationed at Fort Polk, North Carolina. His favorite duty was in the kitchen, where he could identify with "the common man."[45]

While at Fort Polk, Jones kept himself informed of the waning

---

[41] *Amarillo Daily News*, June 18, 1934.

[42] James O. Guleke, chairman, Eighteenth Congressional District, Democratic Party Sworn Affidavit on Election Results: Jones, 38,029; Lockey, 7,187; and Crudgington [whose name remained on some ballots despite his withdrawal], 2,390; James O. Guleke Collection, Nita Stewart Haley Memorial Library, Midland, Texas.

[43] U.S., Congress, House, 65th Cong., 1st sess., 1917, 55, pp. 114, 1220–21, 3147, 3543, 5146, 5760, 7243, 7293.

[44] Scrapbook I, MJP; Jones, *Marvin Jones Memoirs*, pp. 40–41; Alben W. Barkley, *That Reminds Me*, pp. 112–116.

[45] Scrapbook I, MJP; U.S., Congress, *Biographical Directory of the American Congress, 1774–1961*, pp. 728, 1138.

war. Early in November a revolution broke out in Germany, and sailors in Kaiser Wilhelm's fleet mutinied against going on what they considered a hopeless mission against the British navy. On November 9 the kaiser abdicated, and two days later German officials agreed to end the fighting, signing armistice terms in a railroad car in the Forest of Compiègne. Late that month Jones received a discharge, and he returned to Congress, a veteran.

In the meantime the Texas legislature had redistricted Jones's congressional area, so that in 1919 he represented the Eighteenth, not the Thirteenth, District. The eastern part of his old district remained in the Thirteenth, but changes had occurred in the west. The new Eighteenth District included fifty-three counties with a population of 257,170.[46] But that was not an immediate concern as far as his reelection was concerned.

Altogether some fourteen million men had died on battlefields during the war. Millions of others had been wounded. Still the war-ending Treaty of Versailles, supported by President Wilson, quickly encountered much opposition in the United States because it included the League of Nations Covenant calling for American participation in an international body. Many Americans remained isolationist, and they opposed such participation.

President Wilson lobbied for the covenant in person, traveling into the Middle West and the West, arguing in behalf of the League of Nations. Jones predicted success. If the Versailles Treaty came to an early vote, he said, the Senate would pass the measure. Speaking in Fort Worth on April 19, 1919, he became more specific. He foresaw five-to-one Senate ratification of the League of Nations Covenant, declaring that senators would never have nerve to refuse the president's request.[47]

But Jones's prophecy came to nothing. Wilson's lobbying was stopped by illness, then a stroke. The Senate was never to approve participation in the league.

---

[46] U.S., Congress, *Official Congressional Directory, 65th Congress, 1st Session*, p. 111; U.S., Congress, *Official Congressional Directory, 66th Congress, 1st Session*, pp. 115, 491; U.S., Congress, *Official Congressional Directory, 67th Congress, 2d Session*, p. 114; U.S., Congress, *Official Congressional Directory, 72d Congress, 2d Session*, p. 114.

[47] COHP-MJP, pp. 181–183; scrapbook II, MJP.

Other matters occupied Jones's thoughts and efforts during this postwar period: assuring a wise system of paying and collecting the huge war debts, striving for limits on the future size of the army and of the federal government itself, seeking to economize in federal spending, supporting prohibition and woman suffrage, advocating greater national security (especially during the postwar red scare), and, as always, seeking greater benefits for farmers of his district.

Early in 1919 he urged Congress to extend payment of the war debt incurred by the United States government over a forty- to fifty-year period. He reasoned that paying the estimated indebtedness of $26,736,302,274.52 in a shorter period would "break down the business spirit of the Nation, interfere with our commercial opportunities, and lessen the initiative of practically every business and working man in the United States largely because a shorter payment of the debt would result in higher corporate and personal taxes for all Americans." When a House colleague, Rufus Hardy, wondered aloud whether Jones had overestimated the federal war debt, especially since European nations owed the United States billions of dollars, Jones replied:

While it is true that the other nations owe us money and will ultimately pay it, I do not believe they will be able to repay us the principal, at any rate, for a long period of time; and I doubt whether it would be wise for us to endeavor to collect too rapidly from those nations, because that would make it necessary for them to ship gold into this country; and we would have an oversupply of gold and they would have an undersupply of gold.[48]

At the same time Jones argued against keeping a large army—in this case a proposed permanent body of 175,000 soldiers backed up by a standby volunteer force of 537,000 men. He remembered seeing graves of American soldiers near Paris. That had compounded his feeling that militarism was contrary to the ideals of democracy. He urged, without success, that the total number of regulars and volunteers be kept below 205,000, remarking that "a pistol-toting man would sooner or later get into a fight."[49] He believed that "the world has learned, through bitter experience, the way to settle rival-

---

[48] U.S., Congress, House, *Congressional Record*, 66th Cong., 1st sess., 1919, 58, pp. 1709–11; see also scrapbooks I and 1, MJP.

[49] Ibid., 2d sess., 1919, 58, p. 4139.

The Formative Years, 1916-1920 43

ries between nations is for each to build up its own resources rather than tear down the neighboring commonwealth, and that the contests of the future will be creative and constructive rather than destructive."[50]

Jones also wanted a smaller bureaucracy. In 1919 the Bureau of War Risk Insurance maintained headquarters in Washington and offices in forty-eight states. The House Committee on Interstate and Foreign Commerce recommended that fourteen new regional offices be established to meet postwar demands. Congressman Warren Gard of Ohio led a fight against the proposal, and Jones joined him. The House accepted the Gard amendment and saved one million dollars.[51] Jones also helped block congressional attempts to make the Council of National Defense a permanent body.[52]

Jones urged care, too, in allowing veterans' benefits, particularly to survivors of men whose deaths were claimed to have been service-connected. But Jones, frugal-minded though he was regarding benefits, manifested compassion for veterans, particularly for youths who had falsely enlisted as minors without parental consent and had been found out. He sponsored an amendment by which Congress removed the stigma of the "blue discharge" given these youths, and he warned over-zealous recruiters to require birth certificates from future enlistees.[53]

During these years prohibition and woman suffrage attracted nationwide attention, and Jones supported both movements. As a youth in a class experiment he had been startled by observing the effect of alcohol on a raw egg and had wondered what alcohol might do to a human brain. Further influenced by prevailing religious sentiment in his district, he cast a supporting vote for the Eighteenth Amendment.[54] He also went on record in favor of woman suffrage, although he was not a leading spokesman for it. He was aware that in Amarillo potential women voters outnumbered men 2,112 to

---

[50] Ibid., 65th Cong., 3d sess., 1919, 57, p. 3715.

[51] Ibid., 66th Cong., 2d sess., 1920, 59, pp. 7357-75.

[52] Ibid., 3d sess., 1921, 60, pp. 897-899; Jones, *Marvin Jones Memoirs*, pp. 50-51.

[53] Jones, *Marvin Jones Memoirs*, p. 55; U.S., Congress, House, *Congressional Record*, 66th Cong., 3d sess., 1921, 60, pp. 2599-2600.

[54] COHP-MJP, pp. 172-174.

2,072.⁵⁵ In his district were "mossyback gentlemen" who did not appreciate his vote, but a newspaper account characterized him as a "win-the-war Democrat" with a "constructive brain" and a belief in "the world of today and not the world of the sixteenth century."⁵⁶

Jones's "world of today" soon included the red scare. When it burst upon the nation after the end of World War I, it was accompanied by spirited speeches in Congress. Minnesota's Walter Newton charged that the Wilson administration should use stronger means to curb anarchical activity. Jones urged congressional support to enforce existing legislation. When in 1919 congressmen debated whether to allow Victor Berger, a Socialist, to take his seat in the House, Jones associated Berger's party with anarchy: "unpatriotic, un-American and . . . undesirable in the country."⁵⁷ Jones believed in freedom of speech, but he refused to sanction unlimited freedom. He observed, "When a man is unwilling to abide by the wishes of the majority, but insists by processes of treachery and violence upon inculcating the doctrines of force and the saddling of his ideas upon the people through the medium of fear, he becomes the most dangerous character in a free republic."⁵⁸ Jones's stand, publicized through the efforts of journalist Bascom Timmons, won approval in the Panhandle.⁵⁹

Work in behalf of his district won for Jones further local support. He sponsored legislation that placed the Oklahoma Panhandle and most of West Texas in the central time zone instead of the mountain zone, as previously decreed by the Interstate Commerce Commission. He and Senator John B. Kendrick of Wyoming won a reduction in freight rates on cattle feed. He fought continually, but with infrequent success, to procure more efficient and less expensive rail service for his constituents. In doing this, he always opposed government management of the railroads, preferring private opera-

---

⁵⁵ Jones, *Marvin Jones Memoirs*, pp. 38–39; U.S., Congress, House, *Congressional Record*, 65th Cong., 2d sess., 1917–18, 56, pp. 810, 9136.

⁵⁶ Undated clipping, scrapbook 1, MJP.

⁵⁷ U.S., Congress, House, *Congressional Record*, 66th Cong., 1st sess., 1919, 58, pp. 7586–87.

⁵⁸ Ibid.

⁵⁹ *Lockney* (Texas) *Beacon*, October 28, 1919; *Panhandle* (Texas) *Herald*, November 7, 1919; "Individual Voting Record, Honorable Marvin Jones, 66th Congress," MS, MJP.

The Formative Years, 1916–1920   45

tion as the lesser of two evils. But he also fought railroad privileges, such as government loans and guaranteed income on freight. In 1920, despite Jones's opposition, Congress passed the Esch-Cummins Act, which enlarged the scope and power of the Interstate Commerce Commission in regard to railroads (assuring a 6 percent net freight profit and allowing loans and guaranteed incomes—the very benefits Jones opposed).

By this time Jones had become generally frustrated. He deplored the lack of activity in his own committee assignments, and he abhorred the bureaucratic inefficiency he saw all around him. Restless for action, he proposed reducing House membership. In a speech delivered on January 18, 1920, he observed that the House had some sixty committees and that of that number about twenty labored with some consistency but only five or six did momentous work. He concluded, "New members coming to the House, not being able to get on an important committee and finding that they cannot take much part in the work of the House, frequently get to doing departmental duties and other incidental things, and cease to take much of an interest in the affairs of the House."[60]

Jones's solution was simple. He would reduce House membership to a total of 307 and create twenty committees, with all work to be distributed equally among them. Veteran congressmen easily defeated these proposals by a vote of 203 to 27.[61] So ended Jones's activities during his formative years in Congress.

[60] U.S., Congress, House, *Congressional Record*, 66th Cong., 1st sess., 1919, 58, p. 7648.
[61] Ibid., pp. 1648–80.

4.

The Harding Years

When Marvin Jones made his speech proposing House changes, the roaring twenties were drawing near, although neither he nor anyone else could have anticipated the events of that decade. Jones's speech was given on January 18, 1920. Eleven days after that the Eighteenth Amendment (prohibition) became effective, and organized crime quickly moved in to profit from illegal distribution of liquor.

The postwar year 1920 proved to be a momentous one. Federal agents throughout the country arrested hundreds of persons suspected of being Communists or anarchists. The Senate continued to refuse to ratify the Versailles Treaty and the League of Nations Covenant. Toward the end of the year American women won the right to vote, upon ratification of the Nineteenth Amendment. About the same time census takers completed their nationwide count: 105,711,-000, including more than 5 million immigrants. Sinclair Lewis's novel *Main Street*, appeared, as did F. Scott Fitzgerald's *This Side of Paradise*. The first licensed broadcasting began, over Radio Station WWJ in Detroit. Nicola Sacco and Bartolomeo Vanzetti were arrested in Massachusetts and charged with murder in connection with a payroll robbery.

Foremost in Marvin Jones's mind that year, however, was the political situation. As a loyal Democrat he became concerned about party leadership, which had been lacking since the stroke that had incapacitated President Wilson. Public speculation about the president's mental and physical health was taboo for Democrats. One careless word would evoke the awesome wrath of party stalwarts like Carter Glass, who would teach a lesson in discretion to the man who had not learned to keep his mouth shut.

Outside Washington the nation had tired of Wilsonian idealism and talk about the League of Nations. Domestic problems—demobilization, unemployment, and the high cost of living—appeared more important than diplomacy.

On June 8, 1920, Republicans met at Chicago and nominated Warren G. Harding of Ohio for president and Calvin Coolidge, governor of Massachusetts, for vice-president. Three weeks later Democrats met at San Francisco and selected their ticket: Governor James M. Cox of Ohio for president and Assistant Secretary of the Navy Franklin D. Roosevelt of New York for vice-president.

Harding won much support with his campaign for a "return to normalcy." He foresaw, during a Harding administration, a renewal of business, labor, and agricultural stability. The Democrats, on the other hand, included in their platform support of the widely unpopular League of Nations Covenant and for the Versailles Treaty.

Many voters were blaming the Democrats' occupancy of the White House for serious agricultural problems, overlooking the possibility that the Republican-dominated Congress might be a factor. The nation was in a postwar business slump, and farmers were suffering most of all. In the last six months of 1920 farm income declined as surpluses of agricultural commodities reduced the prices of the ten leading crops by 57 percent. Meanwhile farm bankruptcies increased, and land values declined. The Federal Reserve System failed to respond effectively. James Shideler has observed: "With the end of the Sixty-sixth Congress, farmers could point to no legislative achievements that gave genuine promise of relief. The farm situation was going from bad to worse, and Congress was capable only of talk."[1]

Jones predicted a Democratic victory in the presidential election. He urged voters of his Eighteenth District to support the Democratic ticket because "the failure of the Republican party to enact any reconstruction legislation in fourteen months' control of Congress, refusal to revise tax laws urged by the President, and continued extravagant appropriations, show that little or nothing is to be

---

[1] James H. Shideler, *Farm Crisis, 1919–1923*, p. 75. For good accounts of the problems of this era see ibid.; Robert K. Murray, *The Harding Era: Warren G. Harding and His Administration*; and Robert K. Murray, *The Politics of Normalcy: Governmental Theory and Practice in the Harding-Coolidge Era*.

expected of that party in the future."² His own reelection, with no effective opposition, was taken for granted.

Senator Pat Harrison of Mississippi, national director of the Cox-Roosevelt effort, asked for Jones's assistance in September, as the presidential campaign intensified.³ Jones accepted, glad to get away from Panhandle politics that had become boring to him and happy to be active again in exciting political work. He campaigned in Kentucky, Indiana, Missouri, and Oklahoma, often speaking two or three times a day.⁴

In his talks Jones sought to play on the fears of rural Americans who suspected any shifts from agrarian to industrial influence in Washington. Jones pointed out that when the Republicans had gained control of Congress the speakership had passed from an agricultural state (Missouri and Champ Clark) to an industrial state (Massachusetts and Frederick H. Gillett). Such talk was persuasive among some farmers, but Jones's thinking also influenced city voters, and Democratic leaders wisely refrained from calling on him to solicit Democratic support in urban areas.

When November 2 came, the entire Democratic effort ended in abysmal failure. Harding won by a landslide, 16,152,000 to Cox's 9,147,000. Farmers as well as urban dwellers had voted to put the Republicans in office and give them control of Congress. The Senate of the new Sixty-seventh Congress consisted of 59 Republicans and 37 Democrats. In the House, the Republicans posted their largest victory, winning 301 seats against only 131 for the Democrats.

In the days before the Sixty-seventh Congress convened, disappointed Democrats readjusted their depleted ranks and committee assignments. With an aim of advancing his own position, Jones began cultivating friendships among congressmen likely to retire in the not-so-distant future, leaving their assignments vacant. These men could be expected to have a voice in saying who would succeed them.

Jones also conferred frequently with John Nance Garner, the Texas member of the powerful House Ways and Means Committee,

---

² *Claude* (Texas) *News*, June 18, 1920.

³ "Jones on Speaking Tour for Democracy," *Tribune* (n.p.), August 17, 1920, scrapbook 2, Marvin Jones Papers; hereafter cited as MJP.

⁴ Scrapbook 2, MJP.

and, more important for Jones, a member of the House Committee on Committees. Garner made the committee assignments of Texas representatives. Jones, a lawyer and parliamentarian, wanted an assignment to the House Committee on the Judiciary.[5]

Another Texan interested in the same job, Hatton Sumners, had seniority over Jones. After wavering between the Judiciary and Agriculture committees, Sumners chose the Judiciary, largely to use his influence in getting a federal building for Dallas. Despite Jones's pleas Garner refused to recommend two Texans to the Judiciary Committee, and Jones was forced to move in another direction.[6]

Jones was always a bitter loser, whether in a bridge game or in politics, but he muffled his disappointment and asked Garner to give him an assignment to the Agriculture Committee. In time Garner agreed, promising Jones a place on the committee when James Young of Kaufman, Texas, retired.[7]

Despite the interests of many constituents, Jones's own concern in agriculture actually had been secondary to parliamentary procedure and the judiciary. Previously he had taken stands on agricultural legislation only when the farm bills reached the floor of Congress.[8] After his new appointment, however, Jones became in every respect an agrarian advocate, although he continued to think of himself as a lawyer first. When the new session began, he devoted his considerable charm and talents to working with Gilbert Haugen's Agriculture Committee.[9] He went frequently to the Library of Congress, talked agricultural politics with lobbyists at the Congress Ho-

---

[5] Marvin Jones, interview with author, August 12, 1971; Marvin Jones, interview with Dean Albertson, Columbia Oral History Project, 1952, p. 215, hereafter cited as COHP-MJP. Unless otherwise noted, all interviews and correspondence citing Jones refer to Marvin Jones.

[6] Jones, interview with author, August 12, 1971.

[7] COHP–MJP, p. 215.

[8] Ibid., pp. 214–226.

[9] The committee consisted of sixteen Republicans and six Democrats. The Republicans, ranked by seniority, were Gilbert Haugen, James C. McLaughlin, Charles B. Ward, Fred S. Purnell, Edward Voight, Melvin D. McLaughlin, Carl W. Riddick, J. N. Tincher, Thomas S. Williams, James H. Sinclair, Edward D. Hays, Charles J. Thompson, Fred S. Gernerd, Frank Claque, John D. Clarke, and J. Kuhio Kalainaole. The six Democrats, also ranked by seniority, were H. M. Jacoway, John W. Rainey, James B. Aswell, David H. Kincheloe, Marvin Jones, and Peter Ten Eyck. U.S., Congress, *Congressional Directory, 67th Congress, 1st Session*, p. 196.

tel, and stayed up late reading and analyzing bills before committee meetings on the following day. He made it a point to familiarize himself with agricultural legislation proposed since 1917 by congressional farm blocs, which were then in an embryonic stage (between 1917 and 1920 three farm groups—the Farmers' National Council, the National Board of Farm Organizations, and the Grange—established Washington offices). The power of these blocs was to fluctuate during the 1920's, and they were to form constantly shifting coalitions.

Most of the time Jones found himself in agreement with the cotton bloc, largely because both he and they sought export markets for agricultural surpluses. But though the blocs—cotton, corn, wheat, and others—formed shifting coalitions, all these interests were included in a larger congressional group called the farm bloc, which was dedicated to assuring the enactment of legislation in the general interest of farmers. In the House this group had only limited political influence, even though its membership numbered from seventy-five to one hundred members, because it lacked organization and experience.

Although Jones tended to agree with the cotton bloc, he avoided close social contacts with the farm lobbyists who had invaded Washington in recent years. He stayed well clear particularly of the lobbyists who represented what he considered radical organizations like the Farmers' Union and the Nonpartisan League. His association with lobbyists was generally limited to those occasions when they were testifying before the House Committee on Agriculture. There, however, the spotlight was on Chairman Gilbert Haugen of Iowa, who could bless or block bills, and Jones was only a junior member of the minority party. Lobbyists dared not tinker with this political status quo.[10] Jones was to remain a relatively minor committee member for several years.

Nevertheless, his influence and prestige showed some slight gains at this time, for two reasons. First, the flood of farm bills brought on by lobbying and other activity caused a change in House operations. Previously individual congressmen had been able to analyze for themselves the various agricultural proposals. Now, however, they were forced to rely more on the judgment of the House

---

[10] COHP-MJP, pp. 215–217.

Committee on Agriculture and, at least somewhat on Jones's work there.[11] Second, Jones developed a smooth working relationship with Committee Chairman Haugen, even though Haugen was, of course, a Republican.

Haugen, a veteran congressman and respected lawmaker, was straightforward and placed a premium on sincere, hard-working committeemen. He was not adept at keeping order, however, and he tended to let his committee run wild. Despite his method of operation he resented and even feared some opposition members like Democratic leader James Aswell of Louisiana, whose caustic remarks often upset him, but he could show open affection for genial Democrats. Jones took advantage of this opportunity.

Jones studied Haugen's strengths and weaknesses. He sincerely respected Haugen's knowledge of agriculture. He could see that certain of Haugen's personal characteristics hid an image of hard-working chairman. Jones thought Haugen "slow in his mental process— he drove a mental ox cart," which contributed to the Iowan's lack of charisma. Further, Haugen's manner of speech left most congressmen straining to understand him. Haugen permitted members to express their opinions with little restraint. Long, disorganized, unproductive meetings resulted from this excessive tolerance. Jones concluded, however, that, although the Iowa Republican certainly failed in achieving greatness, he deserved much credit for developing national farm legislation.[12]

Jones's own thinking in regard to 1921 farm legislation included opposition to protective tariffs. One reason was his fear that tariffs would backfire and hinder world marketing of American farm produce. The Harding administration, on the contrary, saw protective tariffs as beneficial.

[11] Ibid., pp. 218–225. Anderson contended Congress had other blocs and that "bloc" voting might not have been a strange development in House operating procedures. He noted that there was a beer bloc, a tariff bloc, a sales-tax bloc, and a railroad bloc. He did, however, substantiate the contention that by December 1921 representatives were under increasing pressure from their constituents to enact some kind of farm legislation. Sydney Anderson, "The Latest Thing in Blocs," *County Gentlemen* 86 (December 31, 1921): 3–4, 21. See also Theodore Saloutos and John D. Hicks, *Twentieth-Century Populism: Agricultural Discontent in the Middle West, 1900–1939*, pp. 321–341.

[12] COHP-MJP, pp. 202–206.

In April 1921 Congress debated an emergency tariff that would increase duties on meat, corn, wheat, sugar, corn, and wool.[13] The farm bloc supported the bill, but Jones voted to send it back to committee because it was basically protective and not for the primary purpose of collective revenue. After farm-bloc supportive efforts intensified, Jones yielded and voted for the bill. He justified his new position "in the hope that the plight of the farmer and livestock raiser may be somewhat relieved." Furthermore, he believed that the Republicans might try to pass a higher tariff, and the emergency tariff seemed the lesser of two evils.[14]

Jones's support in 1921 of limited economic nationalism reflected the desires of many, but not all, of his constituents. The *Amarillo News* observed that Jones voted "in the interest of the people of his country, without haggling over the possible effects such action will have on his next campaign."[15] For the rest of his time in Congress, however, he would oppose protective duties, and later he would seek to modify the emergency tariff through an export debenture plan that proponents claimed would restore agricultural prosperity in the United States. Under this plan exporters would receive government debentures with face values equal to differences between the world-market price of the commodity exported and a domestic evaluation based on that price plus the tariff. The exporter would be allowed to sell these debentures to importers of foreign goods so that they could use them to pay tariffs on those imports. The debentures would sell for their approximate face value and would avoid more burdensome methods of collecting equalization fees.

Jones's support of that plan, however, still lay in the future when, on July 13, 1921, he spoke in the House against high protective tariffs. He traced the history of the word "tariff" to Moorish Spanish, asserting that throughout its existence the word had meant "forced contribution of the many to the few," and warned that tariffs would hinder world marketing of American surpluses. Nevertheless,

[13] Murray, *The Harding Era*, p. 125.
[14] Marvin Jones, "Individual Voting Record, 67th Congress, 1st Session," MS, MJP; "The Farm Bloc—A Peril or a Hope?" *Literary Digest* 71 (December 24, 1921):10–11; COHP-MJP, p. 190.
[15] *Amarillo News*, April 22, 1921.

a higher tariff that Jones had foreseen and feared passed the House eight days later in the form of the "Fordney bill." Jones attacked it as partisan, big-business legislation.[16] After further congressional work, however, it was to become law, the Fordney-McCumber Tariff. The House approved it on September 15.[17]

The Harding administration expressed satisfaction about the extent of agricultural relief afforded by the emergency tariff, but to most farmers it seemed little more than crumbs from the congressional dinner table. The farm bloc pushed for new legislation. Jones and other representatives blocked a move to adjourn Congress without substantial farm relief. Faced with a bipartisan rebellion, Harding yielded. In the summer of 1921, Congress passed five measures: the Packers and Stockyards Act, which prohibited certain unfair and monopolistic practices; the Future Trading Act, which eventually provided supervision of "contract markets" in a manner beneficial to farmers; amendments to the Farm Loan Act of 1916 that favored borrowers; and the Emergency Agricultural Credits Act, of further benefit to farmers. Eventually the War Finance Corporation was revived to rush aid to farmers through loans and to promote foreign trade.

Jones gave much thought to all this legislation while it was being debated. Regarding plans to regulate packers and stockyards, for example, Jones opposed a government takeover of those businesses, as some individuals advocated, but he also opposed practices of packers and stockyards that took advantage of the producer. The first action, he thought, would represent socialism, which Jones consistently fought. The second action would represent government regulation, and, though Jones generally opposed more government control, he realized the occasional necessity for it, especially in correcting abuses. He drafted an amendment to the Packers and Stockyards Act that prohibited certain attempts at price-fixing, but it failed. Jones thought that the act that finally became law was a very small step indeed toward eliminating abuses.

[16] Marvin Jones, *The Tariff Bill, July 13, 1921*, p. 8; see also U.S., Congress, House, *Congressional Record*, 67th Cong., 1st ses., 1921, 61, pp. 3708–3709.

[17] COHP-MJP, pp. 258–261; Murray, *The Politics of Normalcy*, pp. 66–67; Marvin Jones, "Individual Voting Record, 67th Congress, 1st Session, 67th Congress, 2d Session," MJP.

Regarding the other farm legislation, Jones championed government regulation of agricultural speculators, whom he likened to fleas on a dog; supported moves to make more government money available in loans to farmers at lower interest rates; and opposed attempts to allow local banks a 2 percent commission on transactions. The loans, he said, should be arranged directly with government agencies. Throughout all this generous lawmaking, however, Jones remained basically conservative, never favoring great raids on the treasury by any group.

He was also a conservationist, through experience on his father's farm. The Jones family had relied on guesswork and intuition rather than on scientific study to enhance productivity of their land. Horace Jones had supervised the building of crude earthen dams and terraces. The boys, working mule-powered plows, had cut contour furrows on hillsides and had planted crops to stop gully washing. Jones's conservationism would later expand to encompass broad aspects of land policy and use. Regarding the Alaskan domain, he would, in time, declare opposition to the United States government's parting with any land without keeping all oil, gas, and mineral rights.[18] To prevent speculation by large companies, Jones advocated further restrictions on land ownership. But, inconsistently, Jones was intrigued by a proposal concerning Muscle Shoals, on the Tennessee River in Alabama.

In 1921, Henry Ford offered the government five million dollars for a one-hundred-year lease on the federal hydroelectric plant there. The industrialist said that his primary purpose would be to use the plant in producing cheap fertilizer for farmers. This proposal appealed to Jones. In the Senate, Vice-President Calvin Coolidge sent the idea to the Agriculture Committee. In the House, Speaker Frederick Gillett of Massachusetts, in a political maneuver, referred the bill to the Military Affairs Committee. This shocked the House Agriculture Committee members, and Jones persuaded his colleagues to ask Gillett to send the bill to Agriculture. Most Democratic champions of Ford's proposal feared that a bitter controversy over committee power would doom their efforts, but Jones wanted to fight

---

[18] U.S., Congress, House, *Congressional Record*, 67th Cong., 1st sess., 1921, 61, p. 7270.

the issue on the House floor. Calmer congressmen warned Jones against this policy, and he yielded to pressure. The Ford bill failed. Thirty-one years later Jones would blame himself for this "mistake." Jones always believed, erroneously or not, that Ford's plan would have guaranteed cheap fertilizer for the American farmer[19] and that it failed largely because Republicans and some other congressmen from industrial states feared that their industries "would come trooping South."[20]

In time, however, Jones would change his mind about government ownership of Muscle Shoals, along with many other conservative southern Democrats who eventually accepted it. He was to cast his first vote favoring the project on February 20, 1931.[21] Later still, following President Franklin D. Roosevelt's endorsement, Jones would vote for Muscle Shoals and Tennessee Valley Authority bills during the New Deal's "hundred days."

That lay a decade away, however. In the early 1920's agriculture continued to experience a severe depression. The Joint Commission of Agriculture Inquiry, convened under the leadership of Representative Sydney Anderson, a Republican from Minnesota, recommended in 1922 that the federal government encourage improved farm-cooperative organizations, expansion of agricultural credit, reform of federally licensed warehouses, reduction of freight rates, improved grading of agricultural commodities, expansion of research and statistical data gathered by the Department of Agriculture, greater cooperation between the Department of Agriculture and state agricultural colleges, and additional provisions for agricultural attachés in foreign countries to promote the sale of farm surpluses.[22] Jones supported these remedies. Generally, however, he believed that

---

[19] Scrapbook 1, MJP; U.S., Congress, House, *Congressional Record*, 67th Cong., 1st sess., 1921, 61, pp. 6767–68; Preston J. Hubbard, *Origins of the TVA: The Muscle Shoals Controversy, 1920–1932*, pp. 28–146; COHP-MJP, pp. 369–370.

[20] Unidentified clipping, scrapbook 2, MJP.

[21] COHP-MJP, pp. 425–427; Jones, "Individual Voting Record, 70th Congress, 2d Session; 70th Congress, 3d Session; 71st Congress, 1st Session," MJP; Richard Lowitt, *George W. Norris: The Persistence of a Progressive, 1919–1933*, pp. 457–467, 556, 567–568.

[22] COHP-MJP, pp. 213–215; U.S., Congress, Joint Commission of Agricultural Inquiry, *Report of the Joint Commission of Agricultural Inquiry*.

officials of the Harding administration responded inadequately to farm problems.

After passage in early 1922 of the Capper-Volstead Cooperative Marketing Act, a law allowing farm cooperatives favored status with respect to antitrust and income-tax legislation, the House plodded forward with a study of the agricultural appropriations bill. Republican Floor Leader Frank Mondell of Wyoming warned against any big drain on the treasury, but Democrat James Aswell of Louisiana sought increased appropriations and expansion of programs —especially in regard to the Department of Agriculture's statistical division, warehouse-legislation reform, the program of foreign agricultural attachés, and research in agricultural colleges and universities. Jones backed Aswell. He knew that the Harding administration intended to give monetary support to the failing merchant marine, and he believed that American agriculture deserved equal consideration.[23] Apparently the thought never struck him that expansion of the merchant marine might help sell agricultural surpluses on the world market. Another major consideration before the Sixty-seventh Congress was legislation that would become known as the Intermediate Credit Act, an effort to provide additional relief for agriculture. Jones argued that the bill would not benefit the small farmer because its administration would not be at the grass-roots level. Eventually, however, he voted for the bill as a temporary remedy for farm finance.

As the months of Harding's administration became one year, then two and more, gossip about misconduct of administration officials became widespread in Washington. It developed that President Harding (like President Grant after the Civil War), had made a number of unwise appointments and (also like Grant) soon found himself surrounded by corruption without admitting or even realizing its inception. Furthermore, Harding was no real leader. The greatest achievement of his administration (or so it appeared at the time) was the 1921–1922 Washington Naval Conference and an ensuing international agreement to limit arms, but all this had been brought about through the initiative of others.

In April 1922, Senator John B. Kendrick of Wyoming, acting

---

[23] U.S., Congress, House, *Congressional Record*, 67th Cong., 2d sess., 1921, 63, p. 3627.

on information he had received from his state, asked Secretary of the Interior Albert B. Fall why certain oil fields in Wyoming, known as the Teapot Dome, reserved for the United States Navy, had been leased, as he had heard, to an oil company owned by Harry F. Sinclair. His question initiated the official queries that would in time expose corruption in many areas. Fall would be found guilty of accepting a bribe in leasing naval oil reserves. Other Harding officials would be found guilty of fraud, bribery, and conspiracy. President Harding himself heard of impending publication of many other charges during a visit to Alaska. Shaken by what he heard, he traveled southward to San Francisco and died there August 2, 1923, of complications not exactly defined even today. He was succeeded by Vice-President Calvin Coolidge.

Jones remained convinced that Harding had been victimized by his advisers. He thought that Harding was personally honest, even if the easygoing president did not understand human nature or take much interest in public affairs. Jones had known that many Harding men were getting away with all kinds of improprieties.

Within the Democratic National Campaign Committee, however, a sense of frustration prevailed. The Democrats had neither the congressional power nor the key people to take political advantage of the situation. They seemed to Jones like young boys pulling wild grapevines from a tall tree. Jones recalled:

Four or five of us used to tug at the vines fastened in the tree top. It looked like nothing was going to come down, and we would just about give up. Some boy would say, "Let's give one more tug," and we would give it another tug and the whole vine would turn loose and fall, and we would have all the grapes we wanted.[24]

Nevertheless, truly delicious political fruit did not fall into their hands.

During the Harding years Jones emerged as quiet and cautious, with a flair for emotional oratory and the habit of sponsoring legislation through proposing amendments. In partisan matters he stood with the Democrats, although he sometimes acted independently and rashly—as in the Muscle Shoals controversy. Jones's scope of ideas had not yet risen to the national level.

[24] Marvin Jones, "Individual Voting Record, 67th Congress, 4th Session," MJP; COHP-MJP, pp. 261–280.

5.

The Crusade for the
Export Debenture Plan

IN December 1923, President Calvin Coolidge delivered his first annual message to Congress. He declared support for lower taxes, government economy, and enforcement of prohibition. Radio sets carried his message, delivered in his nasal twang, to thousands of listeners.

The same month three issues began competing for Marvin Jones's time and attention: the forthcoming elections of 1924, the question of Philippine independence, and debate on the Export Debenture Plan (to be described in Chapter 6), which Jones felt was a better answer to agricultural problems than a plan proposed as a series of bills by Senator Charles McNary of Oregon and Representative Gilbert Haugen of Iowa, although the plan was actually formulated by agriculturalists Charles Brand, George N. Peek, and Hugh S. Johnson, who had the backing of Secretary of Agriculture Henry C. Wallace (the father of Franklin D. Roosevelt's secretary of agriculture). The plan, which came to be known as the McNary-Haugen Plan, was a highly complex and slow-in-fulfillment arrangement whereby farmers would be assured by the government of receiving, in regular money and scrip, the much better prewar prices for their crops.

The forthcoming election was expected to have an incumbent campaigning for return to the presidency—always a difficult obstacle for the opposing party to overcome. Jones, as a member of the Democratic National Campaign Committee, hoped to sway many rural voters away from Republican support because of the continuing farm problems.

Calvin Coolidge, however, had brought the fresh aroma of honesty to the White House, even if he was evidently devoid of personal charm and color and even if investigators continued, during Coolidge's first months as president, to probe into earlier wrongdoing by Harding appointees.

True to expectations, the frugal Coolidge had immediately named domestic problems as the nation's first concern, with emphasis on tax reduction and government economy. The president's solutions for agriculture included tax reductions, cheaper fertilizer, better credit, expanded cooperative marketing, and greater railroad efficiency coupled with lower freight rates. He added highway construction and reforestation projects to his list of agricultural priorities.

These very ideas had been advocated by Marvin Jones and other Democrats and by many of Coolidge's fellow Republicans during the Harding administration. One of Coolidge's biographers, Donald McCoy, later observed, "It was the [program] of a man who sought to satisfy most people by picking up the things they want and carrying them so long as they cost [only] a little."[1] Coolidge's agricultural policies seemed neither progressive nor reactionary.

The president's domestic concerns lost out in priority and publicity to the continuing investigations of the Harding-era scandals. Capitol Hill Democrats, although frustrated by lack of power, approached the forthcoming election vowing not to let voters forget the moral decay of the Harding era. Republicans themselves showed some division. Many feared rejection at the polls and deemphasized their party identity. Especially conspicuous among these were northwestern Republicans elected to Congress with Non-Partisan League support.

Meanwhile, during the cold months of December and January, the Coolidge administration encountered increasing pressure from farmers to get something done besides investigating scandals. Many of them braved ice and snow to visit the Washington headquarters of the Farmers' National Council. There they urged enactment of the Norris-Sinclair bill, which would set up a government export corporation, repeal of the Esch-Cummins Transportation Act and the Fordney-McCumber Tariff, replacement of the secretary of agriculture by the Federal Trade Commission as administrator of the Pack-

[1] Donald R. McCoy, *Calvin Coolidge: The Quiet President*, pp. 200–201.

ers and Stockyards Act, convening of a world farm conference, and other actions. Mail sacks brought even more unsolicited advice from individuals and organizations. Congressional hoppers filled with drastic solutions. The McNary-Haugen movement had its inception at this time.

Early in 1924, President Coolidge examined with favor the Norbeck-Burtness bill, which would provide farmers of northwest-central states $50 million in loans to help them diversify their production and end their dependence on wheat as their sole crop. The president sent a message to the House Agriculture Committee expressing his support.

Jones attacked Coolidge's recommendation and, in fact, his entire agricultural policy in "The President and the Farmer," a speech delivered on January 29, 1924. Jones called Coolidge vague and indecisive about help for farmers. Jones asked which of the forty bills lying in neat piles before the committee the president really wanted passed. He waved in his hand an assortment of Republican-initiated bills, and remarked, "If the President meant all these bills I have here, then no such rainbow has been painted in the farmers' political sky since the days of 'sockless' Jerry Simpson."[2] He singled out the Norbeck-Burtness bill for specific criticism. It was, Jones said, impractical and primarily a political document. He saw the entire situation as irrational executive leadership.

Jones suggested some solutions, among them immediate repeal of the Fordney-McCumber Tariff:

If you repeal the iniquitous tariff, which gives to the interests the power to sell to the farmer at outrageous prices, you will do something.... These bills and this message [from Coolidge] are striking at the [farm] problem from the wrong angle. The trouble is not production. The farmer is producing. . . . He simply wants equality of opportunity. That he has never had. We should tackle the machinery of distribution rather than the machinery of production. . . . Distribution is where the farmer gets the hot end of the poker, . . . but the biggest single thing is to repeal the tariff bill.[3]

[2] U.S., Congress, House, *Congressional Record*, 68th Cong., 1st sess., 1924, 65, p. 1634. See also scrapbook 3, Marvin Jones Papers, hereafter cited as MJP; Murray Benedict, *Farm Policies of the United States, 1790–1950*, pp. 215–216; Gilbert C. Fite, *Peter Norbeck: Prairie Statesman*, p. 107.

[3] U.S., Congress, House, *Congressional Record*, 68th Cong., 1st sess., 1924, 65, pp. 1634–35.

Doggedly determined, on April 1 Jones sought to bind Coolidge to the Harding scandals. In a speech he called "The Republican Street Parade and G.O.P. Circus," Jones mentioned the principals in the Harding scandals, including among the performers "Kareful Kal" (Coolidge), "the only politician in captivity who has even been able to hold office for twenty-five years and always have himself photographed milking a cow or pitching hay when notified of his nomination."[4] Jones was certain that Coolidge would not be returned to office in the wake of the Republican scandals, but he was blinded by provincialism. He was still not much more than "the Panhandle Kid" in some ways. He failed to detect Coolidge's appeal as a moralist and assumed that the Republicans would nominate, instead of the former vice-president, Speaker of the House Frederick Gillett or Senator Henry Cabot Lodge of Massachusetts or Senator Hiram Johnson of California—men of real presidential timber, in Jones's estimation. He felt certain that Coolidge did not meet that description.[5] The Republicans surprised him. When their convention met in Cleveland early in June, they nominated President Coolidge for reelection. His running mate was Charles G. Dawes of Illinois.

Jones was a member of the Texas delegation to the Democratic National Convention, which met in New York City late the same month. Jones and the other Texas delegates were committed to California's William Gibbs McAdoo, son-in-law of Woodrow Wilson. When arguments arose concerning the best-qualified Democrat, however, Jones remained silent. He feared that conflict would wreck his party's chances.[6]

Conflict did indeed nearly disrupt the convention, and Jones and his sister Metze, who made the trip with him, looked on helplessly. A fight over the Ku Klux Klan and tension between rural and urban Democrats developed. Unfortunately, McAdoo was linked with the Ku Klux Klan through receipt of a retainer's fee. Al Smith of New York, opposed to the Klan, emerged as a strong candidate,

---

[4] Marvin Jones, *Marvin Jones Memoirs*, ed. Joseph M. Ray, pp. 73–74.

[5] Scrapbook 2, MJP; Marvin Jones, interview with Dean Albertson, Columbia Oral History Project, 1952, pp. 264, 310–311; hereafter cited as COHC-MJP. Unless otherwise noted, all interviews and correspondence citing Jones refer to Marvin Jones.

[6] See Lee N. Allen, "The Democratic Presidential Election of 1924 in Texas," *Southwestern Historical Quarterly* 61 (April 1958):474–493.

but Smith was a Catholic and an easterner, and that alienated many delegates from the South and West. Peace did not come even after a plea by William Jennings Bryan (who was making what proved to be his last appearance before a Democratic convention) that delegates ignore the Klan issue and other divisions and get on with the business of defeating Republicans. After 102 unsuccessful ballots the exhausted Democrats finally nominated John W. Davis of West Virginia for president and Governor Charles W. Bryan of Nebraska, brother of William Jennings Bryan, for vice-president.

After the convention, in an attempt to stimulate unity, some New York Democrats invited Jones to make a Fourth-of-July speech at Tammany Hall. The opportunity excited him. He was eager to speak to a big-city audience and to play a national political role, but he also feared the appearance would backfire at home, where the Klan influence there was still strong. If one believed Amarillo courthouse gossip, then Jones himself had once been a Klan member, only to realize his mistake and have his name quietly removed from the rolls.[7] Reluctantly Jones declined the New York invitation.

In election year 1924 several other political parties entered the campaign, a division that was expected to hurt the Democrats more than the better-unified Republicans. The strongest of these parties appeared to be the Progressive party (backed by the American Federation of Labor), the Farmer-Labor party, and the Socialist party. The Progressive nominees were Senator Robert M. La Follette of Wisconsin for president and Senator Burton K. Wheeler of Montana for vice-president.

During the early days of the ensuing presidential campaign, Jones, who had no political opposition himself, campaigned for Davis and Bryan in his home district and other Texas districts. When the Progressives sent Senator Wheeler into Texas on a speaking tour,

---

[7] "Tammany Asked Jones to Make Fourth Address," *Amarillo Evening Post*, June [?], 1924, scrapbook 3, MJP; COHP-MJP, pp. 309–310. Was Jones ever a member of the Ku Klux Klan? I have been unable to document an answer. A version of the story is that, during the high tide of Klan activity in Panhandle, Jones became a member but did not play an active role. When Klan membership became a political liability, one of Jones's campaign managers had Jones's name erased from the membership rolls. A similar action seems possible with regard to Jones's brief marriage, which made him an "official bachelor."

the Democratic National Committee called on Jones to counter him. Later Jones asked to campaign also in rural areas of Illinois, Indiana, Kentucky, Colorado, Iowa, Missouri, Kansas, and Oklahoma. There he stressed the Republican scandals and observed that "the past four years have been filled with corruption, and the people will not vote for the maintenance of materialism."[8] He also emphasized the ability of candidate Davis, but he could not persuade rural farmers to embrace the corporation lawyer from West Virginia. Jones came to realize too late that people were tired of the scandals issue and in 1924 wanted only peace and tranquillity. When the campaign ended in November, Silent Cal Coolidge's huge victory came as no surprise, even to Jones.

After the election the issue of Philippine independence claimed much of Jones's attention. He favored giving the Philippines their freedom. One reason for his position was his nationalism in regard to foreign affairs. Another was his support of American farmers and ranchers, including those in the dairy industry. During the 1920's farm organizations began demanding independence of the islands so that tariffs could be imposed on agricultural imports—especially on coconut milk, which competed with American dairy products. Coconut milk added to skimmed milk, for instance, made a respectable canned-milk substitute. Testimony before the House Agriculture Committee failed to show any genuine nutritional harm from this "filled-milk" product, however, and Jones supported the manufacturers' right to sell it as long as the contents were clearly printed on the label. When that compromise failed, Jones sided with dairy-state representatives who said that the filled-milk industry sought to deceive the unsuspecting public and that Congress must prohibit this method of marketing.[9]

Another statement of Jones's support of Philippine independence came in 1923, when he argued that Filipinos should be given self-government because they are in much better condition to handle their own affairs than a great many of these other little countries

---

[8] "Congressman Jones Declares Democratic Party Should View Election on Bad G.O.P. Record." See also various clippings, scrapbooks 2, 3, MJP; COHP-MJP, pp. 311–319.

[9] See Benedict, *Farm Policies of the United States*, pp. 269, 271–272; John D. Hicks, *The Republican Ascendancy, 1921–1933*, pp. 255–257; Paul H. Clyde, *The Far East*, 3d ed., pp. 619–621; COHP-MJP, pp. 270–274.

that we recognized at the conclusion of the great World War. Furthermore, Jones argued, the Filipinos seemed to have been maturing in their ability to govern themselves until the United States sent General Leonard Wood to the Philippines as administrator. Jones disliked Woods's strong-arm tactics, called them directly opposed to congressional intent on the Philippines' future, and said that they showed why a military man should never be named to head a civilian government.

Arguments that most Filipinos favored continued American administration of the islands made little impact on Jones. Whether or not they wanted independence, they were ready for it, in Jones's estimation.

In 1925 he had a chance to visit the Philippines and see for himself. On June 11 he and eleven other congressmen boarded the naval transport *Chaumont* for a trip to the Orient—his first. Jones and colleague David Kincheloe observed with interest Philippine farm families and the islands' agriculture, especially the fields of sugarcane, but they were appalled to see military fortifications. The congressional party proceeded to Shanghai, Hong Kong, and Japan before returning to the United States by way of Guam and Hawaii.[10]

The trip increased Jones's fears that continued United States involvement in the Orient would result in eventual war with Japan. Speaking at the First Methodist Church in Denton, Texas, after his return, Jones observed that the islands were the weakest link in the American "empire" and that fundamental conflicts existed in Filipinos' and Americans' concepts of government that would make future efforts at Americanization costly and ineffective. The feasible alternative, Jones said, was to grant the islands self-determination (the Philippines would finally become fully independent after World War II, on July 4, 1946, in accordance with terms of the Tydings-McDuffie Act of 1934).

After returning to Washington from his trip to the Orient, Jones continued to pound away at the coconut-milk issue. Speaking before the House, he described it as a "battle between the coconut and the

[10] COHP-MJP, pp. 329–332; clippings, scrapbooks II, 2, 3, MJP. With Marvin were Otis Wingo, Daniel Garnett, S. D. McReynolds, Ralph Gilbert, Maurice Thatcher, John Miller, Charles R. Crisp, James Begg, Walter Lineberger, Luther A. Johnson, and David Kincheloe.

cow. In that kind of battle, I am inclined to favor the American cow."[11]

His concern, however, extended to encompass Texas cotton. He had become increasingly alarmed by the competition of coconut with cottonseed oil as an ingredient in oleomargarine. "This is a crisis not only for the dairy products but for cottonseed," he said. "it is a crisis for peanuts; it is a crisis for all domestic oils, because this country is being flooded with foreign oils."[12]

But for the rest of the decade Jones would give top priority to his fight for his Export Debenture Plan as an alternative to the McNary-Haugen plan. As early as 1922 the House Agriculture Committee had begun considering what was to become known as McNary-Haugenism, whose origin actually had preceded that date. Gilbert C. Fite, in *George N. Peek and the Fight for Farm Parity*, traced the progress of the movement that began in December 1921, when Peek and Hugh S. Johnson originated an "equality for agriculture" plan. Peek and Johnson argued that the agricultural tariffs inherent in the then-current policy of economic nationalism had the continuing problem of crop surpluses. Any equality for agriculture thus had remained nothing more than a dream among farmers, because they bought equipment and other necessities in a protected market and sold their agricultural surpluses in highly competitive world markets. To benefit farmers, Peek and Johnson proposed modifying the tariff structure by establishing a government corporation to purchase surplus products from the domestic market, permit the domestic price to increase behind the tariff wall, and then sell the commodities on the world market. If prices should fall drastically, corporation losses could be curtailed through equalization fees paid by farmers on the commodities sold. This plan was described in detail by Peek and Johnson in a book, *Equality for Agriculture*. It attracted much attention among farm leaders and congressmen.[13]

[11] "The Coconut and the Cow," speech, February 25, 1931, MS, MJP.

[12] Ibid; see also scrapbook 4, MJP; Marvin Jones, "The Remarks of Marvin Jones," *Congressional Record* Scrapbook, vol. 2 (69th Cong., 1st sess.), pp. 5360–63, MJP (Jones's remarks on the floor of Congress were collected in four scrapbooks, now among his papers); *New York Times*, March 11, 1926; "The Coconut and the Cow," speech, MJP.

[13] Gilbert C. Fite, *George N. Peek and the Fight for Farm Poverty*, pp. 38–58; George N. Peek and Hugh Johnson, *Equality for Agriculture*.

The agricultural conference of January 1922 provided Peek another opportunity to gain support for the plan. At the same time Peek met individually with some members of the House Agriculture Committee. When he talked with Jones, Peek faced some hard questioning about the proposed equalization fee.

Jones wanted to know the amounts of the fees for wheat and other commodities. Peek's responses varied from "a few cents" to twenty cents. Jones, a suspicious, stubborn man, doubted these general responses (it might be observed also that Jones was a "salesman" himself and not easily hoodwinked).

Other ideas from the January agricultural conference filtered into Capitol Hill cloakrooms. For example, Senator George Norris of Nebraska wanted a competitive government corporation to buy farm products and sell them abroad, much like the War Finance Corporation. Some legislators proposed revival of the controversial Ladd-Sinclair bill from the previous Congress, to expand functions of the United States Grain Corporation. The Gooding bill would have authorized a $300 million government corporation to purchase surplus wheat. Kansas Republican Edward Little favored a plan to permit the secretary of agriculture to purchase surplus commodities and make loans to farmers. South Dakota Republican Charles Christopherson proposed that the Department of Agriculture fix prices of basic agricultural commodities. The last idea was completely unacceptable to Jones, who nevertheless focused immediate attention on all these bills, which were already in the hopper as the new Sixty-eighth Congress began discussions of agricultural policy.[14]

In January 1922, the McNary-Haugen bill came before both House and Senate. The government corporation thus established would purchase and sell eight surplus commodities—swine, flour, wheat, cotton, wool, cattle, sheep, and corn. The House would appropriate $200 million for the corporation's activities.

When the House Agriculture Committee conducted hearings on the proposal, Jones listened carefully to testimony in behalf of the bill by Peek, Chester Davis, W. W. Hirth, and others. Corn-belt congressmen and certain other farm-bloc representatives favored pas-

---

[14] Ibid.; COHP-MJP, pp. 240–244; Benedict, *Farm Policies of the United States*, pp. 207–208.

sage. Southern congressmen were not united, but all the representatives, Jones included, hoped for expanded foreign markets for surplus commodities. A sense of urgency prevailed, and Jones hoped to eliminate procedural defects in the bill and perfect its administrative features.

Jones had doubts about the bill's policy objectives, and these doubts intensified as debate proceeded. He believed that the bill created an artificial prop for farm products, and he argued that reduction of the tariff would be a better solution. Virginia's Walton Moore joined Jones in denouncing the Fordney-McCumber Tariff as a failure.

Jones also believed that McNary-Haugenism would lower the price of cotton. Congressmen from other cotton-producing districts expressed a similar fear. As a result Jones sought to limit coverage to wheat, flour, swine, cattle, and dairy products, but all of his work proved futile because the McNary-Haugen plan failed to win approval. Jones thought that the bill's defeat amounted to political obstructionism and that Congress could perfect it in later sessions.[15]

During these years of debate on agricultural policy came a most difficult decision for Jones. On January 18, 1924, the House created the World War Veterans' Committee. John Nance Garner and Finus Garrett approached Jones asking him to accept an assignment to the committee, which would concern itself primarily with war-risk-insurance claims. Jones had actively supported veterans; now he could have the ranking Democratic position on their committee, and it would assure him a chairmanship as soon as the Democrats regained control of Congress.

But Jones became suspicious about Garner's motives. Garner told him that the Democrats needed a skilled parliamentarian to head the committee and that during the next election the Democrats would dramatize the bonus issue. The World War Veterans' Committee would, however, have much less prestige than the Agriculture Committee. Jones suspected that Garner might be wanting a Texan on the House Agriculture Committee whose views were more in line

[15] COHP-MJP, pp. 285–300; A. B. Genung, *The Agricultural Depression Following World War I and Its Political Consequences*, pp. 27–28; U.S. Congress, House, *Congressional Record*, 68th Cong., 1st sess., 1924, 65, pp. 9453, 9936, 9945–46, 10036.

with those of southern congressmen and who had not voted in favor of McNary-Haugenism. Eventually Jones declined to leave the Agriculture Committee, preferring less actual power for the time being, and continued to focus his attention on farm problems.

After Coolidge became president on his own in 1925, he created the President's Farm Commission to investigate agricultural conditions and recommend legislation. Making up the membership were basically conservative agriculturists headed by Robert D. Carey of Wyoming. That same year, in three different reports, the commission recommended as agricultural remedies reduction of freight rates, readjustment of tariffs, and establishment of a federal cooperative marketing board. These recommendations were later included in the Capper-Haugen bill. Jones led southern representatives in denouncing all of this with an intensity that was increased by earlier House refusal to appropriate funds for an agricultural experiment station in his district.

Jones depicted Coolidge as a false friend of agriculture and as one who lacked initiative and creativity. The president, said Jones, boxed national policy on the meddlesome tariff, which gave agriculture an Achilles' heel. Jones's opinions were echoed by other congressmen and by newspaperman Edgar Howard, who editorialized in his *Columbus* (Nebraska) *Daily Telegram* that "the pretended friendship of the Coolidge Administration toward agriculture is a joke." On the other hand, Jones drew a stinging rebuke from his close friend "Poly" Tincher of Kansas, who told legislators to ignore Jones's stated views because Garner and certain other influential Democrats would honor recommendations made by the President's Farm Commission and not treat the report like a political football.[16]

Disgusted, Jones began seeking his own solution to agricultural problems. His lukewarm support of the McNary-Haugen bill evaporated. Eventually he proposed the Export Debenture Plan. This plan had been the subject of lectures Professor Charles L. Stewart

---

[16] U.S., Congress, House, *Congressional Record*, 68th Cong., 2d sess., 1925, 66, pp. 60, 2801–2807; *Fort Worth Star Telegram*, February 1, 1925; *New York World*, February 1, 1925; Edgar Howard, "Fooling the Farmer Again," *Columbus* (Nebraska) *Daily Telegram*, February 3, 1925; "Capper-Haugen Bill Put the Dealers on Top," *Farmer's National Magazine*, March 1925.

had delivered in May 1924 at the University of Illinois. In February of the following year Marvin Jones introduced a measure (H.R. 12346) that was a forerunner of the McKinley-Adkins bills. This embryonic version of the Export Debenture Plan allowed customs officials to issue to farm associations certificates stating the amount and domestic value of their products at the time of exportation. When the certificates were filed with the secretary of the treasury, the government would pay 10 percent of the domestic value of the products. The bill restricted certificate redemption to wheat, cotton, corn, rice, cattle, and swine.[17]

The following year the Export Debenture Plan was included in the McKinley-Adkins bills of January 1926. Jones urged their support. Meanwhile, he, with Louis Taber of the National Grange and John Ketcham, a Michigan representative who owed his seat to Grange support, devoted long hours to drafting a more sophisticated domestic allotment bill. This was a move to capitalize on Coolidge's now-known hostility to McNary-Haugenism.

Thus, while Jones opposed the Fordney-McCumber Tariff, he maintained some allegiance to economic nationalism, and he never was a believer in unlimited free trade. He preferred to modify the tariff to capitalize on possibilities of obtaining new agricultural markets and to assure equity between industrial and rural America. Concurrently, he refused to accept the thesis that a farm surplus was the number-one problem for agriculture, and he deplored acreage-control proposals. He realized that a surplus made the Fordney-McCumber Tariff ineffective in raising farm prices, and he observed that "you might just as well attempt to dam the Mississippi River with toothpicks as to undertake to lift the price of farm products generally through the medium of a tariff."[18]

Jones always considered commodity distribution, not quantity of production, the primary difficulty. Every bushel of corn, he reasoned, could feed some hungry person somewhere in the world. He assumed that markets for American surpluses were available, but

[17] Joseph Standiffe Davis, *The Farm Export Debenture Plan*, p. 2; H.R. 12346, February 18, 1925, MJP; Jones, "The Remarks of Marvin Jones," *Congressional Record* Scrapbook, vol. 2 (69th Cong., 2d sess.), pp. 3873–74, MJP.

[18] Marvin Jones, "The Tariff, the President, and the Farmer," flyer to constituents, January 7, 1926, MJP.

government purchases of food for hungry Americans did not logically follow, because (like most other Americans) Jones reasoned that capitalism generated its own social welfare. Since the prime issue for American farmers was expansion of distribution, it made little difference where the expansion occurred—abroad or at home. Success would come with effective salesmanship. Thus Jones justified his Export Debenture Plan, which utilized the tariff structure.

To equalize the tariff and to increase the flow of agricultural products into the market, Jones worked to strike cattle from the list of commodities receiving support from McNary-Haugenism. He also supported flexible provisions for government activity by urging passage of an amendment that stated:

> ... in the case of any or all of such basic agricultural commodities ... [when] a substantial number of cooperative associations or other organizations representing the producers ... are in favor of the commencement by the board of operations in such ... then the board shall declare its findings and commence operations in respect.[19]

Jones's position on cattle ran against that of the plains rancher, but he avoided political retribution by attacking the packer, long a whipping boy of rancher interests. He sought to place any equalization fees on meat already in packers' cold storage, but he was unsuccessful.[20]

From 1925 through 1927, Jones further refined his ideas on the Export Debenture Plan. He was supported by the conservative National Grange, which had the greatest influence on his thinking of any farm organization. Jones met frequently with Louis J. Taber of the Grange and John Ketcham, a Michigan Republican and former Grange lecturer, to discuss new legislation and share opinions. After the Grange voted to support the Export Debenture Bill at its 1926 convention, Taber came before the House Agriculture Committee to speak in favor of the Adkins bill. During 1927, Jones introduced two export debenture bills (H.R. 17025 on February 8, 1927, and H.R. 19247 on February 19, 1927), but neither won House approval.

The following year Jones introduced a bill (H.R. 12893) simi-

---

[19] Jones, "The Remarks of Marvin Jones," *Congressional Record* Scrapbook, vol. 2 (69th Cong., 1st sess.), p. 9140.

[20] Ibid., pp. 9104–07, 9140, 9399, 9404, 9648; John T. Schlebecker, *Cattle Raising on the Plains, 1900–1961*, p. 117.

lar to one sponsored by his friend Ketcham. Meanwhile, in the Senate, Hattie Carraway of Arkansas urged acceptance of export debenture.[21]

During the spring of 1928, President Coolidge invited Jones, Ketcham, and Taber to the White House for a conference and gave his own blessing to the Export Debenture Plan. At that time the McNary-Haugen bill held the spotlight in the House Agriculture Committee, and it contained an equalization fee that Coolidge disliked. The president had, in fact, concluded that the fee was unconstitutional, after conferring with William D. Mitchell, later Hoover's attorney general. Still Coolidge saw that passage of the Ketcham-Jones bills offered a way to sidestep the issue. As a result he urged Congress to substitute export debenture for the McNary-Haugen bill then being considered.[22] From that point on, Republican Coolidge had Democrat Jones's undying admiration.

Ketcham and Jones considered strategy. Talking to cloakroom audiences, the two men contended, erroneously, that the export debenture concept had been sanctioned by Alexander Hamilton as part of the original tariff system for the nation. The emphasis on Hamilton, the patron saint of the 1920's, manifested Jones's adherence to the business-oriented philosophy of the age and cemented a base between Jones and conservative elements, whether Democrat or Republican. His continuing references to Hamilton in this regard revealed that some Jeffersonian-minded agrarians adhered to cooperative business government, in contrast to cooperative federalism, as the means to strengthen the political foundations of the nation. But Jones's views certainly were not shared by all, nor did all farm organizations agree with him. The nation lacked experience with export bounties, despite a brief and unsatisfactory encounter with production bounties on sugar, and his plan died in committee, where the advocates of McNary-Haugenism reigned supreme. On March 26, 1928, the committee rejected the Export Debenture Plan by a vote

[21] Jones, telephone conversation with author, March 27, 1974; H.R. 9371, January 16, 1928, H.R. 10656, February 7, 1928, H.R. 10762, February 9, 1928, H.R. 12893, April 11, 1928, MJP; L. J. Taber to Fred S. Purnell, March 14, 1928, MJP; Joseph S. Davis, "The Export Debenture Plan for Aid to Agriculture," *Quarterly Journal of Economics* 43 (February 1929):250–277.

[22] COHP-MJP, pp. 340–342; Jones, interview with Jerry N. Hess, 1970, transcript, Harry S. Truman Library, Independence, Mo.

of thirteen to eight and then approved the Haugen bill fifteen to six. Congress later passed the Haugen bill, but Coolidge vetoed it on the grounds that it would tend to fix prices and encourage overproduction. Possibilities of farm relief ended for the session.[23]

At that time Coolidge was in his final months as chief executive, having declared in 1927, "I do not choose to run for President in 1928." In June the Republicans, meeting at Kansas City, nominated Secretary of Commerce Herbert C. Hoover of California for president and Senator Charles Curtis of Kansas as his running mate. Two weeks later Democrats met at Houston and nominated Governor Alfred E. Smith of New York and Senator Joseph T. Robinson of Arkansas.

Of more immediate concern to Jones was the Democratic primary in his own Eighteenth District. This time he would face what seemed to be strong opposition. J. Ross Bell of Paducah, a prominent district attorney, was campaigning against Jones on a platform of restricting immigration, curtailing Washington bureaucracy, obtaining aid for water conservation, keeping the federal government out of business, prohibiting congressmen from raising their own salaries without approval by voters, and enacting legislation against speculation in the commodity markets.[24] But these issues quickly proved to be secondary. Bell soon directed his appeal to rebellious Democrats who opposed Al Smith for president for either of two main reasons: Smith was an unpolished man, and—worse—he was a Catholic. Bell hoped to ride Herbert Hoover's coattails into the House of Representatives.

Jones replied that he would vote a straight Democratic ticket because "the Democratic party was fighting for certain principles long before either Smith or Hoover was born . . . [and] it would be fighting for those same principles long after both of them had passed

---

[23] Davis, *The Farm Export Debenture Plan*, pp. 242–265; Jones, interview with author, March 22, 1971; Tom Connally to W. B. Yearny, February 15, 1928, and A. C. Perry, telegram to Tom Connally, April 19, 1928, Thomas T. Connally Papers, Manuscript Division, Library of Congress; U.S., Congress, House, *Agricultural Surplus Control Bill: Minority Views*, H. Rept. 1141, pt. 3, 1st sess., 1927; "Advantage of the Export Debenture Plan Clearly Stated by Congressman Jones of Texas," *National Grange Monthly*, April 1928.

[24] *Spearman Reporter*, October [?], 1927, MJP.

from the stage of action."²⁵ Jones also emphasized his position as the second-ranking member of the House Agriculture Committee and his support for farmers. He won the primary, 52,226 to 28,667, but his subsequent campaigning for Al Smith failed to show much influence. The Democrats lost the presidential election, and even Jones's Eighteenth District went for Republican Hoover.

The new president quickly showed himself an opponent of Jones's Export Debenture Plan. Hoover contended that a proposal, eventually to become the Agricultural Marketing Act, held the remedy for agricultural distress. Jones and some of his colleagues hoped to persuade Hoover to their viewpoint, but after they made a visit to the White House for that purpose, Hoover remained convinced that Jones's Export Debenture Plan would increase the surplus, cause greater taxation, raid the treasury of $200 million a year, and help mostly wheat and cotton to the disadvantage of other commodities. Furthermore, the president told the congressmen, he would veto the Export Debenture Plan, if necessary—and the McNary-Haugen bill too. Thereafter Ketcham's role in the Export Debenture Plan diminished, and Marvin Jones held center stage in the House as its leading advocate.

Jones continued to fight for his proposal, but without success. In June 1929 he appeared on an NBC radio program with three other agriculturists and argued in behalf of the plan, but he failed to arouse much support. It never captured the imagination of either the rural or the urban public. What little success Jones won came from already favorable publications like the *Fort Worth Star-Telegram*, which editorialized, "If the export debenture plan is a subsidy, so is the protective tariff."²⁶ The editorial stated further that agriculture had a special case because farmers produced a surplus, and that, therefore, "the problem for agriculture is not protecting the home market but disposal abroad of surplus home products. The export debenture plan is the simplest way for solving this problem, while keeping the solution true to the principle of protection as applied in the tariff."²⁷ But on June 13 the House formally voted, 250 to 113,

²⁵ COHP-MJP, p. 376.
²⁶ "Debenture or Tariff—Both Are Protection," *Fort Worth Star-Telegram*, April 23, 1929.
²⁷ Ibid.

to eliminate the Export Debenture Plan. In the Senate members yielded to President Hoover and eliminated the plan from the agricultural marketing bill.

Even those defeats failed to silence Jones, who would continue to advocate the plan in later congressional sessions. In the process he would ignore a resolution passed by the Seventh Annual Convention of the Texas Farm Bureau Cotton Association favoring the McNary-Haugen bill and supported by five Texans on Capitol Hill: Senators Morris Sheppard and Earl Mayfield and Representatives Henry Wurzbach, Morgan Sanders, and J. J. Mansfield. Other Lone Star congressmen besides Jones, however, continued to oppose McNary-Haugenism: John Box, Rayburn, Sumners, Buchanan, Clay Briggs, Daniel Garrett, Connally, Fritz Lanham, and Elmer Hudspeth.[28]

Jones also directed his attention toward acquiring new markets for cotton. The basic problem was that the cotton producers suffered from a surplus that resulted in low prices. American farmers faced competition not only on the world market, from the Mediterranean, but also within their own national boundaries. Cotton producers in the Deep South, for instance, competed with newer producers in other areas, such as the Southwest. Because science and technology had expanded the "cotton kingdom" into the Texas Panhandle, Jones's Eighteenth District averaged approximately 700,000 bales during the period 1926–1930. Jones thus had an interest in cotton farming, and he favored congressional action to help solve problems.

As early as 1926 he had exerted serious efforts to help cotton farmers. That year he had introduced a bill (H.R. 14245) that cut Department of Agriculture publication of estimates of cotton cultivation and storage because speculators had been reaping harvests from fluctuating prices. Jones's bill provided for publishing only three reports a year—in July, September, and December. Some changes were made, but the final bill (H.R. 15539) was still much the same bill that Jones had originally proposed. Further, he received support

---

[28] Jones, "The Remarks of Marvin Jones," *Congressional Record* Scrapbook, vol. 2 (71st Cong., 1st sess.), pp. 157–159, 2526, 2578, MJP; ibid. (72d Cong., 2d sess.), p. 609, MJP; H.R. 15553, December 20, 1930, MJP; *New York Times*, April 20, 1929, and June 8, 1929. For the views of a senator who favored the Export Debenture Plan, see Fite, *Peter Norbeck: Prairie Statesman*.

The Crusade for the Export Debenture Plan 75

from the administration, as well as from the two Texas senators, who introduced similar bills in the Senate. In February 1927 the bill became law.[29] It was a personal victory for Jones, who thus sought to increase cotton prices through domestic-market mechanisms.

During 1926 and 1927 the magnitude of the cotton crop (some 18 million bales) ignited Jones into action. In 1927 he sponsored many bills, each of them allocating $50,000 from the United States Treasury to be used in finding new uses for cotton.[30] Unless that could be accomplished, he believed, the industry would suffer drastic decline.

In April 1928 one of his bills passed Congress and became law. Later Jones described the aim of the law, known as the Jones Act: "I secured the passage of a measure providing for a permanent study and investigation into new uses for cotton—the placing of it in channels into which it has not heretofore gone."[31] The Jones Act sanctioned work already being conducted by Bonney Youngblood and Arthur W. Palmer of the Bureau of Agricultural Economics and Edward T. Pickard of the Bureau of Standards of the Commerce Department.[32] Youngblood, a former director of the Texas Agricultural Experiment Station, may have influenced Jones. In any event Jones was confident that the measure would provide real relief to farmers. He elaborated later, in an article in the *New Republic*:

If the money is loaned to take a million bales of cotton off the market, it will help temporarily, but when it is again thrown on the market it will depress it. But if a new use is found for a hundred thousand bales, it is forever lifted and the price of the commodity will necessarily be enhanced.

For years the South has been selling her cotton in other markets at

[29] H.R. 14245, December 7, 1926, H.R. 15345, December 7, 1926, and H.R. 15539, January 18, 1927, William M. Jardine to Jones, December 14, 1926, Jones to Pat Daniel, May 9, 1928, and *Dallas Morning News*, December 18, 1926, MJP; U.S., Congress, House, Committee on Agriculture, *Hearings: Cotton Crops Reports, H.R. 14245*.

[30] H.R. 458, December 5, 1927, H.R. 5517, December 5, 1927, H.R. 8224, December 21, 1927, and H.R. 11579 February 29, 1928, MJP.

[31] Marvin Jones, "The New Kingdom of Cotton," speech before U.S. House of Representatives, December 6, 1928, flyer to constituents, MJP.

[32] H.R. 11579, February 29, 1928, MJP; U.S., Congress, Senate, *Report 711*, 70th Cong., 1st sess., 1928. The act passed the House on March 7, 1928, although the $50,000 appropriation was stricken. The basic ideas for research met with Hoover's approval. Herbert Hoover to Jones, February 28, 1928, MJP.

prices named by the buyer and purchasing supplies in those same markets at prices named by the seller. This had made a sort of stepchild of the South, economically speaking. . . . At the shrine of cotton practically every southerner has bowed the head and bent the knee. . . . The South has within her own borders and at her own threshold the raw materials for the building of a wonderful prosperity. She has the climate, she has the power, and her people have the determination to translate these resources into her own development. She is building her own plants, and with the strength and sinew of her own fiber, in the loom of her own genius, and with the industry of her own hands she is weaving the garment of her future glory.[33]

During the next two years achievements in cotton research dramatized the importance of the Jones Act. By 1930 representatives of the Cotton Textile Institute had traveled more than fifty thousand miles advertising cotton products and emphasizing new uses in clothing, road construction, and sidelines, such as manufacture of cotton bags for use in power laundries and for retail packaging of fruits and vegetables and blending cotton with rubber in tire manufacture. Jones and others hoped that increased domestic consumption of cotton would solve the surplus problem without crop restrictions, but the levels of supply and demand did not change greatly. Cotton prices continued their sharp declines (as did the prices of almost everything else in the American economy at the time). Some estimates credited the Jones Act, combined with activities of the New Uses for Cotton Committee, with increasing domestic consumption by as much as 10 percent, but the measure proved to be too little too late. Nonetheless, the developments had impact. Breakthroughs in research and technology gained new importance. Further, even some of the failures helped by setting the stage for a different approach during a future presidential administration.

In 1930, after two years of the Hoover presidency, that future administration was still two years away. In June 1929 the Agricultural Marketing Act became law; through it Congress hoped to stabilize farm prices by means of the Federal Farm Board, which aided in financing of agricultural markets. But the entire nation was on the verge of a ruinous depression. On October 24, 1929, panic selling set in on the stock market, and it became worse. By mid-November

[33] Marvin Jones, "A New Kingdom of Cotton," *New Republic*, April 1929, pp. 9, 59.

The Crusade for the Export Debenture Plan 77

paper losses were estimated at $26 billion. Then in June 1930, President Hoover's signature on the Smoot-Hawley Tariff raised duties so much that international trade was drastically reduced and added to economic depression. In December conditions had become so bad that Hoover asked Congress for $100 million to $150 million to begin a public-works program and reduce unemployment.

Because of the deepening depression Jones had easier campaigning in his 1930 bid for reelection. James Cade, an Amarillo attorney, ran against him and criticized him especially for his support of Al Smith two years earlier. But voters were not interested in Smith now; they wanted experienced congressional leadership, and Jones exhibited it. The *Motley County News* observed:

Even those who disagree with Mr. Jones occasionally on public issues appreciate the manner in which he looks after the interests of all his constituents, and of the record he has made. No man writes to him that he does not receive an answer, and when congress has adjourned he always returns to Texas to visit his people and learn their wants and needs.[34]

Jones spent a minimal amount of money and easily defeated Cade, 70,134 to 14,422.[35]

On the national level the Republicans were still the party in power, and voters showed some reluctance to change habits. In campaign speeches Jones attacked the Republican tariff policies and frequently exhibited for amusement a "Hoover Lucky Pocket Piece," which the Republicans had issued in the election of 1928. The coin, about the size of a half dollar, displayed a picture of Hoover and Dawes on one side and on the other the words: "Good for four more years of prosperity." Jones liked to flip the coin and let it land on a table with a dull thud.

Despite the deepening depression no landslide developed for the Democrats. They eventually won control of the House but by a scant margin and even then only after the deaths of some newly elected Republicans had changed numbers. Voters sent to the House

---

[34] *Motley County News*, July 17, 1920.

[35] "Statement of Receipts and Expenditures of Marvin Jones for Nomination for Representative in the Congress of the United States," 1930, MJP; Narwood Beville, chairman, Democratic Executive Committee, 18th Congressional District, to Secretary of State [of Texas], August 23, 1920, MJP.

218 Republicans, 216 Democrats, and 1 Farm-Laborite. Before Congress could convene, however, deaths and special elections gave the House to the Democrats, 220 to 214.[36] Senate Republicans lost eight seats but remained in control there.

The Democrats thus failed to capitalize greatly on unfavorable economic conditions, but Marvin Jones was on the verge of a rise to considerable power in the House.

[36] COHP-MJP, pp. 414–417.

6.

The First Crisis of Jones's Leadership

DEATHS of elected Republicans had allowed Democrats to organize the House of Representatives for the next congressional session. Now another death, this time of a Democrat, allowed Marvin Jones to move up to chairmanship of the House Agriculture Committee. Louisiana's James Aswell, who was heir apparent to the chairmanship held by Republican Gilbert Haugen and stood to profit by Democratic organization of the House, suddenly died. Second to Aswell in party seniority was Jones, and he inherited the post at the age of forty-nine.

Jones was not the only prominent Texan in the House to gain a chairmanship. Hatton Sumners chaired the Judiciary Committee; Sam Rayburn, the Committee on Interstate and Foreign Commerce; Guinn Williams, the Committee on Territories; Fritz Lanham, the Committee on Public Buildings and Grounds; and J. J. Mansfield, the Committee on Rivers and Harbors. Furthermore, John Nance Garner occupied the Speaker's chair. The entire Texas delegation had increased its power and prestige, but Jones held a key position. Additionally he was popular among his fellow Texans, and they elected him chairman of the state's delegation to Congress. Jones presided over meetings of this close-knit group, in which members discussed effects of legislation upon their state, but Jones exerted his principal effort in the Agriculture Committee.[1] The recent election had changed the growing membership of the Agriculture Committee

---

[1] U.S., Congress, *Biographical Directory of the American Congress, 1744–1961*, pp. 361–366, 493; "Texans Who Head House Committees," *Fort Worth Star-Telegram*, December 16, 1931; "Marvin Jones Is Chairman of Texas Delegation," *Ochiltree County Herald*, December 10, 1931; Lionel V. Patenaude, "The Texas Congressional Delegation," *Texana* 9 (Winter 1971):3–16.

from fifteen Republicans and six Democrats to thirteen Democrats and ten Republicans. Of the Democrats only Jones and Hampton Fulmer of South Carolina remained from the previous session. That enhanced the chairman's prestige among new Democratic members, who looked to Jones for advice and leadership. Nonetheless, Republican members anticipated passage of legislation that would cut across party lines, since they were only three votes from the majority. Further, with support from the executive branch, they certainly would not be considered dead. Finally, new power and prestige might easily draw wavering mavericks into their corral.[2] It was apparent that the Democratic majority lacked experienced leadership despite Jones's previous work.

Chairman Jones assumed the routine responsibilities of appointing the committee's professional staff, calling meetings, preparing agendas, directing hearings, taking results to the House, and leading debates on reported measures. From the beginning he faced a Republican president and worked with only slim Democratic majorities in his committee on the House floor. These circumstances forced him to employ cautious bipartisanship. He retained Katherine Wheeler as committee clerk from Haugen's chairmanship, needing her experience to ensure continuity of operations. He named as appointments secretary Mrs. Lotus Van Huss, an efficient, strikingly beautiful woman. Former Amarillo reporter Hollis Schrieber became editorial assistant. Later, after 1933, the staff would include also the most brilliant assistant Jones ever had—vivacious Mrs. Altravene Clark Spann, constituents secretary and later assistant committee clerk.[3] Day-to-day operations rested on the shoulders of this loyal staff, permitting Jones and committee colleagues to concentrate on policy.

As chairman, Jones sought to decrease committee friction on the House floor and thus avoid furnishing ammunition to opponents

[2] U.S., Congress, *Official Congressional Directory, 72d Congress, 2d Session*, p. 192; Charles O. Jones, "Representative in Congress: The Case of the House Agriculture Committee," *American Political Science Review* 55 (June 1961):358–367.

[3] After Jones retired from Congress, Mrs. Clark, a widow, married John M. Spann. Before that she and Jones had dated, but he believed that he was too old for marriage. Jones thought that Mrs. Spann and Lady Bird Johnson were the two smartest women he ever knew. Altravene Clark Spann, interview with author, March 23, 1973.

of his agricultural legislation. He also stressed efficiency. Unlike Haugen, Jones insisted on promptness. Members soon discovered that he would not tolerate thirty-minute delays for a quorum to gather. He informed committeemen that meetings would begin promply at 10:00 A.M. and that, if possible, they would end at a predetermined time. He set a two-to-three-day maximum on appearances by witnesses to avoid petty friction. In public he never addressed Mrs. Van Huss as Lotus or Mrs. Clark as Altravene, but he usually called Schrieber by his first name. In committee he addressed his colleagues formally, although in private he was on a first-name basis with them.[4]

Bachelor Jones came to consider the agriculture committee his "family." By nature he was soft-spoken and mild-mannered, and he created a mood for conciliation. He avoided official Washington society, which he regarded as "a great time waster," and preferred small dinner parties with a few close friends.

For entertainment he liked an occasional game of bridge, which he always played to win, or reading biography or light fiction. When time permitted, he might retreat to a lake nearby for some fishing. Each spring he took his staff on a picnic. Usually, however, he sought relaxation after a hectic day by joining Sam Rayburn on a walk around the Capitol grounds, discussing politics.[5]

He always was known as a loner, a "man's man" respected by colleagues, but from a distance. Consequently, newspapers devoted more coverage to colorful congressmen: Garner, Huey Long, Edward Cox, Martin Dies, the Bankhead brothers, and Rayburn. Jones was no adventurer in social relations; he considered politics his life.

---

[4] Ibid.; Marvin Jones, interview with Dean Albertson, Columbia Oral History Project, 1952, pp. 419–421, hereafter cited as COHP-MJP; Marvin Jones, telephone conversation with author, March 10, 1975. Unless otherwise noted, all interviews and correspondence citing Jones refer to Marvin Jones.

[5] During his congressional career bachelor Jones roomed with Sam Rayburn and Hatton Sumners for brief periods. Politics became these men's lives when all three became committee chairman: Jones of Agriculture; Rayburn of Interstate Commerce (and later Speaker); and Sumners of the Judiciary. D. B. Hardeman, interview with author, August 17, 1972; George Mahon, interview with author, October 15, 1971; Altravene C. Spann, interview with author, March 23, 1973; Ray Tucker, "The New Head Man," *Country Home*, February [?] 1933, scrapbook 2, Marvin Jones Papers; hereafter cited as MJP.

After Jones had become chairman of the Agriculture Committee, he became more of a pragmatist, with a passion to achieve obtainable goals. Nothing vexed him more than to lose political battles. For that reason he would expand his already considerable ability to work with people who had diverse personalities—individuals like the urbane Franklin D. Roosevelt and South Carolina's rustic senator, Cotton Ed Smith.

When Jones took over as chairman, new problems threatened American agriculture. The Federal Farm Board had failed, and the government had abandoned emergency commodity buying. As a result gross farm incomes nosedived, although production costs remained obstinately high. Net farm income also dropped drastically—64 percent from 1929 to 1932—but production levels remained about the same, piling up more surpluses.

Trying to cope with their dilemma, farmers cut their consumption expenditures sharply, spent their liquid assets, and borrowed money. They complained that the agricultural community had become too dependent on insurance companies and loan sharks for long-term loans and too dependent on local banks for intermediate and short-term loans. Perceptive agrarians urged reforms in the Federal Land Bank and the federal intermediate-credit banks. Congressmen heard these complaints and considered the general situation. Not all agricultural enterprises were foundering. The larger and more efficient ones, in fact, continued to prosper.[6] Consequently, many congressmen wondered whether the complainers should not be striving for greater efficiency rather than crying for federal aid.

A leadership crisis slowed efforts to solve the problems. National agricultural organizations failed to join in a unified plan of action.[7] President Hoover, having pushed his Agricultural Marketing Act through Congress, retreated from further expansion of govern-

---

[6] Lester V. Chandler, *America's Greatest Depression, 1929–1941*, pp. 53–66.

[7] Murray R. Benedict, *Farm Policies of the United States, 1790–1950*, pp. 269–275; William R. Johnson, "The National Farm Organizations and the Reshaping of Agricultural Policy in 1932," *Agricultural History* 37 (January 1963):35–42; U.S., Congress, House, Committee on Agriculture, *Hearings on Marketing of Farm Produce*, 72d Cong., 1st sess., May 4–25, 1932.

ment activity and did not offer effective executive leadership.[8] At the same time legislators were strongly bound by tradition and somewhat lacking in original ideas about how to deal with the unprecedented situation. Congress continued to support increased distribution rather than curtailment of production, and Jones followed that pattern. In committee, at least, sentiment continued for cooperative marketing, McNary-Haugenism, the Export Debenture Plan, or tariff policy.[9]

Democrats were at a disadvantage in producing any bold new relief measures for farmers. The party did not control the White House or the Senate and had only a paper-thin majority in the House. The majority, precarious as it was, was of little help. Still another difficulty worked against House Democrats. Journalist Bascom Timmons discussed it: "A party that has been for a long time in the minority and schooled in the critical opposition tactics of an anti-Administration force is not easily converted into a responsible working unit, willing to take a unified stand on legislation and accept the blame for it if it fails."[10] Worse, every legislator realized that the 1932 campaign actually had started before the Seventy-second Congress convened, and the partisan splits inevitably widened despite a few efforts at unity. Secretary of Agriculture Arthur Hyde was not a farmer himself, and that alienated Marvin Jones, who rarely met with him.

Congressmen did seek solutions through the many farm bills that filled the hopper, but most of them represented experiments with little real chance of enactment. Members of the Agriculture Committee had a sense of futility in view of Hoover's opposition to McNary-Haugenism and the Export Debenture Plan.[11] Every phase of the American economy, in fact, seemed to be going downhill.

Jones attempted to bring some order by defining basic goals: "Economies should be practiced wherever possible, excessive salaries

---

[8] Harris Gaylord Warren, *Herbert Hoover and the Great Depression*, pp. 168–187; Albert A. Romasco, *The Poverty of Abundance: Hoover, the Nation, the Depression*, pp. 97–124.

[9] Benedict, *Farm Policies of the United States, 1790–1950*, pp. 272–273; "Jones Hopes to Help Farmers," *Fort Worth Star-Telegram*, December 16, 1931.

[10] Bascom N. Timmons, *Garner of Texas: A Personal History*, p. 137.

[11] Jones did not completely agree with the interpretation presented in this book; COHP-MJP, p. 423.

reduced, a free circulation of money restored, the control of local affairs returned, restored to local people, and Mellonism should be destroyed."[12] He continued to blame the headaches of production control on haphazard agricultural distribution, and he insisted that other problems of agriculture were interrelated with a scarcity of currency, needed agricultural-banking reforms, and reduction of the tariff. Outdated legislation and federal bureaucracy held down agriculture, Jones asserted, but he shared his committee's doubts that extensive legislation could pass the current congress.

Jones decided to try an indirect approach. He began thinking about seeking to win acceptance of his Export Debenture Plan by making it an amendment to tariff bills. A promising opportunity came in January 1932, when the House discussed James W. ("Billy") Collier's bill authorizing the Tariff Commission to change rates that interfered with foreign trade. Collier proposed to transfer certain items to the free list and to increase or decrease tariff rates on certain other commodities. Collier balked, however, when Jones solicited his support. Moreover, Massachusetts Representative John McCormack called Jones's idea well meaning but impractical.[13] Jones had no choice but to withdraw his proposal.

That same January, Congress in prompt reply to a Hoover request debated and passed the bill providing for the Reconstruction Finance Corporation. Jones expanded the bill's potential assistance for agriculture to a total of $200 million on January 14, when he introduced an amendment providing that no less than $50 million be allocated to specified intermediate-credit banks, agricultural credit corporations, livestock credit corporations, and agricultural associations.[14]

Debate on the amendment drew from Jones one of the most concise statements he ever ventured as a solution to the depression:

I think an expansion of the currency within reasonable limits would do more to restore the country than any other one thing. That would be

[12] Marvin Jones, "The New Congress," flyer to constituents, scrapbook 5, MJP.

[13] Jones to U.S. Tariff Commission, November 30, 1931, MJP; Marvin Jones, "The Remarks of Marvin Jones," *Congressional Record* Scrapbook, vol. 3 (72d Cong., 1st sess.), pp. 1923–27, MJP.

[14] Jones, "The Remarks of Marvin Jones," *Congressional Record* Scrapbook, vol. 3 (72d Cong., 1st sess.), MJP.

simple. It would be direct. It would stimulate both agriculture and industry. With one-third more gold than we had in 1920 and twenty percent less money in circulation, we can expand on a perfectly sound basis.[15]

The amendment passed the House by a narrow margin, 120 to 112. On the following day, however, Jones voted against the bill he had been responsible for amending. The House passed it by a vote of 335 to 56. Earlier Jones had indicated the reason for his disapproval by warning that the bill did not strike at the main cause of the depression: the concentration and unequal distribution of wealth, with its corresponding result—destruction of agriculture's purchasing power. Still, his no vote remained largely a mystery until 1952, when he recalled that the bill failed to provide assistance to all people and corporations, regardless of size, who could offer adequate security. The bill, he said, had been too conservative.[16] In future votes Jones changed his position yet again. After a House-Senate conference committee retained the Jones amendment, he supported the conference report. President Hoover signed the bill on January 22, 1932, but Secretary of Agriculture Hyde did not use all the funds allocated for agriculture. Only $69 million had been administered when the session ended.

The House Agriculture Committee took another financial step in February 17, 1932, when it reported a resolution (H.J. Res. 292) that granted the secretary of agriculture power to make advances or loans to individuals up to a total of $10 million and thus assist agricultural credit corporations and livestock loan companies that did business with federal intermediate-credit banks. The bill also allowed individuals to borrow money to purchase stock in the corporations and obtain loans from them.

Jones had persuaded Democratic leaders to assign the bill to his Agriculture Committee rather than to the Banking and Currency Committee, where it would encounter stronger Republican opposition. Eastern Repubicans resented Jones's behind-the-scenes maneuvering, carried out on the premise that agriculture was the foundation of America. Robert Luce of Massachusetts observed:

[15] Ibid., p. 1957.
[16] Ibid., pp. 1956, 2081.

It is frequently brought to our attention that agriculture is the mainstay of our country.... I do not desire to discuss whether the brain, the heart, or the lungs are more important to the body, but I point out that if you lend money to men engaged in agriculture in order to enable them to buy stocks in corporations, you will be confronted next with the proposal that the same thing be done for other lines of activity.

Another Republican, William Stafford (from Milwaukee) called the measure socialistic.[17]

The bill proposed a "permanent solution" that gave agriculture a preferred position in the nation's financial picture. Jones, supported by his committee, presented a strong defense of the bill against Republican critics, citing establishment of the Reconstruction Finance Corporation as a precedent. Further, he revealed that he and Secretary of Agriculture Hyde had carefully gone over the bill and that Hyde had even suggested some of the provisions. New York Representative Fiorello H. La Guardia, who frequently supported Jones, reminded opponents that they had supported the RFC bill, which allowed loans to corporations, but that now they deemed loans to individuals impractical and even Bolshevistic.

The bill passed the House, 151 to 35, and Hoover signed the measure.[18] Jones was showing increasing power in matters of farm finance, an area previously under the control of the Banking and Currency Committee.

Jones's committee now began considering problems involved in utilizing Federal Farm Board surplus commodities. Cotton and wheat held in Federal Farm Board storage totaled millions of bales and bushels, and an economy-minded Capitol Hill wanted to avoid storage charges. Motivated by economics rather than philanthropy, congressmen considered giving surplus commodities to the Red Cross for distribution. While the House Agriculture Committee members deliberated on this proposal,[19] the Senate passed a bill giving forty million bushels of wheat to the Red Cross for processing into flour and distribution to the needy, who were growing in

[17] Ibid., p. 4153.
[18] Ibid., pp. 4149, 4152, 4153, 4160, 4166, 4180.
[19] Ibid., pp. 4729–31; COHP-MJP, pp. 430–431; Foster Rhea Dulles, *The American Red Cross: A History*, p. 291.

numbers as the depression worsened. Time was of the essence; some Americans were starving. Frustrated by Jones's apparent lack of concern, Representative Hamilton Fish, Jr., charged him and his committee with unreasonable delay and partisan action. Fish's criticisms were matched by Louis Ludlow of Indiana, sponsor of the House version of the Senate bill. Jones branded their attacks as unjust, unfair, and untrue and offered an elaborate denial of partisanship. His committee had held hearings on the bill and had discovered that many commodity interests wanted the bill expanded to include their own products.

Another obstacle became apparent. The Federal Farm Board had borrowed funds for expenses in regard to wheat, and several middle-western representatives favored a reapportionment of funds to pay the board's debts before the wheat was distributed. Others proposed that the government, instead of distributing the wheat, weighted with an overhead of interest and storage costs, use appropriated funds to buy wheat in the open market for distribution to the needy. The discussions naturally led to an allied topic: the federal government's role in providing surplus food for the needy. If government responsibility was to prevent starvation, some men argued, then significant relief called for a larger program. Consensus could not be obtained on that subject in Jones's committee, but Jones himself favored the bill. Later he recalled:

I felt because the Farm Board had the wheat, and it was costing something to carry it, it was more like discarding an old overcoat or an old suit of clothes that is not needed, which made it distinguishable from a dole. And for that reason, I felt it would be wise to go ahead with the relief measure, that it would relieve a portion of the suffering.[20]

Eventually the House Agriculture Committee reported the Senate bill favorably. Its appearance on the House floor sparked patriotic and humanitarian speeches from members of the House Agriculture Committee. Jones himself set the tone when he observed:

We have wheat. It is deteriorating. I do not see any reason on earth why the American government cannot show that warmth of spirit which

---

[20] Jones, "The Remarks of Marvin Jones," *Congressional Record* Scrapbook, vol. 3 (72d Cong., 1st sess.), p. 4731.

will at least enable it to discard old and worthless garments in order to see that its citizens do not suffer from hunger and are not kept in misery and want.[21]

The House passed the bill, 345 to 2, and it became law.[22]

By June 1932, with the Great Depression nearing its low point, farmers needed additional federal relief legislation. On the sixteenth of that month the House began considering a measure (H.J. Res. 418) advocated by Hampton Fulmer of South Carolina to ease the burden carried by the Cotton Stabilization Corporation and to provide further relief for the Grain Stabilization Corporation of the Federal Farm Board. About the same time urban representatives Emanuel Celler and Fiorello H. La Guardia, both of New York, met with Jones and Fulmer to urge additional legislation that would enable the Red Cross to exchange wheat or flour for other food. This provision was included in the bill as finally approved.

The legislation accorded with Jones's philosophy of distribution of agricultural commodities.[23] He supported Fulmer's bill:

> I do not believe any finer disposition could be made of these commodities, which the Government has through these stabilization corporations, than to make this distribution. This will not only feed the hungry, but will get these commodities off the market and prevent them from continuing to be a drag on the market. I believe the commodities in the hands of the stabilization corporations should be disposed of, and I think the program of direct buying and selling under Government supervision, through stabilization corporations should be ended.[24]

Thus Jones readily accepted the measure not only to provide relief for the Farm Board and the needy but also to end the Farm Board's operations.

After a Senate-House conference the bill remained basically intact. It allowed for the distribution of forty-five million rather than forty million bushels of wheat. As a concession to the wheat bloc it gave priority to wheat products in any exchange of commodities. Hoover signed the legislation into law on July 5, 1932. More than five million needy families living in all but seventeen counties across

---

[21] Ibid., p. 5194.
[22] Ibid., pp. 5198, 5214, 5219, 5205.
[23] Ibid., pp. 13195–13200.
[24] Ibid., p. 13195.

the land received processed wheat and cotton products.[25]

While attempting to solve immediate problems, the House Agriculture Committee continued to deal with general farm-relief policy. In February 1932 hearings were held on the Thomas-Swank bill (supported by John A. Simpson of the Farmers' Union), which contained a plan for a fixed domestic price on products manufactured for domestic consumption without production controls. The Department of Agriculture would determine production costs, which would include interests and tax costs. Resulting surpluses could be dumped on the foreign market—or so the sponsors hoped.

The Texas commissioner of agriculture, J. E. McDonald, advocated the plan in frequent speeches before Texas cotton farmers. After analyzing its provisions, however, Jones concluded that it was impractical. He reasoned that if Congress permitted agricultural businessmen to dump surpluses on the foreign market the shock would destroy America's world trade. Furthermore, Jones was a firm opponent of fixed domestic prices. Still, he calculated the shifting political winds. When sufficient support for the bill failed to materialize, his Agriculture Committee turned its attention to other ideas.[26]

Jones brought forth for further consideration his Export Debenture Plan (H.R. 7236). For three weeks he listened to representatives from major farm organizations and concluded with regret that a lack of farm support doomed the bill. Frustrated in attempts to reach an agreement with Jones, representatives of the Grange, the American Farm Bureau Federation (AFBF), and the Farmers' Union had thrown their support to a measure (S. 4536) introduced by Senator Charles McNary.[27] Nicknamed by its opponents the "three-headed monster," the bill called for the Federal Farm Board to use the Export Debenture Plan, a Farmers' Union allotment plan, or an equalization fee advocated by the AFBF. During House

---

[25] Ibid., pp. 14265, 14498; Dulles, *The American Red Cross*, pp. 290–293.

[26] COHP-MJP, pp. 435–439; U.S. Congress, House, Committee on Agriculture, *Hearings on Marketing of Farm Produce*, 72d Cong., 1st sess., February 4–5, 1932; Gilbert C. Fite, "John A. Simpson (1871–1934): The Southwest's Militant Farm Leader," *Mississippi Valley Historical Review* 35 (March 1949):563–584.

[27] U.S., Congress, House, Committee on Agriculture, *Hearings on Marketing of Farm Produce*, 72d Cong., 1st sess., May 4–25, 1932.

Agriculture Committee hearings, however, it soon became clear that the farm leaders had not hit upon a workable solution, and Chairman Jones sent them home to think further on the subject. Then he devoted the remainder of the session to consideration of various domestic-allotment plans.

The committee considered the Hope-Norbeck bill (forerunner of the Jones bill of 1933 and the Agricultural Adjustment Act of 1933), but it died in the House Agricultural Committee from lack of support by agricultural organizations.[28]

During the spring of 1932 the Rainey-Norbeck bill received attention. Of all the domestic-allotment proposals this one showed the most promise of being enacted. Introduced first in the House, it passed the Senate and was then returned to the House for a final decision. The bill contained principles of voluntary domestic allotment advocated by economists William J. Spillman and John D. Black, and it seemed acceptable to agricultural leaders like Earl Smith, Henry A. Wallace, George Peek, and Chester Davis. A capable agricultural legislation drafter, Fred Lee, prepared the final version of the bill. Most of the men involved were close associates of Jones's or soon would be, but personalities counted little in the bill's fate.[29]

Rainey and Norbeck advocated "a free trade price plus the tariff duty for the part of [the producer's] crop which is consumed in the United States . . . without the tariff duty for the part . . . that is exported, this . . . to be arranged by a system of allotments to individual producers of rights to sell the domestic part of the crop in the domestic market."[30] With congressional consent the secretary of agriculture would determine the percentage of cotton, wheat, and hogs to be consumed domestically, and each producer would receive a negotiable adjustment certificate that would be redeemed by the United States Treasury. The bill contained a processing tax to finance these services.[31]

[28] William D. Rowley, *M. L. Wilson and the Campaign for the Dramatic Allotment*, pp. 134–149.

[29] William J. Spillman, *Balancing the Farm Output*; John D. Black, *Agricultural Reform in the United States*, pp. 271–301; George N. Peek with Samuel Crowther, *Why Quit Our Own*, pp. 51–54.

[30] Black, *Agricultural Reform in the United States*, p. 271.

[31] Peek, *Why Quit Our Own*, p. 52.

The First Crisis of Jones's Leadership

The bill represented an attempt to attain the general objectives of the McNary-Haugen proposal and of the Export Debenture Plan. It also represented a last chance for Congress to pass a general agriculture relief bill during the session. Speaker John Nance Garner, however, opposed it.[32] The final decision about allowing the bill to come before the House rested in Garner's hands, but Jones played a key behind-the-scenes role. Although his committee had reported the bill favorably, Jones disagreed with his colleagues because he thought that the bill could never be successfully applied. Among other things, Jones wanted provisions for county and local administration, but those provisions would probably have resulted in House rejection. Eventually, when Garner asked for advice regarding the bill, Jones suggested blocking it because under the circumstances it would be foolish to pass a measure that was not complete, failed to cover all the commodities that should be included, lacked provisions for rotation or adjustments that were essential parts of any successful farm measure, and would bog down as the Farm Board had bogged down.[33] The Speaker acted in accordance with the wishes of his agriculture chairman.

In addition to the reasons Jones gave for rejecting the bill, perhaps he also envisioned the possibility of enacting his Export Debenture Plan if strong Democratic majorities came out of the 1932 election. In the closing week of the session he introduced two such plans, although he realized that they could not pass. He hoped that they would serve as a basis for discussion during the next session.[34]

As Herbert Hoover's first term neared its end, the country had sunk to the depths of what came to be known as the Great Depression. By July 1932, farm purchasing power had plummeted to one-half that of 1929. Five thousand banks, including many rural ones,

---

[32] Gilbert C. Fite, *George N. Peek and the Fight for Farm Parity*, p. 236.

[33] The Senate did recall the Rainey-Norbeck bill on July 14, 1932; however, the House decision had already been made, if not published. COHP-MJP, pp. 463–466. The standard accounts of this action make no mention of the role Jones played in the decision-making process. See Peek, *Why Quit Our Own*, p. 52; Christina M. Campbell, *The Farm Bureau and the New Deal*, pp. 49–50; Gilbert C. Fite, *Peter Norbeck: Prairie Statesman*, pp. 158–167.

[34] H.R. 12571, June 10, 1932, and H.R. 12645, June 15, 1932, MJP.

had closed in the past two years. Unemployment had increased greatly; monthly wages of people still working had dropped to 60 percent of the 1929 total. Industrial volume had sunk even lower—to half that recorded in 1929. Some politicians obviously were in trouble, but not Jones. He went into the 1932 Democratic primary without opposition.

Thus blessed, he took a low-key approach to the election. In early spring he had declared his allegiance to Garner, should the Texan win the Democratic presidential nomination. Jones knew that Garner had presidential fever, but when their talk turned to the vice-presidency, Garner showed little enthusiasm. Still, Garner stressed, no man in public life could decline his party's call. Jones agreed with Rayburn, however, that New York Governor Franklin D. Roosevelt stood the best chance of being nominated.

On June 14 the Republican convention met in Chicago and chose President Hoover and Vice-President Curtis to run for a second term. Republican campaigners warned that it would be dangerous to change parties in mid-depression.

On June 27, Democrats gathered in the same city, Chicago, for their national convention. Jones did not attend. Work kept him at his Washington desk, but he followed developments. On the fourth ballot the delegates chose Roosevelt. Jones's favorite, Garner, was Roosevelt's running mate. The Democratic platform called for, among other things, aid to farmers.

After the convention Jones, with Silliman Evans and Tom Connally, went to Hyde Park, where he met Roosevelt for the first time. He came away with the impression that Roosevelt had too much spirit and was superficial. Jones also realized, however, that he had met a master politician and an almost certain winner. Roosevelt's magnetic charm appealed to Jones.[35]

Roosevelt conferred with many farm leaders and congressmen even before the election, seeking possible solutions to agricultural problems. Jones quickly found himself outside FDR's inner circle, for several reasons: he was a southwesterner; he favored the Export Debenture Plan, and he wanted fewer changes than Roosevelt's ad-

---

[35] Marvin Jones, *Marvin Jones Memoirs*, ed. Joseph M. Ray, pp. 85–86; COHP-MJP, pp. 440–447.

The First Crisis of Jones's Leadership

visers were advocating. Nevertheless, Jones supported Roosevelt and the party without qualification.

Speaking in Topeka, Roosevelt suggested that any federal program to aid agriculture must be financially self-sustaining, must benefit producers of surplus commodities like cotton, wheat, hogs, and tobacco, and must not pollute the already glutted foreign market. Furthermore, he said, Congress should distribute government aid through existing agencies and through decentralized agencies outside Washington to avoid expanding the federal bureaucracy. Government programs must be voluntary, he said, must operate on a cooperative basis, and must have the support of most of the producers. By speaking to principles rather than to a specific program, Roosevelt won the support of diverse agricultural elements.[36]

Jones campaigned for the Democratic candidates in many states, continually focusing on the failures of the Hoover administration to provide relief for agriculture. It was easier to win by recalling unfulfilled promises than by expounding on theoretical solutions, and as farm prices declined, farmers became even more receptive to Democrats who offered hope for the future.

Jones later recalled:

> Hoover had promised a chicken in every pot and two cars in every garage, but after four years he sat baffled, looking around the corner for prosperity, while surplus food piled up and farm mortgages were being foreclosed.
>
> In contrast, the Democrats had nominated a vigorous candidate with a golden voice, a sparkling personality, and a record of accomplishment, who was assuring people that he [Roosevelt] would at least take action to remedy the desperate situation.[37]

November 8, 1932, brought a great Democratic victory. Roosevelt received 22,810,000 votes; Hoover, 15,759,000. Democrats won firm control of both Senate and House. In accepting the nomination, Roosevelt pledged a new deal for the American people.

Two weeks after the election, on November 22, Roosevelt met with President Hoover and others in Washington to discuss matters that might come before the forthcoming lame-duck session of Congress (a phenomenon that has since been eliminated). Roosevelt also

---

[36] Frank Freidel, *Franklin D. Roosevelt: The Triumph*, pp. 349–350.
[37] Jones, *Marvin Jones Memoirs*, p. 85–86.

met with Democratic congressional leaders in the Mayflower Hotel to discuss general goals for his new administration. Those leaders suggested waiting until after the inauguration before initiating strong legislative programs.[38]

Increasingly depressed agricultural conditions, however, cried for something from Congress now. Farmers were destroying crops and shooting livestock rather than transport them to market and suffer additional losses. At the same time starvation stalked the cities. Because of potential farm revolt, congressional efforts might soothe discontent by demonstrating the sincerity of the Democrats' intentions.

Garner informed Roosevelt that Jones knew more about agricultural legislation than anyone else in Congress. The vice-president-elect urged Roosevelt to confer with Jones immediately, and the president-elect talked with Jones on the following day.

As Jones recalled the conversation:

... he [Roosevelt] did say that the situation was so desperate that no matter who got the credit for it, he thought there should be some legislation passed. He felt that was the key to the whole process of recovery, and he said if we could pass it, fine, and if we couldn't pass it, we would know who was responsible for its failure.[39]

Following this meeting Jones faced the most difficult task of his congressional career. Roosevelt went on to Warm Springs, Georgia, where he liked to relax, but Jones remained on Capitol Hill, charged with the responsibility of passing a farm bill despite a hostile, defeated president, a Congress with 158 lame-duck members, and at least temporary disunity among Democrats.

A few days later Roosevelt telephoned Jones that Henry Wallace, William I. Myers, Henry Morgenthau, and other supporters would arrive in Washington soon to discuss agricultural legislation. Roosevelt emphasized his hopes for legislation patterned in accordance with campaign promises and his request that Congress pass a farm bill during the lame-duck session.

At 10:00 A.M. on December 3 discussions began with Wallace, Jones, Morgenthau, Myers, M. L. Wilson, Rexford Tugwell, Fred-

---

[38] COHP-MJP, pp. 475–476; Raymond Moley, *After Seven Years*, pp. 72–78.

[39] COHP-MJP, pp. 482–483.

eric Lee, and Mordecai Ezekiel in the Agriculture Committee Room of the old House Office Building. South Carolina Senator Cotton Ed Smith, in another of his temper tantrums, boycotted the meeting. Initial general agreement came only on the need to increase farm prices and to establish a marketing fee on commodities that would make any proposed farm measure self-sustaining.

The extent of federal aid and the form it should take were the real sore spots. Production controls, which Jones preferred to call "production adjustments," were frequently discussed, but Jones himself had other priorities. He suggested that the group

> contemplate a measure for correcting freight-rate discrimination, a measure for refinancing farm mortgages which were being foreclosed by the thousands, and a provision for financing a control program that would enable us to handle the surplus. . . . we should try to get an adjustment, crop rotation or something, that would enable us to keep these unwieldy surpluses from piling up and rotting in the bins and granaries . . . and . . . the whole operation should be linked to soil conservation and rebuilding.[40]

The conferees eventually agreed that a farm bill should be drafted, one that embodied some principles of a voluntary domestic-allotment plan urged by M. L. Wilson. Since Smith was absent, the bill's sponsorship fell solely to Jones. He began the work of conferring, drafting legislation, holding hearings, listening to a wave of criticism, and attempting compromise.

On January 3 he introduced a bill (H.R. 13991) to the newly reconvened Congress. Based on the domestic-allotment plan, the bill provided for parity and gave immense power to the secretary of agriculture, who had authority to control acreage and withhold issuance of certificates unless the acreage had been reduced. Commodities were restricted to hogs, wheat, cotton, and tobacco—with adjustment charges levied on the first domestic processing of those items. The surplus problem was attacked by acreage control primarily, rather than by production control, because Jones maintained that acreage restrictions would suffice while the nation explored new methods of food distribution. The bill contained Jones's wish that this temporary

---

[40] Ibid., pp. 486–487; John M. Blum, ed., *From the Morgenthau Diaries: Years of Crisis, 1928–1938*, pp. 38–41.

program would be extended by the president upon recommendation by the secretary of agriculture.[41]

Jones faced two barriers: a divided committee, which did not give its chairman unanimous support, and a rebellious Congress. Jones sought to counter them by taking the offensive. He launched into a crusade that painted agriculture as the cornerstone of America. Then he stressed the tireless work of his committee, a need for parity, and the bill's provisions. He conjured up an agrarian utopia in which

> every farmer in America shall eat bread from his own fields and meat from his own pastures, and distributed by no creditor and enslaved by no debts, shall sit amid his orchards and vineyards and barnyards and gardens, planting his crops in their seasons, and growing them in independence, making wheat and cotton his clean surplus and selling them in his own markets, in his own time and manner, and not at a master's bidding, taking his pay in cash and not in a receipted mortgage, which while it ends a portion of his debts, does not restore his freedom—then will be dawning the fullness of a new day.[42]

Fearing that the United States might become overindustrialized and believing that all great nations in world history had had a strong pastoral element, Jones proclaimed that the bill preserved American agriculture.

When opposition seemed certain to kill any chance of passage, some of his colleagues advised Jones to wait until the next session to make the fight for his bill. Jones replied, "Hell, no. I've never deserted on the field of battle in my life. I'm going to finish this bill and bring it to a formal vote, if I'm the only one who votes for it."[43]

After all the criticism and conflict the bill eventually passed the House, 203 to 151, but it died in the Senate, where opponents succeeded in victimizing it with many amendments based on unsound economics.[44]

---

[41] H.R. 13991, January 3, 1933, MJP; COHP-MJP, pp. 519–520.

[42] Jones, "The Remarks of Marvin Jones," *Congressional Record* Scrapbook, vol. 3 (72d Cong., 2d sess.), p. 1351.

[43] Jones, interview with author, August 12, 1971.

[44] It should be noted that the fate of the Jones bill did not end all House efforts for agriculture. Additional cotton was provided to the Red Cross, and crop-loan bills were passed as a result of the Agriculture Committee's action.

The First Crisis of Jones's Leadership

Jones's defeat did not lack positive aspects. He had demonstrated courage in the face of unsurmountable problems. Many Texas congressmen had followed his leadership even after the bill was condemned by a resolution in the Texas state senate. Jones's understanding of agriculture expanded, and he won increased respect from House leaders and from Roosevelt, who now realized that Jones was no ordinary legislator. In fact, a bond between the two men had been sealed. New Deal agricultural policy had begun with the Jones bill, which was a forerunner of the Agricultural Adjustment Act.

On January 20, Roosevelt came through Washington on another trip and visited with Jones. The president-elect recalled Jones's earlier advice about waiting until after the inauguration to submit farm legislation, and now he acknowledged its accuracy. Then the two men turned their discussion to strategy for the approaching session.

After the conference photographers took pictures of Roosevelt with the agriculture chairman on the back platform of Roosevelt's train. This symbolized to Jones Roosevelt's acceptance of him as a member of the team. Afterward Jones displayed on his desk a print of the photograph. It quickly became a treasured memento.

The Jones bill, however, was the most significant agricultural bill before the House during that session. Ibid.; *New York Times*, February 11, February 16, and February 21, 1933.

7.

The Hundred Days

On Inauguration Day, March 4, 1933, a cloudy sky kept the sun from shining on depression-ridden Washington. Despite the morning gloom a smiling, apparently confident president-elect brightened the inaugural parade. Roosevelt was accompanied by outgoing President Hoover, who had the look of a loser in a fight with a lion.

At noon the procession reached Capitol Hill. Roosevelt and Hoover proceeded to the Senate chambers to watch the swearing-in ceremony for Vice-President "Cactus Jack" Garner, the salty sage of Uvalde, Texas. After that the official party made its way through a crowd of legislators, diplomats, and government officials to a special stand erected on the east wing. There Chief Justice Charles Evans Hughes administered the oath of office to Franklin Delano Roosevelt.

At 1:06 P.M. the new president began speaking to the throng standing before him and to millions of individuals listening on radio. On this "day of national consecration," he assured the people, "this great nation will endure as it has endured, will revive and will prosper." Sitting with other House dignitaries, Jones admired FDR's choice of words that "the only thing we have to fear is fear itself." At first it seemed ironic, then warmly reassuring, that they came from the mouth of a man—a polio victim—who knew well the meaning of fear and pain. Refreshed, revitalized, Jones forgot the tension of the past session as he thrilled to each inaugural-day activity.[1]

Within days Roosevelt summoned all the Democratic congres-

---

[1] Marvin Jones, interview with Dean Albertson, Columbia Oral History Project, 1952, pp. 547–558, hereafter cited as COHP-MJP. Unless otherwise noted, all interviews and correspondence citing Jones refer to Marvin Jones. See also James MacGregor Burns, *Roosevelt: The Lion and the Fox*, p. 163; Edward Robb Ellis, *A Nation in Torment*, pp. 267–272.

sional chairmen to the White House and elaborated on desires expressed in the inaugural address. Jones listened and anticipated leading his agricultural committee without worrying about partisan opposition from the Senate or from the chief executive. After all, there were hardly enough Republicans left to create much partisanship. Now, he thought, his committee could make real progress on refinancing farm mortgages and meeting other problems of agriculture. Jones focused on short-term solutions for immediate problems. He had no long-range plan of his own; nor did he enjoy theoretical discussions of agricultural policy like those often engaged in by some of Roosevelt's agricultural lieutenants. Jones listened and reserved the right to exercise his own independent judgment.

In the early days of the New Deal three important philosophies were present, according to Paul Conkin, in *Tomorrow a New World*: purist, modern Hamiltonian, and government activist. Jones had more in common with purists who still believed in Jeffersonian liberalism, but he saw through the superficial espousal of this liberalism by business groups. Like the purists, Jones favored fiscal responsibility and a restrained federal bureaucracy. He had little in common with modern Hamiltonians, who welcomed a centralized government. He wanted a government based on "those vulgar masses which Hamiltonians distrusted," but he also wanted expanded government aid for agriculture.[2] Like the government activists, he desired greater economic security.

Jones always preferred the counsel of agricultural organizations and plain dirt farmers to agricultural economists and social scientists. He lacked confidence in the "socialistic" approaches of "a great many so-called bright boys who felt that business and the entire make-up of the country could be made over almost by waving a magic wand in the form of legislative enactments."[3]

From the day of Roosevelt's inauguration Jones considered himself a New Dealer. During those desperate times he saw government's duty to be to "humanize and to link the individual rights and

[2] Paul K. Conkin, *Tomorrow a New World: The New Deal Community Program*, p. 5; Marvin Jones, "The Remarks of Marvin Jones," *Congressional Record* Scrapbook, vol. 3 (73d Cong., 2d sess.), pp. 9049, 11862; ibid., vol. 5 (76th Cong.), pp. 13631–38, Marvin Jones Papers, hereafter cited as MJP.

[3] COHP-MJP, pp. 645–648; See also Marvin Jones, "The Essentials of Farm Legislation," radio address, March 18, 1933, MJP.

opportunities."⁴ Thus he moved toward uncommon support of a program described by historian Richard Kirkendall: ". . . in its basic farm legislation, the New Deal was, in effect, urging the farmer to participate in, rather than resist, the development of a collectivistic or organizational type of capitalism" and to become part of the larger world of business, science, and the city in increasing respective demands for help upon the government while "at the same time moving reluctantly with, rather than against, the development of a collectivistic type of capitalism."⁵

Jones's committee supported him in the early days of the New Deal. The committee included nineteen Democrats and eight Republicans. Even the senior Republicans posed no great threat. No Democratic challenger to Jones's leadership appeared. Republicans Gilbert Haugen of Iowa, Fred Purnell of Indiana, and John E. Ketcham of Michigan and Democrats William Larsen of Georgia and William Nelson of Missouri had left the committee. Only two aspects of their influence remained: commodity interests and conflicts over the extent of federal government involvement in relief.

Liberal committee members like Democrats John Flannagan of Virginia and Hampton Fulmer of South Carolina and Republican Gerald Boileau of Wisconsin immediately favored extensive government action. Centralists like Democrats Wall Doxey of Mississippi, Cap Carden of Kentucky, David D. Glover of Arkansas, and James G. Polk of Ohio and Republican Clifford Hope of Kansas differed from the liberals principally on the degree of government involvement. Conservatives—including the ranking Republican member, John D. Clark of New York, and Democrats Harry Beam of Illinois and Richard Kleberg of Texas, Jones's classmate of University of Texas days—favored closer restrictions on government activity and usually supported the interests of the agricultural processors.

Jones alternated between liberal and center. His closest advisers in those days came from the center: Doxey (Jones's own Democratic

---

⁴ COHP-MJP, pp. 645–648.

⁵ Richard S. Kirkendall, "The Great Depression: Another Watershed in American History," in *Change and Continuity in Twentieth Century America*, ed. John Braeman, Robert H. Brammer, and Everett Walters, pp. 156–157, 161–162; COHP-MJP, pp. 547–548, 645–648; Jones, "The Essentials of Farm Legislation"; James MacGregor Burns, *Roosevelt: The Lion and the Fox*, p. 163.

lieutenant) and Kansas Republican Hope, whom Jones especially liked.

The committee members looked out as usual for their own districts' major commodities, even though the larger issue of farm relief absorbed them. Some of the more effective commodity spokesmen were Fulmer and Doxey for cotton; Glover, for rice; Carden and Flannagan, for tobacco; Colorado Democrat Fred Cummings, for sugar; Hope and Iowa Republican Fred Gilchrist, for wheat; Boileau, for dairy products; and Kleberg, for cattle. Packers found a spokesman in Harry Beam. Jones's interests cut across commodity politics, concentrating primarily on farm financial issues, but he kept a watchful eye on cotton, cattle, and, to a lesser extent, wheat.[6]

Jones's work for the New Deal actually antedated Roosevelt's presidency. On the day before the inauguration Henry Morgenthau, Jr., told Jones that Roosevelt wanted him and Bill Myers to prepare an executive order calling for consolidation of various farm lending agencies. Jones replied that he had never read an executive order, much less written one. Morgenthau insisted that Jones proceed, assuring him that Roosevelt respected his opinions on farm finance.

Other reasons, however, possibly lay behind Roosevelt's request. The president-elect wanted to get the support of the House Agriculture Committee—especially since, in the Senate, Cotton Ed Smith could be counted on to be obstinate. Probably, too, Roosevelt wanted to draw Jones closer to the new administration by getting him involved and committed and by weakening his potential conservative leanings. Finally, Roosevelt realized that Jones would know what would be politically possible, while Bill Myers, more familiar with Cornell University than with Capitol Hill, would not.

Jones agreed to help. Myers wrote the drafts. In the evenings Jones met with Myers to make revisions. Eventually they created an order that would establish the Farm Credit Administration, abolish the Federal Farm Board structure, and promote economy and efficiency by taking various lending agencies (such as land banks, intermediate-credit banks, and other agricultural lending agencies) within the federal government and placing them in one centralized bureaucratic structure. They sent the draft to Roosevelt for his approval.

[6] COHP-MJP, pp. 550–556; Mrs. Altravene Clark Spann, interview with author, March 23, 1973.

Both Jones and Myers knew that the order could not stand without implementation by legislation. Later they would work on drafting a bill that would become known as the Farm Credit Act. In the meantime Jones wondered about Roosevelt's delay in issuing the order.[7] At that time the New Deal was alive with action. Henry Wallace assumed the post of secretary of agriculture. Farm leaders flocked to Washington to discuss solutions to farm problems. Suggested revisions of the Agricultural Adjustment Act began to emerge. Roosevelt ordered a "bank holiday" from March 6 through March 9 in an effort to halt the widespread failures of those institutions, and when banks began reopening under some new controls, confidence had been restored. Large-scale runs and failures ceased; stocks went up.

Farm income continued to be sickly, however. It had sunk to new lows through continued high operating costs, increased numbers of farm mortgages, overproduction, high prices at which farms changed ownership, difficulties in finding and maintaining foreign markets, and natural disasters like bad weather. Jones believed that legislative solutions could not cope with everything. In this he differed from certain of Roosevelt's lieutenants, who felt more confident about the effectiveness of new laws.

A bill to increase farm income was drafted by Lee, Ezekiel, Peek, Wallace, and others. It gave the secretary of agriculture great power to reduce acreage and to fix farm-commodity prices. The drafters expected Jones to be a loyal New Dealer and to sponsor the bill in the House, but Jones still believed that the road to farm prosperity lay in lower taxes, lower transportation costs, and mortgage relief. Furthermore, he had determined not to be a rubber stamp for every piece of Roosevelt legislation.

Moreover, in this instance Jones believed that the drafters had proceeded unconstitutionally. He refused to support the bill as originally drafted and even walked out of heated committee hearings for breaths of fresh air. Sponsorship of the bill fell to Hampton Fulmer,

---

[7] Jones, interview with James S. Ward, assistant to the administrator, Agriculture Stabilization and Conservation Service, October 11, 1967, pp. 6–7, in the possession of James S. Ward, Washington, D.C.; hereafter cited as Jones to Ward.

second-ranking Democrat on the Agriculture Committee,[8] but Jones retained behind-the-scenes power and worked for compromises by the drafters.

Few bills can stand up to a chairman's opposition in the committee room, and in return for Jones's support changes were made. As originally drafted, the bill gave Secretary of Agriculture Wallace power to reduce acreage through "agreements with producers or otherwise," but at Jones's insistence the committee omitted "otherwise" and substituted "by other voluntary methods," thus emphasizing a self-determining concept. Other changes included permitting farmers who overproduced in one year an opportunity to apply that production to the next year's allotment, making provisions for fines and imprisonment of government officials who engaged in commodity speculation, and granting processors of exported commodities refunds of processing taxes. The committee also followed the chairman's views in saying that funds from the processing tax should go to the United States Treasury rather than to individual farmers as proposed in the original draft; but, like Jones, they focused on Supreme Court approval rather than a clearly conceived plan of social consciousness.

After all the changes had been made, Jones still expressed some reservations about the bill, but he agreed to support it when it came before the House. He considered the bill a temporary experiment and compromised with the intention of working to repeal it later. The bill came to the House floor on March 21, 1933, under a rule prohibiting amendments. Jones spoke for the bill on the basis of party unity by declaring that, in these emergency times, he would "follow the man at the other end of the Avenue."[9]

Opponents charged that the proposal was impractical and con-

---

[8] For an excellent general discussion see Van Perkins, *Crisis in Agriculture: The Agricultural Adjustment Administration and the New Deal: 1933*, pp. 49–78. See also John E. Pearson, "Cotton Policies and the Economic Welfare of Cotton Producers," Ph.D. dissertation, Indiana University, 1956, pp. 103–114. William E. Leuchtenberg, in his excellent *Franklin D. Roosevelt and the New Deal*, noted that "the House quickly passed the farm bill without changes but the Senate balked at speedy action" (p. 49). I respectfully disagree with this generalization. Scrapbook, 5, MJP; Jones to Ward, October 11, 1967, 1–5; COHP-MJP, pp. 558–565, 575–588, 591–598.

[9] Jones, "The Remarks of Marvin Jones," *Congressional Record* Scrapbook, vol. 3 (73d Cong., 1st sess.), p. 578, MJP.

ferred too much power. Even Jones's close friend, Republican Hope of Kansas, observed, "If it is right and proper to have an agricultural dictator, I am glad that it is going to be Secretary Wallace."[10] In a sort of defense Jones remarked that greater executive power had been established in the Packers and Stockyards Act, passed by a Republican administration.

On March 22 the House passed the measure by an overwhelming vote, 315 to 98.[11] After that the bill went to the Senate, and the House turned to problems of farm finance.

The very next day the House Agriculture Committee began deliberating proposals aimed at easing the farm-mortgage burden. A few days later, on March 27, Roosevelt used the executive order (6084) drafted by Jones and Myers to consolidate all farm-credit agencies into one new organization, the Farm Credit Administration, to take effect May 27. The president followed the executive order with an appeal to Congress to pass legislation providing lower interest rates for farm-mortgage refinancing, with reduction of payments on the principal of the original loan.[12]

During the spring of 1933 sponsors of farm-credit legislation had to consider the effects on American farmers who were not in serious difficulty. Other factors to be considered included the general agricultural credit rating, the status of creditors as well as of debtors, and a desire to prevent farm families from declaring bankruptcy.

Debate on the subject sparked wide differences of opinion. Garner later said to Morgenthau, "Until you came along Mrs. Garner and I average 16 percent a year on our money, and now [as a result of the Farm Credit Administration] we can't get better than five percent." Morgenthau remarked that Garner's attitude was in striking contrast to that of Marvin Jones, who "had seen his father and mother struggle helplessly against high-interest notes."[13]

Jones was determined that the Agriculture Committee, not the

[10] Ibid., p. 682.
[11] Ibid., pp. 756, 759–768.
[12] Perkins, *Crisis in Agriculture*, p. 53; Franklin D. Roosevelt, *Public Papers and Address: 1933*, pp. 85–90.
[13] Morgenthau stated that "Jones, a sharecropper's son, had seen his father and mother struggle helplessly against high-interest notes until it killed them." As previously noted, Jones's father was a small yeoman farmer who later became an insurance agent. Marvin's mother was alive in 1947. See also

Banking and Currency Committee, would handle matters of farm finance. On April 2 he met with Henry Steagall of Alabama, chairman of the Banking and Currency Committee, and asked him to let the Agriculture Committee handle the legislation. Steagall bristled and refused, but he did agree to a two-day delay to discuss the matter with his own committee. In the meantime both committees solicited House support despite a personal appeal from Speaker Henry Rainey to "calm down, boys." A fight seemed certain.

On April 4, Jones proposed before the House that Roosevelt's suggestions about farm mortgaging be submitted to the Agriculture Committee. Steagall immediately opposed the motion, basing his arguments on House rules giving the Banking and Currency Committee jurisdiction over public credit, farm-loan acts, the Federal Reserve System, and related matters. Furthermore, he warned, such a precedent would enable the Agriculture Committee to take from the Ways and Means Committee jurisdiction over agricultural tariffs.

Steagall stood on solid ground with his arguments. Finally the debate became a disputation of semantics. Which word was most important, "farm" or "credit?"[14] Jones argued that "farm" held more importance, and he insisted that under the current legislative calendar his committee could bring the bill back to the House floor more quickly. Not voiced was another consideration: a deep, years-long distrust of Steagall's committee by Jones and other agrarians. They knew that the members of the Banking and Commerce Committee favored higher interest rates. Jones added a plea "to see the question of agriculture torn from the bankers of the Nation and to have agriculture stand on its own bottom."[15] Those arguments persuaded a few urban legislators like Detroit's Carl Weideman to agree with Jones that existing banking laws discriminated against agriculture.

The logic of Jones's arguments resulted in a political upset. The

---

Case, "Farm Debt Adjustment during the Early 1930's," p. 176; Henry Morgenthau, Jr., "The Morgenthau Dairies: The Paradox of Poverty and Plenty," *Colliers* 120 (October 25, 1947):25. Arthur M. Schlesinger, Jr., *The Age of Roosevelt: The Coming of the New Deal*, p. 45.

[14] Jones, "The Remarks of Marvin Jones," *Congressional Record* Scrapbook, vol. 3 (73d Cong., 1st sess.), pp. 1209-10, MJP.

[15] Ibid., pp. 1216-17.

House voted 172 to 83 to send the emergency farm-mortgage bill to Jones's committee. Ever since that time the Agriculture Committee has retained dominance in the area.

Bill drafters John O'Brien and Gerald Morgan helped the Agriculture Committee put the bill in final form: federal land banks could issue up to $2 million in farm-loan bonds, refinance farm mortgages held by mortgagees other than federal land banks, raise the maximum amount of loans from $25,000 to $50,000, and reduce interest rates on all loans from 5.4 percent to 4.5 percent. The last provision was especially important because of the existing $8.5 billion in farm mortgages and $3.5 million in other debts that farmers had amassed at an average interest rate of 6.1 percent.

The bill also permitted debtors a five-year moratorium on payment of the principal, as long as they paid the interest. The government guaranteed investors both interest and principal on the bonds.[16]

The emergency farm-mortgage bill became title II of the Agricultural Adjustment Act, which was signed into law by President Roosevelt.

While some analysts charged the Agriculture Committee with failure in its farm-finance efforts, Murray Benedict concluded that the committee confronted the most pressing emergency of the times. The Emergency Farm Mortgage Act was one of the most practical and important steps that could be taken, curtailing the retraction of credit from the agricultural sector of the economy. Loans provided by the act permitted refinancing and a way to ease economic discomfort and hostility. Now loans could be made up to 75 percent of the value of the farm.[17] The nonfarm financial situation also relaxed.

On Capitol Hill the Senate had cautiously considered the bill. Senator Smith had voiced reservations about it and had sought means to strengthen his own cotton program. The Senate had added two important amendments: the Norris-Simpson and the Thomas amendments. The first permitted the secretary of agriculture to establish minimum prices on basic crops that were consumed domestically.

---

[16] U.S., Congress, House, Committee on Agriculture, *Agricultural Credit, Emergency Farm Mortgage Act of 1933: House Report to Accompany H.R. 4795*, 73d Cong., 1st sess., April 10, 1933, H. Rept. 35.

[17] Murray R. Benedict, *Farm Policies of the United States, 1790–1950*, pp. 281–282; *New York Times*, April 14, 1933; "Congressman Jones Has Some 'Mighty' Pens of Roosevelt on Display," undated clipping, scrapbook 5, MJP.

Despite administration opposition the amendment passed in the Senate, 47 to 41. Senators also passed the Thomas amendment (as title III) on April 28 by a vote of 64 to 21. This amendment permitted the president to inflate currency by devaluing the gold dollar, allowed the government to issue currency up to $3 billion, and made silver acceptable for payment of international debts.[18]

Representatives of the House and Senate agriculture committees met immediately to iron out differences. House members Jones, Clark, Hope, Doxey, and Fulmer conferred with the Senate delegation, which was made up of Smith, McNary, Fletcher, Thomas, and Wagner. Secretary Wallace opposed the cost-of-production plan, and House members backed him. In conference, however, senators secured support for sixty-seven of their amendments, most of which were primarily concerned with perfecting amendments, excluding cattle and sheep as basic commodities, and strengthening Smith's cotton plan. But the most important elements of the Emergency Farm Mortgage Act remained basically unchanged.[19]

On May 12, 1933, Jones received one of the pens the president had used to sign the act into law. Roosevelt distributed them among the farm leaders, congressmen, and administration officials he deemed principally instrumental in the bill's inception. Jones's efforts in behalf of title II had already been publicly acknowledged.

Jones continued to strengthen his number-one priority, farm finance, on May 25, when he introduced a bill (H.R. 5890) designed to furnish long-term credit to farmers. This was the third and concluding step in farm-finance revision begun with Roosevelt's executive order of March. The bill was drafted by Jones and Myers with some help from Morgenthau. As before, Myers assumed the principal role of author, with Jones the enactor. The legislation allowed divisions of the Farm Credit Administration to make production and marketing loans and amended certain other agricultural financial legislation. It liquidated joint-stock land banks by creating new credit agencies that featured a central bank with twelve regional

[18] General studies of the Senate action can be noted in Perkins, *Crisis in Agriculture*, pp. 49–78, and David Conrad, *The Forgotten Farmers*, pp. 19–36.

[19] *New York Times*, May 5, 1933; U.S., Congress, House, Committee on Agriculture, *Relieve the Existing National Emergency by Increasing Agricultural Purchasing Power: Report to Accompany H.R. 3835*, 73d Cong., 1st sess., May 5, 1933, H. Rept. 100.

banks to lend funds to cooperatives. Twelve production credit corporations were established to provide financial assistance and supervision to local units. As Benedict explained, in *Farm Policies of the United States,* this new financial structure consisted of

> the twelve land banks, for making mortgage loans; the twelve intermediate credit banks, for making production and marketing loans; the thirteen banks for cooperatives, for making loans to cooperatives; and the twelve production credit corporations, for creating an adequate local mechanism whereby the intermediate credit banks could research and serve the individual farmer.[20]

Jones and Myers took their rough draft of the bill to the White House for Roosevelt's approval. The president looked it over and urged the authors to keep interest rates as low as possible consistent with sound operations. Six days later the House debated and passed it. The Senate suggested fifty-eight amendments, most of which were accepted by the House. On June 10, 1933, both House and Senate passed the bill.[21] Roosevelt signed the Farm Credit Act into law in the closing week of his first one hundred days.

Jones had proved himself. Henry Morgenthau, Jr., said:

> Especially do I wish to express my admiration for... Marvin Jones, to whom probably more than to any other man in Congress is due the nation's gratitude for the untiring and wise effort he devoted to the drafting and enactment of the Emergency Farm Mortgage Act of 1933, and the Farm Credit Act of 1933 and other legislation for the benefit of agriculture enacted in the 100 days of this year.[22]

Throughout this momentous New Deal period Jones had focused his attention on problems of agriculture. His responsibilities had prevented detailed consideration of other New Deal measures. He had confined his speeches on the House floor to agriculture, and in them he generally supported the Roosevelt program. In other areas of relief or reform, however, his vote could not be taken for granted by the administration. It varied. He maintained his commitment to the TVA, and he favored relief work to improve highways.

---

[20] COHP-MJP, p. 620; H.R. 5790, May 25, 1933, MJP; Benedict, *Farm Policies of the United States,* p. 282; *New York Times,* June 1, 1933.

[21] Jones, "The Remarks of Marvin Jones," *Congressional Record* Scrapbook, vol. 3 (73d Cong., 1st sess.), p. 5690, MJP.

[22] "Morgenthau Praises Jones," undated clipping, scrapbook 6, MJP.

He welcomed creation of the Home Owners' Loan Corporation and obtained for Amarillo one of the four Texas-based Home Loan Corporation banks. On the other hand, he voted against creation of the Federal Emergency Relief Administration and the National Industrial Recovery Act. Like most other farm spokesmen, he had long been skeptical of business combinations, and he continued to demand strict enforcement of antitrust laws.

Jones had always distrusted strong measures taken for recovery and relief. To him the New Deal in its earliest days had moved too fast, seemed too impractical, and manifested an insufficient constitutional foundation. He was mostly pleased with the part he had played in obtaining some farm relief. Yet he had been disappointed in other areas, particularly the failure of Congress to provide exclusive federal ownership and operation of the Federal Reserve System and its failure to provide increased federal aid to refinance farm and city home mortgages.[23]

Thus Jones returned to Texas in mid-July, 1933, to renew political contacts, visit relatives, and rest. His only political speech was delivered in Pampa on July 19, when he spoke on his legislative activities to 250 businessmen and ranchers with conservative leanings. He attacked the Hoover administration, paid loyal tribute to the Democratic party, praised Roosevelt the man, and generally established an I-follow-my-leader stance. He declared that something positive had been done to help the nation and his district, but he admitted that he would not have supported many New Deal measures except in the economic emergency that gripped the nation. Federal relief, he said, should be given "only in the name of mercy as a temporary measure."[24] Then turning to his new priorities for the forthcoming session, Jones insisted that the issuance of currency must be taken from the hands of "international bankers." The solution must be public ownership of banks.

Careful analysis of his speech might have produced concern among liberals and conservatives alike, but the speech, an honest statement of his views, aroused no adverse comment. Jones's activ-

[23] Jones to "Friend," form letter, June 27, 1933, MJP; Jones to Franklin D. Roosevelt, July 11, 1933, MJP; Roosevelt to Jones, July 21, 1933, MJP.

[24] "Throngs Hail Marvin Jones at Reception," unidentified clipping, scrapbook 5, MJP.

ities had not been widely publicized, partly because of his own desire not to call dramatic attention to himself and partly because Texas constituents, like their modern-day counterparts, were politically apathetic to something no more alarming than a banquet speech.

8.

The Expansion of the AAA

Marvin Jones's supporters in Amarillo wanted to express their appreciation to him for his work during the first hundred days of the New Deal. They planned a political rally and an old-fashioned barbecue for July 31, 1933. Wilbur Hawk, publisher of the *Amarillo News-Globe*, hired a famous Panhandle chef, John Snyder, to prepare a "fealty feast" and invited everyone to come to the Tri-State Fairgrounds for the celebration. On the eve of the festivity, however, Jones received a telegram from Washington urging him to return to participate in a conference on wheat and cotton allotments under the Agricultural Adjustment Administration. Jones left for the capital as soon as he could pack.

The meetings continued through August. In them Jones again worked for the folks at home. He asserted that crop estimates for the nation were too high but that those for Texas were too low. To prove his point, he used statistics compiled from Texas railroad records. He contended that the low estimates would deprive Texas wheat farmers of $3,038,790 in government payments. He succeeded in preventing drastic monetary reductions to Texas farmers, especially those of his district.[1]

After the meetings Jones remained in Washington and spent the next three months preparing for the forthcoming congressional session. A wide variety of matters vied for his attention, but drought relief took precedence. By 1933 dry topsoil was swirling in what would become known as the Dust Bowl. While the greatest tragedy

---

[1] "Marvin Jones Says Acreage Set Too Low," undated clipping, scrapbook 2, Marvin Jones Papers, hereafter cited as MJP; "Marvin Jones Called to National Capitol on Important Matters," undated clipping, scrapbook 5, MJP.

was still to come, the farmers and ranchers of the region had already begun to suffer; the ribs were showing under the hides of scrawny Panhandle cattle who hunted for the sparse grass on the dry, windswept ranges. Jones urged Hugh Johnson, head of the National Recovery Administration, to ask "all mortgage and loan companies, or other companies holding either farm or city mortgages, . . . to formulate a code by the terms of which they will agree to refrain from foreclosure for a period of three years on all farm and city properties on which interest and taxes are kept paid during that period."² Jones also sought government feed loans and lower transportation rates for the stricken area. He appealed personally to President Roosevelt on September 26:

In 17 counties of northwest Texas there has been the worst drought period within the memory of any living man. In many instances the soil has been blown away to the clay. It was my understanding that this territory was to be included within the program in the sixty million dollars provided for relief.³

After deliberations that Jones thought took too long, Roosevelt designated a special fund of $8,900,000 for drought and flood relief. Then Harry Hopkins cut the funds by 40 percent, alleging that Texas did not need that much relief. Jones exploded:

It is an outrageous situation when the federal administration, including the public works board, Secretary [of the Interior] Ickes, the Relief Administration and all departments concerned agree to a relief program, [which] then has the approval of the President who signed his name to the order calling for the issuance of funds, to have one of the President's employees, Mr. Hopkins, stand in the way and refuse to do not only what he is told to do but what he agreed to in my presence.

Never had Jones been so angry. The president did not care to antagonize the Agriculture Committee chairman further. He conferred with Henry Wallace, Ickes, and Hopkins on October 20 in a hastily summoned meeting.⁴ What transpired was never reported publicly,

---

² "Code for Mortgage Companies Providing Moratorium Asked," *Houston Chronicle*, August 14, 1933.

³ Marvin Jones to Franklin D. Roosevelt, September 26, 1933, MJP. Unless otherwise noted, all interviews and correspondence citing Jones refers to Marvin Jones.

⁴ Jones to Henry A. Wallace, Special Board of Public Works, October 11, 1933; *Dalhart Texan*, October 19, December 5, 1933; Jones to Wallace, Octo-

but the Texas congressman got his drought-relief funds. The *Amarillo News* lauded his efforts:

> There hasn't been any vacation for Congressman Marvin Jones. He has been constantly on the job in Washington, helping to speed up farm relief administration and giving his personal attention to specific problems affecting the Panhandle. . . . The result was that Texas wheat growers, mostly in the Panhandle, are the winners by several thousand dollars. . . . The most outstanding bit of work performed by the Panhandle's congressman, however, has been his untiring efforts for speedy action on the $5,000,000 emergency road grant for the drought district.[5]

During the rest of the year Jones polished preliminary drafts of more farm-credit legislation and a bill to include cattle as a basic commodity. Desiring once more to assess ranchers' sentiment and to spend the approaching holidays with his relatives, he returned to his district, made an extensive tour of the Panhandle, and visited the King Ranch in South Texas to discuss farm and ranch problems with owner Richard Kleberg, an Agriculture Committee member. Not surprisingly, he won Kleberg's support for his forthcoming move to provide relief to cattlemen.

When Congress reconvened in January 1934, legislators discovered that more farms had passed into the hands of creditors despite the recent legislation. Conditions remained especially acute in drought-stricken areas. Jones, who represented one of the nation's most severely depressed districts, realized that the original fund of $200 million for land-bank loans was not nearly enough to meet the needs.

Within a week after the session began, Jones brought before the Agriculture Committee a bill providing for creation of the Federal Farm Mortgage Corporation to operate with the Farm Credit Administration in issuing up to $2 billion in bonds for use in refinancing farm mortgages. Later on the House floor Jones stymied attempts to

---

ber 4, 1933; Henry G. Knight, "Memorandum: A Plan for Control of Wind Erosion in the Region of Southwestern Kansas, Southwestern Colorado, Northwestern Oklahoma and Northwestern Texas in Connection with Agricultural Relief That May Be Offered Those Farmers of the Region Who Are Suffering Seriously from the Effects of Drought and Severe Wind Erosion on Their Lands," September 6, 1933, National Archives, Washington, D.C., Record Group 16.

[5] "Marvin Jones on the Job," undated clipping, *Amarillo News*, MJP.

substitute other loan plans and to make the FFMC bonds liable for state and local taxes. Congress passed the bill, and Roosevelt signed it into law.[6]

In earlier, more placid days ranchers had insisted on independence from government. Now, however, the forces of nature were eroding that attitude. By June 1933, prominent men like Dolph Briscoe, president of the Texas and Southwestern Cattle Raisers' Association (and father of a future governor), had appealed to Wallace for government aid in the face of drought.

Jones had long been aware of the problems ranchers faced.[7] He had talked with Panhandle cattlemen like Jay Taylor, Julian Bivins, and Grover Hill, Jones's long-time confidant. Taylor recalled later:

> We suggested a slaughtering and canning program of 10 million cattle in the drought area which would put a lot of unemployed people to work and would provide thousands of cans of good, nutritious meat for the needy. Jones saw immediately the need for this and we went from his office to Senator Connally, who quickly said he would join him in [proposing what would become] the Purchase Act. [My] activities were simply to assist in the drawing up of the bill, [and] help sell the idea to Henry Wallace and President Roosevelt and as many members of Congress as it was possible for me to contact. I worked out of Marvin's office and he was very, very helpful in giving advice and guiding us in our very amateurish methods of lobbying.[8]

Despite the disastrous dought, however, not all ranchers agreed on the desirability of government aid. Many of them proclaimed their independence from meddling. If government aid was to come, a consensus in favor of federal action had to be presented to Depart-

---

[6] E. C. Johnson, "Agricultural Credit," in U.S. Department of Agriculture, *Yearbook of Agriculture: 1940*, pp. 743–751; H.R. 6670, January 10, 1933; Marvin Jones, "The Remarks of Marvin Jones," *Congressional Record* Scrapbook, vol. 3 (73d Cong., 2d sess.), p. 719, MJP.

[7] Jones, interview with James S. Ward, assistant to the administrator, Agriculture Stabilization and Conservation Service, October 11, 1967, pp. 48–51, MJP; hereafter cited as Jones to Ward. For general background of the rancher's plight see John T. Schlebecher, *Cattle Raising on the Plains, 1900–1961*, pp. 134–140; C. Roger Lambert, "Texas Cattlemen and the AAA, 1933–1935," *Arizona and the West* 14 (Summer 1972):137–154; Irvin May, Jr., "Welfare and Ranchers: The Emergency Cattle Purchase Program and Emergency Work Relief Program in Texas, 1934–1935," *West Texas Historical Association Year Book* 47 (1971):3–19.

[8] Jay Taylor to author, June 18, 1974.

ment of Agriculture officials and congressmen. That would require the support of a substantial segment of politically prominent farmers and ranchers.

At Henry Wallace's suggestion representatives of the American National Livestock Association, the Texas and Southwestern Cattle Raisers' Association, and the Panhandle Livestock Association met in Denver with other ranchers and representatives of the federal government (headed by Victor A. Christgau, assistant administrator of the Agricultural Adjustment Administration) to discuss ways of increasing cattle prices. Jones sat in on the discussions. A visit to the Denver stockyards shocked the Panhandle congressman and made Jones realize that the ranchers' dilemma was not localized in Texas but was a real and dangerous threat throughout the Southwest.

After the meeting Jones accompanied federal officials on a trip to Salt Lake City to confer with sheepmen. On the way their automobile became overheated. They had to pay ten cents a gallon for water, which (as they learned) service-station operators hauled from as far as twenty miles away. On every side they saw the sufferings of man and livestock, the ravages of wind and drought. These experiences became important factors in the drafting of relief legislation.[9]

Jones later introduced an amendment to the Agricultural Adjustment Act (H.R. 6133) making cattle a basic commodity. This measure provided an opportunity to conduct hearings, to gain farm organization views, and to seek a consensus approach. Senator Connally agreed to introduce similar legislation in the Senate.

Information from hearings conducted by the House Agriculture Committee from January 4 to 26, 1934, revealed that many cattlemen desired government aid but that most of them opposed a processing tax and many feared competition with dairy cattle, should they be included as a basic commodity. Secretary Wallace told the committee that the processing tax should stand and that cattle should not be made a special case. Ranchers continued to lobby in opposition to this position. Wyoming's Senator Robert Carey testified against the processing tax, as did J. E. Brock, of the Wyoming Stock Growers' Association.

At night Jones worked on revisions of his bill with Senator

[9] Jones to Ward, October 11, 1967, pp. 48–51, unidentified clippings, scrapbook 6, MJP.

Connally and committee member Richard Kleberg. With Kleberg's assistance Jones arranged a conference of federal officials, ranchers, and other farm representatives to review the final draft of the hoped-for Jones-Connally Act. The meeting took place in Room 134 of the New House Office Building with Jones presiding. The conferees agreed that cattle should be included in the AAA, with the additional proposal for a $200 million appropriation to the Department of Agriculture to finance production adjustments for dairy and beef cattle. The next day Jones introduced his revised bill (H.R. 7478), and the House passed it on February 6. The measure then went to the Senate.[10]

There the bill encountered greater opposition; senators had previously rejected attempts to make cattle a basic commodity and now faced the humiliating prospect of publicly changing their position. On the other hand, the Roosevelt administration was supporting the bill. Secretary Wallace called for prompt Senate action and sought to win the weighty support of Cotton Ed Smith.

Smith stalled, however, and during the following six weeks senators in committee sought to make a number of changes. Finally the bill emerged on the Senate floor. There senators added relief for other commodities: barley, flax, peanuts, grain sorghums, and rye. An amendment offered by La Follette and adopted by a vote of 41 to 38 provided for $150 million to eradicate tubercular cattle and for appropriations to the Federal Surplus Relief Corporation. Later Jones rationalized to his House colleagues that the purposes outlined in the La Follette amendment were in the main the declared purposes of the House bill.

Loaded with amendments, what would become the Jones-Connally Act finally squeaked by the Senate, 39 to 37, with 20 abstentions. In conference legislators reduced the La Follette amendment allocation to $50 million (at the insistence of the House conferees),

---

[10] H.R. 6133, January 3, 1934, and H.R. 7478, January 30, 1934, MJP; Paul H. Appleby to Jones, January 15, 1934, and Appleby to Jones, January 23, 1932, National Archives, Record Group 233; U.S., Congress, House, Committee on Agriculture, *Include Cattle as Basic Agricultural Commodity, Hearings*, 73d Cong., 2d sess., January 4–26, 1934; Jones, "The Remarks of Marvin Jones," *Congressional Record* Scrapbook, vol. 3 (73d Cong., 2d sess.), p. 3815, MJP.

and the bill passed both houses with little subsequent opposition.[11]

The far-ranging features of the Jones-Connally Act actually came from the skimpy funds provided for in the La Follette amendment. That money brought relief to the neediest and also important measures for control of brucellosis. Jones's fiscally conservative nature prevented him from championing larger federal appropriations. Like other congressmen, he failed to recognize at the time the scope of the Dust Bowl disaster and hoped that rains would alleviate the situation. Still Jones benefited politically because he had begun a program that some ranchers wanted.

At the same time Congress was considering the Jones-Connally bill, problems in administering cotton provisions of the Agricultural Adjustment Act were being discussed on Capitol Hill. Under the provisions of the act cotton-acreage reductions were being nullified by heavier fertilization and by utilization of farm-credit measures that served to increase production. The cotton section of the AAA surveyed reaction to this and other conditions through questionnaires sent to cotton producers. Of those responding, nearly 95 percent favored a congressional increase in the AAA's use of the processing tax, and a majority favored compulsory controls. Adherence to those recommendations would mean a change in policy, because the administration heretofore had stressed voluntary controls.

In an attempt to satisfy the majority sentiment, the Bankhead brothers from Alabama, Senator John and Representative Will, jointly introduced a cotton-control bill. The bill avoided emphasizing its compulsory features, but the intent seemed clear. It provided for levying a tax of 50 percent of the market price on all cotton ginned in the United States and then exempting about 10 million bales from the tax. Farmers would receive transferable tax-exemption certificates for this amount. The bill made cotton grown in excess of AAA

[11] H. A. Wallace to E. D. Smith, February 15, 1934, National Archives, Record Group 16; Jones, "The Remarks of Marvin Jones," *Congressional Record* Scrapbook, vol. 3 (73d Cong., 2d sess.), pp. 3815, 4829, MJP; Jones to Ward, pp. 48–51; 1934 scrapbooks, MJP; Tom Connally Papers, Manuscript Division, Library of Congress; U.S., Congress, House, Committee on Agriculture, *To Include Cattle as Basic Agricultural Commodity Under Agricultural Adjustment Act Administration: Report to Accompany H.R. 7478*, 73d Cong., 2d sess., March 24, 1934, H. Rept. 1051; Henry A. Wallace to Jones, February 7 and February 14, 1934, National Archives, Record Group 16.

quotas unprofitable. Only by suffering heavy penalties could cotton farmers refuse to cooperate.

In February 1934 the House Agriculture Committee began hearings on the bill. Jones hoped to preserve the voluntary principle. Moreover, he contemplated an amendment to the Agricultural Adjustment Act that would guarantee federal benefits to all cotton producers, both landholders and tenants. Finally, he wanted guarantees that large producers who received AAA benefits and then mechanized their farms would not receive full government support. To Jones the Bankhead bill seemed undesirable.

As the hearings continued, however, President Roosevelt personally intervened with a strongly worded letter in support of the bill. Roosevelt contended that crop limitations could thus be maintained—and with the firm approval of cotton farmers.

Jones remained unconvinced. In his office lay sacks of letters protesting the bill. Many cotton farmers, especially those in his district, opposed countywide allotments that would be based (as in the bill) on a ten-year period. As farmers on the frontier of the cotton kingdom they foresaw this provision as discriminating against them and serving only the interests of the older producers of the Deep South.

Jones therefore refused to support the bill. Further, in his questioning of John Bankhead, he predicted that if the bill became law the Supreme Court would declare it unconstitutional because the purpose of the processing tax was for regulation rather than revenue.[12]

Intense pressure came from Democratic leaders. Jones conferred with a Republican colleague, Charles Tobey of New Hampshire, who told him:

> I've talked the matter over with several minority members [of the Agriculture Committee]. We want to vote just as you want us to vote. If you want us to kill the bill, we'll kill it. We'll take care of you in this

[12] John E. Pearson, "Cotton Policies and the Economic Welfare of Cotton Producers," Ph.D. dissertation, Indiana University, 1956, pp. 115–119; undated clipping, scrapbook 6, MJP; Franklin D. Roosevelt to Jones, February 16, 1934, Franklin D. Roosevelt Papers, Franklin D. Roosevelt Library, Hyde Park, N.Y.; Henry I. Richards, *Cotton and the AAA*, pp. 6, 30–42, 163–193; U.S., Congress, House, Committee on Agriculture, *Cotton, Bankhead Cotton Control Bill (H.R. 8402), Hearings*, 73d Cong., 2d sess., February 12–17, 1934.

way. You can fight for the bill just as hard as you want to. ["He knew the pressure that was being placed upon me," Jones injected here, "From the top spots as well as from the Bankheads, who were powerful figures in Congress."] If you want the bill reported, we'll help you report it. . . . There are enough of us, combined with the members of your party [who] are opposed to it. You can make your record any way you want to. . . . If you don't tell us that you want the bill reported out, we're going to vote against reporting it.[13]

Jones openly admitted a lack of enthusiasm for the bill, but he believed that Congress should have a chance to debate it. It went to the House floor. There debate began on March 10. Jones assigned the fate of the bill to Wall Doxey of Mississippi, although he spoke in favor of it himself, largely out of party loyalty. The bill passed, 251 to 115, on March 19.[14] After Senate passage and some changes resulting from work by the House-Senate Conference Committee, Roosevelt signed the Bankhead Cotton Control Act on April 21, 1934. Congress delayed the necessary appropriations, however, until late May.[15]

Jones had thus continued to give the party his loyal support, though with some reservations. Differences of opinion did not necessarily mean differences of principle or the breaking of treasured friendships. Jones had cultivated a personal relationship with John Bankhead, who was administrative spokesman for agriculture in the Senate (not Cotton Ed Smith). Bankhead and Jones were known for their mutual respect.

By September the Bankhead Act had produced increased opposition among cotton farmers, who sought to produce surpluses and profit even with the 50 percent tax. When these dreams failed to materialize, they protested to Congress—particularly to the agriculture committees.

Jones discussed the complaints with Secretary of Agriculture Wallace, who wanted to suspend the Bankhead Act at once in the

---

[13] Jones, interview with Dean Albertson, Columbia Oral History Project, 1952, pp. 684–685; hereafter cited as COHP-MJP.

[14] Ibid., pp. 681–686; Jones, "The Remarks of Marvin Jones," *Congressional Record* Scrapbook, vol. 3 (73d Cong., 2d sess.), pp. 4189, 4193, 4213–14, 4432–35, 4447, 4640–51, 4829, MJP.

[15] Unidentified clippings, John Bankhead Papers, Alabama Department of Archives and History, Mongomery, Ala.; Richards, *Cotton and the AAA*, pp. 163–193.

interest of the few sections that had overproduced. He believed that the act would be unfair to farmers in the drought and flood areas who had fully complied with the program and relied on the value of their excess certificates.

Jones felt, however, that "the 50 percent tax was a wolfish thing" and that AAA officials had worded their ballot to produce a favorable response from cotton farmers. Increasingly Jones doubted the popularity of the Bankhead Act and hoped that the president would intervene. In January 1935, Jones wrote Roosevelt that he had accepted the act as expedient legislation but that he doubted its wisdom as a permanent program. Jones maintained his view that long-range programs should have a voluntary base. He further charged that the act might encourage increased export of American cotton and greater use of cotton substitutes at home.

Jones's hope for presidential intervention soon flickered out. Later when Bankhead sought Jones's support to extend the act, Jones asked and received in return Bankhead's vital support for an automatic appropriation of 30 percent of the tariff revenues to be used by the secretary of agriculture in paying losses on marketing and distribution of surplus farm commodities.[16] This provision was to be section 32, a significant agricultural and relief measure, the only one of its kind during the New Deal, with important potential for future agricultural programs.

Cattle and cotton problems thus had received attention. The problem of sugar remained. Domestic production had benefited from tariff protection, but that was not sufficient to check a downward trend of producers' prices. Efforts to resolve the problem through the Agricultural Adjustment Act had not met with Secretary Wallace's approval.

In February 1934, Roosevelt asked for legislation to increase producers' prices, stabilize production, stop the decline of Cuban sugar imports, and maintain existing acreage without further expansion. Before this an amendment to the Jones-Connally Act, aimed at meeting these objectives, had been discussed by Wallace, Jones, and Smith, but they had failed to find a satisfactory solution. The

[16] Jones to Ward, October 11, 1937, pp. 34–36, MJP; Jones to Franklin D. Roosevelt, January 19, 1935, Roosevelt Papers; Roosevelt to Jones, January 31, 1935, MJP; undated clippings, scrapbook 6, MJP.

three had continued deliberations, often joined by Democratic Senators Edward Costigan of Colorado, Joseph Robinson of Arkansas, and Bankhead.

Eventually the request from Roosevelt himself motivated a reluctant Jones to sponsor a House bill making sugar beets and sugarcane basic commodities under the AAA (Costigan would introduce a similar bill in the Senate). Until then Jones had manifested little interest in sugar except for use with "coffee and strawberries." Even then Jones insisted that he would not compromise his belief that the processing fee should never be more than the amount of tariff reduction.

As soon as debate began, Congress faced intense pressure from various groups opposed to production quotas, import restrictions, and other provisions. This powerful opposition forced sponsors to introduce a revised bill that increased to 1,550,000 tons the quota for domestic beet-sugar producers. Costigan also persuaded cosponsor Jones to abandon the fixed-quota system and to provide that the secretary of agriculture could base quotas for producing areas other than the continental United States on an average three-year period from 1925 to 1933. The House bill further provided that western sugar-beet producers must prohibit child labor and must provide minimum wages for workers. On April 5, 1934, the House passed the bill without significant opposition.

The scene now shifted to the Senate Finance Committee, chaired by Democrat Pat Harrison of Mississippi. The committee was deluged with protests from Puerto Rican and Hawaiian sugar producers and government officials. Meanwhile, the sugar-beet producers, whose demands had been met, were urging immediate action because of the approaching planting season. Harrison's committee approved the bill, 11 to 6, but not before Republican Senator Arthur Vandenberg of Michigan had modified the child-labor provision to allow regulation but not require abolition of child labor. The senators also eliminated the minimum-wage provision before passing the bill, 49 to 18, on April 19.

In conference senators accepted the basic House measure, and representatives agreed to Senate amendments. They compromised on the domestic-sugar-beet quota, reducing it 500,000 tons. Despite further protests from the Puerto Rican senate and the Hawaiian

Sugar Planters' Association, Congress approved the conference report. President Roosevelt signed the bill on May 9, 1934, in the presence of a group of people, from which Jones was conspicuously absent.[17]

This law, which became known as the Jones-Costigan Sugar Act, stood as an exception to the legislation that bore Jones's name in that he played only a minor role in its policy determinations. The president had wanted prompt action and had simply arm-twisted Jones.

By June the Seventy-third Congress was speeding toward adjournment, but one congressman was hoping to get action on further agricultural-relief measures. William Lemke of North Dakota was pushing the Frazier-Lemke farm-bankruptcy bill in the House. Lemke's measure would allow farmers a five-year moratorium on mortgage foreclosures. During that time a farmer need pay only rent on his place. In the meantime the farm could be reappraised, and the debtor would owe this amount regardless of original mortgage.

Roosevelt opposed the bill, as did Speaker Henry T. Rainey of Illinois, and Democrat Hatton Sumners of Texas, chairman of the Judiciary Committee, which was handling it. The measure had reached an impasse in committee, and Lemke was seeking a discharge petition to force the bill out. Speaker Rainey hoped to adjourn before Congress could debate it.

Jones found himself in a race against the clock. Lemke and Oklahoma's Tom McKeown appealed to him to talk to Rainey in behalf of the bill. Jones voiced reluctance. Sumners was a close friend, and, moreover, Jones doubted the constitutionality of the bill.

At the same time it seemed to Jones that most mortgage companies were foreclosing on farms that had been largely paid off. For a hardworking farmer who remained deep in debt, foreclosure seemed less likely. Jones concluded that mortgage companies were taking unfair advantage. Although Jones had opposed earlier measures offered by Lemke, it seemed to him now that the desperate

---

[17] Marvin Jones, *Marvin Jones Memoirs*, ed. Joseph M. Ray, pp. 131–133; Edwin G. Nourse, Joseph S. Davis, and John D. Black, *Three Years of the Agricultural Adjustment Administration*; Jones to Ward, October 11, 1967, pp. 51–53; H.R. 7907, February 12, 1934, and H.R. 8861, March 28, 1934, MJP; *New York Times*, February 13, May 3, and May 10, 1934.

times called for at least consideration of the bill. He reasoned that, if Congress approved it, better legislation could be obtained during the next session. He persuaded Speaker Rainey to let the House debate the bill.

On the floor Jones observed that Congress had passed laws favoring corporations in bankruptcy proceedings and asked whether farmers should not also receive benefits. His arguments helped win House approval for the bill, which also passed the Senate.

Roosevelt faced a dilemma. He wanted to veto the legislation, but congressional leaders threatened to pass it anyway. Roosevelt at length gave in to them.[18] The major agricultural-legislation activity of the Seventy-third Congress had concluded with a reluctant president following congressional leadership.

At the close of the session Jones passed out some political ammunition for use by Democratic candidates running in the forthcoming elections. On June 15 he reviewed agricultural accomplishments of the New Deal. Significant achievements like the AAA, the FCA, the Crop Production Loan Act, drought measures, and the expansion of the AAA to include cattle and other commodities had produced financial benefits for farmers and ranchers. Prices of cotton, wheat, and corn rose with only minimal increases in cost to consumers.[19]

Jones went into the election of 1934 without opposition, so he used the summer for rest and routine visits with constituents—especially cattlemen, whose herds were suffering from the drought. His popularity became obvious again that summer, when twenty-five hundred citizens gathered for a barbecue in his honor. Jay Taylor, Julian Bivins, and Grover Hill sponsored the event on Jack Hall's ranch, near Amarillo. Taylor recalled:

When word got out about the barbecue, cattlemen and farmers all over the Panhandle began calling in and saying, "We want in on this too and we will send some beef."... We hired the great barbecue king, John Snyder, to prepare the meal, and it seems to me he prepared ten or

[18] Edward C. Blackorby, *Prairie Rebel: The Public Life of William Lemke*, pp. 198–201; COHP-MJP, pp. 749–769; Gilbert C. Fite, *George N. Peek and the Fight for Farm Parity*, pp. 271–281; Irvin M. May, Jr., "Peter Molyneaux and the New Deal," *Southwestern Historical Quarterly* 73 (January 1940):309–325.

[19] Jones, "The Remarks of Marvin Jones," *Congressional Record* Scrapbook, vol. 3 (73d Cong., 2d sess.), p. 11862, MJP.

twelve whole calves weighing about five hundred pounds apiece and God knows how many pounds of pinto beans and apricots!

Taylor spoke of Jones as

the most modest man I ever knew or even heard of. He never pushed himself, he never used his high office to browbeat or pressure anybody. . . . He was the greatest friend the cattleman and farmer ever had in Congress, [who] understood quickly and acted wisely in passing legislation to prevent a lot of us from going broke and to enhance agriculture in general.[20]

That year Jones served again on the Democratic National Campaign Committee. On October 1 he summarized the New Deal's agricultural accomplishments over NBC radio and asserted that the recent legislation reflected a majority of farm opinion. Still he cautioned those who complained of the slowness of the program that one could not "expect the President in a few months to sweep all the trash out of the White House which had accumulated there in the last twelve years." Jones suggested that his impatient listeners call in Hoover, "who produced twenty-cent wheat, ten-cent corn, and five-cent cotton."

The same year Jones spoke for Democratic candidates in New Mexico, Kansas, Nebraska, Missouri, Illinois, and Ohio. He contributed at least in part to the victories of Mell Underwood of Ohio, Richard Duncan of Missouri, Charles McLaughlin of Nebraska, and John Dempsey of New Mexico. Roosevelt's popularity remained high, and the party increased its strength in Congress.[21]

---

[20] Jay Taylor to author, June 18, 1974. One of the most significant articles against the New Deal's agricultural policies came from the pen of a resident of the Eighteenth Congressional District: rancher-historian J. Evetts Haley; see Haley, "Cow Business and Monkey Business," *Saturday Evening Post* 207 (December 18, 1934):26, 28–29, 94, 96.

[21] Democratic National Committee, press release, October 2, 1934, MJP; undated clippings, scrapbook 6, MJP. Jones, in *Marvin Jones Memoirs,* p. 115, noted that, when Rainey died, Joseph Byrnes, John McDuffie of Alabama, and John Rankin of Mississippi announced their candidacies for Speaker. Claude Fuller of Arkansas, Sam Rayburn, and Jones announced for Democratic floor leader. Jones withdrew, and McDuffie and Rayburn ran as a team. When Byrnes won, Will Bankhead became Democratic floor leader. The version in the text is based on newspaper accounts in scrapbook 6. Among other minor contenders were James Mead of New York and Illinois's Adolph Sabbath. COHP-MJP, pp. 770–772, contains another version.

Jones also tried, unsuccessfully, to help Speaker Henry T. Rainey that year, but in a nonpolitical way. He had noticed a wan look about Rainey, and the day after Congress adjourned he called at the Speaker's office to ask a favor. Rainey smiled and replied, "If it's reasonable, I'll try to grant it."

"I want you to go somewhere for thirty days where there isn't any telephone, where you won't be bothered, where you don't have any constituents—and rest," Jones said. "You're worn out much more than you realize."

"I can't," Rainey answered, adding that he had already scheduled three weeks of speaking engagements and a trip to Canada.

Jones agreed that Rainey should make the Canadian trip but urged him to cancel the speeches. Rainey promised to take the vacation, but only after making the scheduled speeches. He died, however, before commencing the vacation.[22] Joseph W. Byrns, a Tennessee Democrat, eventually replaced him, although Jones hoped for a time that he himself would win the position.

[22] COHP-MJP, pp. 769–770.

9.

Building the New "Farm House"

WHEN the Seventy-fourth Congress came into being in January 1935, Marvin Jones felt that the Agricultural Adjustment Act needed some revisions if American agriculture was to prosper. Specifically he favored increased federal aid to drought-stricken ranchers and to agricultural scientists engaged in research, but he realized that any sensible program must keep in mind the interests of producer, processor, manufacturer, distributor, and consumer.

Jones had another concern regarding the AAA. He feared that the Supreme Court would invalidate the legislation. It became essential to him that certain recently enacted measures be clad in constitutionality. This concern resulted in caution and delay in Jones's work in behalf of further relief for the farmer.

Another interruption slowed him. Now fifty-three, he was thinking about retiring from Congress. For the past eighteen years he had enjoyed his work in the House. Recent years had been even more satisfying, with Roosevelt as president and Jones himself having greater power, prestige, and popularity than ever.

But he could not forget his first campaign for Congress and his speeches against Stephens's twenty-year service. Jones had begun feeling the years, too. He had especially lost zest for campaigning. Too, he was more and more concerned about financial security. As a congressman he had not sought wealth. Now he concluded that the federal judiciary offered desirable retirement benefits, in addition to the long-term security he had always wanted. Jones began indicating to President Roosevelt that he would like an appellate judgeship.

For now, however, he was a congressman, and he strove to focus on the work of his office. Agricultural leaders, rural sociologists, agricultural economists, and federal officials were attempting to boost income levels, especially of the tenant farmers—the sharecroppers. Some progress had been made, and New Deal officials were suggesting that now was the time to begin a serious attack on the tenant system in the South. Although the tenancy percentage had stabilized during the depression, the nation's expanding population was adding about forty thousand tenants a year.

In Jones's Texas, 57.2 percent of the farms were operated by tenants, a percentage far exceeding the national average of 42 percent. Tenancy in Texas, like that in the Deep South, occurred predominantly on cotton-producing farms, nearly 70 percent of which were operated by tenants. About 2 percent of the Texans were sharecroppers; one-third of all tenants were black.[1]

Jones knew these statistics, but they meant little to him because few blacks lived in his district, and they had virtually no political power. He centered his attention on the yeoman farmer without drawing a conscious distinction on racial grounds or displaying ultraliberal humanitarianism by making proposals for unlimited relief.

In January 1935 rural relief rolls were higher than ever. Suggested solutions were coming to Congress from various sources. Will Alexander used funds from the Rockefeller Foundation and the Rosenwald Fund to prepare reports on the federal government's impact on the economy and on southerners. Alexander and other theorists argued that the AAA existed primarily for the planters' benefit and that Congress should expand the legislation to include agricultural workers. Department of Agriculture officials Rexford Tugwell, Paul Appleby, and M. L. Wilson were studying reports and making recommendations. Jones was fond of Wilson, but he did not have much faith in Tugwell's ideas. As for Alexander, Jones regarded him as a little extreme in some of his views. Jones particularly disliked two ultraliberal lawyers in the Agriculture Department: Jerome Frank and Lee Pressman. Neither man knew a cotton stalk from a weed, snorted Jones, who preferred practical men like Clarence Poe, editor of *Progressive Farmer*, and C. V. Gregory, editor of *Prairie Farmer*.

[1] C. Horace Hamilton, "Break the Backbone of the Tenant System," *Rural America* 12 (October 1934):3–5; C. Horace Hamilton, "Texas Farm Tenure Activities," *Journal of Land and Public Utility Economics* 14 (August 1938): 330–333.

One liberal proposal recommended that federal agencies purchase land held by financial institutions, subdivide it, and sell it to the families already on the land. Alexander and others declared that a federal corporation could handle the land transactions and that federal credit agencies should then assist in improving the production and efficiency of the farms.[2]

Jones sometimes supported ideas from the agricultural left, but generally he was a middle-of-the-roader, and this proposal struck him as extremely impractical as well as socialistic. He questioned the desirability and practicality of the Subsistency Homesteads Program, especially a model project in Reedsville, West Virginia. After making a personal inspection, Jones went away dismayed. The model did not agree with his concept of democracy. Jones doubted that such models would bring much hope to large numbers of farmers, and he reflected the objections of many southerners to a selective tenant-purchase-borrower concept. Jones sought federal funds that would assure the greatest equality of opportunity within the existing system (years later he would reminisce, "I had nearly as much trouble with the rainbow promisers . . . as I did with those who didn't want to do anything at all.")[3]

Specific legislation Jones sought at this time was expansion of the Farm Credit Administration consistent with the general agricultural theme of Roosevelt's State of the Union message of 1935. The president urged clarification, improvement, and consolidation of New Deal agencies to facilitate programs for social security, public works, better homes, work relief, and conservation. The president gave tenant legislation low priority, but Jones immediately began working to broaden the concept of "better homes" to include tenant legislation of a practical sort.

On January 8, 1935, Jones introduced a bill (H.R. 3247) providing for $40 million in additional FCA loans for drought vic-

---

[2] Will Alexander, "Overcrowded Farms," in U.S. Department of Agriculture, *Yearbook of Agriculture: 1940*, 876–886. See also Wilma Dykeman and James Stokely, *Seeds of Southern Change: The Life of Will Alexander*, pp. 202–223; Bernard Sternsher, *Rexford Tugwell and the New Deal*, pp. 262–278; Sidney Baldwin, *Poverty and Politics*.

[3] Marvin Jones, interview with Dean Albertson, Columbia Oral History Project, 1952, pp. 567–570, hereafter cited as COHP-MJP. Unless otherwise noted, all interviews and correspondence citing Jones refer to Marvin Jones.

tims. The measure quickly received congressional approval, and during the next two months Jones continued introducing bills expanding the FCA's functions, through proposals for low interest rates that would aid drought victims and refinance farm homes.[4]

In February, Congress intensified efforts in behalf of the tenant farmer. On February 11, John Bankhead introduced the farm-tenant homes bill of 1935 (S. 1800). In the other wing of the Capitol, Bankhead's partner, Marvin Jones, continued introducing amendments reforming the AAA, but two weeks later he dropped into the hopper a bill (H.R. 6151) calling for reduced interest rates for potential farm purchasers and reduced interest rates on loans by federal land banks to small farmers. By this maneuver he was trying to amend the Federal Farm Loan Act to encourage the ownership of small farms by permitting mortgages in an amount not exceeding $3,500 on the security of farmland, the normal value of which would be not more than $7,000 if the borrower became a bona fide farmer personally engaged in the operation of the mortgaged farm. Jones wanted to restrict interest rates to 2 percent a year.[5]

In a press release issued that same day, Jones said that his tenant bill would decrease speculation and give intermediate-credit banks the same reserve-note privilege enjoyed by other parts of the Federal Reserve System. He remarked also that his bill, though not backed by Roosevelt or the Department of Agriculture, would "enable many renters and sharecroppers to buy and pay for a home." Later (on March 7), as another alternative to Bankhead's bill, Jones introduced the mortgage-reduction provisions of the tenant measure as a separate bill (H.R. 6503). That was consistent with his beliefs. Jones based his tenant-relief program on interest-rate reduction (to preserve farm homes), in contrast to the more liberal position Bankhead took in the Senate.[6]

---

[4] H.R. 3247, January 8, 1935, H.R. 4512, January 23, 1935, and H.R. 5440, February 6, 1935, MJP; *New York Times*, May 11, 1935; James MacGregor Burns, *Roosevelt: The Lion and the Fox*, p. 220; Paul Porter to author June 15, 1973.

[5] H.R. 6151, February 25, 1935.

[6] Press release, February 25, 1935; H.R. 6503, March 7, 1935, Marvin Jones Papers, hereafter cited as MJP; James G. Maddox, "The Bankhead-Jones Farm Tenant Act," *Law and Contemporary Problems* 4 (October 1937): 434–455. Sidney Baldwin, in *Poverty and Politics*, has the most enlightening account of the Bankhead-Jones Farm Tenancy Act history. Baldwin's conclu-

Meanwhile, the Senate had been proceeding differently from the House. There the Committee on Agriculture and Forestry was giving consideration to the government land-purchase and resale plan favored by Will Alexander and other liberals. Hearings began on March 5, 1935, and Senator Bankhead extended a personal invitation to Jones to attend the sessions.

After listening to all the talk, Jones remained unconvinced of the need for practicality of the bill. Moreover, he lacked confidence in the House's ability to pass a major farm-tenant bill during the current session. Bankhead urged him to launch some kind of trial balloon, and the two men began working closely toward that objective.

On March 26, Bankhead and Jones introduced companion bills (S. 2367 and H.R. 7018) that were more conservative than Bankhead's earlier proposal. The bills called for creation of a farmers' home corporation outside the exclusive jurisdiction of the Department of Agriculture, with a board of directors that would include both the secretary of agriculture and the governor of the Farm Credit Administration. The revised measure avoided direct mention of certain objectives: reducing tenant-landlord conflicts, encouraging conservation (legislation concerning which Jones wanted to pass separately), reducing land speculation, and giving government guarantees of economic stability. The compromise manifested Jones's thinking: to ensure greater democracy along Jeffersonian ideals without extensive federal supervision.[7]

---

sions are usually perceptive; however, a mixture of half-correct analysis occurs on page 138, where Baldwin notes that, "reflecting a streak of Populism in his character derived perhaps from an uncle who had been a strong Populist, Jones has had a long history of activity in Congress on behalf of cheap money, and several times he had introduced "bank note legislation." This explanation oversimplifies the complexity of Jones's thought.

[7] Baldwin, *Poverty and Politics*, pp. 133–136; Jones, interview with author, March 22, 1971; John Bankhead to Jones, February 28, 1935, John Bankhead Papers, State of Alabama, Department of Archives and History, Montgomery, Ala.

Responding to requests for an explanation of Jones's concept of the Democratic party and Jeffersonianism, I offer the following comments by Jones:

"The Democratic Party arose from the principles laid down by Thomas Jefferson, the theory being that the National Government should operate largely through local communities, local organizations, and with local control. The

From April to June the upper chamber debated the bill and then passed it during the closing days of the session. In the meantime Jones's committee had held one day of hearings that had been characterized by the chairman's silence. He made little attempt to defend the compromise bill or to solicit support from colleagues.

Democratic Party hasn't always adhered strictly to that priniciple. I regret to say, that, because I wish that it had. I think that, as industry grows and expands, naturally the Federal Government must handle some of these matters that flow across the States. . . .

"The Republican philosophy stems from the Hamiltonian philosophy that the people, in their individual and local capacity, are not capable of Government; that there should be a strong National Government which would set the pattern and practice control, the theory being that the people would be better off than they would be if they were allowed all kinds of mistakes in trying to run their own affairs .

"Between 1920 and 1953 there has been growing in both parties a division of sentiment regarding many things.

"The Democratic Party has traditionally adhered to an emphasis on human rights. They have felt that, while property rights are important, they should not be held superior to human rights. The control of property, with the natural power that comes with that control, shouldn't be allowed to operate in such a cruel fashion as to grind down and deprive individual men, women, and children of their natural and inalienable rights.

"The Republican Party places an emphasis on property rights. They think that property rights should be protected in all respects and that there can't be any human rights separate from property rights. Therefore, they put the emphasis on controlling and protecting the rights of property, on the theory that if you maintain property, somehow the individual will be benefitted by the vast operations in connection with property. . . .

"We frequently mistake policies for principles. There are only a few fundamental principles, and they are as old as the hills. They have been here always. . . . For that reason, the early-day principle, as announced by Thomas Jefferson, of having the control of the policies of the Government largely in the hands of localities and of having the policies that directly affect the people in those localities largely controlled by those people, is largely the single principle of Government operation. While the policy must vary—you must widen the policy and activity—in the process, the same principle remains.

"I think the term 'States Rights' is a sort of slogan that is a misnomer, to some degree. . . . It is the primary function of any government to hold the scales of justice evenly balanced and open the doors of opportunity for people to do things for themselves and to work out their own salvation. It isn't the primary function of government, as I see it, to give healthy, ablebodied people something, but it is the function of government to see that the business of the country is so regulated that it is fair in its operation not only to individuals, but to small concerns and to every business interest of the country." COHP-MJP, pp. 854–865.

Two days after the hearing Jones abruptly introduced something else: a revised version of the Agriculture Bank Note Act. The sudden change in direction of Agriculture Committee work seemed to go far toward verifying charges from liberals that Jones had killed the bill. Later, during July, when the Senate sent its "companion bill" to the House for consideration, Jones immersed himself in proposed reforms of the AAA.[8]

In *Poverty in Politics*, Sidney Baldwin remarked:

> The Texan really had not expanded a great deal of energy and political capital on the measure. . . . he was a shrewd politician and parliamentary strategist who did not believe in lost causes, and in 1935 there was no doubt about it—the Bankhead-Jones bills were a lost cause. Jones knew his Committee on Agriculture—their special commodity interests, their fears, and their flaws—and he had no hope in 1935 of winning their support. His usual strategy was to try to secure a unanimous committee in reporting any bill, because, he believed, passage in the House was difficult enough without having to carry the burden of internal committee differences to the floor. Contrary to some liberals' belief, his behavior was not simply disinterest.[9]

As early summer came to Washington, the bill that Jones had ignored died quietly amid clamor for politically achievable measures like soil conservation and AAA reforms.

During 1935 problems of soil erosion and conservation attracted national attention because of the widely publicized dust storms. These phenomena were not confined to the Dust Bowl. In April a dust storm struck Washington even as a Department of Agriculture soil scientist, Hugh Bennett, was asking for additional appropriations from the Senate Public Lands Committee. In Jones's home district on the southern plains residents of Amarillo and vicinity saw more of the storms, and at closer hand, and they knew that the dark, dry clouds signified devastation of their parched soil.

As early as 1874 federal aid had been initiated to curb soil erosion. That year the Bureau of Chemistry and Soils of the Department of Agriculture had begun encouraging farmers to use scientific conservation methods. Later state agricultural experiment stations

---

[8] Maddox, "The Bankhead-Jones Farm Tenant Act," pp. 434–455; Baldwin, *Poverty in Politics*, pp. 140–156, H.R. 7018 March 26, 1935, MJP; U.S., Congress, House, Committee on Agriculture, *Farm Tenancy*, 75th Cong., 1st sess., 1937, pp. 323–362.

[9] Baldwin, *Poverty in Politics*, p. 153.

and extension services continued the work. In 1928, Hugh Bennett, with strong support from A. B. Conner, director of the Texas Agricultural Experiment Station, and from scientists at Spur and Chillicothe stations, had sought additional research funds from the federal government. Marvin Jones had given them moral support, but before the advent of the New Deal in his support of farm legislation he had emphasized increased consumption of agricultural commodities rather than soil conservation. Bennett's efforts to conserve the soil would become basic agricultural policy during the New Deal.[10]

Early in the Roosevelt administration the National Industrial Recovery Act was aimed partly at increasing employment through use of government money to hire laborers for work in controlling land erosion. Funds for that purpose were allotted to the Department of the Interior, within which was established the Soil Erosion Service. Hugh Bennett became Interior Secretary Harold Ickes's first SES administrator.[11] The Soil Erosion Service pursued its own projects, but they soon conflicted with other soil-conservation work being handled by the Department of Agriculture. Farm leaders became concerned over the bureaucratic maze and asked for clarification.

Marvin Jones helped. He favored Agriculture Department supervision of soil conservation, and he agreed to coordinate such a fight in Congress, provided that wind-erosion relief (which would especially benefit his Dust Bowl district) was included in the program. After much bitter conflict (during which a reluctant Roosevelt attempted to transfer the SES to the Agriculture Department and thereby infuriated Secretary Ickes) Jones and his colleagues succeeded in getting through Congress a bill (the Dempsey Act) granting the secretary of agriculture new powers and giving him supervision over the permanently established Soil Conservation Service.

Marvin Jones had shown his wisdom in helping get the bill passed. He allowed others to take the limelight while he remained in

---

[10] Indispensable background studies for this movement are found in Gladys L. Baker, Wayne D. Rasmussen, Vivian Wiser, and Jane M. Porter, *Century of Service: The First 100 Years of the United States Department of Agriculture*; Murray R. Benedict, *Farm Policies of the United States, 1790–1950*, pp. 112–137, 276–348; and Robert J. Morgan, *Governing Soil Conservation*.

[11] Benedict, *Farm Policies of the United States*, p. 318.

the background. The bill passed without much friction, and Roosevelt signed it in April 1935.

Jones continued to stress soil conservation. He began working to join the Texas Panhandle with areas of New Mexico, Colorado, Oklahoma, and Kansas in a soil-conservation district devoted to solving Dust Bowl problems. When Bennett balked at creating SCS districts cutting across state lines, Jones argued that the Texas panhandle should not be linked with, say, east Texas because of vast differences in climate and vegetation. Jones failed to convince Bennett, but he persuaded House Appropriations Chairman James Buchanan, a fellow Texan, to delay SCS appropriations until Bennett finally gave in.[12]

Jones then found himself in another conflict. Secretary of the Interior Ickes, as it had developed, had not completely given up on an idea of making his domain a department of conservation and public works. Ickes proposed now to exchange the Bureaus of Reclamation, General Land Office, Grazing, and Subsistence Homesteads with the Department of Agriculture in return for Forestry, Roads, and Biological Survey. To gain liberal support, Ickes advocated Rexford Tugwell as undersecretary.

Departmental infighting combined with inept leadership by Roosevelt prevented another compromise, and the dispute went to Capitol Hill. From June 4 to July 13, 1935, the House Committee on Expenditures in the Executive Departments held hearings on the proposal. Witnesses, beginning with Harold Ickes and Henry Wallace, testified in behalf of their vested interests. Marvin Jones, backed by his entire committee, testified that the proposed new department would have vast potential power over too many projects. Moreover, he said, the measure authorized transfers of bureaus by executive order that would wreck operations of other government agencies. He maintained that any such transfers should be made only with congressional consent.[13] Soon after Jones's testimony Ickes's proposal died in the House.

[12] COHP-MJP, pp. 795–811; H.R. 7055, MJP; Morgan, *Governing Soil Conservation*, pp. 1–51.

[13] Arthur Schlesinger, Jr., *The Coming of the New Deal*, pp. 347–349; U.S., Congress, House, Committee on Expenditures in the Executive Departments, *Hearing, Change the Name of the Department of Interior to the Department of Conservation and Public Works*, 74th Cong., 1st sess., June 4–July 17, 1935, p. 94.

Marvin Jones's interest in soil erosion inevitably focused on research. Following discussions with Secretary Wallace and other Department of Agriculture personnel, Jones sponsored a measure (H.R. 6123) providing for greater funding for land-grant colleges to increase cooperative-extension efforts. Then, after discussions with H. H. Finnell (director of the Dalhart Soil Erosion Station), John Bankhead, and Texas A&M officials, Jones drafted a revised bill strongly supported by Ed O'Neal of the American Farm Bureau Federation, representatives of experiment stations, and T. O. Walton of Texas A&M. The two bills proposed that the secretary of agriculture authorize and conduct scientific, technical, economic, and other research into basic agricultural principles and procedures.

Still another version, completed April 1, 1935, contained a significant addition granting the secretary of agriculture power to conduct "research into laws and principles underlying basic problems of agriculture in its broadest aspects," including production, distribution, marketing, conservation, and land and water resources. Annual appropriations would go to agricultural experiment and extension stations. States would receive 60 percent of the federal money on a matching basis. The Farm Research Act, which became law in June 1935, stood as a major New Deal contribution to the continuing federal support of important agricultural research.[14]

That year the Roosevelt administration was giving high priority to revision of existing statutes, as well as to new legislation. The National Agricultural Conference resulted in the drafting of several proposed amendments to the AAA regarding monetary reform, rural credits, national land utilization, cooperative marketing, and greater regulatory powers for the secretary of agriculture.

From the conference emerged a piece of legislation that would achieve the following basic goals: prohibit excess marketing of basic

---

[14] H.R. 6123, February 22, 1933, H.R. 6981, March 25, 1935, MJP; undated clipping, scrapbook 6, MJP; H.R. 7160, April, 1, 1935, MJP; press release, March 23, 1935, MJP; U.S., Congress, House, Committee on Agriculture, *Hearings, Agricultural Research*, 74th Cong., 1st sess., March 29, 1935; H. D. Knoblauch, E. M. Law, and W. P. Meyer, *State Agricultural Experiment Stations: A History of Research Policy and Procedure*, pp. 119, 134, 136, 223, 225; Jones to H. A. Wallace, February 13, 1935, July 12, 1935, MJP; "Hearings before House Committee on Expenditures in Executive Departments on H.R. 6612," MS, MJP; James J. Jardine to M. L. Wilson, August 17, 1935, National Archives, Record Group 16.

agricultural commodities by producers after a two-thirds' vote of the producers; allow the secretary of agriculture to license commodity processors and to refuse licenses to those who handled more than their quota allotment; provide for carrying out Wallace's "ever-normal granary" concept on a modified scale through benefit payments, cash, and loans; clarify language in the original AAA regarding licenses governing marketing operations; permit the secretary of agriculture to request reports from processors of basic commodities; and place the burden of proof on agricultural businessmen whenever the government challenged their practices under the AAA, thus opening agricultural-business records to federal supervision.

Allen Treadway of Massachusetts and others did not enjoy success with another suggested revision: repeal of the processing-tax provision of the Agricultural Adjustment Act. Jones defended the tax. Previously he had declared that the only purpose of the tax was to counter the tariff. Now, however, he accepted the Department of Agriculture assertion that the tax served as a means of reducing surpluses. Jones continually denied that the processing tax materially affected consumer prices, and eventually Treadway's efforts failed. Ironically, the consumer issue brought up by the two men was mostly a smoke screen for other considerations. The consumer did not rank high with Treadway, who favored the New England textile and merchant interests, or with Jones who sympathized primarily with the plight of the producers.

New Deal officials solicited Jones's support to introduce what became known as the Agricultural Adjustment Amendments Act, proposed by the National Agricultural Conference. Jones, however, had his own ideas for revisions. Some of them concerned distribution, in which, of course, he had maintained an interest for years. He argued, for example, that when farm surplus commodities from the free list were sold on the world market an equivalent value of imports should be allowed to enter the country duty-free. Jones also proposed an annual appropriation from tariff revenues for use in distribution. He estimated that farmers made up approximately 30 percent of the American population, and he declared that 30 percent of the tariff collections thus should be used to distribute surpluses on home and foreign markets.

At lunch and in late-night meetings Jones discussed his tariff-appropriation idea with several agrarians. At a meeting with Chester Davis, George Peek, and others Jones penciled his ideas in a rough draft of what was to become the Agricultural Adjustment Amendments Act. The addition became section 32, the first guaranteed annual appropriation for agriculture in United States history. The concept had evolved from the Export Debenture Plan and from McNary-Haugen proposals, so Jones found satisfaction in writing the Export Debenture Plan as a part of New Deal legislation. Later the *New York Times* speculated that Peek had suggested the idea, but Congress enacted the section as it had appeared in Jones's draft.

In March 1935, Congress began a long, bitter fight over the amendments to the Agricultural Adjustment Act. Even Jones's House Agriculture Committee split. Republican August Andresen of Minnesota wanted to scrap everything except section 32. Some members opposed granting the secretary of agriculture broad powers to license producers of basic agricultural commodities. Finally the committee agreed to the licensing of milk, tobacco, and sugar producers. By a narrow margin of thirteen to ten it reported the bill for House consideration.

Meanwhile, the Senate was considering a similar bill. There, however, trouble developed for Jones's section 32. The principal opposition came from Bankhead, who was at the same time working to get House extension for his soon-to-expire Cotton Control Act.

One day Jones suggested to Bankhead that if section 32 received Senate approval the House would extend Bankhead's cotton measure. Bankhead jumped to his feet, paced the floor, and began complaining about the high cost of compromise. Jones remained quiet while the senator stormed. Finally Bankhead agreed.

Jones, however, still had a fight on his hands to get approval for section 32. He faced opposition from a fellow Texan, James ("Buck") Buchanan, chairman of the House Appropriations Committee and an avowed foe of automatic appropriations. After Buchanan had read the bill, he telephoned Jones to complain about section 32—in earthy language. Buchanan demanded to know how an appropriations measure could emerge from Jones's committee.

Jones went to Buchanan's office to assure him that the bill did not represent a personal attack. Jones remarked that both of them had large agrarian constituencies and that section 32 provided price supports and surplus-removal activities that would benefit the many cotton producers in their district. Jones also tried to convince Buchanan that he did not intend any permanent usurpation of power.

This assurance calmed Buchanan, but he suggested that Jones present the measure when Buchanan was absent from the House floor; otherwise he would fight it. Jones followed the suggestion.

Later some congressmen contended that the two men had conspired for the benefit of cotton farmers. Jones denied the accusation, and he told George Peek that section 32 should not be used exclusively for the benefit of any one commodity. Moreover, he declared, under no circumstance should the funds be used only to subsidize foreign marketing.

The proposed amendments to the Agricultural Adjustment Act represented a last-ditch effort to prevent the AAA from being declared unconstitutional. The harsh times had demanded far-ranging and sometimes experimental solutions, the Roosevelt administration contended, but some solutions tended to range too far. On May 27, 1935, the Supreme Court did, in fact, invalidate the National Recovery Administration, and the legislation behind it, in a decision(*A. L. A. Schechter Poultry Corporation* v. *United States*) that the delegations of legislative power exceeded those permissible under the Constitution. By that decision the whole NRA experiment was brought to an end.

Two days after the Schechter decision Senator Joe Robinson met with members of the House and Senate agriculture committees and with Secretary of Agriculture Henry Wallace, AAA Administrator Chester Davis, and USDA Solicitor Seth Thomas to write technical changes in the section on the agricultural processing tax that would meet Supreme Court approval—or so they hoped.

On June 17 a united House Agriculture Committee presented its bill for House consideration. As was his custom, Jones took careful parliamentary precautions to ensure a smooth conclusion. He tolerated opposition, seeing little reason to make enemies needlessly with eventual victory all but certain. In this spirit he withdrew a point of order and allowed Richard Wigglesworth of Massachusetts to lead opposition to the processing tax. In time the House passed the bill, 174 to 40. Later the Senate voted approval too, after insisting on use of its own wording in the section on the rights of claimants to recover processing taxes that had been illegally collected.

The Agricultural Adjustment Amendments Act as signed by the president retained and revised the AAA. Though Roosevelt himself (and Treasury Secretary Morgenthau) voiced some alarm about the drastic new principles in section 32, he signed it into law to get the entire measure. Section 32 became the one original and most lasting of the amendments, and it stood as one of Jones's greatest personal contributions. After the signing, Jones predicted success in saving the constitutionality of the AAA.

In his next budget message, however, Roosevelt would ask for repeal of section 32 on grounds that it prevented accurate budget estimates. Many congressmen resented the president's request, claiming that it was like a dog baying at the moon. Among them was James Buchanan, who was no friend of section 32 but had come to resent Roosevelt's dictatorial tactics. Buchanan threw his support to section 32. The president's request was ignored (section 32 provisions were even strengthened in the following year, in measures providing for purchases of agricultural commodities and in the Soil Conservation and Domestic Allotment act).

During the first year of operation section 32 provided for an expenditure of $92 million. Of this amount the government spent $1 million on export subsidies, $3 million on domestic consumption, and $10.5 million on relief purchases by agencies like the Federal Surplus Commodities Corporation. Thereafter the automatic appropriation was infrequently used, but it provided the Secretary of Agriculture with funds to aid farmers during times of economic hardship.[15]

After the 1935 congressional recess Jones returned to Texas. Government attorney Stanley Reed had asked him to stay in Washington as consultant in *United States* v. *Butler*, in which a district court had ordered the receiver for a bankrupt firm, the Hoosac Mills

[15] Chester Davis to author, March 23, 1973; *New York Times,* January 16, May 1, June 1, June 6, June 19, July 24, August 6, and August 25, 1935; Jones and George Peek, transcript of telephone conversation, August 2, 1935, Harry Coffee and Peek, transcript of telephone conversation, August 6, 1935, and Jones and Peek, transcript of telephone conversation, August 23, 1935, George N. Peek Papers, Western Historical Manuscripts Collections, University of Missouri, Columbia, Mo.; COHP-MJP, pp. 867–887; Edwin G. Nourse,

Corporation, to pay processing taxes required by AAA legislation. It would indeed be a test of the constitutionality of AAA, but Jones felt that Reed had a strong case and that the Supreme Court would uphold it. Moreover, Jones wanted to look after his political fences. He was worried about the impending emergence of a challenger in the Democratic primary.

In December 1935, Jones spoke to a standing-room-only crowd at the Texas Agricultural Association meeting in Dallas. He lauded the virtues of the New Deal agricultural program and received enthusiastic applause. He assured farmers that if the Supreme Court dared invalidate any part of the AAA a Democratic Congress would replace it with better, stronger laws. He contended that American farms were much better off than they had been under Hoover, and the delegates cheered loudly. Speaking at the same meeting, Chester Davis concluded that the AAA would be continued regardless of any adverse Supreme Court decision.

Following his return to Washington in January 1936, Jones learned of the Supreme Court's verdict while talking with Roosevelt and Wallace about new legislation permitting loans for farm tenants. The Court had declared the processing tax unconstitutional. The president accepted the decision, but Jones was stunned. He had not prepared himself for such an outcome. Roosevelt asked him to return later that afternoon to discuss the Court decision and future plans in detail.

At 2:30, Jones met with Roosevelt, Wallace, Cummings, Bankhead, Davis, Myers, and Pressman in the president's office. Roosevelt read Owen Roberts's majority opinion slowly: farming was a local business and not subject to federal regulation under the commerce clause, and the processing tax represented an unconstitutional use of power by Congress. Bitter, sarcastic remarks flowed from the

---

Joseph S. Davis, and John D. Black, *Three Years of the Agricultural Adjustment Administration*, pp. 186–190; H.R. 5585, February 12, 1935, H.R. 6613, April 24, 1935, H.R. 8052, May 14, 1935, H.R. 8492, June 4, 1935, MJP; press releases, July 20, 1935 and July 30, 1935, MJP; Marvin Jones, "The Remarks of Marvin Jones," *Congressional Record* Scrapbook, vol. 3, MJP; James S. Ward, interview with Jones, October 22, 1967, pp. 32–40, 47, in possession of James S. Ward, Washington, D.C.; hereafter referred to as Jones to Ward.

lips of the conferees. They all asserted that the Supreme Court majority had not understood the problems of agricultural marketing. Some of them wanted to draft a constitutional amendment, but Roosevelt discouraged such drastic action. Instead he told them to work toward constitutional legislation containing AAA goals.

Jones's earlier efforts to place processing-tax revenues in the Treasury thus had failed to win Supreme Court approval. Further, Roberts's opinion denied that the government had the power to impose conditions on those who received the federal funds. In so doing, Roberts ignored the historical trend in land grants and federal aid that had begun in 1802. He also failed to understand that the protective tariff actually had served as a taxing device for the regulation of production.

Jones gritted his teeth at the reasoning of the Court majority. In mid-January 1936 he broke his silence in a speech before the Illinois Agricultural Association. He wondered why a national tariff was legal and a national farm program that merely restored the price balance could not be made legal. Jones, like Wallace, believed that the processing tax equated with a farmer's tariff.[16]

New Deal officials now realized that they had no choice but to reevaluate their agricultural policies. The Hoosac Mills decision, by preventing the secretary of agriculture from levying processing taxes, deprived the AAA of its principal source of funds. All government contracts made with individual producers were now illegal. Although the court had not specifically ruled on the Bankhead Cotton Control Act, the Kerr-Smith Tobacco Act, and related legislation, these measures controlling production and marketing were also unconstitutional. Further, the marketing agreements made under the Agricultural Adjustment Act and the Jones-Costigan Act were of doubtful constitutionality, although they remained in effect—as did Jones's section 32.

[16] Jones's recollections differed slightly from newspaper accounts in the scrapbooks. In this instance I have accepted the newspaper accounts. Undated clippings, scrapbooks 6 and 7, MJP; Jones to Ward, 23–26; Chester Davis to author, March 23, 1973; COHP-MJP, pp. 896–910; *United States v. Butler et al., Receivers of Hoosac Mills Corporation*, 297 U.S. 1 (1936); Alfred A. Kelly and Winfred A. Harbison, *The American Constitution: Its Origins and Development*, 3d ed., pp. 744–747; Alpheus T. Mason, *Harlan Fiske Stone: Pillar of the Law*, pp. 405–418.

In the final analysis the New Deal agricultural program had received a critical blow but not a fatal one. The decision left Congress with a moral obligation to compensate those producers who had already complied with the AAA program. Wallace took upon himself the responsibility of assuring farmers that the administration would act promptly for a sound program, and he called on farm leaders to present their views at a meeting on January 10.

At that meeting the Roosevelt administration obtained endorsement of a new set of farm proposals. Howard Tolley set them down in a hastily written draft. After that the administration sought to gain congressional approval. On Capitol Hill, Jones took the lead, promptly calling his committee into executive session. Members discussed substitute measures for the AAA: the previously advocated Export Debenture Plan, a domestic-allotment plan, outright direct relief to farmers, a system of state AAAs financed by federal grants-in-aid, and a program of crop restriction and control through soil-conservation measures.

Jones and Cotton Ed Smith introduced bills for loans to farmers who stood to take losses because of the Supreme Court decision. A joint congressional resolution permitted the secretary of agriculture to meet government commitments and obligations previously incurred under the AAA. Jones, with the vital support of Clifford Hope, James Buchanan, and tough old Republican watchdog John Taber, obtained Department of Agriculture estimates and added $296 million to a deficiency act for these purposes.[17]

Jones then responded to a request from Secretary Wallace and worked for congressional approval of an amendment allowing the government to retain processing taxes when the processor had already passed these amounts on to the consumer. In the Senate, Charles McNary sponsored similar legislation. Thus the processors were kept from taking undue economic advantage.

Because of the Hoosac Mills decision President Roosevelt asked Congress to repeal the Bankhead, Kerr-Smith, and Potato acts since it would be only a matter of time until they were tested before the

---

[17] Murray R. Benedict, *Can We Solve the Farm Problem?* pp. 249–252; clippings, scrapbook 6, MJP; Edward L. Schapsmeier and Frederick H. Schapsmeier, *Henry A. Wallace of Iowa: The Agrarian Years, 1910–1940*, pp. 214–218; H.R. 10213, January 4, 1936, and H.J. Res. 460, January 16, 1936, MJP.

Court. Most Republicans and conservatives sought to use the action for gain in the forthcoming elections. Hamilton Fish, Republican representative from Roosevelt's home district, rejoiced. "We Republicans opposed that legislation at the time," he said, "because we thought it was economic insanity, economic suicide—and in addition unconstitutional." New Hampshire's Republican Charles Tobey remarked, "Thoughtful members opposed these three pieces of legislation because they embodied a philosophy of regimentation and control which they believed un-American, but because of administration pressure they were passed." Another Republican, however, Everett Dirksen of Illinois, claimed to take little pleasure in the action before the House. He wanted voters to realize that some Republicans shared a bit of the disappointment felt by the Roosevelt administration. In his words the situation was similar to that experienced by "the noble king of France. He had ten thousand men. He marched them up a hill, and then marched them down again."[18]

Two weeks later Wall Doxey and Marvin Jones brought to the House floor a soil-conservation and domestic-allotment bill that had passed the Senate, 56 to 20, as a temporary replacement for the AAA. Speaker Joseph Byrns and Jones predicted quick passage of the legislation. Fearing, however, that opponents might try to pass amendments to render the bill unconstitutional or contrary to New Deal policies, they obtained from the House Rules Committee a five-hour limit on debate.[19]

Their careful preparation paid off. Later the *New York Times* observed, "Not a single change was made in the bill as reported to the House without the expressed approval of Chairman Jones of the Agriculture Committee."[20] The House broadened the measure and passed it, 267 to 97. Later the Senate accepted the House revision. As signed into law on February 29, 1936, it expanded the basis of adjustment undertakings, liberalized factors in allotments to states, and increased the agriculture secretary's powers to adjust farm output and determine benefits.

[18] Jones, "The Remarks of Marvin Jones," *Congressional Record* Scrapbook, vol. 4 (74th Cong., 2d sess.), pp. 1498-99, MJP.
[19] H.R. 10500, January 22, 1936, and H.R. 10835, February 3, 1936, MJP; COHP-MJP, pp. 912-922.
[20] *New York Times*, February 22, 1936.

The Soil Conservation and Domestic Allotment Act had been designed by its sponsors as an end in itself as well as a stopgap measure. It provided payments for conservation rather than for production controls. It also transferred to state governments the responsibility for making these payments that would be drawn from federal grants. All of this ensured constitutionality. At the same time the act preserved the AAA's purpose. Marketing rather than conservation was the primary objective. Later, after the New Deal era closed, soil erosion remained a major unsolved problem. By that time, however, New Deal agricultural policies had become acceptable to the Supreme Court, and federal aid continued to flow to agriculture.

Jones characterized Roosevelt's farm program as one that provided justice for the farm family—a justice sanctioned by the Constitution and in accordance with religious principles. Mere political expediency rarely if ever motivated Jones in agricultural legislation. He consistently mixed concern for family welfare, frontier humanitarianism, and Christianity in his considerations.[21]

Work on the Soil Conservation and Domestic Allotment Act had forced the administration to delay tenancy legislation. Finally, late in the session, the Senate passed a bill that amounted to another version of the Bankhead-Jones Farm Tenancy Act. The legislation encountered opposition in the House Agriculture Committee, and it died there as the session ended. Jones returned home for campaigning as the 1936 elections approached. Roosevelt would run for another term; so would Jones.

The state legislature had divided his Eighteenth District. Now Jones would be representing twenty-eight counties rather than fifty-three. The revised district included the Panhandle and extended south through Parmer, Castro, Swisher, Briscoe, Motley, and Cottle counties. These counties had been represented by Jones since 1916, and he seemed secure there, especially since he was chairman of the House Agriculture Committee and could say beyond that, "I'm a Christian and a Democrat."

Some politicians, however, believed that the new district should have a new representative. Moreover, public-opinion samples re-

---

[21] See COHP-MJP, pp. 913–921.

The Jones brothers, about 1907. *Left to right*: Earl, Delbert, Frank, Marvin, and Herbert ("Hub"). Courtesy, Mr. and Mrs. Hub Jones.

Marvin Jones in 1916, during his first campaign for Congress. Unless otherwise noted, all photographs were provided to the author by Marvin Jones.

Participants in a National Grange radio broadcast to its one million members, June 17, 1927. *Seated, left to right*: Senator Arthur Capper, Kansas; Representative Ruth Hanna McCormick, Illinois; and L. J. Taber, master of the National Grange. *Standing, left to right*: Representative John C. Ketcham, Michigan; Representative Jones, Texas; and James G. Farmer, National Grange lecturer.

Representative Jones in the 1920's. Photograph by Harris & Ewing.

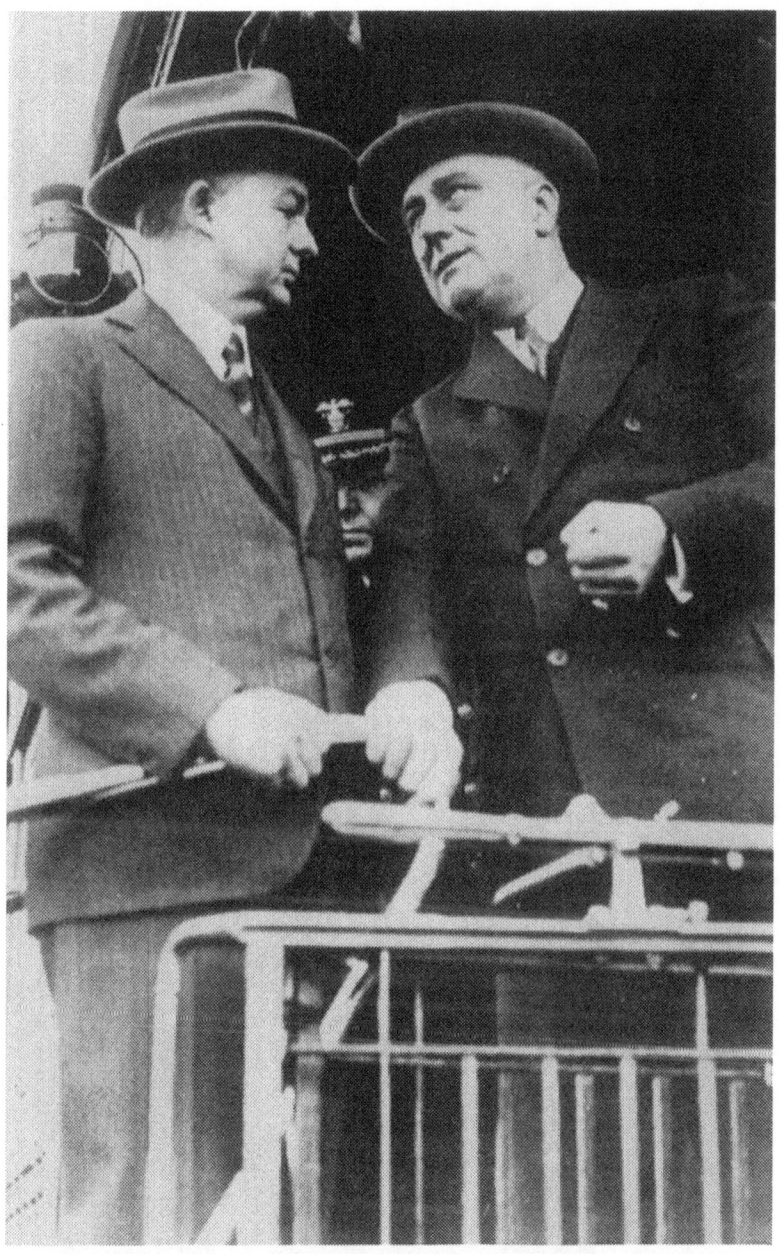
One of Jones's treasured mementos. Jones and President-elect Franklin D. Roosevelt on the rear platform of Roosevelt's private train, Washington, D.C., January 20, 1933. Roosevelt was about to leave for Warm Springs, Georgia, after conferring with outgoing President Herbert Hoover.

President Roosevelt presents the first government check for cutting cotton acreage to William E. Morris, a Nueces County, Texas, cotton grower, July 28, 1933. *Standing, left to right*: Representatives Jones, C. A. Cobb, and E. R. Eudaly, Morris, Representative Richard Kleberg, and Secretary of Agriculture Henry A. Wallace. Franklin D. Roosevelt Library Collection. Courtesy, Underwood and Underwood.

A family picture, taken about 1936. *Seated, left to right*: Jones; his mother, Mrs. Theodocia Jones; and Jones's brother Hub. Hub's two daughters are among those in the back row.

President Roosevelt during a visit to Amarillo, Texas, in 1938. *Left to right*: Roosevelt, his son Elliott, Texas Governor Jimmy Allred, and Texas Representatives Maury Maverick, W. D. McFarlane (behind Maverick), Fritz Lanham, Lyndon Johnson (behind Lanham), and Jones. Franklin D. Roosevelt Library Collection. Courtesy, UPI (Acme).

Jones taking the oath of office as war food administrator. Chief Judge Richard S. Whaley, United States Court of Claims, administers the oath as Secretary of Agriculture Claude C. Wickard looks on, June 29, 1943.

James F. Byrnes, director of Office of Economic Stabilization, and War Food Administrator Jones, 1943.

Chairmen of delegations to the International Food Conference held at Hot Springs, Virginia, May 18 to June 3, 1943.

Left: War Food Administrator Jones as he appeared on the cover of *United States News*, July 1943. *Right*: Judge Jones on a fishing trip, June 1957.

Judge Jones at his desk in the United States Court of Claims Building, February 1949.

Judge Jones, 1959. Courtesy, Mrs. Jeff Neely.

The United States Court of Claims, about 1961. *Left to right*: Judges Donald N. Laramore, Stanley Reed, Marvin Jones (chief judge), Samuel E. Whitaker, and James R. Durfee.

vealed an undercurrent of dissatisfaction with the New Deal and a growing popularity for an old-age-pension scheme called the Townsend Plan. John Miller, who favored the plan, entered the Democratic primary and attacked Jones's twenty-year tenure in Congress as "long enough." Miller also called for long-term loans at low interest rates for small homes and farms, for an increase in the number of civil-service employees, and for higher taxes on luxuries, inheritances, and incomes.[22] His greatest appeal, however, came in his advocacy of the Townsend Plan, which was described in a poem quoted in those days:

> Cheer up, Grandma, have no fears
> If you live a hundred years,
> And be contented along the way,
> The time will come, politicians say,
> When Old Folks will be entitled then
> To a Lavish Pension, "Five and Ten,"
> But of course this must be brought around
> By the way Folks guzzle liquor down.
>
> Now Folks must drink an awful lot,
> To get the tax, you'll be a sot. . . .
> Let little Marv and little John
> Drink cocktails from night till dawn
> They must drink their Bourbon and their Gin
> To pay Grandma her "Five and Ten."
>
> But as for me I'm glad to say
> That folks have found a better way. . . .
> Let's give a pension—the Townsend Plan
> And bring back prosperity to our land.
>
> Let's give the young men work to do—
> The Old Man the leisure he's entitled to—
> Let Grandma sit in the rocking chair,
> And Grandpa sit beside her there—
> They've labored long and earned a rest,
> Old Age should be one of happiness.
>
> Of course Wall Street will rant and moan—
> The Money Bower will cease to own—

---

[22] U.S., Congress, *Official Congressional Directory, 74th Congress, 1st Session*, p. 671; undated clippings, scrapbook 7, MJP; "John R. Miller's

> The Old Man Depression will be forgot,
> And peace and happiness will be our lot.
> For poverty and crime will cease to be.
> Unemployment and fear that stalk the land
> Will fade away with the Townsend Plan.[23]

Jones countered Miller's campaign by reemphasizing the benefits of New Deal programs in the Eighteenth District.[24] He ignored personal attacks on himself and thereby lessened their effect. He refused to endorse the Townsend Plan, despite pressure from a friend, W. W. Parkinson, because he thought it impractical.

Jones's assessment of public opinion in the Panhandle convinced him that he could win the nomination without much trouble. He concluded correctly. These candidates were like two bullfrogs at night: made a lot of noise, but their impact was small. In the 1936 primary Jones defeated Miller by a four-to-one margin, and was thus assured reelection in that Democratic stronghold. After that Jones could focus on the national election.[25]

On June 11, Republicans met at Cleveland and nominated Governor Alfred M. Landon of Kansas for president and Colonel Frank Knox of Illinois for vice-president. The platform criticized New Deal "unconstitutionality" but suggested no alternatives to Roosevelt's programs.

On June 23, Democrats renominated Roosevelt and Garner at Philadelphia. The party stood behind the New Deal record. Optimism flowed from Democratic National Campaign Headquarters. The Gallup Poll indicated that 55.8 percent of the voters favored Roosevelt. The president's support among farmers, however, fell below that figure. To counter the Republican threat there, the Democratic National Campaign Committee planned a bipartisan appeal to farm voters in the corn-belt, Rocky Mountain, and northwestern states. Thus they hoped to garner votes of Independents, Union party members, Farmer-Laborites, and disenchanted Republicans—as well as reluctant Democrats. Furthermore, an independent agricultural

---

Principles," *Hutchinson County* (Texas) *Herald*, July 17, 1936; *Canyon* (Texas) *News*, July 16, 1938.

[23] "Better Days Ahead," *Claude* (Texas) *News*, May 22, 1936.
[24] *Pampa* (Texas) *Daily News*, July 23, 1936.
[25] COHP-MJP, pp. 969–973.

campaign committee would attract the support of national farm organizations whose policies prohibited their direct participation in party politics. In that manner pro–New Deal agrarian representatives like Norris of Nebraska could support the New Deal, and Roosevelt could win with huge majorities that rebellious representatives would never ignore during the next two years. Late in August when Landon intensified his attack, Democratic leaders took belated action to force him on the defensive.

Until August 24 loosely organized New Deal state committees operated independently in fourteen states. On that date they joined together in an organizational meeting in Des Moines. They agreed that the primary emphasis must focus on producing New Deal victories in Colorado, Illinois, Indiana, Iowa, Kansas, Montana, Minnesota, Missouri, North Dakota, Nebraska, Ohio, South Dakota, Wisconsin, and Wyoming. As the campaign intensified, national leaders would coordinate activities but would avoid endangering Roosevelt's new political coalition of urban voters. From the Des Moines meeting a campaign organization called the Roosevelt Agricultural Committee materialized. William H. Settle of Indiana, a member of the board of the American Farm Bureau Federation, was elected chairman. William S. Bradley, formerly of Centerville, Iowa, and head of the Corn Loan Division of the Commodity Credit Corporation, was elected secretary-treasurer. Completing the roster of key organizational personnel were Paul A. Porter, special counsel for the AAA and a journalist with experience in Oklahoma and Georgia, and Mrs. Altravene Clark, from Jones's own staff. These people were loyal Democrats with close ties to the soil and to the federal government. They planned to attack Landon's farm policies and defend New Deal programs.

But where did Jones fit into the national campaign picture? From 1917 to 1933 he had served on the Democratic National Campaign Committee. Now the committee again called on Jones for assistance. After his own decisive victory in the Democratic primary, his help and agricultural expertise were solicited by Roosevelt's campaign manager, James A. Farley, who asked him to go to Chicago in September to serve as an adviser to the Roosevelt Agricultural Committee. Jones would coordinate speaking activities of congressional spokesman for the New Deal. He quickly accepted.

The committee's activities included producing pamphlets, coordinating funds among Democratic National Headquarters and local organizations, and appealing to farm voters through radio addresses and public speeches. The Democratic National Campaign Committee allocated $335,000 for these purposes and sent an additional $27,000 collected in fund drives. Of the total spent by the committee $272,609, or approximately 50 percent, went to state organizations.[26]

To counter further Landon's appeal to middle-western farm voters, Democratic leaders and President Roosevelt himself toured that drought-stricken area in August and returned in October for another campaign swing. Roosevelt spoke of farm-tenancy legislation as a priority item. The moralistic Secretary of Agriculture Wallace denounced Landon's program as a battle waged against the Democrats' heavenly farm by a Republican hell, but Wallace did not have the experience or the innate interest in politics to be an effective campaigner. Jones and Paul Porter joined in making personal appeals to the farm voters. A radio program begun by Porter, called the Roosevelt Sunrise Hour, particularly attracted interest. Every morning from 5:45 to 6:00 from October 12 through election day it was beamed to farm families, at a time when most of them would be at the breakfast table. From his Chicago microphone Porter spoke on "Why I Am for Roosevelt," presented recorded interviews with Wallace and others, and twice scheduled Jones to explain what might be expected to happen to the farm program if Landon was elected.[27]

A speech by Landon in Topeka, Kansas, on September 18 resulted in Jones's assumption of another role, that of stalking-horse. When Landon lamented government regulation of agriculture, Jones responded on the very same day that farmers should first analyze

---

[26] Paul Porter to author, June 15, 1973; Roosevelt Agricultural Committee, *Agriculture in the 1936 Presidential Election*, microfilm, Texas A&M Library, College Station, Texas; Donald R. McCoy, *Landon of Kansas*, pp. 291–295; H. A. Wallace to William S. Bradley Papers, in the possession of Mrs. William S. Bradley, Austin, Texas; scrapbook 7, MJP.

[27] Roosevelt Agricultural Committee, *Agriculture in the 1936 Presidential Election*; Schapsmeier and Schapsmeier, *Henry A. Wallace of Iowa*, pp. 228–233; Paul Porter to author, June 15, 1973; Marvin Jones, "The Republican Street Parade and the G.O.P. Circus," typescript of speech, October 23, 1936, MJP.

the results, particularly the increased income. After that Jones kept the pressure on the Republican nominee.[28]

On September 22, in Des Moines, Landon outlined his agricultural program. Landon wanted (as had Hoover) increased consumption of farm products through increased national employment, retirement of submarginal lands, and effective marketing agreements. He wanted also research to find new uses for agricultural commodities, federal subsidies of exported surpluses, and increased conservation measures. The latter should especially benefit owners of family farms, Landon said, and give drought-relief aid to tenants. Finally, the Republican nominee wanted crop and seed loans, a crop-insurance program, and efficient bureaucratic operations.[29]

The main difference between Alfred Landon and Marvin Jones actually centered on their choice of the political party that could best achieve these goals and the means that party would use. Jones favored greater government involvement, but he opposed Landon's protective tariff. If Republicans objected to large AAA payments to farmers, Jones asked, what about large tariff benefits to industry?

The tariff was the key to Jones's quick responses to Landon. The Texan believed that farmers as well as industrialists should enjoy benefits.[30] His arguments and his sincerity proved persuasive. The *Columbus* (Nebraska) *Daily Telegram* editorialized that if Jones "might be heard by all the people in Nebraska the vote would be practically sold for Roosevelt," because Jones had

a way of getting right close to his hearers, convincing them as a friend appeals to a friend. No man who hears Marvin Jones has any doubt of his sincerity. His language is clean and pure and his stories and anecdotes amplify his own argument. President Roosevelt has many men-lovers in America but none more devoted to him, none more ably promoting a great cause in which President Roosevelt is both the heart and the brain.[31]

That November, Roosevelt won a smashing victory. The popular vote gave him 27,753,000 to Landon's 16,675,000. Roosevelt

[28] See McCoy, *Landon of Kansas*, pp. 144–149, 176–180, 197–201, 275–276, 286–288, 291–312; Marvin Jones, press release, September 18, 1936, MJP.

[29] McCoy, *Landon of Kansas*, pp. 302–303; Herbert Hoover, *Addresses upon the American Road, 1933–1938*, pp. 101–112.

[30] Marvin Jones, "What's Landon's Farm Plan?" speech, MJP.

[31] *Columbus* (Nebraska) *Daily Telegram*, October 13, 1936.

carried every state but Maine and Vermont. Democrats also won approximately 80 percent of the seats in the House and Senate.

Jones and his close friend Grover Hill went to New York City before election day. There, as results came in that November 3, 1936, they saw and heard a tumult like that of Times Square on New Year's Eve.

Later Farley wrote Jones, "I am taking this opportunity to express to you my personal appreciation for the splendid leadership which was an inspiration to those who assisted you."[32] Jones had indeed inspired confidence among his colleagues. Moreover, he had demonstrated again that he could be an extremely competitive campaigner, though the outcome also showed that Roosevelt's Agricultural Committee had overestimated Landon's appeal. Furthermore, the composition of the House Agricultural Committee remained the same—and Jones remained firmly in charge.

[32] Scrapbook 7, MJP.

10.

The Climactic Year in Congress

AFTER the 1936 election Jones relaxed in the Panhandle. There he visited brothers and sisters, laughed and cracked jokes with local reporters and politicians, and went to church with old friends. The vacation, however, was cut short at the insistence of President Roosevelt, who called him back to Washington to work on farm-tenancy legislation.

Earlier, in September, Roosevelt had asked Jones and Bankhead to begin preparing such legislation. The same month Roosevelt had also appointed the Committee on Farm Tenancy to recommend solutions for the problem. The president urged members of the committee to consult with Jones and Bankhead and to make their report no later than February 1, 1937.

Jones remained dedicated to the concept that legislation should help competent farm tenants become owners. He urged this in stating his opposition to the use of federal funds to create large-scale collective farms. Actually, however, he sought to walk a tightrope, for several political reasons. One was that a majority of members of the House looked with disfavor on tenancy legislation, deeming it impractical. Another was that he wanted to avoid alienating men like Rexford Tugwell, Lawrence Westbrook (chairman of the advisory board of the Works Progress Administration), and R. W. Brown (president of the Missouri Farm Bureau), who viewed farm tenancy in the broader socioeconomic arena and favored more federal aid.

Jones noted arguments presented before the Committee on Farm Tenancy and concluded that at least two plans might pass Congress. One of them provided for government purchase of tracts of land that would then be improved and sold. Jones opposed this suggestion on grounds that the government should not obligate itself to that extent. More acceptable to him was a financial-credit approach in which local committees would purchase farms with government funds and sell them to worthy tenants selected by the same committees.

Jones's thinking on this issue reflected that of many other men who have achieved success through their own efforts. Jones placed less emphasis on socioeconomic assistance and more on provision of opportunities for hard-working individuals. Continuing conversations with a long-time friend, banker Charles Peery, strengthened Jones in his preference for local control and an insistence that recipients earn their farms. Local committees could best judge the applicants' characters, Jones believed, and the government would be protected against massive random aid that might harm the American stereotype of hard-working citizenry.

Jones insisted also on establishing low interest rates and on selling farms only to persons who lived on the premises. He observed: "Everyone knows that the Republic is anchored in the homes of this country. The immortal songs like 'Home Sweet Home' and 'The Little Gray Home in the West' were not written about a rented shack, but were inspired by the thoughts of home in a real sense."[1]

When he began planning legislative strategy, he realized that Senator John Bankhead's injured feelings must be soothed. The Alabaman had been deeply disappointed by the way the last congressional session had ended. Though in ill health and convalescing at home, Bankhead had kept abreast of developments. He had earlier expressed optimism about quick passage of tenancy legislation, and when it had stalled, he had written letters saying that the House Agriculture Committee was bottling up the legislation, implying that Jones could not control his own committee.

Bankhead had been correct to some extent. Many members of the House felt that, although farm-tenancy legislation "was desirable, a fine thought and a fine purpose, it was just like a great many other theoretical ideas and would not stand in the light of reason and the

---

[1] Marvin Jones, *Marvin Jones Memoirs*, ed. Joseph M. Ray, pp. 128–129; scrapbook, 7, Marvin Jones Papers, hereafter cited as MJP. See also "The Nation-Wide Problems of Farm Tenancy," *Congressional Digest* 16 (February 1937):53.

logic of analysis."[2] Despite the Democrats' campaign promises of 1936, many congressmen opposed the use of federal funds for those whom society marked down as economic failures. The factors of sectionalism, commodity interests, and partisan politics mingled with FDR's desires to cut federal spending and fed a pervasive negativism within the House Agriculture Committee.

Jones sought to change things, including Bankhead's antagonism, when he returned to Washington. Relations improved so much that on January 5 and 6, 1937, Jones and Bankhead introduced their bills, each known as the Farmers' Home Act (H.R. 8 and S. 106), containing nearly identical provisions. The legislation would create the Farmers' Home Corporation with an initial appropriation of $50 million, to be followed by another appropriation during the next ten years. In drafting the measure, Bankhead had furthered his goal of using appropriations rather than funds raised through special bond issues.

Jones began his committee hearings on January 27, before any report was made by the Committee on Farm Tenancy. This aroused some displeasure among Agriculture Department officials, but Jones had felt all along that there had been little use in calling that committee. When reporters questioned his motives, Jones responded that, considering the difficulties encountered in the last session, Congress should take advantage of every minute. Actually, however, Jones's action was largely a gesture of independence.

In his opening statements to the Agriculture Committee, Jones reminded his colleagues that their immediate purpose would be to listen to and analyze procedures promoting home ownership with long-term financing. He urged them to focus on method and management and to decide whether the Agriculture Department, the Farm Credit Administration, or another agency should control the tenant program.[3] At the same time Jones prepared arguments that,

---

[2] John Bankhead to James H. Chappell, November 30, 1936, and Bankhead to Associated Press, December 3, 1936, John H. Bankhead Papers, State of Alabama, Department of Archives and History, Montgomery, Ala. Unless otherwise noted, all interviews and correspondence citing Jones refer to Marvin Jones.

[3] H. R. 8, January 5, 1937, MJP; Sidney Baldwin, *Poverty and Politics*, pp. 177–185; James G. Maddox, "The Bankhead-Jones Farm Tenancy Act,"

he hoped, would pacify representatives who feared that tenant legislation would reward inefficiency. As Sidney Baldwin noted:

Calmly but persistently, Jones reminded the hostile members of his committee that stabilization of farm commodity prices, reduced interest rates for farmers, adjusted tax rates on farm land, and promotion of productive efficiency and improved marketing in agriculture, and other general goals has already been addressed in other legislation, but that in all fairness, something special was needed for that class of farm people who were incapable of deriving benefits from general farm prosperity.[4]

On February 17 the Committee on Farm Tenancy released its report. It stressed currency expansion rather than soil conservation, and the need for technical-assistance programs for tenants.

Two days later Secretary of Agriculture Wallace testified before Jones's committee and criticized the limitations of the Farmers' Home Act, which excluded migratory workers and omitted submarginal-lands programs from its considerations. He also urged longer leasing of land and greater federal-state cooperation in tenancy matters.

Wallace clashed with Jones over the extent of government control of the land to be sold to tenants. The secretary maintained that the government should keep control, through contracts, for twenty years, to establish ownership on a strong foundation. Jones wanted to issue tenants a conditional title to the land at the end of a five-year prohibitory period and make a full transfer of title whenever the tenant paid the mortgage. Jones reasoned that this would provide an incentive for the mortgagee to repay his loan promptly. He also believed that the government would exert sufficient control through the mortgage-payments schedule. Wallace's plan, he concluded, might discriminate against ambitious tenants.[5]

The difference with Wallace was by no means the only one Jones faced. Within his committee reemerged strong feeling against

---

Law and Contemporary Problems 4 (October 1937):441–443; U.S., Congress, House, Committee on Agriculture, *Farm Tenancy*, 75th Cong., 1st sess., 1937, pp. 10–11, 112.

[4] Baldwin, *Poverty and Politics*, p. 180.

[5] Murray R. Benedict, *Farm Policies of the United States, 1790–1950*, pp. 358–362; U.S., Congress, House, Committee on Agriculture, *Farm Tenancy*, 75th Cong., 1st sess., 1937, pp. 215–274.

large-scale government land purchases. Some members believed that the plan would be a socialistic rewarding of inefficiency. For them and, in fact, for moderates like Marvin Jones—parity prices and expanded markets remained the logical cornerstones for future farm prosperity.

That view crossed party lines. South Carolina's Hampton Fulmer, the second-ranking Democrat on the committee, said that any government proposal to make landowners of tenant farmers would be "just like pouring so many millions of dollars in a rat hole." The ranking committee Republican, Clifford Hope, shared Fulmer's fears. Only the programs for submarginal lands and rehabilitation loans won committee approval. By a vote of thirteen to eleven the group refused to go further.[6]

This development and others forced Jones to confer with John Bankhead and agricultural-legislation draftsmen. They prepared a new measure to achieve at least some of the stated objectives of the Committee on Farm Tenancy. On March 20, Jones met with President Roosevelt and others to discuss the proposed legislation. After winning approval there, Jones introduced a farm-security bill (H.R. 6240) nine days later.[7] The measure provided $40 million for loans to tenants, sharecroppers, and farm laborers. Combined with it was a $75 million rural-rehabilitation-loan program and a $70 million conservation program for submarginal lands. The bill also provided for creation of the Farm Security Administration as a division of the Department of Agriculture and gave the secretary of agriculture broad powers of administration. It omitted the controversial provisions for large-scale government land purchases.

[6] The vote in opposition to tenancy-loan provisions was thirteen against to eleven for. Those voting against were Republicans Clifford Hope (Kans.), John Kinzer (Pa.), Charles Tobey (N.H.), August Andresen (Minn.), Clare Hoffman (Pa.), and Bert Lord (N.Y.). Democrats opposed were Hampton Fulmer (S.C.), James G. Polk (Ohio), Richard Kleberg (Tex.), Walter Pierce (Oreg.), Scott Lucas (Ill.), Frank Hook (Mich.), and Harry Coffee (Nebr.). In favor were Democrats Marvin Jones (Tex.), Wall Doxey (Miss.), John Flannagan (Va.), John Mitchell (Tenn.), Fred Cummings (Colo.), Fred Biermann (Iowa), Harold Cooley (N.C.), Emmett Owen (Ga.), William Nelson (Mo.), Harry Beam (Ill.), and Progressive Gerald Boileau (Wis.). *Philadelphia Record*, April 1, 1937.

[7] U.S., Congress, House, *Farm Security Act of 1937*, confidential committee print, March 25, 1937, MJP; Jones to John Bankhead, April 7, 1937, Bankhead Papers.

Members of the House Agriculture Committee rejected the $50 million authorization for tenant loans. Jones suggested setting a lower figure, and the committee consented to $30 million. The provision for local control remained, to Jones's satisfaction. With Fulmer endorsing the measure, the committee reported it favorably five days after its introduction. Under pressure from the administration Jones planned to let proponents reinstate the land-buying provision through amendment on the House floor.[8]

Now, however, opposition developed from the House Rules Committee and from Agriculture Department officials Alexander and Appleby. The two men feared that local administrators would favor their friends with the loan program. Rules Committee members considered Roosevelt's current economy drive and the appropriations authorized by the measure and declined to let it reach the House floor.

Jones tried a third time. On June 17 he brought out a measure (H.R. 7562) in which appropriations for the submarginal-land program were slashed. On the following day it was approved by the Agriculture Committee. Ten days later the House began debate.[9]

Jones himself spoke eloquently for the bill:

> As long as it is possible for a man to return to his home after a day of labor in the office or in the field, and find awaiting him all the things that home means, we will have a substantial and patriotic citizenship. The first thought of the pioneers who founded this country was to own a piece of land. . . . This desire to own the land was responsible for the ring of the ax that made possible access to the land. It was responsible for the creak of the western-bound prairie wagons as the early settlers made their way to western homesteads. Unfortunately in the complex economic structure that has developed within the last few decades, much of this contact has been lost.[10]

The House passed the bill.

In the Senate, where sponsorship had fallen to John Bankhead,

---

[8] H.R. 6240, April 18, 1940, MJP; undated and unidentified clippings, scrapbook 7, MJP; Baldwin, *Poverty and Politics*, pp. 182–183.

[9] Baldwin, *Poverty and Politics*, p. 183; H.R. 7562 June 12, 1937, undated and unidentified clippings, scrapbook 7, MJP; U.S., Congress, House, Committee on Agriculture, *Farm Security Act of 1937*, H. Rept. 1065.

[10] Marvin Jones, "The Remarks of Marvin Jones," *Congressional Record* Scrapbook, vol. 4 (75th Cong., 1st sess.), p. 6452, MJP.

the bill contained a provision for government purchase of land. In House-Senate committee this provision was removed. Then, to win support in both houses of Congress, the committee named its draft the Bankhead-Jones farm-tenancy bill. Essentially it was the House version.[11] On July 13, 1937, the day after the conferees' report, the House passed the bill. Two days later the Senate followed suit.

The act failed to achieve total relief for tenants. It merely sanctioned the FSA officially without actually providing a foundation for the creation of the agency. Hard-core poverty remained. As it developed, more qualified applicants appeared than the appropriation could satisfy. Thirty-four applicants applied for every loan made under the Bankhead-Jones provision, which amounted to only about ten loans a county. Nevertheless, the legislation was a step forward —a relatively short one, in keeping with the modest idea of credit of the day. But the federal government had embarked on a commitment to ease the poverty conditions.[12] Its most important return was to come during World War II, when (as rural sociologist C. Horace Hamilton said) FSA families, representing only 7 percent of the nation's farmers, accounted for much larger increases than that in food production. Thus the family farm had showed its capacity for serving the nation.[13]

While the final draft of the Bankhead-Jones Act disappointed Bankhead and agrarian congressmen who sought greater federal action, if Marvin Jones had not shared their goals, they would never have gone that far. Of all the House committee members, Jones stood as the leader in manifesting concern for a national program rather than one drawn on sectional or commodity lines.[14] While this round of events had not proved to be one of his more glamorous leadership battles—indeed, he had lost most of the skirmishes—he

---

[11] U.S., Congress, House, *Bankhead-Jones Farm Tenant Act,* 75th Cong., 1st sess., July 12, 1937, Bankhead Papers.

[12] Paul V. Maris, "Farm Tenancy," in U.S. Department of Agriculture, *Yearbook of Agriculture, 1940,* pp. 899–900; Baldwin, *Poverty and Politics,* pp. 189–192.

[13] C. Horace Hamilton, "Statement of Farm Security Administration," MS, 1943, courtesy of Dr. C. Horace Hamilton, Raleigh, N.C.

[14] See Marvin Jones, "The Present Significance of Farm Tenancy," MS, MJP.

had stubbornly fought for a farm-tenancy bill and had prevailed in the end.

Throughout that congressional session Jones fought for greater opportunity for farmers through additional financial aid. In January 1937 he introduced a bill providing for low-interest loans that would help in planting and harvesting the year's crops, with administration in the hands of county agents. The measure actually supplemented the Bankhead-Jones Farm Tenancy Act, providing aid to tenants and yeoman farmers.[15] After the bill passed Congress, another Texas representative, Luther Johnson, correctly observed that

for many [farmers] there will always be more or less a depression, and the Government in helping the unfortunate who need help cannot find a class that is more needy or more deserving than those tenant farmers who farm on a small scale and who without these loans during the past few years would have been wholly unable to earn a livelihood.[16]

In June 1937, President Roosevelt, in an economical mood, vetoed other financial-aid legislation intended to extend low interest rates on federal land-bank loans. He acted without bothering to consult Jones, who then lead in seeking to override the veto. Roosevelt had reasoned that because of swelling farm prices the government need not continue the low interest rates, which amounted to government subsidization. Jones replied that low interest rates saved many farmers from becoming tenants themselves and adding to relief costs. He substantiated his arguments with statistics, expressions of farm philosophy, and personal reminiscences. He told his colleagues:

Many of you have lived on a farm as I have. If so you know the very great burden of paying high interest rates when the living must be made from the production of the farm. If the rates remain high, there is little hope of paying off these obligations and becoming in the full sense free men.[17]

The legislation passed over Roosevelt's veto.

[15] H.R. 1545, January 5, 1937, MJP.

[16] Jones, "The Remarks of Marvin Jones," *Congressional Record* Scrapbook, vol. 4 (75th Cong., 1st sess.), p. 393, MJP.

[17] Ibid., p. 7121; Franklin D. Roosevelt to Jones, June 8, 1937, MJP. Roosevelt argued that interest rates concerned not only farm loans but also the HOLC, the PWA, and the RFC. Roosevelt also sought the support of William Myers of the FCA and Clarence Cannon, chairman of the House Appropriations Committee, as well as Senators Robert Wagner and Alben Barkley.

Considerations other than agricultural monopolized Jones's thoughts in February 1937, when Roosevelt sent Congress his proposal to pack the Supreme Court and thus assure favorable decisions on New Deal legislation. On the very day Roosevelt acted, February 5, Jones happened to be relaxing on one of his occasional fishing trips with Democratic friends Lindsay Warren of North Carolina, fellow-Texan Sam Rayburn, and Bob Doughton of North Carolina. Roosevelt's move surprised Jones, although rumors about it had circulated in congressional cloakrooms. When Jones returned to Washington, he consulted his trusted colleague Hatton Sumners, chairman of the House Judiciary Committee. Sumners convinced him that the president had blundered.

Jones himself did not object to Supreme Court or other federal-judiciary reforms, but he maintained that no president should add justices in order to change Court opinions. Such a move, he knew, would introduce dangerous precedents for the future and threaten the separation of powers. He privately suggested to friends a better solution for long-term reform: appoint justices to the Court from the circuit courts, giving representation to all sections of the nation—a representation that should be achieved in other government bodies too. That would ensure fairness, Jones said. He elaborated, saying that government officials frequently lack understanding of the issues that arise in a section of the country with which they are unfamiliar. No doubt Jones made his suggestion with an idea of avoiding future court decisions similar to *United States* v. *Butler*, but he did not publicize it for fear of jeopardizing his dream of being named to a federal judiciary post. His friend Sumners knew where he stood, and that was sufficient. Moreover, the House Judiciary Committee had the responsibility of dealing with Roosevelt's proposal, and Jones was not looking for a hornet's nest.

The president's scheme soon ran into trouble. Jones attributed it to a belief that most congressmen—including him—considered the Supreme Court the ultimate safeguard of American liberty and a basically nonpartisan body. Further, Roosevelt was not universally loved on Capitol Hill, where personalities and tender egos often clashed. Jones commented later that "Roosevelt was a rather dominant character. As frequently happens in reference to that kind of character, there were some people who had a sort of 'I hope you choke' feeling for him, even in his own party."[18]

Eventually Roosevelt lost the battle, but he won the war when judicial changes enabled him to gain more favorable decisions. The conflict also, however, strengthened the anti–New Deal coalition.

Conflict over the court-packing scheme made it impossible to achieve consensus on a general agricultural program, at least for a time. Jones hoped that the Soil Conservation and Domestic Allotment Act would serve as a policy basis throughout the session. He believed that general farm reforms were ill-advised, and he pleaded with his colleagues to concentrate on problems of tenancy, crop loans, crop insurance, conservation, and drought relief.

During this time Secretary Wallace was urging support for a general farm program based on the ever-normal-granary idea. In February he called farm leaders to a conference in Washington. Representatives from the American Farm Bureau Federation, the Farmers' National Union, the Grange, the National Co-operative Council, and the Farmers' National Grain Corporation attended, along with Agriculture Chairmen Jones and Cotton Ed Smith. The court-packing furor delayed decisions there, too, but eventually Wallace prevailed on Jones to get the House Agriculture Committee to discuss general legislation. Jones commented pessimistically, but he agreed to hold hearings on agricultural relief. The hearings began on May 17.[19]

Meanwhile, to get the ball rolling for general agricultural-policy revisions, the AFBF had drafted a bill that House Agriculture Committee member John Flannagan introduced. In the Senate, James Pope and George McGill introduced a similar measure, but Chairman Smith opposed it, which made its chances slim indeed. The measure called for crop controls under a nationally administered program and thus abandonment of the state and regional concept of the Soil Conservation and Domestic Allotment Act, a provision that immediately brought opposition from Jones. Also included were

---

[18] Jones, interview with Dean Albertson, Columbia Oral History Project, 1952, p. 976; hereafter cited as COHP-MJP.

[19] Edward L. Schapsmeier and Frederick Schapsmeier, *Henry A. Wallace of Iowa: The Agrarian Years*, pp. 238–241; Marvin Jones, "On Capitol Hill. . . . ," *National Farm News* 2 (January–February 1937):1; undated and unidentified clippings, scrapbooks 7 and 8, MJP.

provisions for Wallace's ever-normal granary, benefit payments on basic crops, and commodity-credit loans. Farm income would be aided by Commodity Credit Corporation loans at specified percentages of parity prices on a sliding-scale tariff foundation.

Wallace favored the bill, and Roosevelt himself urged its passage during the hearings. Jones moved slowly on the legislation, however, and with a marked lack of enthusiasm. He believed that the proposal had a lot of "trigger work" in it, and he determined that the committee would examine all aspects very carefully before doing anything to upset the soil-conservation program. Besides, most members of the Agriculture Committee felt that they had a farm act that was functioning satisfactorily. The plan must show conclusive proof that it would improve American agriculture.

The ranking Republican on the committee, Clifford Hope, opposed any form of compulsory control and echoed Jones's cautious approach. Other opposition formed, too, and the Grange and the National Cooperative Council soon denounced the measure.[20]

Actually, Jones was not hostile to all the provisions of the Flannagan bill, and he was rather sympathetic to Wallace's ever-normal-granary concept. Still Jones wanted the bill to have sufficient safeguards to ensure sufficient soil conservation and lower freight rates and provide regional research laboratories. Frequent talks with Wallace, however, increased Jones's fears that "soil conservation" was merely an expression to Department of Agriculture officials. He doubted that the bill would materially assist the federal soil-conservation program. He also doubted the constitutionality of compulsory production controls and their attendant provisions, the fiscal soundness of the bill, and its fairness to cotton producers. All of this discouraged Chester Gray, an AFBF legislative representative, who observed that without Jones's strong support the bill could not pass.[21]

---

[20] Christiana M. Campbell, *The Farm Bureau and the New Deal*, pp. 111–113; Orville M. Kile, *The Farm Bureau through Three Decades*, pp. 233–239; press release, May 24, 1937, Franklin D. Roosevelt Papers, Franklin D. Roosevelt Library, Hyde Park, N.Y.; undated and unidentified clippings, scrapbook 7, MJP.

[21] U.S., Congress, House, Committee on Agriculture, *General Farm Legislation: Hearings*, 75th Cong., 1st sess., May 17–June 10, 1937; undated and unidentified clippings, scrapbook 7, MJP.

Jones may have believed that he could kill the measure by stalling and expressing doubts and thus gain time to prepare his own legislation. He called John O'Brien and Gerald Morgan to his office and asked them to begin drafting a bill that included the ever-normal granary, soil conservation, county committees, section 32, a $10,000 limit on payments to any farm, protection for tenants, agricultural research, and a surplus-reserve-loan corporation to facilitate financing and freight-rate adjustments.[22]

While Jones's comprehensive approach was being drafted, letters poured in to the Texan urging passage of the Flannagan bill. On July 12, Roosevelt sent Jones a letter prepared with Wallace's help. The president said:

> ...once more my hope that your Committee will go forward and that sympathetic consideration may be given by Congress: first, to the continuation of the present conservation program as the foundation of the long-time plan; second, for the assurance of abundance for consumers by storage of substantial reserves of feed for use in years of crop failures; third, for protection of farm prices and farm income.[23]

Roosevelt urged prompt action on the bill because, he said, emergency conditions and even a crisis during the next session could result in hastily drafted legislation.[24] Ironically, the president called for immediate action by the committee at the very time when relations were severely strained between the chief executive (along with the AFBF) on one side and Jones and the House Agriculture Committee on the other.

Tension mounted further when Jones introduced a measure (H.R. 7972) that he hoped would become the Agricultural Adjustment Act of 1937, prepared with the help of Morgan and O'Brien. The Grange threw its support behind the bill, but the Senate delayed recommendations on agricultural legislation when Cotton Ed Smith rebelled against current lobbying tactics and sought the opinions of "one-gallus" men.

Wallace tried to soothe the situation and at the same time win

---

[22] COHP-MJP, pp. 1020–22, 1029–30; H.R. 7972 (July 22, 1937), MJP; H. A. Wallace to the President, June 18, 1937, Roosevelt Papers; James S. Ward, interview with Jones, October 11, 1967, pp. 27–33; hereafter cited as Jones to Ward.

[23] Franklin D. Roosevelt to Jones, July 12, 1937, Roosevelt Papers.

[24] Ibid.

approval of the Flannagan bill. He requested a conference with Speaker Bankhead, Jones, Rayburn, and Doxey. The secretary appealed to Jones on the basis of party unity, but that only increased Jones's irritation. He replied, "I do not accept a lecture in good grace from someone who is a Johnny-come-lately as far as the party is concerned." Jones told Wallace that the Flannagan measure was inadequate and that if other Democratic congressional leaders attempted to pass it he would "fight it as hard as I can."[25]

Wallace then sought to persuade Speaker Bankhead to oppose Jones, but Bankhead refused to intervene, saying that no one in the House could prevail over Jones in agricultural matters.

Jones did not want a complete break with Wallace, but tension remained high. The split briefly flared in public when Jones went on radio to defend the provisions of his own legislation. He said that he recognized the inadequacy of the current Soil Conservation and Domestic Allotment Act in solving problems caused by huge surpluses of major crops, and he urged farm groups to give congressmen their views so that common goals might be reached.

In the speech Jones avoided widening the breach with Wallace by focusing on Roosevelt, and in a sympathetic way at that. Jones remarked that

> the President of the United States, with his great heart and mind, is earnestly desirous of seeing a sound, practical, permanent farm program evolved as soon as possible and written into the law of the land. I believe we will be able to accomplish this, if with an attitude of conciliation and patience, all the groups concerned dedicate themselves to the task.[26]

Roosevelt retreated on the Flannagan legislation. He and Jones agreed that an immediate adjournment of Congress would be satisfactory if the two agriculture committees would return to Washington six weeks before a special session. The decision reflected growing difficulties between the chief executive and Congress. Roosevelt's court-packing attempt had helped bring on the trouble. Even loyal New Deal supporters had been antagonized by the action. Moreover, the Texas congressman refused to be a rubber stamp for the admin-

---

[25] COHP-MJP, p. 1030.
[26] Marvin Jones, "Representative Marvin Jones Discusses Farm Legislation Over CBS," speech, July 29, 1937, MS, MJP.

istration, and he would not allow his committee to become one. All these factors and others doomed AAA revisions for 1937. Agricultural legislation had ended for the session.

Jones longed to see the farmers of his district and hear their reactions. Throughout September and up to mid-October he discussed farm problems with constituents. Meanwhile, members of his committee and the Senate Agriculture and Forestry Committee were conducting similar surveys. All these studies confirmed his opinion that farm organizations still had not come up with a widely supported general policy.

In Texas, however, Jones discovered at least one generally stated desire: cotton farmers wanted federal loans for surpluses produced during good years, and they favored controls that would hold production in line with demands of domestic and export consumption. These farmers welcomed increased government assistance. They requested establishment of a federal cotton-research laboratory in their region. Further, since Texas occupied a premier position among cotton-export states, they voiced fears of losing foreign markets.

On October 14, 1937, Jones went to Taylor for a major meeting of cotton producers sponsored by the East Texas Chamber of Commerce. More than 1,500 farmers attended, as did Texas Congressmen Jones, Kleberg, Nat Patton, and W. R. Poage, Texas Commissioner J. E. McDonald, and Burris Jackson, vice-president of the Texas Cotton Association. Jones listened and decided to support cotton-commodity legislation. Since cotton occupied a unique place in American exports, he made it a priority for his future farm proposals.[27]

As the autumn of 1937 came to the nation's capitol, Secretary Wallace insisted that President Roosevelt notify Marvin Jones and Cotton Ed Smith of the impending congressional session and remind them of their agreement to begin preparing legislation. Roosevelt told

[27] Marvin Jones, "Hon. Marvin E. [sic] Jones Explains Proposed Farm Program," *Cotton Digest* 10 (October 16, 1937):5, 14–15; clippings, scrapbook 7, MJP; *Kiplinger Agricultural Letter*, letter 229, October 16, 1937, Edward O'Neal Papers, State of Alabama, Department of Archives and History, Montgomery, Ala.; N. C. Williamson, president of American Cotton Cooperative Association, to Henry A. Wallace, October 5, 1937, Wallace to M. W. Thatcher, October 21, 1937, and Wallace to Jones, October 20, 1937, National Archives, Washington, D.C., Record Group 16.

Jones that the current agricultural conservation program was wrecking farm prices and that surpluses were mounting. The president added that he was not asking for conservation to be shelved; he was only insisting that the new farm bill be economical but expanded to include the ever-normal granary and to protect both producers and consumers against extreme market fluctuations. Roosevelt emphasized the inefficiency of price-stabilization measures through agricultural financial policies.

Jones went to work. He first conferred with Wallace and then talked with the Agriculture Committee. To meet constitutional requirements, he decided to substitute marketing control for direct production control, through authority based on congressional power to regulate interstate and foreign commerce. On November 24 he introduced a measure (H.R. 8505) designed to ensure economic freedom for farmers and protection against scarcity for consumers. He won Speaker Bankhead's pledge to bring up the bill quickly for debate on the House floor.[28]

Now Roosevelt watched with relish what soon became a House-Senate race with agricultural bills. The Senate was readying the Pope-McGill bill. The House was playing catch-up with the Jones bill. Jones's power and prestige were on the line. Later he recalled those days:

> The Farm Bureau was trying to pass the bill in the Senate before we could pass my bill in the House. If they did that, the Pope-McGill bill would come over to the House and whatever we put in it, it would still be the Pope-McGill bill. We could amend it and turn it into our bill, but it would still have the Senate number, which was the identification for the bill they introduced. To a degree, they would get credit for the bill. The Farm Bureau felt that they could secure its passage through the Senate first.... Some of the members from districts where the Farm Bureau was strong threw a few little monkey wrenches, but they could not get anywhere.[29]

Jones faced another problem: strong opposition from a minority of his committee led by Gerald Boileau and August Andresen. Their

---

[28] COHP-MJP, pp. 1035–37. See also H. A. Wallace to Franklin D. Roosevelt, October 13, 1937, Roosevelt Papers; Roosevelt to Jones, October 20, 1937, MJP; undated and unidentified clipping, scrapbook 8, MJP; H.R. 8505, November 24, 1937, MJP.

[29] COHP-MJP, p. 1043.

opposition prevented the bill from going to the floor with solid committee backing. Texan Wright Patman fanned the flames higher with a petition containing one hundred congressional signatures urging that the "Second AAA" be sent back to Jones's committee for the addition of a guaranteed minimum price for farm products.

Jones refused to compromise. He worked a political trade with urban representatives by backing minimum-wage-and-hour legislation in return for their support of his bill. He was forced to compromise in another area, however, when an amendment was passed granting the secretary of agriculture greater powers to make CCC loans. Jones preserved the bill's essential components, however, and it passed the House in December by a vote of 242 to 157.

In the Senate the bill ran into some trouble: Cotton Ed Smith's inherent hostility to New Deal–supported measures and preferences by other senators for the Pope-McGill bill. The Senate increased farmers' benefits and delayed until 1939 the specified $10,000 limitation for individual producers. In that form the bill passed the Senate. In February, House-Senate conferees agreed to the provision for the ever-normal granary, including penalties for noncompliance.

Finally, on February 9, 1938, the Second AAA bill passed the House by a vote of 263 to 135. Senate approval followed within a week. Roosevelt signed the new legislation, calling it an effort to balance prices.[30]

Included in the act were amendments to the Soil Conservation and Domestic Allotment Act and new provisions for freight rates on agricultural commodities, loans, parity payments and marketing quotas, and cotton and crop insurance. Jones retained the tenancy legislation; Wallace won his ever-normal granary and greater powers to control surpluses. The secretary could now control overproduction through soil-conservation payments, loans, and marketing agreements. The act extended the life of the Federal Surplus Commodities Corporation and created the Federal Crop Insurance Corporation, as

---

[30] Undated and unidentified clippings, scrapbook 8, MJP; *New York Times*, January 5, 30, and 31, February 7, 10, 15, and 19, 1938; Jones, "Remarks of Marvin Jones," *Congressional Record Scrapbook*, vol. 4 (75th Cong., 2d sess.), pp. 2129–32, 2259–60; H. A. Wallace to Jones, February 18, 1938, National Archives, Record Group 233; press release, February 10, 1938, MJP; Kile, *The Farm Bureau through Three Decades*, pp. 233–239.

well as federal research laboratories. It preserved the AFBF's concept of parity and protected cotton and corn producers.

With general farm policy updated by the Agricultural Adjustment Act of 1938, Jones decided to get a head start and supplement it before the 1938 election with amendments concerning cotton. On March 17 he introduced a bill (H.R. 9915) that would tack a marketing agreement onto the Second AAA. It proposed to give the secretary of agriculture power to allocate to each state in which at least 3,500 bales of cotton had been produced in any of five preceding years sufficient acreage to ensure a minimum state production of 5,000 bales. It would also provide relief to farmers whose 1937 cotton crop had been damaged by hail, drought, flood, or boll weevils. This strategy—crop insurance tied to a marketing agreement—had been well calculated by Jones.

Farmers who suffered during the 1937 depression would have crop insurance with a guaranteed 90 percent of parity for one year on any soil-depleting crops for which the AAA had established special acreage allotments. The measure was meant primarily for the relief of cotton, tobacco, and potato producers, but it also would give help to Illinois farmers whose fields had been ravaged by floods for the past three or four years and to farmers who had lost crops in warehouse fires. Despite these generosities Jones had failed to reach one of his most desired goals: standardization of relief with an amendment giving needy farmers the same eligibility for employment as persons already on the relief rolls. The bill passed the House and then the Senate, which consented to local determination of cotton acreage rather than a determination made solely by AAA officials.

The creation of a cotton-research laboratory was a matter of immediate concern. Huge surpluses of cotton sat in the warehouses, and neither federal nor state legislation had succeeded in effectively reducing production. Texas cotton producers and Texas A&M had supported past efforts to find new markets and new uses for cotton, and for good reason, since Texas led the nation in production and exports. Various research proposals had been advocated by T. O. Walton, president of Texas A&M; A. B. Conner, director of the Texas Agricultural Experiment Station; Burris C. Jackson of the Texas Cotton Association; "Cotton George" Moffett of the Texas

House of Representatives; and the East Texas Chamber of Commerce. They had been defeated, however, in their efforts to create a state-financed cotton-research laboratory. Texas legislators had decided that they would not tax or appropriate funds to give cotton special consideration to the detriment of research in grain, animal diseases, and other fields.

By October 1937 most Texas farm leaders had agreed to seek federal funding for a Texas cotton laboratory, to be established at Texas A&M. Elmore Torn, agricultural director of the East Texas Chamber of Commerce, remarked to Jones:

Any additional uses which will increase domestic consumption and probably also world consumption will directly benefit the man who grows the cotton. Also there is a desire on the part of many people in Texas to improve the quality of their cotton, but unfortunately they are not in a position financially to buy the proper planting seed to accomplish this.[31]

Within a week following passage of the Second AAA, Texas and other cotton-producing states had begun vigorous campaigns to acquire cotton laboratories. Texas and Mississippi emerged as principal contenders. Texans placed their faith in Marvin Jones to bring them a federal laboratory; Mississippians relied on Senator Theodore Bilbo's efforts. Jones conferred with Roosevelt and joined Sam Rayburn and Luther Johnson in petitioning Secretary Wallace and other Department of Agriculture officials to support the Texas location. Jones pointed out that Texas lay almost in the center of the cotton belt, which stretched from the Atlantic Coast to California and had the climate and soil conditions of both western and eastern cotton-producing areas.

---

[31] Elmore Torn to Jones, November 29, 1937. It should be noted that competition for a research laboratory existed between Texas Tech University and Texas A&M University. Jones favored Texas A&M because it was the land-grant college with longer-term activity and interest in the project. He avoided direct confrontation on the issue by urging Texas Tech to solicit the aid of Representative George Mahon. Jones to Franklin D. Roosevelt, March 4, 1938, Roosevelt Papers; James Jardine, Director of Research, U.S. Department of Agriculture, to Jones, May 18, 1938, T. O. Walton to Jones, July 11, 1935, A. B. Conner to Jones, August 30, 1935, A. B. Conner to Henry A. Wallace, November 6, 1935, Herbert Harrison, vice-president and general manager, East Texas Chamber of Commerce, to Jones, February 17, 1937, A. B. Conner to Jones, March 16, 1938, Clifford B. Jones to Jones, December 22, 1937, Jones to Clifford B. Jones, January 4, 1938. MJP.

The Climactic Year in Congress 169

Roosevelt refrained from endorsing Jones's request, saying that Henry Wallace would make the final decision. Texans responded that they deserved a laboratory since under the Bankhead-Jones Act crop laboratories had already been established in South Carolina, Alabama, Mississippi, Idaho, Iowa, Illinois, and Pennsylvania.[32]

Months of waiting followed. Then, on December 14, Henry Wallace announced that four research laboratories would be established: in Peoria, Illinois; New Orleans; Philadelphia (in Wyndmoor); and San Francisco (in Albany). Jones was angry. He felt betrayed, but he let others do the protesting. South Carolina's Hampton Fulmer demanded that Wallace "state just one good reason, based on common sense, and fairness to the cotton-growing states, why the State of Louisiana, and the City of New Orleans, located in a state which has for its major farming operation the growing of sugar cane and rice, should be given this Research Station."[33]

Economic and political considerations had combined to defeat Jones and his fellow Texans. Urban New Orleans had better communication and transportation facilities than did the Texas A&M campus, in then-isolated College Station. Moreover, by establishing the laboratory in a neutral city, officials had avoided involvement in

[32] State-wide Cotton Committee of Texas to Members of Texas Delegation in Congress, February 24, 1938, Jones, Sam Rayburn, and Luther Johnson to Henry A. Wallace, March 3, 1938, Jones to Franklin D. Roosevelt, March 9, 1938, Roosevelt to Jones, March 11, 1938, A. B. Conner to Jones, March 17, 1938, MJP.

[33] Jones observed that the notices had been sent to congressmen's offices in their districts rather than to their Washington offices. He noted that, since the letters had been sent out after the announcement and because of his daily contact with Wallace on the matter, protocol had been lacking. When the January issue of *American Cotton Growers* credited Bilbo with establishing the cotton-research laboratories, Jones detailed the achievements of both men. Both had made contributions to cotton research as provided in the Second AAA. Hampton Fulmer to Henry A. Wallace, December 13, 1938, MJP. See also the following materials in MJP: A. B. Conner to Jones, May 16, 1938; California-Arizona Cotton Association, resolution, undated MS; Burris C. Jackson to Jones, July 22, 1938; James T. Jardine to Burris C. Jackson, August 25, 1938; Sam Rayburn to Jones, November 1, 1938; H. T. Herrick, chairman, Special Survey Committee, to Jones, December 12, 1938; Jones, press release, December 14, 1938, MS; Jones to Henry A. Wallace, December 15, 1938; Wallace to Jones, December 19, 1938; Wallace to Fulmer, January 5, 1939; Jones to Stanley Andrews, editor, *American Cotton Grower*, January 23, 1940; Andrews to Jones, January 30, 1940.

a heated rivalry between the Mississippi and Texas agricultural experiment stations. Roosevelt had not favored stretching the taxpayer's dollar by using available resources at land-grant universities.[34]

Later Jones reflected that the achievements of 1938 had been a fitting climax to his career. The New Deal agrarian-reform period actually ended with the Second AAA. The two days before the congressional session closed, Jones proclaimed the agricultural achievements of the New Deal and called the Second AAA and improved interest rates for farmers the high points of the session. He charged his colleagues to "go forward until the struggle for equality for agriculture is finally won."[35]

[34] Thomas R. Richmond, interview with author, December 22, 1975.
[35] Marvin Jones, "The Remarks of Marvin Jones," *Congressional Record* Scrapbook, vol. 4 (75th Cong., 3d sess.), appendix, p. 2842, MJP.

11.

Congressional Sunset

IN 1938, when President Roosevelt tried to purge a number of Democrats who had opposed his New Deal, Marvin Jones was certainly not among them. He faced scant opposition in the congressional election and really did not need the support of Roosevelt, who, however, when he visited Amarillo on July 11, spoke highly of Jones:

> We are fortunate in Washington in having as chairman of the Agricultural Committee of the House of Representatives a man who has a well-rounded knowledge of the agricultural programs in every part of the United States. He and I have discussed many times the great objective of putting agriculture and cattle raising on a safe basis—giving assurances to those who engage in these pursuits that they will not be broke one year and flush the next.[1]

Jones had warned Roosevelt against attempting the purge, but the president had ignored him. Jones deplored Roosevelt's decision to intervene in state elections, observing:

> The ballot is about the only instrumentality for maintaining a free government. It is the only way an honest choice can be made of the servants who are to administer the public affairs. The hills and the valleys of the old world are bleaching with the bones of men who lost their lives in the struggle of people to the plains of liberty. About all they have left to show for these sacrifices and the sacrifices that the early-day patriots went through in this country, is that little piece of paper which we call the ballot.[2]

Jones enjoyed greater success in the election than the president.

---

[1] Franklin D. Roosevelt, "Address Delivered by the President of the United States at Amarillo, Texas, July 11, 1938," mimeographed, Marvin Jones Papers, hereafter cited as MJP.

[2] Marvin Jones, interview with Dean Albertson, Columbia Oral History Project, 1952, p. 1075; hereafter cited as COHP-MJP. Unlesss otherwise noted, interviews and correspondence citing Jones refer to Marvin Jones.

The man from the Panhandle won the Democratic primary (and thus reelection) by a four-to-one majority. He determined not to risk crossing swords again with the president, because he wanted, now more than ever, appointment to a federal judgeship.

At the time there was a vacancy on the Circuit Court of Appeals in the District of Columbia. Jones wanted to stay in Washington, and he sought the appointment. He thought his chances were good.[3] On August 31, 1938, he wrote the president:

> I have always wanted to do judicial work, feeling that whatever talent I have is in that field, and feeling, also, that the chance of retaining the progress of the past years depends as much upon the personnel of the courts as upon the legislative enactment.[4]

In 1938, Jones was fifty-six. He hoped to begin his judicial career before old age overtook him. Moreover, he wanted financial security and the opportunity to remain near the seat of power. However deeply he loved the Panhandle—and love it he did—few men have had a stronger case of Potomac fever. At home Panhandle newspapers speculated about Jones's judicial dreams, and contenders emerged for his job in Congress. The congressional campaign of 1940 actually began a few months after the 1938 Democratic primary.

In Washington, Roosevelt stalled on Jones's request. The congressman persisted, because he feared that the president's power would wane considerably during what he assumed would be the last two years of his administration. Late in November the president was visiting his favorite retreat, at Warm Springs, Georgia. Jones requested and received an appointment with him there. He arrived on November 29, ostensibly to discuss crop-control legislation and criticisms of cotton policies by the New Orleans Cotton Exchange.

Jones met with the president at 2:00 P.M. They toured the area in Roosevelt's Ford, with the president at the wheel. As they drove around the countryside, Roosevelt monopolized the conversation and confined his remarks to a superficial description of his Georgia farm. The president knew very well what Jones was after.

---

[3] Jones to Marvin McIntyre, secretary to the President, August 1, 1938, Franklin D. Roosevelt Papers, Franklin D. Roosevelt Library, Hyde Park, N.Y.

[4] Jones to Franklin D. Roosevelt, August 31, 1938, Roosevelt Papers.

Eventually Roosevelt turned to the subjects of conservation and tenancy legislation. Finally he took up Jones's request for a judicial post and asked the congressman to withdraw it. Roosevelt said that he feared for the fate of the Second AAA in a Congress that was continually manifesting independence of the chief executive and that he wanted trusted New Dealers to remain in key positions.

Jones, who assumed that Roosevelt would not run for a third term, replied that he feared the chief executive elected in 1940 might be unreceptive to his request for a judicial appointment. Roosevelt said, "I am not going to promise you this particular place [on the circuit court], but I assure you, you will be taken care of. But I want you to stay on the Hill for a while, if you will, and help handle the program up there."[5]

After that the president returned to the cat-and-mouse game for which he was famous. He played on Jones's well-known desire to remain in Washington by offering him a judgeship far from the city, on the Fifth Circuit Court of Appeals in New Orleans. As Roosevelt had anticipated, Jones chose to await a position on a Washington court. Meanwhile, in Jones's district rumors of an impending appointment persisted throughout the next two years, eroding his political base.

For Jones the satisfying days in Congress were largely ended. As Europe moved closer to war and inevitably attracted United States involvement, Roosevelt shifted priorities, including increased farm production in place of controls. His administration stopped initiating significant agricultural legislation. Moreover, increased Republican strength, plus growth of a conservative coalition, made consensus difficult. Commodity strength grew in the House Agriculture Committee. The composition of the committee was now sixteen Democrats and eleven Republicans. Each party had a territorial member. Jones lead a committee that lacked enthusiasm for new legislation. His call for the Interstate Commerce Commission to re-

---

[5] Marvin McIntyre to Jones, August 25, 1938; Jones to McIntyre, November 24, 1938, MJP. Jones's account in COHP-MJP, pp. 1055–62, varies from documents in the Roosevelt Papers. For example, the visit occurred in November rather than in the summer; see "President Is Caustic as to Cotton Group," clipping, scrapbook 9, MJP. The principal reason for Jones's visit was to gain a judicial appointment; crop-control legislation was secondary.

duce all export freight rates on agricultural commodities rang hollow. It was a product of the past, and it fell far short of the "urgent call for unity and action" that had characterized previous committee sessions. Comprising the agenda now were amendments to the Agricultural Adjustment Act and the Soil Conservation and Domestic Allotment Act; some attention to farm finance and tenancy, agricultural research, and cotton and wheat legislation; and reorganization of the Department of Agriculture. Of these items only the USDA reorganization was new.

Jones delayed announcing trends and goals for the committee until February 4, 1939, when he announced that he would seek more efficient payment of government funds to farmers and an earlier preparation of acreage allotments so that farmers could make detailed plans before planting crops. Also, he said, he hoped to base legislation for benefit payments on farm acreage actually being cultivated plus land planted in soil-building crops and on other practices.

Five weeks later, on "The National Farm and Home Hour," he conceded that "only minor changes will be made in this year's program" and predicted that they would not become effective before 1940. He also praised the achievements of the AFBF and promised to continue efforts to restore agriculture to the level of industry.[6]

After that Jones appeared on the House floor with a bill (H.R. 3800) that placed a $10,000 limit on the amount an individual could receive in soil-conservation payments. In an effort to protect the cash tenant and prevent his removal from the land by the landlord, Jones wrote into the bill provisions that allowed landowners to receive benefits also.[7] Large landowners opposed the bill. It passed the House but failed in the Senate.

During 1939 the House Agriculture Committee sponsored eighteen technical amendments to agricultural legislation of previous sessions. Jones successfully supported an amendment permitting the application of conservation payments on crop-insurance premiums and the use of section 32 funds for school-lunch programs, but he failed to win approval of measures encouraging absentee owners to sell farms to tenants.

[6] Jones, speech, "National Farm and Home Hour," March 11, 1939, MJP.
[7] H.R. 3800 (February 7, 1939), MJP.

Roosevelt issued an executive order transferring the FCA to the Department of Agriculture and did not bother to consult Jones beforehand, perhaps knowing that Jones (along with members of the Grange, the AFBF, and other farm organizations) believed that the independence of the FCA should be maintained. Jones retaliated by preparing for introduction during the next congressional session a farm-credit bill that would assure the FCA's integrity.

The year 1939 gave the cotton farmer little to cheer about, including cotton legislation from past sessions. Although acreage allotments had declined from the previous year, the government still controlled one-third of the acreage, and because of generous federal loans domestic prices were higher than the world-market prices. When the nation's cotton exports fell to their lowest level in sixty years, Wallace consulted with Jones, Bankhead, Smith, and Allen Ellendar of Louisiana, but they failed to agree on a solution.

Various ideas were pushed. Jones was under constant pressure from Texas Panhandle cotton producers to discontinue AAA and soil-conservation payments and allow unlimited acreage. Ed O'Neal of the American Farm Bureau Federation advocated an export subsidy program similar to that for wheat, but the American Cotton Shippers' Association would not go along. Cotton Ed Smith championed selling loan cotton for three cents a pound to growers who would reduce their allocated production under the present farm program by amounts equal to their purchases. Smith's scheme would increase price-adjustment payments up to five cents a pound for farmers who marketed their cotton instead of storing it under government loans. Jones argued that the secretary of agriculture already had the power to deal with the crisis. Jones declared that Wallace could use funds accumulated under section 32 to facilitate export of cotton and distribute cotton domestically through relief channels.

Administration officials agreed with Jones. On March 28 the president announced the goals for the economy, including orderly merchandising of surplus cotton, protection for producers, and maintenance of the United States position in the world market. Roosevelt urged Congress to guarantee payments of $1.25 a bale to producers who released their cotton on the world market and moderate payments for all cotton exported after the plan went into effect.

Jones acted on the president's request by suggesting a plan for subsidizing the utilization of domestic cotton, paying export losses, and releasing some cotton to flow into the world market on a competitive basis. Producers and manufacturers would be protected from a flow-back of cotton to the domestic market through marketing-quota provisions. Jones organized these ideas into a bill and secured its endorsement by the House Agriculture Committee.

A bitter fight broke out between Jones and Senators Bankhead and Smith, who contended that Jones's proposal would cause hardships for southern cotton farmers. Throughout March and early April, Secretary Wallace, Bankhead, Smith, and Jones held conferences. Eventually Bankhead agreed to support the Jones program of export subsidies. All legislative remedies proved unsuccessful, however. It took a world war to raise cotton prices.[8]

To solve other farm problems, Jones pleaded for new legislation based on soil conservation, distribution of surpluses by subsidizing low-income families, and additional loans to prevent commodity-price collapse. Jones thus moved toward a socioeconomic philosophy of farm legislation that he would not have accepted eight years earlier.

Simultaneously the battleground for House agricultural policy shifted from the Committee on Agriculture to the Committee on Agricultural Appropriations, and Jones played a lesser role. Many congressmen had become disillusioned with the results of farm legislation and were unsympathetic to increased appropriations. Their coolness also reflected a change of priorities. The reform spirit had waned; partisan politics and foreign affairs had taken on greater importance. On September 1, 1939, Hitler's Germany invaded Poland, and two days later Great Britain and France went to Poland's aid. World War II had begun, and though the United States would remain at peace for two more years, tension gripped the nation.

[8] U.S. Department of Agriculture, *Compilation of Soil Conservation and Domestic Allotment Act as Amended, Agricultural Adjustment Act of 1938, as Amended, Federal Crop Insurance Act as Amended, Sugar Act of 1937, Appropriation Items Relating Thereto, and Miscellaneous Laws*; H.R. 4386, March 7, 1939, MJP; press release, July 28, 1939, MJP; Gladys L. Baker, Wayne D. Rasmussen, Vivian Wiser, and Jane M. Porter, *Century of Service: The First 100 Years of the United States Department of Agriculture*, p. 217; COHP-MJP, pp. 1079–80; unidentified clippings, scrapbook 8, MJP; Franklin D. Roosevelt, press release, March 28, 1939, MJP; Jones, press release, April 3, 1939, MJP; H.R. 7171, July 12, 1939, MJP.

Jones's primary goal in Congress continued to be help for farmers. From January 24 to 30, 1940, he held hearings on yet another effort (H.R. 6768) to encourage farm sales to tenants by absentee owners. Jones wanted the government to guarantee these loans 100 percent. The secretary of agriculture, he said, should have the power to sell the notes to private lenders. Jones admitted that the bill would give special consideration to the small farmer, but he denied that it constituted a raid on the federal treasury.[9]

At the end of the hearings Jones sought increased appropriations for tenancy, but House Agricultural Appropriations Committee Chairman Clarence Cannon disagreed and argued that Jones's committee should produce a bill standardizing farm prices at no less than 100 percent of parity. Nevertheless, on February 2, Jones introduced an amendment to the agricultural-appropriations bill providing $25 million to aid farm tenants. This proposal won the support of Roosevelt, Wallace, and the Bureau of the Budget.

Jones called on his fellow representatives to approve a balanced attack on the farm problem. He and like-minded colleagues received much urban support when they compared tenancy appropriations with slum-clearance funds and promised to vote for urban assistance.[10]

Cannon still disagreed. He declared that Jones's amendment amounted to an "Arabian Nights entertainment scheme and would not solve the tenant problem." The veteran Missourian saw in Marvin Jones "a man of many parts, a word painter, a golden-throated orator who plays upon the emotions of the House as a master musician plays upon the keys of a mighty organ."[11] Cannon argued that even after years of agricultural legislation farmers had not achieved prosperity and said that he would not support any bill unless it guar-

[9] H.R. 6768, June 9, 1939; MJP. For a different interpretation of the county committees see Louis Cantor, *A Prologue to the Protest Movement*, p. 154; U.S., Congress, House, Agriculture Committee, *Hearings: To Promote Farm Ownership by Amending Bankhead-Jones Farm Tenant Act to Provide for Government Insured Loans to Farmers*, January 24–30, 1940.

[10] Jones declined to vote for the Wagner-Steagall act on slum clearance. Jones, "The Remarks of Marvin Jones," *Congressional Record* Scrapbook, vol. 4 (76th Cong., 2d sess.), 1940, pp. 775–778, 781–790, 831–836, 971–1026, MJP.

[11] Ibid., pp. 1021–22.

anteed farm prices. Congress followed Cannon's advice and rejected Jones's amendment, 135 to 149.¹²

In early March, Jones opened hearings on additional farm-credit legislation. Two months earlier Secretary Wallace had urged Jones to reconsider a measure (H.R. 7342) to extend time and lower interest on land-bank loans. The principal issue soon became whether the FCA should be an independent agency to operate under Department of Agriculture supervision. Among those who favored USDA control were A. G. Black, acting governor of the FCA, and representatives of the National Farmers' Union. They voiced support for the bill. Black's testimony, however, aroused Jones's fears; Black seemed to him ultraliberal.

The views of Albert Goss, who wanted to restore the independence of the FCA, made more sense to Jones. Goss, a member of the Grange and a former land-bank commissioner, led the attack against the bill, a vaguely worded measure. Joining him were members of the American Farm Bureau Federation, the American National Livestock Association, and the American Bankers' Association. With consensus unattainable, Jones permitted the bill to die in committee rather than risk a bitter, fruitless fight on the House floor. That solution could be called characteristic of him.

Jones chose another approach. With Chester Davis' assistance he wrote a bill (H.R. 7342) that would achieve the administration's goals by providing loans to federal land banks for refinancing farm-loan bonds by the Federal Farm Mortgage Corporation and by changing the method of fixing interest rates on land-bank mortgages. Jones introduced the legislation on May 21. It passed the House in June. In the Senate, however, John Bankhead's opposition killed it. Although Jones doggedly lobbied for it later, when other congressmen reintroduced it, the bill never became law. It was Jones's last major attempt at legislative reform.¹³

---

¹² Ibid.

¹³ Henry A. Wallace to Jones, January 13, 1940, National Archives, Record Group 16; H.R. 7342, July 24, 1939; H.R. 9843, May 21, 1940; H.R. 9973, May 31, 1940, MJP. Nor was this bill the last Jones helped pass. For example, later in the session he helped pass H.R. 9859, May 22, 1940, providing for feed and seed loans, MJP; U.S., Congress, House, Committee on Agriculture, *Hearings: Farm Credit Legislation*, March 7–April 5, 1940; COHP-MJP, pp. 1100–1109.

About that time Jones was anxiously awaiting a promised announcement from President Roosevelt regarding a judiciary appointment. When it came, on April 9, 1940, Jones learned that he had been appointed to the court of claims providing he would serve the rest of his congressional term, as the president had earlier requested, and take part in the 1940 campaign.

This success led to temporary pressures. Hampton Fulmer, heir apparent to the Agriculture Committee chairmanship, insisted that Jones relinquish it to him immediately so that he could use the prestige of the position for his own reelection in South Carolina.[14] Jones resented the demand, naturally enough, and refused to resign.

Jones encountered other pressures from his home district. Many voters wanted him to stay where he was. Amarillo Mayor Ross Rogers pleaded:

You simply must continue to serve this district ... and your country in its time of need. Men like you must stay in harness to help fulfill America's destiny of maintaining a seat of order and of freedom, of establishing a citadel so strong in its defense that by our own example the world can be eventually redeemed and pacified and made whole again.[15]

During the spring of 1940 the presidential campaign got under way seriously. Robert Taft, seeking the Republican presidential nomination, went after farm support in a speech on May 18 in Des Moines, Iowa. A week later Jones replied to the speech in a nationwide radio address. He attacked the Republican farm program of the 1920's and reminded voters of the inadequacies of the Hoover administration. Jones emphasized:

We are no longer the beaten and prostrate nation that was turned over by the Republicans in early 1933, but stand today a vigorously united, and powerful people [who] can bend tremendous energies and vast wealth to the task of maintaining peace, or if our shores are menaced, to prosecute war victoriously.[16]

On June 3, Roosevelt told Jones that he intended to run for a

---

[14] COHP-MJP, pp. 1105–1106; Edwin Watson to Franklin D. Roosevelt, April 11, 1940, Franklin D. Roosevelt Papers; Hampton Fulmer to Jones, May 4, 1940, MJP.

[15] Ross D. Rogers to Jones, June 1, 1940, MJP.

[16] Jones, press release, May 25, 1940, MJP.

third term. The president then asked Jones to seek reelection himself and remain in the House during the next few years, which were sure to be troubled ones. Jones assured Roosevelt of his support during the forthcoming campaign, but he repeated his great desire to go to the Court of Claims. Roosevelt insisted, and Jones yielded to the point of saying that he would permit his name to be entered in the Democratic primary.[17]

Jones's vacillation brought him trouble. Previously announced candidates for his job were intensifying their efforts, his office staff told him. Newspaper editors in his district felt that they had been double-crossed and wrote critical editorials. The *Panhandle Herald* commented, "Marvin Jones would be guilty of a disgraceful act, especially after he had obtained confirmation as a judge on the U.S. Court of Claims. . . . Should Jones make the run-off this newspaper pledges in advance to support the candidate who opposes him." The *Spearman Reporter* said, "So far as the average citizen of the Panhandle is concerned, they love Marvin Jones, but the whole affair stinks to the high heavens." Ed Bishop of the *Dalhart Texan* wondered whether Jones's reelection could solve the crisis facing the nation. Bishop told his subscribers, "Personally I don't believe the reelection of Mr. Roosevelt or the relection of Marvin Jones or any other congressman is going to have a great deal to do with our entry in the war."[18]

After two days of torment Jones sent the president a letter in which he declined to run again. He said that many contenders for his congressional seat were his loyal supporters who had believed him earlier when he announced his original decision not to run. Among the candidates, he said, was a former law partner, E. T. ("Dusty") Miller. Jones concluded that the president's request could result in a bitter local election fight that might be detrimental to Roosevelt as well as to Jones.[19]

To Miller, Jones wrote:

---

[17] See Jones to Edwin M. Watson, June 6, 1940, Jones to Ross D. Rogers, MJP; telegram, June 6, 1940, Roosevelt Papers; COHP-MJP, pp. 1109–11.

[18] *Amarillo Times*, June 10, 1940. This article quotes from a number of Panhandle weekly newspapers.

[19] Jones to the President, June 5, 1940, MJP.

The only reason I permitted my name to be filed was at the urgent insistence of the President of the United States. He called me both Saturday and Sunday nights and insisted that, in view of the crisis confronting the country I should remain in my present post during the emergency. . . . I saw him late yesterday afternoon for a long conference. . . . I went down to tell him I could not run as some of my friends had entered the race and I felt that on account of them I should not run. I had not made up my mind until that time. Only then did I agree. . . . No one else had an influence upon my decision.[20]

In retrospect, constituents of the Eighteenth Texas District knew that one of the nation's most powerful congressmen had protected their interests during the New Deal years. The federal government had constructed many new public buildings throughout the district—notably post offices and the new Veterans Administration hospital in Amarillo. Jones had played a key role in securing them.[21] Amarillo became the site of one of four Home Owners' Loan Corporation banks when Jones secured the support of William F. Stevenson, a former colleague in Congress and later chairman of the national board of the corporation, which determined the location of new banks. Congress also created the Northwest Texas Judicial District, with the courtroom in Amarillo.[22]

Jones had ardently supported soil-conservation measures and had increased federal spending in Amarillo as nature's wrath struck the Eighteenth District ever harder. As the major Texas city in the Dust Bowl, Amarillo became the site of a regional office to aid drought victims, as well as a regional headquarters for the Soil Conservation Service. Amarillo gained these additional benefits through Jones's alliance with James Buchanan, chairman of the House Committee on Appropriations.[23]

[20] Jones to E. T. Miller, June 4, 1940, MJP.

[21] For references to text see *Memphis Democrat*, February 2, 1931; *Dalhart Texan*, November 20, 1936; *Amarillo Globe*, November 25, 1936. Evidence of Jones's role in securing a veterans' hospital is seen in his testimony before the Federal Board of Hospitalization. See also L. H. Ryan to Jones, July 5, 1936, Jones to General Frank T. Hines, April 16, 1931, Bruce E. Autry to Jones, October 21, 1938, Arthur Capper to Jones, July 23, 1938, Carl Hatch to Jones, July 25, 1938, John J. Dempsey to Jones, June 27, 1938, MJP.

[22] H.R. 7967, February 14, 1934, Jones to Gordon Browning, chairman, Subcommittee on the Judiciary, U.S. House, February 21, 1934, W. M. Sutton, secretary, Amarillo Bar Association, to Jones, March 14, 1934, MJP.

[23] Jones to Marvin McIntyre, April 9, 1935, MJP; *Dalhart Texan*, April

Rural inhabitants of the Panhandle also benefited from Jones's representation by obtaining federal funds for emergency road-building and livestock-feeding programs throughout the district (as well as part of New Mexico and Colorado). Dalhart became the site of the nation's first dry-land soil-conservation project.

Jones was active in water conservation as well. Aided by New Mexico's Carl Hatch and Oklahoma's Wesley Disney, he successfully urged the construction of the Conchas Dam on the Canadian River. Roosevelt approved the needed funds.[24] During the recession of 1937, Roosevelt granted Jones's request for $10 million in WPA projects, and the Panhandle Water Conservation District received $4,750,000 of those funds.[25]

Jones realized also his constituents' transportation needs. He supported expanded federal funds for farm-to-market road projects, which also provided work for needy constituents.[26]

Can monetary value be placed on Jones's assistance to his constituency? Walter Wilcox, senior specialist in agriculture for the Congressional Research Service, believed that such a valuation was impossible to determine accurately for the years before 1940. Some figures are available, however. During the years to 1938, $37,179,-681.05 in AAA payments were made to the Eighteenth District. FCA loans during the period amounted to $29,349,364. Post offices valued at $1,353,011 were constructed. Civilian Conservation Corps camps were maintained in five counties at various periods of time (figures for various WPA projects and other federally sponsored programs are unavailable).[27] And of course, the value of these programs in sustaining and benefiting human life can never be measured.

15, 1935; E. P. Spiller, secretary and general manager, Texas and Southwestern Cattle Raisers Association, to Jones, September 21, 1935, "Sidelights by Marvin Jones: The Problem of Soil Erosion," March 23, 1935, MJP.

[24] U.S. Department of the Interior, press release, October 9, 1934, Mary E. Bivens Memorial Library, Amarillo, Texas; *Amarillo Daily News*, January 30, 1935.

[25] Jones, "The Remarks of Marvin Jones," *Congressional Record* Scrapbook, vol. 4 (75th Cong., 1st sess.), p. 5005, MJP; *Amarillo Daily News*, June 17, 1939; *Pampa News*, August 26, 1937.

[26] Jones to Franklin D. Roosevelt, September 23, 1933; Jones to Henry A. Wallace, Special Board of Public Works, October 11, 1933, MJP; COHP-MJP, pp. 690–692; Jones to Roosevelt, November 12, 1935, MJP.

[27] Walter W. Wilcox to author, October 18, 1973.

Of equal significance, Jones consistently sought solutions to his district's most pressing problem: agriculture. The people were convinced that they needed him—until he accepted the appointment to the court of claims. Most of them thought that Jones sympathized with them and had the ability to meet their needs. Nevertheless, he could not reverse the trend toward retirement from the House, even if he had wanted to. Indeed, the sun began going down on Jones's congressional career the first moment he began thinking seriously about a judicial appointment.

Jones still had the rest of his term to serve out, nevertheless, and he still had the presidential campaign ahead of him. Roosevelt began soliciting advice from him and from other influential Democrats.

In the Cosmos Club and the National Press Club rumors were heard that Jones might replace Garner as the nominee for vice-president, but Jones later said that he never wanted the nomination. Apparently Roosevelt did consider him for Garner's place but knew that Jones would probably refuse the offer, coveting as he did the security of the judicial appointment.

When Roosevelt named Henry Wallace as his running mate, Jones refrained from comment. He respected Wallace for his knowledge of agriculture and for his high character but had long ago concluded that he was too idealistic and liberal and lacking in experience in political campaigning. Jones wished that Roosevelt had chosen a more able politician, like James Byrnes or Sam Rayburn.[28]

Early in August, Paul Appleby asked Jones to campaign for Roosevelt, helping especially in farm issues. Appleby elaborated:

The President and the Secretary will need to pitch their speeches on a high level where they will stress the catastrophic proportions of world happenings, with the implications being clear that the time demand the services of a President who has given his life to thinking about politics —international affairs and the government—as contrasted with a man

---

[28] At any rate, Jones believed that he was being considered and deliberately rebuffed Roosevelt's advances. Jones wanted the lifetime security of the court of claims. Furthermore, he held Byrnes and Rayburn in high esteem and thought that they were more capable than he. In 1938 or in any other year Jones did not want to be designated the vice-presidential nominee. Jones to W. J. Miller, May 17, 1938, COHP-MJP, pp. 1111–22; Johnnie Simms, transcript of telephone conversation with author, June 14, 1973.

[Wendell Willkie, nominated by the Republicans at Philadelphia in June] who belatedly and suddenly has become interested in politics because he wants to be President.

Appleby wanted Jones to choose topics for Wallace's speeches and to anticipate questions from the public so that the campaign committee could prepare answers in advance.[29]

Careful planning went into Wallace's initial campaign venture in his home state, Iowa. Party leaders planned for Speaker Will Bankhead to accompany him as a sign of Democratic solidarity. At the last minute, however, Bankhead declined the invitation because, "to use a farming term, you and Marvin Jones have been yokefellows for over seven years in working out and executing an agricultural program . . . that has been so sound and serviceable that even the Republican platform and their candidate for President unite in endorsing its unchanged continuation." With this send-off the Speaker pledged his support of the national ticket.[30]

The Democrats selected the site for Wallace's opener with great care. Des Moines was certain to provide a receptive audience for a native Iowan. Jones helped Wallace prepare a fighting speech on foreign affairs. In his introduction of the nominee he sought to win farm support, and no doubt he did. Jones presented Wallace as a true agrarian who had helped agriculture combine with industry to keep America a democracy while other nations were turning to dictatorships.

Wallace's campaign then moved into Illinois, Missouri, and Kansas. Jones and another speech writer, Clifford Gregory, former editor of the *Prairie Farmer*, went along. Jones served chiefly as a cheerleader for Wallace, but occasionally he suggested solutions to serious problems confronting the nation. At Galesburg, Illinois, he recommended conscription of industry as well as agriculture in any war effort—an idea he had supported from the beginning of his congressional career.

Behind the scenes Jones called in his many political debts. He had made as many contacts as the nonpolitical Wallace had missed. Following the Illinois swing, during the first week in September, Jones returned to Washington. The new House speaker, Sam Ray-

---

[29] Paul Appleby to Jones, August 8, 1940, MJP.
[30] William B. Bankhead to Henry A. Wallace, August 21, 1940, MJP.

burn, had asked him to participate in congressional consultations, report to Roosevelt on the progress of the campaign, and help draw up a list of congressmen for speaking engagements in the Middle West.[31]

During the ensuing weeks Jones sandwiched campaign activities between congressional duties.[32] Most of Jones's campaign speeches focused on benefits of the farm program and praise of Roosevelt and Wallace as guardians of national defense. In October, to a nationwide radio audience, Jones mentioned that "a good beefsteak is an important element in national defense," emphasizing agriculture's role in American security. "When famine and want begin to stalk across the battlefield," he said, "the skeleton of defeat leers at the captain of that army." The campaign produced a Democratic harvest. Wallace acknowledged Jones's skillful assistance not only as a campaigner but also as a political mentor.[33] For his part Jones looked forward to the serenity of the court of claims.

Throughout his congressional career Jones had, of course, campaigned for agriculture, and during the closing months of his last term in Congress he gave two important speeches. The first, on July 1, 1940, entitled "The Land—Our Ultimate Security," contained political overtones, as he reviewed New Deal accomplishments and emphasized "land" in a powerful statement of his agrarian philosophy (that philosophy will be analyzed in chapter 16).[34] The second speech came on November 18, on the eve of his resignation, when he delivered with humor and a touch of sadness a speech he called

---

[31] Jones recommended to Lucas that effective speakers would include Ewing Thomason, Lyndon Johnson, Albert Gore, Wall Doxey, Fritz Lanham, Harold Cooley, Stephen Pace, Robert Ramspeck, and John Sparkman. He also recommended fifteen minute political broadcasts over radio. Democratic National Committee, press release, August 29, 1940, MJP; unidentified clipping, scrapbook 10, Jones to Franklin D. Roosevelt, September 14, 1940, Jones to Scott W. Lucas, September 10, 1940, MJP.

[32] Rayburn's rise to the speakership corresponded with his gentlemen's agreement with his friend Jones. By this time Jones was destined for the court of claims; if Jones could have become Speaker, he might have remained in Congress.

[33] Unidentified clipping, scrapbook 10, Jack Houston to Jones, November 7, 1940, H. A. Wallace to Jones, November 8, 1940, MJP.

[34] Jones, "The Remarks of Marvin Jones," *Congressional Record* Scrapbook, vol. 5 (76th Cong., 2d sess.), 1940, pp. 9132-37.

"Sidelights on Congress."[35] There he reviewed his twenty-four-year service to the people of the United States and preached a political sermon. The one-time Methodist Sunday-school teacher remained a moralist with a deep faith in his country. He warned congressmen never to let bitterness enter political issues to destroy personal friendships. He appealed for strong character: "The supreme test of any man's courage in a legislative way comes when he is required to show courage and yet be under the imputation of lacking in courage." He commented that

when a representative is industrious and has something to say and will say it truthfully, no more generous audience [than the House] can be found anywhere. On the other hand, if he is not informed, if he talks when he has only half-baked information, if he undertakes to deceive the House, the House can be merciless, even almost cruel.

He spoke of the necessity for compromise. Seldom did men win approval for and vote for legislation that exactly reflected their thinking and desires. Compromise was the essence of democracy. He warned that "a people's government cannot survive unless its citizens are willing to take an interest in its affairs.[36]

When he finished speaking, fellow congressmen rose to their feet and applauded him vigorously. Many of them paid tribute to him. Clifford Hope, ranking Republican on the Agriculture Committee, spoke first. He said that under Jones's leadership a huge amount of agricultural legislation had been passed—largely because Jones possessed the rare art of getting people to work for and with him. Jones had exercised his own independent convictions, Hope said, and had given strength and confidence to his colleagues.

August Andresen, who had frequently opposed Jones, praised his efforts. The volatile Georgian Edward Cox confessed that he always got a moral cleansing from Jones. Fulmer called him a student of the Bible and a great parliamentarian (an accurate statement, according to House Parliamentarian Lewis Deschler). Wall Doxey, John McCormack, and the Texas delegation joined in the praise. Kansas Republican U. S. Guyer lamented the loss of his old golf partner. The conservative Republican Hamilton Fish, perhaps wel-

---

[35] Ibid., pp. 13631–33.
[36] Ibid.

coming the retirement of the powerful New Dealer, was lavish in praise. He observed that "for twenty years I have served with Marvin Jones, and as a member of the minority, I am glad to testify that in all these years there has never been a finer nor an abler member of this House than he."[37] Like funeral eulogies, farewell orations contain some substance, some qualities dimly seen, and some traits conveniently overlooked. Retiring from Congress was a shrewd, determined, quietly ambitious legislator who mixed a good sense of humor with moralism and agrarian romanticism.

Where did Marvin Jones stand against the backdrop of his contemporaries? Clearly he was the dominant agricultural specialist in the House and one of the most respected agriculturalists in Congress.[38] Because of Jones's prestige, knowledge, and ability Roosevelt knew that his support was vital to the passage of New Deal legislation. Jones's idea of service, an extremely important personality trait, sometimes resulted in his support of New Deal legislation without any profound conviction about its worth and kept him from taking strong stands against some legislation that he did not really approve.

As a member of the Texas delegation Jones maintained a left-of-center position. One could not label him a liberal Texan in the tradition of Maury Maverick, nor did his beliefs align him with conservatives like Kleberg. His dearest friend, Sam Rayburn, had closer ties to the New Deal, and within this progressive center Ewing Thomason stood at Jones's left. Like many other Texas congressmen Jones supported the New Deal because it had been proposed by a Democratic administration that had successfully provided procedures and solutions.

In this regard, during the New Deal's early years Jones displayed little social consciousness but devoted his major efforts to economic stability and farm prosperity. This emphasis continued

---

[37] Ibid., pp. 13633–38.
[38] See George B. Tindall, *The Emergence of the New South, 1913–1945*, vol. 10 of *A History of the South*, ed. Wendell H. Stephenson and E. Merton Coulter, pp. 391–432; Gary Dunn, "The West Texas Delegation and the New Deal: 1937," MS, Southwest Collection, Texas Tech University, Lubbock, Texas; Lionel V. Patenaude, "The Texas Congressional Delegation," *Texana* 11 (Winter 1971):3–16; Irvin M. May, Jr., "Marvin Jones: Agrarian and Politician," *Agricultural History* 51 (April 1977):421–440.

throughout his congressional career; yet, to his credit, the scope of his social consciousness increased over the years. He shared southern support of domestic allotment, and he displayed the streak of liberalism that most southern representatives showed in their support of government aid. Like his contemporaries from the Great Plains states, he advocated soil conservation and the need for tariff equality. Although his district lay in the Great Plains, it contained southern as well as western influences. His interest in farm finance cut across sectional lines and enabled him to rise above the pressure of commodity interests.

Finally, Marvin Jones the agrarian advocate manifested the depression back-to-the-land movement and the Jeffersonian image of rural independence. How would Marvin Jones the federal judge modify and apply these concepts?

12.

Transition Time

WHEN Marvin Jones succeeded the deceased Thomas S. Williams as a judge of the United States Court of Claims, he attained a long-term goal. The court was a creation of Congress. It was established in 1855 as an advisory council to determine the legitimacy of lawsuits filed by Americans against the federal government. The court had appellate-level rank, but it also had certain original jurisdiction through a trial court of commissioners. Only the United States Supreme Court could overrule appeals of the court's decisions.

In the years since its founding, the court's jurisdiction had gradually been expanded to include eleven categories of cases, but it had second-class status among federal circuit courts of appeal. When Jones was appointed to the court, it was concentrating on claims against the government involving taxes, contracts, civilian pay, military-service pay, patents, and transportation.[1]

In the winter of 1940, Jones moved into the Court of Claims Building at Pennsylvania Avenue and Seventeenth Street. The aging structure had been occupied originally by the Corcoran Art Gallery, and it was more appropriate to house art than the law. Clerks and secretaries were squeezed in among the judges. Storage space overflowed with paper and books. The building was a serious fire hazard —about which the Washington Fire Department was well aware. The structure was deteriorating: passersby were sometimes struck by pieces of crumbling mortar and debris. Inside, the high ceilings

---

[1] The best published summary of the court of claims is United States Court of Claims, *A Symposium: The United States Court of Claims*. The symposium articles originally appeared in *Georgetown Law Journal* 55 (December 1966 and March 1967).

and handsome architectural design did little to ease the discomfort.[2]

Chief Judge Richard Whaley, a sixty-six-year-old South Carolinian, presided. He was a large, balding man with wispy white hair; gold-rimmed spectacles, without earpieces, resting serenely on a large, pointed nose; and an impish smile. Whaley overshadowed Jones in size as well as judicial experience.

Jones's hair was now touched with gray and had begun to recede, but his high-arched eyebrows retained their darker shade. His boyish face, though still pleasant, had become rather jowly, but his lips remained firmly set, and his eyes were still piercing.

The docket of seventeen hundred cases severely taxed the five-man court. At a frantic pace to reduce the load, Whaley's judges heard more than forty cases a month, retiring to their chambers to make decisions. Whaley assigned opinion writing to associate judges, who did the work with the help of law clerks.

During Jones's first two years he established discernible trends in his evolving legal philosophy. His cornerstone was a reliance on congressional intent; he gave legal precedents lower priority. He avoided judicial activism, observing: "We have no right to pass on the wisdom of legislation. Our duty is simply to construe its practical effect, giving meaning to the language used and finding the intention of the Congress as disclosed by the language which it used in the special act."[3]

Jones established himself as a practical judge. He relied on his clerks to supply legal precedents for his views, preferring to analyze their summary notes rather than engage in deep research. Jones then took the legal precedents and wrote his opinions in layman's language.[4]

[2] "Report of the Architect of the Capitol on Companion Bills S. 3445 and H.R. 9873, 84th Congress, Providing for the Construction, Equipment and Furnishing of a Building for the United States Court of Claims and Their Purposes, March, 1956," MS, undated clippings, scrapbook 10, Marvin Jones Papers, hereafter cited as MJP.

[3] In the course of research it was necessary to read all of Jones's opinions. For a sampling see Marvin Jones, *Should Uncle Sam Pay—When and Why? Selected Opinions of Marvin Jones; Christopher S. Long* v. *United States*, 83 Ct. Cl. 544 (1941).

[4] *Phillips Pipe Line Corp.* v. *United States*, 94 Ct. Cl. 462 (1941); *B. R. Brucklin* v. *United States*, 96 Ct. Cl. 457 (1942); *J. H. Crain and R. E. Lee Wilson, Jr., Trustees of Lee Wilson and Company, and Business Trust* v.

Transition Time

In that early period Jones maintained his agricultural connections. He returned to Capitol Hill for visits with friends and meetings of the Texas delegation. Two of his major concerns remained soil conservation and expansion of the Surplus Marketing Administration relief program. He was still seeking administration approval of his agricultural goals.[5]

On December 7, 1941, however, his thought and those of virtually every other American turned to war. When the Japanese attacked Pearl Harbor, the United States became an active participant in World War II. That involvement would have an effect on Jones's career.

In October, 1942, James F. Byrnes acceded to a request from Roosevelt and resigned from the Supreme Court to take over the Office of Economic Stabilization, created in October and November of that year to formulate programs and resolve disputes among agencies whose actions affected economic stabilization. Its primary goal was to stabilize the cost of living during the war. To that end the OES was empowered to develop a comprehensive national policy controlling prices, wages, subsidies, and profits and to oversee rationing. Departments and agencies like the Department of Agriculture and the War Labor Board retained their responsibilities, but they were subject to policies determined by the OES.

United States, 96 Ct. Cl. 443 (1942); *Nolan Brothers, Incorporated* v. *United States*, 98 Ct. Cl. 41 (1942). It may be asked why Jones did not accept more Indian cases. It seems logical that a southwestern judge would manifest more concern. A number of reasons can be suggested: (1) Indian cases were highly detailed and historically complex affairs; certainly for an inexperienced jurist they were unattractive assignments; (2) there were more experienced judges to handle such cases; (3) Jones had a preference for contract cases and those where recent congressional intent held interest; (4) since he was from the Southwest with a frontier heritage, he may have believed that others would approach these problems with less bias and more justice. I believe that the last reason was the primary one.

[5] Marvin Jones to Franklin D. Roosevelt, January 13, 1941, Roosevelt to Jones, January 31, 1941, Jones to Dillon Myer, administrator, Agricultural Conservation and Adjustment Administration, April 29, 1942, MJP; Jones, interview with Dean Albertson, Columbia Oral History Project, 1952, pp. 1140–42, hereafter cited as COHP-MJP. Unless otherwise noted, interviews and correspondence citing Jones refer to Marvin Jones.

Acting as advisers to the OES were the Economic Stabilization Board, made up of the secretaries of the Departments of Labor, Commerce, Agriculture, and Treasury; the head of the Office of Price Administration; the chairman of the War Labor Board; the director of the budget; the chairman of the Board of Governors of the Federal Reserve System; and two members each representing agriculture, business, and labor, who were appointed by the president.

Byrnes became the nation's unofficial president for domestic affairs. Under his leadership responsibilities were broadly delegated. In the area of supply and distribution, for example, food differences between the Office of Price Administration and the secretary of agriculture were referred to the War Production Board. The OES itself adjudicated issues involving the price of agricultural commodities. The OES did not have the power to create food programs, and, with the division of responsibility on price policies between the OPA and USDA, the OES preferred to enter the picture only when issues had been clearly defined or when it became apparent that there was a good chance of arbitration. That procedure was in keeping with the training of the judges and lawyers in the OES, who saw themselves in a courtlike situation.

As shortages developed, rumors circulated in Washington that Roosevelt would create a war food administration similar to the one set up in World War I, independent of the Department of Agriculture. From late September into December top-level discussions were held on the creation of such an agency. Donald M. Nelson, chairman of the War Production Board, wanted to control the War Food Administration as well, but Secretary of Agriculture Claude Wickard, who also wanted control, opposed Nelson's plans. Also favoring food-management control by the secretary of agriculture were the American Federation of Labor, the National Farmers' Union, and former President Herbert Hoover, who had had experience in such management in World War I.

The decision fell to James Byrnes. He sought advice from his one-time congressional colleague Marvin Jones and even hinted that Jones should leave the court and head the new office. Jones was pleased but declined. The security of the court position appealed to him. Jones advised Byrnes to create the War Food Administration under USDA control. He further recommended that veteran AAA administrator Chester Davis head the program.⁶

On the night of December 3, 1942, Jones and Byrnes met again in Byrnes's Shoreham Hotel apartment. As they dined, Byrnes told his guest that the president had signed an executive order establishing the War Food Administration and that Roosevelt wanted Jones as administrator. Byrnes assured Jones that an executive order would permit him direct communication with the president and independence from Wickard. Jones would direct food production and distribution, and the secretary would supervise related USDA programs. Should Jones need to control those programs as well, Byrnes said, Roosevelt would shift them to the War Food Administration.

Jones declined to follow Byrnes's example and resign from the judiciary, but he did not rule out a temporary administrative assignment. If Roosevelt insisted, he said, he would take a temporary leave of absence with the provision that his salary would be paid by the court rather than by the executive.

Byrnes then attempted to gain Jones's approval of a move to get rid of Wickard. "The President will appoint you Secretary of Agriculture if you will accept it," he said.

"I don't want to be Secretary of Agriculture," Jones replied, "but I think it [the WFA] ought to be under one head so that there will be no possibility of friction."⁷

Disappointed at Jones's response, Byrnes promised to talk with Roosevelt the following morning and to report Jones's recommendation that Wickard have complete control of the new office. The next morning, however, Byrnes did not call the president immediately. He waited until 11:45 A.M. and called Jones to see whether a night's

---

⁶ James F. Byrnes, memorandum to Roosevelt, November 2, 1942, Byrnes to Jones, October 19, 1942, and enclosure of Claude Wickard to Donald M. Nelson, October 19, 1942, James F. Byrnes Papers, Clemson University, Clemson, S.C.; Dean Albertson, *Roosevelt's Farmer: Claude R. Wickard in the New Deal*, pp. 310–322; Gladys L. Baker, Wayne D. Rasmussen, Vivian Wiser, and Jane M. Porter, *Century of Service: The First 100 Years of the United States Department of Agriculture*, p. 295.

⁷ COHP-MJP, pp. 1144–46; for a slightly different version with a similar thesis see Albertson, *Roosevelt's Farmer*, pp. 329–330.

sleep had changed his mind and, if not, to inquire about changes Jones would require before going into the administrative job.

Jones told him:

If a man like Chester Davis were in charge of that piece of machinery, I would be perfectly happy to go over and do any kind of a job that might have some promise of being helpful, but that is not the picture. The other man is there, and I feel even more strongly that if I were to go over under this other man—Claude Wickard—that I would run into difficulties that might embarrass both the president and you, and the Lord knows you have enough trouble as it is.

Jones urged Byrnes to tell the President where he stood. "If that is fully placed before the President," Jones said, "and he understands it and he still wants to draft me, I am willing to take a leave of absence for the duration—the court is willing to give it—and come over and do the best I can."[8]

Byrnes promptly relayed Jones's message to Roosevelt, and that afternoon he told Jones of the president's response. On the following day Roosevelt issued Executive Order 9280 giving the secretary of agriculture full responsibility for the country's food program as Jones had advised. It was the second major Department of Agriculture reorganization of the war period. Specifically, it gave power to the secretary to publish policies affecting food purchases and procurement by federal agencies; to determine civilian, military, domestic, and foreign food requirements; to formulate policies to meet those needs; to make allocations and assign food priorities; and to control food distribution to the various channels. Wartime food strategy had already been established for the War Food Administration. The Office of Economic Stabilization, headed by Byrnes, would mediate disputes between the Department of Agriculture and other agencies, and within the USDA the new Food Production Administration and Food Distribution Administration would eventually implement the president's order.[9]

As 1943 dawned, a somber picture was drawn by farm experts. American agriculture faced lower production at a time of greater consumer demand. Widespread hunger could be prevented, but

[8] Telephone conversation between Jones and Byrnes, December 4, 1942, MS, MJP.
[9] W. M. Kiplinger, *Kiplinger Agricultural Letter*, letter no. 368, January 2, 1943; U.S. Bureau of the Budget, *The United States at War*, p. 324.

officials anticipated serious shortages of farm labor, machinery, and fertilizer. Price subsidies too would be down.

Early in the year Byrnes addressed a luncheon meeting of the Texas delegation and afterwards offered Jones a ride from the Hill toward the White House. As Byrnes's automobile maneuvered through the heavy traffic on Pennsylvania Avenue, the South Carolinian offered Jones a position as his personal assistant. When Jones stepped out of the car, Byrnes asked him to come to his office the next day to talk about it.

Jones knew that working with Byrnes would be more agreeable than working with Wickard alone. Jones and Byrnes shared mutual respect and friendship, and they had a common bond in the legislative work that had created the Farm Credit Association.

In mid-January, Jones secured Whaley's consent to a leave of absence, completed his court assignments and decisions, and moved into Byrnes's office as agricultural adviser. Jones heard complaints about price controls and black-market operations. Packers claimed continually that illegal slaughter of livestock prevented them from purchasing the animals and selling profitably at ceiling prices. On the other hand, OES, WFA, OPA, and USDA officials heard ranchers charge that low prices prevented them from receiving equitable returns. They also complained about scarcities of machinery, fertilizer, and livestock feed.

Jones got at the truth through Grover Hill, from whom he learned that Wickard's USDA was plagued by internal dissention over policies, regulations, and personalities. All of this interfered with maintaining producer-processor interests, and many of the problems finally arrived at the OES for Jones's adjudication.

Wickard, lacking congressional experience and close connections there, faced a Congress that was in a nasty mood. Legislators were beseiged with complaints about scarcities of beans and potatoes and demands for more food. Many farm representatives opposed the administration's proposals to stimulate production through subsidies. They feared that lower prices would result eventually in agricultural legislation based on a policy of creating a scarcity of food to achieve higher prices for farm products and provide farmers with parity.

With this producer-consumer conflict constantly worsening,

Jones's prestige rose. USDA officials and other Washington observers respected his insight. His congressional record demonstrated that he favored production. He maintained that the cause of agricultural problems lay not in excessive production but in distribution. The change of times and opinions enhanced the importance of Jones's long-held ideas.[10]

Naturally, then, Jones supported Wallace, Davis, and Wickard in advocating increased production. They sought to convince farmers that it was their patriotic duty to increase output. To preserve farm prosperity and stimulate wartime production, Jones wanted the USDA to use section 32 funds that were earmarked for promoting increased consumption. But a rebellious Congress proved hostile to that proposal.

Jones and others suggested that Wickard announce an increased-production policy and then request congressional consent. Jones further advised Wickard to substitute the term "incentive payments" for "subsidies" when he talked to congressmen about farm moneys. Wickard followed the advice.

The secretary of agriculture received the expected hostile reception when he appeared before the House Committee on Appropriations. Chairman Clarence Cannon remarked that the administration had been showing a lack of respect for congressional authority from the beginning of the war. Cannon told Wickard to design policies to benefit the consumer at the producer's expense. Why? Because such policies would prevent increased prices for food and agricultural goods and necessitate achieving parity with congressional appropriations rather than with artificial supports in the marketplace. The "incentive" appropriation failed.[11]

Stymied in Congress, Jones turned to a public-relations campaign to gain support for Wickard's policies. In speeches and question-and-answer sessions he suggested that the secretary of agriculture form a land army, under the principle that food was an important weapon in the arsenal of democracy. Draft deferments

---

[10] COHP-MJP, pp. 1154–59, 1368; Albertson, *Roosevelt's Farmer*, 361–362; William Kiplinger, *Kiplinger Washington Letter*, January 16, 1943; Kiplinger, *Kiplinger Agricultural Letter*, letter no. 370, January 30, 1943.

[11] Albertson, *Roosevelt's Farmer*, pp. 358–361; Walter W. Wilcox, *The Farmer in the Second World War*, pp. 132–134.

would be granted to assure manpower to plant and harvest crops. Jones went on to praise congressional efforts to extend agricultural credit and assured farmers that allocations of farm machinery and supplies would meet demands. He pledged above all that the administration would not steal the farmer's pocketbook. Roosevelt supported the farmer's right to a fair profit, Jones said. To ensure that profit, Jones continued to urge incentive payments to American farmers to encourage them to produce enough staples not only for home consumption but also to help feed the Allies. Jones added that these payments should stop immediately after the end of the war. By these means, he suggested, the government might avoid extensive rationing.[12]

Jones's responsibilities grew as the OES assumed a greater role in initiating farm policies. Jones received and digested daily reports concerning food production, soil-conservation efforts, and fertilizer needs. To farmers and ranchers he explained government policies in simple, direct language, avoiding the vaguely worded instructions set forth by many bureaucrats. On Capitol Hill, Jones served as Byrnes's liaison. He listened as congressmen relayed the desires of their constituents. Many complained about Secretary Wickard's procedures, and Jones reported all of this to Byrnes. Eventually Byrnes called Wickard to his office to explain why ceiling prices should not be placed on live hogs. Byrnes was not satisfied with the answer. Three days later, on March 11, 1943, Wickard returned to explain problems of farm labor.[13] Under the strain Wickard buckled. Byrnes had never held the secretary in high regard; now he declared that Wickard's usefulness as war food administrator had ended.

During the same month Byrnes, Jones, and Roosevelt discussed yet another reorganization of the USDA. Byrnes favored reestablishing a separate war food administrator. Again Jones argued that Wickard was the best man for the job. Byrnes replied, "Well, we feel that a separate administrator should be put in," implying that he and Roosevelt had already decided the issue.

[12] "Judge Marvin Jones on WSB," February 22, 1943, MS, MJP.
[13] H. A. Bennett to Jones, March 8, 1943, MJP; Albertson, *Roosevelt's Farmer*, pp. 368–369; Marvin Jones, *Marvin Jones Memoirs*, ed. Joseph M. Ray, pp. 148–150; Jones, interview with Jerry Hess, 1970, pp. 68–70, Harry S. Truman Library, Independence, Mo.

On the morning of March 18, Jones went to his office and heard from Byrnes: "We're going to get a new war food administrator, and we will probably make a decision at the meeting of the Mobilization Committee today. I am confident that they will select you, and I felt I should warn you in advance."

Later that day James Byrnes, Frank Knox, Henry Stimson, and Harry Hopkins met to discuss the matter. After a few minutes they asked Jones to join them. Jones immediately began trying to forestall being named war food administrator. "Well, I have a man in mind who is the best man in the United States for that position," he told the committee in his most charming manner. He began extolling Chester Davis' achievements. His portrait of Davis proved to be so thorough and persuasive that the committee forgot about Jones and chose Davis.

All of this angered Jimmy Byrnes. Soon afterward he barged into Jones's office and yelled, "You're the damnedest fellow I ever saw! They called you in there to tell you that you had been selected as war food administrator!" Jones replied only that Davis had the best credentials if Wickard's removal was absolutely necessary.[14]

Later that day Byrnes conveyed to Roosevelt Jones's opinion: "Marvin Jones knows the Department intimately. He says that the Agriculture Committee regarded Davis as the ablest representative the Department has had. Because he [Jones] knows the man and the Department, I would take his judgment."[15]

Roosevelt followed the advice. On March 26 by executive order he created the War Food Administration as an independent government agency, with Davis as its head.[16]

Why did Jones decline the offer? For one thing, he feared accepting a grief-laden job that was also a man killer. The position involved too much politics, and, though Jones was a veteran politician, he doubted his ability to succeed. By 1943 he observed that two different approaches to increased production had evolved. One idea, favored by many congressmen, called for establishing prices of agricultural commodities at a level that would ensure production.

[14] COHP-MJP, pp. 1159–63.
[15] James F. Byrnes, "Memorandum for the President, March 18, 1943," MS, Byrnes Papers.
[16] Executive Order 9322, March 26, 1943, Byrnes Papers.

Jones sympathized with this view. Administration officials, on the other hand, advocated freezing agricultural prices and using subsidies to increase production. Unwilling to risk confrontation with Congress over this issue, he declined the WFA post and remained as Byrnes's assistant.[17]

Jones did not leave Davis on a limb, however. He knew from firsthand experience the perils of federal bureaucracy, and he warned Davis, who was then president of the St. Louis Federal Reserve Bank, not to resign his position but to take a leave of absence. Then he added a pat on the back: "I believe you can handle it all right, but you are going to have a great deal of grief."

"I know it," replied Davis, who already doubted that Roosevelt had given him sufficient power. Nevertheless, his concept of duty compelled him to accept the position.[18]

On April 8, 1943, Roosevelt issued a hold-the-line order that included price reductions financed by subsidies. This meant that the federal government would pay farmers the difference between the lower price and the one that had existed earlier. The president thus hoped to control mounting inflation; from October 1942 to April 1943 the cost of living index had risen 4.3 percent. Roosevelt had consulted neither Jones nor Davis before issuing the order. Byrnes had prepared the first draft. He explained it to his two assistants and stated his reluctance to permit any modifications.

This procedure irritated both Jones and Davis. Jones proposed exceptions to the order, including farm prices. Byrnes refused to listen to any arguments. Tempers flared. Davis shouted, "If this is going to stand the way it is, I might as well go home."[19] At that point Byrnes consented to minor changes. Jones and Davis realized that they had lost and turned their attention to other matters.

One was a study of the nutritional needs of the Allies. From the beginning of the war the United States Department of Agriculture and the National Research Council had discussed this problem, as had the British Food Mission and the Combined Food Board. In 1943 the Department of State decided to expand the talks through an international conference that would include all Allied

[17] COHP-MJP, pp. 1164–67.
[18] Ibid.
[19] Ibid., pp. 1178–79; James F. Byrnes, *Speaking Frankly*, p. 19.

nations. On March 31, 1943, President Roosevelt issued invitations to the first United Nations Conference on Food and Agriculture. The meeting was to take place at Hot Springs, in western Virginia, from May 18 to June 3.

The proposed agenda included (1) plans for postwar production, imports, and exports of food and other agricultural products, (2) plans for improving nutrition and worldwide food consumption, (3) discussion of possible international agreements and agencies to ensure efficient food production and simultaneously guarantee producers a fair return, and (4) discussion of commercial agreements that would enable countries to maintain adequate markets for their own surpluses.[20]

In mid-April, Jones learned that he would head the United States delegation. At Roosevelt's insistence Jones also became president of the conference.

He seemed an unlikely choice for the role of international diplomat. An unimposing five-foot-nine-inch, 165-pound Texan whose quiet hobbies included fishing, playing bridge, watching western movies, reading biographies, and singing religious hymns like "When They Ring the Golden Bells," he did indeed have his shortcomings in foreign affairs. Roosevelt knew about them, however, and made sure that behind Jones were some experienced authorities: Josephine Schain, Paul Appleby, W. L. Clayton, Thomas Parran, and Murray Lincoln.[21] Moreover, the United States was the major supplier of food for the Allies during the war, and Jones's support of increased production coincided with the Allies' needs. Equally important, Roosevelt wanted the meetings held in secrecy; hence he chose isolated Hot Springs for the site and counted on the tight-lipped, publicity-shy Jones to be discreet. The president wanted a politician who knew how to be quiet in front of the press.

---

[20] G. Baker et al., *Century of Service*, pp. 325–326; American Freedom from Hunger Foundation, *World Food Congress: United Nations, Yearbook of the United Nations, 1946–1947*.

[21] Technical advisers included Emilio G. Collado, Paul C. Daniels, R. M. Evans, George S. Haas, W. H. Sebrell, Louise Stanley, H. R. Tolley, Leslie A. Wheeler, Leroy D. Stinebower, Theodore Achilles, Walter Brown, Allen Bonnell, Phillip Green, Gove Hambridge, Julius Wendzel, and Clarke Willard; unidentified clippings, scrapbook 10, MJP. See COHP-MJP, pp. 1230–31, for Jones's reaction to bureaucratic reorganization.

When Jones learned of the new assignment, he hurried to Byrnes and asked him whether it meant a demotion. Byrnes replied, "It will last only about three weeks, and I want you back here as soon as the conference is over. I want you to continue here just as you are, but this conference job has to be done."[22]

These assurances failed to quiet Jones's anxieties, but he had little choice. Then, unexpectedly, an uncharacteristic desire for publicity began to show itself. Now Jones was predicting that banning the press from the conference, as the president had planned to do, would cause widespread criticism. Jones's apparent desire to enter the limelight irked Roosevelt. He told Jones, "There is not any reason why in the morning newspapermen should sit and watch me shave and watch me do various things,"[23] implying that Jones, too, should avoid publicity. Responsibility for the delegates' safety and a consideration for national security had necessitated the ban, Roosevelt said. Eventually, however, he relented and allowed newsmen to establish headquarters in a nearby building and interview delegates at the end of each day's work.[24] Jones still favored holding the conference in the same manner as an open session of Congress, where House members debated issues on the floor rather than in closed executive sessions. But Roosevelt was known as "the Boss" for good reason.

Fortunately for Jones, the State Department handled the preliminary work of the conference. Warren Kelchner, chief of the Division of International Conferences, supervised administrative details. The department prepared a statement of general goals. Jones sent the list to American farm leaders and educators for suggestions. Replies were mostly favorable, and organization proceeded smoothly.[25]

On the eve of the conference Roosevelt wrote Jones:

The broad objectives for which we work have been started in the Atlantic Charter, the Declaration of the United Nations, and at the meeting

[22] COHP-MJP, pp. 1180–81.
[23] Ibid.
[24] Ibid.
[25] Cordell Hull to Jones, April 20, 1943, W. L. Clayton to Jones, May 3, 1943, H. R. Tolley to Jones, May 3, 1943, E. G. Nourse to Jones, May 7, 1943, John D. Black to Jones, May 8, 1943, E. J. Kyle to Jones, May 12, 1943, MJP.

of the twenty-one American republics at Rio de Janeiro in January, 1942. It is the purpose of this conference to consider how best to further these policies in so far as they concern the consumption, production and distribution of food and other agricultural products in the postwar period.[26]

Jones conveyed Roosevelt's "Four Freedoms" theme in his initial speech to the delegates. "It is indeed fitting that the first of these world conferences should deal with food," he said, "because freedom means little to people with empty stomachs." Then he expanded his agrarian philosophy from a domestic one to one of worldwide scope: "The world starts with food. Life cannot be sustained without it."[27] Taken together, Jones's opening comments presented a statement of consensus upon which all delegates could build programs. Many participants, however, considered them just so much verbiage.

More criticism came after Jones's next act. He departed from traditional diplomatic formality and asked the respective delegates to stand, with the hope of thus encouraging a spirit of cordiality among the nations. Some newsmen and State Department officials deplored the act as uncouth.[28]

In the weeks that followed, Jones presided over the conference, chaired the general committee (consisting of one member from each delegation), and attempted to create a permanent organization to continue the work of the committee. He listened as delegates from Western Europe called for more shipments of American food, but he left technical details of policy to Paul Appleby, who soon also assumed the role of acting chairman of the United States delegation, leaving Jones to preside over the conference.

Jones's prediction about criticism in the press proved valid. Bitter cartoons deplored the secrecy of the meetings. The *Washington Star* commented:

> If it is true that the representatives of the nations will discuss only the question of feeding the starved or half-starved countries, there can be no reason whatever for not permitting the reporters to have free access to the meetings and telling the people of the United States why the

---

[26] Roosevelt to Jones, May 14, 1943, MJP.
[27] Unidentified clippings, scrapbook 14, MJP.
[28] Ibid.

present effort and rationing should be continued, if necessary, for some time after the war is over.[29]

On the other hand, said the same writer, if the food problems "are only a blind and a screen to cover discussions of other political matters," freedom of the press was being abused even more drastically.[30] Objections to secrecy also came from a number of congressmen, who feared that the proceedings might obligate the nation. Michigan Republicans Frederick Bradley and Homer Ferguson introduced a resolution that would make complete information available to Congress. The Democratic congressional leaders, however, promised that any United States commitments would get careful scrutiny by the House Appropriations Committee. This assurance quieted some of the dissent. Nevertheless, congressional criticism forced Jones to modify press restrictions during the very first week of the conference. Even after that, criticism continued, including a comment by Eleanor Roosevelt that Jones had exhibited amateurish leadership.

After the conference adjourned in June, Jones reported the results to the House Agriculture Committee and promised that an interim commission would study international aspects of increased production, soil-conservation efforts, freer exchange of commodities, and the development of industry to complement agriculture. He assured representatives that the United States had not signed and would not sign any giveaway agreements.[31] By convening the assemblage, the United States had restored the morale of the Allies without overextending commitments at a time when many Americans were grumbling about rationing and food shortages.

Jones discovered that, during his absence from Washington, Davis had fallen out of favor with Byrnes and Roosevelt. Davis, a

[29] Ibid.
[30] Ibid.
[31] Ibid.; Jones to Mrs. Franklin D. Roosevelt, June 12, 1943, Cecil R. King to Mrs. Halcyon R. Stone, May 25, 1943, E. K. Gaylord to Jones, June 9, 1943, MJP; Jones, *Marvin Jones Memoirs*, pp. 152–156; United Nations Conference on Food and Agriculture, *Final Act and Section Reports*; U.S., Congress, House, Committee on Agriculture, *United Nations Conference on Food and Agriculture: Hearings*, 78th Cong., 1st sess., June 22, 1943. It may be noted that Jones's recollections primarily concerned the Russian delegation. While other groups, like Britain and France, had closer ties to the United States, Jones was most interested in the Russians.

stubborn man, had repeatedly clashed with Byrnes over production and freeze orders—and Byrnes was not a man to be pushed. Moreover, changes had been made. In another reorganization Byrnes had become head of the Office of War Mobilization. Fred Vinson, who had resigned from the court of appeals, had taken over the Office of Economic Stabilization. Byrnes had considered Jones for the OES position, but he thought Jones would be biased for agriculture and against labor. When Jones returned to Washington on June 15, Byrnes told him that he could remain as his assistant in the OWM but that Vinson also wanted him to continue in the OES position. A few days later Vinson himself followed up by promising Jones a free hand in agricultural matters.

Jones declined the offer. He considered Vinson a friend, but he preferred to be near the power—Byrnes and Roosevelt. The OWM would be what amounted to an appellate court in agricultural matters, and as Byrnes's assistant Jones would have greater freedom of operations as well as more influence.

Soon after Jones's return to Washington, Roosevelt announced a general agricultural subsidy and freeze order. Jones favored equal treatment of agriculture and labor in regard to wartime controls, but he reluctantly concurred with the president's decision.

Chester Davis opposed the move outspokenly and, with the belief that authority to determine overall food policies should be vested in one central agency, submitted his resignation. Jones considered trying to squelch the conflict until tempers cooled, but Byrnes would not be denied his long-awaited chance to get rid of Davis. Byrnes suggested that Roosevelt accept Davis's resignation and offer the War Food Administration position either to Jones or to Milo Perkins.[32]

Meanwhile, Roosevelt had taken his own action. Before accepting Davis's resignation, he had telephoned Jones and demanded that he resign his position on the court of claims and assume full responsibility for the War Food Administration. Jones, fearing that Roosevelt wanted an opportunity to make a change in the court of

[32] Byrnes to Roosevelt June 19, 1943, Byrnes Papers; Byrnes to Roosevelt, July 25, 1943, Franklin D. Roosevelt Papers, Franklin D. Roosevelt Library, Hyde Park, N.Y.; U.S., Bureau of the Budget, *The United States at War*, p. 400.

claims, told the president that Rudolph ("Spike") Evans should be named to the job. If Evans refused, Jones said, the president should name either Grover Hill or Jay Taylor. Both men knew ranching and farming from firsthand experience. Jones then suggested that the WFA should have a representative on the War Mobilization Committee.

Roosevelt gave up on the telephone conversation and summoned Jones to the White House. When Jones arrived, he was ushered into the president's office. There he encountered Roosevelt, Byrnes, and Hopkins. The president again insisted that Jones accept "the draft," and he was in no mood to hear a negative answer. On the other hand, Jones was proving again to be a stubborn man who refused to be cowed.

Eventually Byrnes interceded with a compromise that would permit Jones to continue his leave of absence from the court of claims and still become a member of the War Mobilization Committee. Jones finally accepted the job with this stipulation: "I will take a leave of absence, which the court is willing to give me. If I can serve under these circumstances in wartime, I'll go over [to the WFA], but I'm not going into that milling herd without a horse."[33]

After the meeting Jones explained to Byrnes, "A man who goes over there and does that job right is going to irritate so many people that I doubt whether he could be confirmed to any official position after it is over."[34] Jones anticipated that he would last a year in the new job, but at least his future security had been assured. He was sworn in as war food administrator by Chief Justice Richard Whaley of the court of claims on June 29, 1943.

In Jones's initial statement as war food administrator he attempted to touch all bases and appeal for consensus. "In accepting the responsibilities of the office of War Food Administrator," he said, "I do so with the firm belief that nothing is more important to the war effort and our domestic economy than a sound and acceptable food production and distribution program." His emphasis was on increased production, naturally enough, rather than on distribution problems. He envisioned crises in the former because of shortages

[33] Jones, COHP-MJP, pp. 1272-73.
[34] Ibid.

of farm machinery repair parts, storage facilities, and farm labor. Furthermore, he said, increased production required more seed, fertilizer, and credit and an assurance to farmers of a fair profit for their labors. He predicted that rationing would be necessary to provide food for United States armed forces and civilians and the Allies. He concluded with high praise for Davis's service and urged his staff to remain.[35]

Jones's appointment was a manifestation of Roosevelt's craftiness. Congressmen had been considering some legislation of which the president disapproved, and the legislation would have given more powers to Davis, whom most congressmen liked. Pending at the very time Jones was assigned to his new job were bills making Davis a food czar with power to ration food and regulate food prices. Congressional sentiment for this move evaporated when Davis resigned.

As for Jones's appointment, congressional reaction ranged from high praise to caustic comment. Harold Cooley of North Carolina, August Andresen of Minnesota, and Eugene Worley, Dick Kleberg, and Ewing Thomason of Texas praised the appointment. A moderate position was taken by Georgia's Richard Russell, who said, "While I have every respect for the ability of Marvin Jones, we can ill afford to spare men of the character and caliber of Chester Davis in these times of emergency." At the negative extreme stood Republican Reid Murray of Wisconsin, from Jones's old committee, who remarked:

Regardless of many of the sins of the New Deal agricultural program, which Mr. Jones has been a party to, I hope he will not follow such a course during wartime. I do not even want to mention to him the fact that he has been one of the leaders of an agricultural program that gives 6,400 farmers in the great state of Texas a subsidy of $12,000,000 a year, which is more than the farmers in thirty-five other states obtain. I hope Mr. Jones can measure up to his responsibilities.[36]

Despite the occasional criticism Congress quickly confirmed Jones.

While farm organizations had wanted Jones to succeed Wickard,

---

[35] Office of War Information, press release, June 29, 1943, MJP.
[36] U.S., Congress, House, *Congressional Record*, 78th Cong., 1st sess., 1943, 89, pp. 6746–48.

Jones's close association with Roosevelt's policies had somewhat tarnished his luster. Nonetheless, James G. Patton, president of the Farmer's Union, praised Jones's appointment as a "promising omen for the working farmers of the country in this period of great crisis." Other farm leaders cautiously approved of Jones with expressions of support or suggestions for future policy as noted in the comments by Jones's long-term associates Ed O'Neal, Fred Brenckman of the Grange, and W. I. Myers. Ezra Taft Benson wrote: "American farmers and the nation are indebted to you for your years of selfless service and now look forward to further progress under your leadership as War Food Administrator." T. O. Walton, president of Texas A&M, told him: "You will probably recall that on November 11, 1942, I wrote you expressing the hope that if the responsibility of National Food Administrator were offered to you, you would accept it.... I believe you have a firmer grasp of the Nation's food problems than any man of my acquaintance."[37]

The *New York Times* disagreed. That newspaper observed in an editorial:

It is evident from the resignation yesterday of Chester C. Davis as War Food Administrator that the President was forced to choose between a good man and a poor policy, and that he chose the poor policy. Mr. Davis could not go along with the subsidy program which is the Administration's newest white rabbit. In Marvin Jones, the President has found a successor to Davis who will no doubt support his policies enthusiastically.[38]

Jones had anticipated the criticism. He had accepted the challenge, although reluctantly. Now a master agricultural politician headed the War Food Administration.

[37] *Washington Post*, June 30, 1943; Edward A. O'Neal to Jones, July 1, 1943, F. H. La Guardia to Jones, June 30, 1943, Fred Brenckman to Jones, July 1, 1943, Ezra T. Benson to Jones, July 2, 1943, T. O. Walton to Jones, June 30, 1943. National Archives, Record Group 16.
[38] *New York Times*, June 29, 1943.

13.

The War Food Administrator

Jones moved into his new post with typical caution. Many members of Davis's staff realized that eventually they would be replaced with individuals whose thinking was closer to Jones's, and they chose to take positions in other wartime agencies. The new WFA leaders included Jones as head, followed by Grover Hill, Wilson Cowen, and Ashley Sellers, in that order. Hill, Jones's long-term friend and political adviser, moved into Jones's private office, to the occasional irritation of visitors who wanted a private word with Jones. Hill's presence turned the office of the WFA administrator into a slice of Texas, with robust humor and slow drawl, and the atmosphere was not always appreciated by visitors.

It soon became apparent that Jones did not feel at home with administrative details. In his current style of decision making, he instinctively avoided bureaucratic channels, red tape, and committee meetings. Jones took great pride in his ability to select his advisers, in whom personal loyalty was more important than a long climb up the administrative ladder. That basis for selection also irked entrenched Washington civil servants and gave Jones a reputation of being a poor administrator.

After choosing the members of his inner circle, Jones gave them extensive powers within their respective areas.[1] Jones wanted them to use their initiative and not come to him asking how he wanted something done. Lower-level staff members had to please Cowen and Sellers, who had power to hire and fire.

During the first weeks new, subtle procedures began to emerge consistent with Jones's concept of weak, figurehead leadership. Each

---

[1] Murray Benedict, *Farm Policies of the United States, 1790–1950*, p. 427; Paul Porter, interview with author, June 15, 1973.

office day began with a brief staff meeting to discuss policy matters, especially those regarding food. Ideas were shared and reports given. Specific policy decisions usually were made outside these meetings, but Jones's aides could maintain their self-esteem through expression of opinions. Jones took immediate steps to remove the WFA from the spotlight by deemphasizing his role and his personality. He insisted that letters and press releases refer to "War Food Administrator" rather than to him by name. He did not want the program tied to fluctuations in his popularity.

Jones had to contend with conflict as soon as he took office. Congress was considering issues in regard to continuing the Commodity Credit Corporation and its price subsidies and rollbacks. Henry Steagall, chairman of the House Banking and Currency Committee, had introduced bills prohibiting use of federal funds for subsidies or rollbacks unless specifically approved by Congress.

Three days after Jones took over as war food administrator, a crisis arose when the president, without a word to Jones, defied Congress by vetoing a bill extending the life of the CCC. This action affected the WFA since Jack Hutson, WFA production head, also served as president of the Commodity Credit Corporation. Jones spoke out against further rollbacks. Treasury Secretary Henry Morgenthau joined him in advocating a temporary hold-the-line policy. Jones insisted that this policy must not become permanent, however, and he opposed setting so low a limit on staple crops as to discourage production.

Jones soon began feeling frustrated. He was operating without clear-cut directives from Roosevelt, as Davis had been forced to do. This meant that anyone who assumed War Food Administration leadership probably would be considered a weak executive.

Jones continued to adhere to his philosophy of less bureaucratic control. He sought to increase production by appeals to local and county officials. Unwilling to risk confrontation with the president, Jones proceeded on a very cautious course. He did a great deal of listening. He was still closely in tune with congressional desires and with those farm organizations opposed to subsidies, and he doubted that Congress would appropriate sufficient funds to ensure adequate agricultural production.

On Jones's desk at the time were Office of Price Administration ceilings awaiting the administrator's signature. They had been held over from the days of Chester Davis, and the OPA wanted prompt action. Jones delayed action on them until he could analyze issues involving specific commodities, maintaining that the government should not put ceilings on crop production at that time. OPA arguments that further delay would increase consumer prices and hurt the middleman failed to convince him. As always, his inclination was to support producers in producer-consumer conflicts. The OPA, on the other hand, responded to consumer demands.

The climax came in a meeting with Roosevelt, Byrnes, and OPA officials two weeks after Jones became war food administrator. The president said that, with food prices increasing, Jones should sign the ceilings promptly. Roosevelt wanted a rollback on the commodities. Jones countered with a proposal that the United States follow the Canadian policy of fixing prices for commodities and then making periodic adjustments. Later an increase in wages could be allowed to absorb the increased cost of living. Roosevelt replied that he was opposed to an increase in the cost-of-living index.

Jones refrained from splitting with Roosevelt, but later he sent Paul Porter and Jack Hutson to persuade Vinson to pay subsidies out of Reconstruction Finance Corporation funds. Eventually a compromise was reached in which both the RFC and the WFA paid for subsidies.

While the House Agriculture Committee began considering farm-production goals for 1944, the House Banking and Currency Committee deliberated the fate of the Commodity Credit Corporation and its lending authority. At the same time Jones planned to deflate the issue of prices versus subsidies through a publicity campaign calculated to increase agricultural production among American farmers by voluntary methods. If successful, the plan would provide the nation cheaper food by creating surpluses.

In his campaign Jones decided to emphasize the failure in 1943 to meet production goals of dairy products and to show that food needs would be even greater as the Allies moved into Europe. American farmers would be expected to produce most of the food for civilian populations, thus coming under Allied control. To make his appeal more effective, Jones requested specific information regarding immediate needs, but administration officials feared that baring this secret information would produce disturbing controversies and interfere with reaching overall objectives.[2]

Jones launched his campaign on August 9, 1943. It was appropriately called "Food Fights for Freedom." Helping publicize the effort were the Office of War Information, the Office of Price Administration, the Office of Civilian Defense, and the War Advertising Council. Americans were educated about the necessity of producing more food and yet conserving what they produced. The planting of victory gardens was urged on citizens who had facilities for growing their own food. Jones emphasized that, "in spite of our enormous production and in spite of our high level of consumption, there will continue to be short supplies of various foods at various times." To meet needs, he said, there "will be no restriction of food production. All-out production is needed."[3]

In September, Jones revealed to the House Agriculture Committee plans for food production in 1944. The WFA intended to mobilize food production through state and county agricultural war boards and to arrange for the use of prisoners of war and imported laborers from Mexico and Caribbean islands to alleviate the critical farm-labor shortage.

Jones told the committee that in 1942 civilians had consumed 86 percent of American food production but that he anticipated a drop to 75 percent during the next year. At the same time the WFA hoped for a record harvest (in 1940) of 380 million acres, with large increases in high-protein crops and vegetables. He predicted that the WFA would have to allocate feed to ensure a balanced production of livestock, dairy products, and poultry. He said that

[2] Marvin Jones, interview with Dean Albertson, Columbia Oral History Project, 1952, pp. 1281–82, 1298, hereafter cited as COHP-MJP; Marvin Jones, telephone conversation with Henry Morgenthau, Jr., July 7, 1943, Henry Morgenthau, Jr., Papers, Franklin D. Roosevelt Library, Hyde Park, N.Y. Jones was afraid that the conversation was being recorded and spoke reluctantly. During wartime that was not an unusual procedure. Jones to Franklin D. Roosevelt, August 9, 1943, Marvin Jones Papers, hereafter cited as MJP; John D. Goodloe to Jones, August 13, 1943, National Archives, Record Group 16. Unless otherwise noted, interviews and correspondence citing Jones refer to Marvin Jones.

[3] Morse Salisbury to War Food Administration employees, November 19, 1943, Jones to C. A. Dykstra, July 14, 1943, Vernon D. Beatty to Marvin Jones, December 8, 1943, National Archives, Record Group 16; Marvin Jones, *How Food Saved American Lives*, pp. 7–21.

Congress could help by increasing funds available to the Commodity Credit Corporation.

Jones then continued his support of CCC operations by appearing before the House Banking and Currency Committee and recommending that Congress give the CCC $500 million additional funds to fulfill guarantees of higher crop prices for 1944. After analyzing the agricultural scene, he concluded that

> the best way to get production is to have a definite support price that will last throughout the season. It should be high enough to cover the added risks and hazards that go with increased production. And it should be announced early. This means that the government should stand ready to buy any surplus of a commodity that might not flow into the regular channels at the time, and to absorb whatever loss may be necessary.

When Congress proposed to extend CCC operations with the reservation that use of funds would be for subsidies, Jones cautioned members that such a plan would jeopardize the entire stabilization process and reduce all support prices to current ceilings—with the disastrous result of hampering production.[4]

Jones carried his appeal beyond the halls of Congress. He spoke at agricultural conventions. To the National Grange he explained: "If there are no controls we shall have inflation. The stabilization lines have been drawn. Where to draw that line has been problematical, but we have done the best we can."[5] Jones's remarks converted few Grangers to the idea of subsidies, but he impressed them with his sincerity. He visited with other agricultural leaders and with congressmen seeking to persuade them at least to consider administration views before rejecting them.

Public-relations activities consumed most of Jones's time in 1943. He deflated an issue that threatened to wreck Roosevelt's anti-inflation and food programs. The *Farmer-Stockman* observed, "The facts are that Marvin Jones has poured oil on the water and has quieted and subdued the storm around the WFA which swept overboard his two predecessors."[6]

---

[4] Harold D. Smith to Jones, September 24, 1943, Jones to Henry B. Steagall, October 21, 1943, National Archives, Record Group 16.

[5] Unidentified clippings, scrapbook 12, MJP; Jones to James F. Byrnes, "Report: The 1943 Food Situation, September 10, 1943," National Archives, Record Group 16.

[6] Unidentified clipping, scrapbook 12, MJP.

Jones further placated Congress somewhat by obtaining the resignation of Farm Security Administration head C. B. ("Beanie") Baldwin, who had alienated legislators. When Congress threatened to eliminate FSA funding, Jones (who of course wanted the FSA continued) persuaded Baldwin to step out of the way.

Filling Baldwin's shoes proved difficult. Some persons urged the promotion of Roy W. Hudgens, acting FSA administrator. Jones disagreed. He had little respect for Hudgens, and he felt that the new chief should come from outside the agency.

Jones offered the position to former North Carolina congressman William Umstead (who later became United States senator and then governor of his state). Umstead declined. Jones then turned to Ralph McGill, editor of the *Atlanta Constitution*. That veteran editor also begged off, saying that he had lost key personnel to the war effort and could not leave the newspaper. Next Jones considered appointing the personable Joe C. Scott, president of the Oklahoma State Board of Agriculture, but Scott rebuffed his overture. Finally Jones gained the consent of Frank Hancock, a southern moderate and a former member of the House Banking and Currency Committee.[7]

When 1943 closed, the nation's output of food had risen 32 percent above the 1935–39 average and 5 percent above the record production of 1942. Farmers had received good prices; the parity index had increased from 157 to 188. During that year the WFA issued more than nine hundred orders affecting food distribution and developed price supports for thirty-nine farm products at a cost of $350 million.

Shortages of farm labor and equipment continued to plague farmers, however. Draft deferments helped in some areas, but it is worth noting that American farmers accomplished their 1943 production record with nearly four million fewer workers.

Jones's success as head of the WFA could be attributed to better use of agricultural methods by farmers, favorable weather,

[7] COHP-MJP, pp. 1312–17; James G. Patton to Jones, October 30, 1943, Jones to Patton, November 1, 1943, Ralph McGill to Jones, October 2, 1943, Joe C. Scott to Jones, October 26, 1943, National Archives, Record Group 16. For background on C. B. Baldwin's difficulties with Congress see Sidney Baldwin, *Poverty and Politics: The Rise and Decline of the Farm Security Administration*, pp. 365–396.

and pure luck. Walter Wilcox remarked: "A partial crop failure in 1943 or 1944 would have been a major calamity catching the War Food Administration entirely unprepared. The difficulties involved both faulty planning and faulty price incentives."[8]

Jones would have agreed about the elements in his success. He never pretended to be an accurate economic prognosticator nor was he a man for all seasons. The *Chicago Sun* observed:

[Jones] has done little toward originating new ideas, but he has made great strides in taking the kinks out of programs already in operation. ... [The] core of his policy from the beginning has been to cut regulations and regimentation to the bare minimum, find out what Congress and the farmers want before announcing any program, and stay off speaking forums and out of the press as much as possible.[9]

During the Christmas, 1943, holidays Jones vacationed in the Texas Panhandle. He listened to complaints, observed farmers and ranchers at work, and acted to alleviate some local problems. When he discovered that livestock feed was scarce, he ordered fifty extra carloads of high-protein supplement shipped to the area, saying: "Livestock people from Maine to Idaho are pleading for more protein feed. The livestock producers in the Panhandle and the Southwest may rest assured that the available supply of feed will be distributed as equitably as possible."[10]

That did not completely pacify unhappy ranchers. The *Amarillo Daily News* concluded that cattlemen would have 20 percent less high-protein feed than in the preceding year and charged that the federal government had abandoned cattlemen. Jones understood the ranchers' plight and was sympathetic, but at the same time he knew that conditions had resulted not only from government inaction but also from cattlemen's failure to support the WFA program.[11]

As 1944 began, the WFA was concerned not only with congressional relations and a lack of storage and farm machinery but also with demands from the Soviet Union for more food. Furthermore, secret plans were being made for the invasion of France, and the government considered the stockpiling of essential food and

---

[8] Walter Wilcox, *The Farmer in the Second World War*, p. 67.
[9] *Chicago Sun*, February 24, 1944.
[10] WFA staff meeting minutes, January 3, 1944, MJP.
[11] Scrapbook 13, MJP.

other agricultural goods a critical necessity. The WFA protested to Fred Vinson that general wage freezes for farm labor would be a threat to increased production. Higher industrial wages had already enticed many laborers to cities.[12]

A reorganization of WFA also occurred as the new year began. Jones designated Bart Boyd to centralize WFA price policies and establish better liaison with the OPA. Moreover, during this time the Agricultural Adjustment Agency, Farm Security Administration, and Soil Conservation Service became independent of general War Food Administration jurisdiction. The WFA Food Distribution Division became the Office of Production, and the Food Distribution Administration emerged as the Office of Distribution. Jones cut the power of the CCC, and that agency lost its prestigious number-one position in the WFA structure. Jack Hutson lost some power, too, over the Agricultural Adjustment Agency, the Farm Security Administration, and the Soil Conservation Service.

These developments surely resulted from criticism of use of CCC funds for subsidies and from Jones's belief that Hutson was trying to undermine the power of the WFA (verification of this conclusion cannot be documented, however). By that time men favorable to the liberal programs of Henry Wallace (Appleby, Hendrickson, and Baldwin, for example) had begun their exodus from government. In their places came moderates and conservatives (including Lee Marshall, Frank Hancock, and—on Jones's recommendation—Undersecretary of Agriculture Grover Hill). This signaled American farmers' disenchantment with Roosevelt and his vice-president and an increasing conservatism among them. By January 1944 political fever had infected Washington, and Jones's name as a dark-horse candidate for the vice-presidency was heard in some conversations.[13]

Jones concerned himself with making further appeals for increased food production. He visited Capitol Hill to solicit support for expanding the CCC and for the victory-garden campaign. During the next few months the WFA supervised community canning projects. As a guest on the popular "Fibber McGee and Molly" radio show he said: "Women from the cities and towns and boys'

[12] Jones to Fred M. Vinson, January 10, 1944, MJP; COHP-MJP, p. 1354.
[13] COHP-MJP, pp. 1359–72; unidentified clippings, scrapbook 12, MJP.

and girls' clubs have done their part. Twenty million victory gardens produced eight million tons of fresh vegetables." At the National Victory Garden Conference in February he urged the planting of 22 million home gardens in 1944, since the United States would export 27 percent of its food during the year, and there would be 2 percent less food available for domestic consumption.

These activities constituted only a small part of WFA work, but they attracted more popular attention than the highly specialized and detailed problems of commodity regulation, production, and distribution. Few people today may remember the WFA, but many will recall the appeals to plant a victory garden.

In early March the WFA announced price supports for farm products that corresponded to the trend of 90 percent of parity for basic commodities. The delicate balance between supply and demand and between production and distribution remained, and the WFA did not seek to increase production without considering the other problems, such as food storage and transportation.[14]

In mid-1944 reduction of livestock brought on what would prove to be a continuing consumer-producer conflict between the OPA and the WFA. Neither federal policy nor federal power could establish effective distribution controls from producer to consumer. Black-market operations practiced by local processors brought producers higher prices for their livestock.

Still another problem presented itself that year. When American farmers responded to WFA appeals with overproduction of pork, fruits, and vegetables, a severe shortage of packaging containers and storage facilities developed, with the result that food spoiled. Moreover, by late spring transportation problems were preventing effective distribution. On May 3, Jack Hutson recommended halting meat rationing until the domestic market could absorb the increased production. Jones concurred, as did Hill. Jones emphasized, however, that press releases should stress that the suspension was only temporary. He said:

The fact that we have sufficient food supply now isn't any assurance that we'll have enough later. A great deal of food is perishable. We not

[14] WFA staff meeting minutes, February 1, February 10, March 20, 1944, MJP; U.S. Department of Agriculture, press release, March 4, 1944, MJP; unidentified clippings, scrapbook 12, MJP; Jones, *How War Food Saved American Lives*, pp. 108–109.

only have to have continuation of outstanding work and ability of farmers to continue that [production] and essential machinery to carry on, but we have to be favored with good weather conditions.[15]

A bureaucratic conflict erupted over the decision. The OPA, under Chester Bowles, contended that its powers included rationing and that the WFA should restrict itself to ensuring sufficient production and supply. In mid-May, however, all meat except beef roast and steak was temporarily removed from rationing. No clear-cut directive on who had responsibility for rationing came from either Congress or the president. Jones stubbornly maintained that the WFA had the responsibility. He based his argument largely on Executive Order 9250 and on subsequent orders regarding WFA powers. Eventually James Byrnes made the decision—in favor of Jones's interpretation. The director of the War Mobilization Board ruled that after the WFA had consulted with the OPA the WFA would be perfectly justified in making a determination about civilian rationing that was contrary to the advice and wishes of the price administrator.[16] Even this ruling failed to forestall future arguments between the two agencies, the one consumer-oriented, the other concerned with producers.

Similar disagreements soon arose concerning vegetable rationing. In September the WFA removed canned vegetables from rationing, thus making them harder to find on shelves because hoarders bought them up in great quantities. Bowles urged greater OPA powers.[17] This time Jones won again. He did not always have his way; in a later dispute he was overruled. He always contended, how-

---

[15] Press releases, May 5 and May 12, MJP.

[16] See Victor A. Thompson, *The Regulatory Process in OPA Rationing*, pp. 269–270; Wilcox, *The Farmer in the Second World War*, pp. 180–181; WFA staff meeting minutes, May 3, 1944, May 4, 1944, July 19, 1944, Chester Bowles to Jones, May 15, 1944, "The Solution to the War Food Administrator," July 26, 1944, MS, Jones to Chester Bowles, May 17, 1944, Bowles to Jones, June 7, 1944, National Archives, Record Group 16.

[17] Chester Bowles to Jones, September 12, 1944, Jones to James F. Byrnes, September 14, 1944, "Representatives of Organizations with Consumer Interest to Marvin Jones," September 29, 1944, memo, Bowles to Jones, November 10, 1944, Jones to Bowles, November 20, 1944, Fred Vinson to Jones, December 22, 1944, National Archives, Record Group 16; WFA staff minutes, August 8, 1944, MJP; Jones, interview with Jerry N. Hess, April 20, 1970, COHP-MJP, pp. 1402–1405.

ever, that the danger of spoilage in stockpiled supplies should be considered when deciding about food rationing.

Some observers then and later accused Jones of having other motives. Allan Matasow, in *Farm Politics and Policies in the Truman Years*, contended that the War Food Administration pursued a "bareshelves" policy of production from the latter half of 1944 until the end of the war so that American farmers would be assured high prices. Jones denied this charge in an interview for the Harry S. Truman Library. In trying to resolve the dispute for himself, the student of the period should examine the effects of rationing and price controls on WFA production policies.[18] In that endeavor the following chronicle of Jones's activities during that time may be of help.

On May 16, 1944, Jones spoke at Orangeburg, South Carolina, stressing the need for increased production and praising the American farmer. He also warned that the temporary halt of rationing would not last. One month later, on June 11, he appeared at Roosevelt's request before the Massachusetts Retail Grocers' Association Convention at Boston. He urged grocers to support the administration in its encouragement of food conservation.

From June 26 to July 14, Jones toured regional WFA offices and inspected crops. In speeches in Dallas and Oklahoma City he predicted that some shortages would ease during the following winter. About the same time he participated in a "March of Time" film, in which he urged increased crop production. The film was shown in theaters across the country.

During these months morale in the WFA remained high. Though farm problems like labor shortages and transportation difficulties remained troublesome, generally the situation was good. Eggs and hogs were in surplus. Favorable weather brought another record year for American agricultural production, especially for dry beans, dry peas, flaxseed, soybeans, corn, wheat, potatoes, and burley tobacco.[19]

[18] See Thompson, *The Regulatory Process in OPA Rationing*, pp. 269–272; Jones, *How War Food Saved American Lives*, Allen J. Matasow, *Farm Politics and Policies in the Truman Years*, pp. 3–4; Bela Gold, *Wartime Economic Planning in Agriculture*, p. 319.

[19] Stephen Early to James F. Byrnes, April 10, 1944, Roosevelt Papers; clippings, scrapbook 13, MJP; Jones, "March of Time," June 13, 1944, MS,

During the summer Jones began modifying his policy of all-out production. On August 23 he reemphasized that the postwar situation would require maintenance of peak production levels, but he warned against repeating mistakes that had been made after World War I. The United States, he said, "should produce all of the food products that we can dispose of both at home and abroad; but after reaching that point . . . [there is] no reason for piling up a lot of commodities that are essentially perishable."[20] Two days later he elaborated on this idea before the House Special Committee on Post-War Economic Policy and Planning.[21] Still later, in a confidential memorandum prepared for the Bureau of the Budget on October 17, he explained:

> In the event of a German collapse before the 1945 planting season, stocks in the hands of Allied governments, plus the new production, will result in the emergence of surpluses for many commodities after the harvest. . . . A very different situation will of course emerge should hostilities in Europe continue into the summer. Needless to say, it is this contingency that makes it impossible for the War Food Administration to assume at this time, in planning the next year's production goals, a return to a prewar production pattern. Should hostilities continue till after the 1945 planting season, production of most strategic commodities will be barely adequate for meeting known firm requirements. Hence, we must at this stage, plan for high production, and at the same time, must prepare to deal with embarrassing surpluses.[22]

Five days later Jones remarked to members of the National Restaurant Association that an end of the war in the European theater would eliminate one phase of the war effort. He added that, although rationing had been imposed only because of national crisis, "a wise Congress has realized the necessity for stabilizing farm prices in the period of adjusted production that must follow the cessation of war demands. The Steagall Bill provides that we shall maintain the price support program for a period of two years after the war."[23]

MJP; Jones, *How War Food Saved American Lives*, pp. 121–125; WFA staff meeting minutes, June, July, 1944, MJP; War Food Administration, *Final Report of the War Food Administrator: 1945*, p. 101; Jones to Elmer Davis, July 14, 1944, MJP.

[20] WFA staff meeting minutes, August 23, 1944, MJP.

[21] Jones, *How War Food Saved American Lives*, pp. 126–133.

[22] Jones to Bureau of the Budget, "World Food Outlook, 1945–1946," October 7, 1944, memo, MJP.

[23] Marvin Jones, "Today's Food Problems," October 12, 1944, MS, MJP.

This speech brought a stern rebuke from President Roosevelt, who warned Jones to control his tongue:

> ... at a most critical time when production of essential supplies vital to the war effort must be kept at a high level, speculative public statements by responsible military and civilian public officials at home and abroad indicating an early termination of the war tend to curtail production of essential war materials. It is highly necessary that this condition be remedied and to this end all government officials are directed to refrain from such public statements.[24]

Jones and Vinson, director of the Office of Economic Stabilization, had not yet formulated long-range plans for a nation facing a choice between expanding consumption and production restrictions. Congressional appropriations to achieve parity and the president's support would be necessary in either event.[25] Jones told Vinson, "It is my judgment that every possible effort should be made to have expanded production and expanded use all along the line insofar as it is possible to do so."[26] These were not the words of a man who advocated a bare-shelves policy.

Later Jones cited some figures regarding the food situation in 1944. He estimated that, even though one-fourth of the year's production was reserved for military, lend-lease, and foreign-relief purposes, American civilians had 7 percent more food than in any of the five years before World War II.[27] The factors responsible for this yield, he said, were the patriotism of the American farmer, good weather, soil-conservation practices, the use of commercial fertilizer, congressional appropriations, and the assistance of the War Food Administration. As a result farm income had risen to a record high, four times higher than that of 1932. "This favorable position which has been achieved by agriculture," Jones remarked, "does not mean that the farmer has fared better than the rest of the economy. The farmer ... achieved this despite serious shortages of manpower and farm machinery."[28]

[24] Franklin D. Roosevelt to Jones, December 12, 1944, MS, MJP.

[25] Fred Vinson to Jones, November 21, 1944, National Archives, Record Group 16.

[26] Jones to Fred Vinson, December 9, 1944, National Archives, Record Group 16.

[27] Jones to James F. Byrnes, "Agriculture's Wartime Constitution," December 15, 1944, memo, National Archives, Record Group 16.

[28] Ibid.

The War Food Administrator 221

During the first weeks of January 1945 many matters vied for Jones's attention. Among them was continuation of farm-labor deferments. Jones looked for guarantees that the 1945 farm crop could be harvested with a minimum of spoilage, yet he knew that the use of prisoners of war must come to an end before long, and he also knew that movement to the cities was continuing.

A second matter was yet another reorganization. Jack Hutson resigned to become Vinson's aide. Hutson, an agricultural economist, was a career Department of Agriculture employee. His *modus operandi* never accommodated to Jones's concept of loyalty.

Still another matter regarded legislative action. Jones appeared before Congress in January 1945 to support a bill extending the life of the Commodity Credit Corporation and increasing its borrowing power from $3 million to $5 million. In testimony before the Senate Banking Committee, Jones advocated gradual abolition of farm subsidies after the war, with farm prices to be maintained near current levels. When Senator Robert Taft observed that if subsidies were abolished either consumer food prices must rise or farm prices must fall, Jones exempted commodities primarily for export. He assured his staff that although Congress might cut the $2 million increase the Commodity Credit Corporation would still have enough funds to continue its work.[29]

WFA production goals included a push for increased acreage and particular emphasis on increased production of milk and hogs and a larger slaughter of cattle to satisfy consumer demands. Crop goals in February 1945 included a 3 percent increase in acreage and greater production of sugar beets, flaxseed, dry beans, potatoes, and tobacco.[30] Privately Jones opposed higher wages for farm workers, but he worried about an adequate supply of labor and estimated that four million civilians would have to be recruited from Mexico, Canada, and the Caribbean islands to meet the farmers' needs.

Later that month he reported to the Agriculture Subcommittee of the House Appropriations Committee: "Shortage of skilled farm labor is perhaps the most serious problem confronting farmers.

---

[29] January 26, 1945, AP release, clipping, National Archives, Record Group 16; WFA staff meeting minutes, January 31, 1945. MJP.

[30] Unidentified clippings, scrapbook 13, MJP.

About 1,650,000 farm men have gone to the armed forces, and 3,500,000 farm men and women of working age have left the farm largely to take non-farm jobs in the last four years."[31] Farm laborers drawn from among Japanese evacuees from the West Coast, prison inmates, conscientious objectors, and others had been insufficient, he said, and he urged Congress to allow more Latin-American workers to enter the United States. He predicted that during the critical year 1945 the nation would have large supplies of eggs and citrus fruit and adequate wheat production but shortages of meat, butter, canned fruits and vegetables, potatoes, rice, and sugar.[32]

The changing food situation soon forced Jones and Byrnes to review their production policies again. Aided by agricultural economist D. A. Fitzgerald, Jones concluded on March 15 that, "regardless of the progress of the European war, available supplies of food in the United States in 1945 will not be adequate to meet all the requirements that have been submitted, including a partial return to a more normal pattern of civilian consumption."[33] Removal of processed foods from rationing had caused Americans to eat too much in 1944, producing a food shortage in 1945. With a few seasonal exceptions no food surpluses were anticipated. Moreover, predicted expansion of military operations in the Pacific would no doubt increase demands for food. With greater demands being made on the American farmer, Congress began taking steps to provide price supports.[34]

Later that March, Jones issued a statement on the food situation that was designed to stress the seriousness of the problem without causing hysteria. Some items were "less than the over-all requirements," Jones said, but "there is sufficient [food] if it is properly distributed and shared to assure our people a good, wholesome diet."[35]

[31] Marvin Jones, "Statement before Agriculture Subcommittee of the House Appropriations Committee," February 26, 1945, MS, MJP.
[32] Ibid.
[33] Jones to James F. Byrnes, March 15, 1944, National Archives, Record Group 16.
[34] For background see George W. Auxier, *Industrial Mobilization for War*, vol. 1.
[35] U.S. Department of Agriculture, press release, March 19, March 23, 1945, MJP.

A pleasant interruption came in Jones's work schedule when he received an invitation to dinner at the White House. Jones accepted at once. He was pleased and flattered to be able to renew his social contacts with the president. When Jones arrived at the White House, he and Roosevelt and other guests engaged in friendly banter. At dinner he sat near Justice and Mrs. Robert Jackson and Canadian Ambassador Leighton McCarthy and his wife. Later he recalled:

> We sat at an elongated table. . . . The President sat [at one end] and Mrs. Roosevelt [at the other] and the rest of us [were seated] along the table. The President looked terrible. He was very thin, looked very tired, would talk a little while, sometimes sort of brighten up, then he would lapse back, and his mouth would come open. That is the first time I realized that he could not last very long. I knew he had not looked well and had had his difficulties. Everyone was familiar with that fact. When the dinner was over and we visited a little while, I walked home. I lived at the University Club at that time. As I walked out of the front door of the White House, a man said, "Do you want a car called?"
> I said, "No, I am going to walk home. It is just three blocks." I walked home very much depressed, because it did not look like the man had strength enough to last very long.[36]

Food-shortage speculations intensified. More criticism was heard, including charges that the WFA had held down production and was wasteful with the surpluses that had been produced. The charges led to congressional investigations beginning in April 1945 and lasting until mid-June, when legislators gave the WFA what amounted to a wrist slap.

There was considerable sentiment for consolidating the WFA and the OPA. Called to Capitol Hill, Jones defended his agency, with Wickard at his side:

> ... let me sound a solemn warning: A food supply is a continuous thing; food begins to disappear the moment it is produced—you cannot keep it for a record. We cannot supply our future demands for food with current and past surpluses. Temporary and local supplies are something we are fortunate enough to enjoy now, and they are the direct result of the fact that our farmers produced it and our distribution programs conserved it; and that the unknown, such as the weather and other factors, operated more in our favor than in our disfavor. But we cannot always depend on that. The only way, then, to ensure this same fortunate posi-

[36] COHP-MJP, pp. 1412–13.

tion for next year is to continue all our efforts for maximum production and efficient distribution.[37]

On April 12, 1945, word came from Warm Springs, Georgia, of President Roosevelt's death. Jones was stunned along with the rest of the nation, although he had seen for himself that Roosevelt's health was failing.

With the advent of the Truman administration and the end of the war in Europe Jones began longing to return to the court of claims. On May 22, 1945, he sent his resignation to President Truman and repeated his desire to return to the court of claims effective no later than June 30. "Now ... that victory in Europe has been achieved," he wrote, "I feel that the work of the Department [of agriculture] and War Food could well be carried on by the Secretary of Agriculture, probably with somewhat less expenditure of funds."[38]

Truman accepted the resignation on the following day. He wrote:

> It was a most difficult assignment. The needs of our armed forces, of our Allies, and of our own civilian population called for the highest degree of competence in food production, management and distribution. It is to the everlasting credit of the War Food Administration that even after supplying the great demands made upon us from all over the world, the American people as a whole not only did not go hungry but actually enjoyed a better diet than in the days before the war.[39]

Jones held his last WFA staff meeting on June 27, 1945. He praised the efforts of his personnel and embarked on some philosophizing of the agrarian kind:

> We do best when we master material things and bend them to the higher spiritual purpose.
>
> When a man lifts up his eyes and looks beyond the mechanics of the universe, he truly begins to grow. He looks back over the receding road of the past and then forward through the clouds that overhang the future. Beneath and above things he seeks the law—not temporary, man-

---

[37] WFA staff meeting minutes, May 2, 1945, MJP. See also Jones to Clinton P. Anderson, May 9, 1945, MJP; Jones to Members of the Senate and the House of Representatives, May 19, 1945, National Archives, Record Group 16.

[38] Jones to Harry S. Truman, May 22, 1945, MJP.

[39] Truman to Jones, May 23, 1945, MJP.

The War Food Administrator 225

made rules, but the universal law. He wants to know how the earth was formed and the stars made. He knocks at the very gates of heaven and asks why.

All through my life I have tried to remain close to the soil, for there is found the setting for wisdom's jeweled ring. There is something in contact with the earth that tends to build character—and I have needed a good deal of building. Farm people live close to nature and therefore close to God. Of all people they come nearest to being free. They believe in liberty, equality, manhood, fair play, and freedom from every form of new and old world caste and privilege and from the tyranny of wealth and birth. They swung the first axe that rung in the wilderness of this country. . . . They have fought in its battles from the beginning. . . .

I came to this organization on leave of absence to do a wartime assignment. I did not seek the place. I did not wish it. I came as a soldier would go at the request of his commander. I am proud of the record of the War Food Administration. . . . On that record we stand ready at all times to be judged.[40]

What should be the verdict on Jones the administrator? He was sensitive, kind, and even-tempered, yet with a stubborn streak. He retained Byrnes's confidence and maintained good relations with Congress that past WFA administrators had not enjoyed. But never did he enjoy government administration for its own sake, and certainly he never had any enthusiasm for it. He delegated too much trust and responsibility to his subordinates, but he felt that his strengths lay elsewhere. Certainly those areas were demanding ones: he worked seven days a week.[41]

Jones enjoyed some support within the USDA, and, as James Ward, a perceptive USDA career servant, noted, "The young blood had to go to the war and the old-timers in the USDA knew what Jones would do, and they weren't about to tangle with him."[42] The WFA reflected the characteristics of its administrator, who was inclined to work on immediate problems rather than devise long-range policies. In contrast to Byrnes, Jones only reluctantly admitted that problems existed, disliking to make forthright public statements. That was a facet of his personality, however, not a bent toward deception.[43]

[40] WFA staff meeting minutes, June 27, 1945, MJP.
[41] Samuel Bledsoe, interview, 1954, John B. Hutson, interview, 1952, Rudolph M. Evans, interviews, 1952, 1953, Columbia Oral History Project.
[42] James S. Ward, interview with author, August 10, 1972.
[43] Wilson Cowen, interview with author, June 29, 1972.

He succeeded despite these shortcomings. Jones's leadership was ideological and public-relations-centered rather than bureaucratic. In a time of wartime tension Jones was a healer, a conciliator, and a harmonizer of interests. He championed increased production and kept morale high among American farmers as the recognized number-one priority. While he failed to achieve a utopian solution, the WFA, aided by favorable weather, was reasonably successful in meeting its production goals. When the inevitable bureaucratic conflicts occurred, Jones knew how to avoid the less important ones. He was lucky, and he used that good luck to make the bureaucratic system work. All these actions were enhanced by his spiritual appeals to the finer instincts of humanity.

14.

Chief Judge, United States Court of Claims

Jones returned to the sanctuary of the court of claims with a feeling of relief. He was now sixty-three, and the two years as war food administrator had been hard ones. Even before his return to the court, plans regarding him had been discussed. James Byrnes, Chief Judge Richard Whaley, and President Truman had agreed that upon Whaley's retirement Jones would become chief judge because of his administrative experience and his congressional ties. Moreover, the other judges liked him.

Not everyone concurred. Leroy Cobbin, a lawyer from Camden, New Jersey, disputed the appointment. He argued that Jones's recent absence from the bench disqualified him for the position. Jones answered Cobbin, declaring that he had absented himself from the bench only to serve on a special assignment—as had other judges and justices: John Jay, who had served as special envoy to England for George Washington; Owen Roberts, who was appointed to help investigate the Pearl Harbor disaster; and Robert Jackson, who served as chief counsel for the Nuremberg trials.[1]

During his years on the court Jones displayed humor, humility, and a strong sense of justice. Frequently he discarded judicial language for the words of the common people. Jones sensed that other judges had greater scholarly intellect and knowledge of precedents and cases. He retained the congressman's desire to convince.

He knew human nature. His personality prevented drastic chal-

[1] M. Leroy Cobbin, "Testimony before Senate Judiciary Committee," March 13, 1947, "Memo, Reply to Objections to Mr. Leroy Cobbin to the Confirmation of Marvin Jones as Chief Justice of the United States Court of Claims," undated MS, O. R. McGuire to Alexander Wiley, March 26, 1947, Carl McFarland, council Member, American Bar Association to Francis Inge, June 12, 1947, Marvin Jones Papers; hereafter cited as MJP.

lenges to his power within the court, and he made certain that he was the one who delegated that power. Moreover, he knew Congress, and that knowledge proved valuable at a time when the court needed appropriations for the new facilities. He knew that in politically conscious Washington good judges and justices had to be good politicians too. Moreover, many powerful post–World War II congressional leaders had been former New Deal colleagues of his and had watched him operate in their own formative years. Jones's close friendship with Sam Rayburn combined with bipartisan respect to confirm Jones as chief judge. But circumstances gave him the opportunity to contribute his own unique brand of justice.

To determine Jones's judicial philosophy, historians must rely on written opinions, because his personal papers available to researchers reveal little behind-the-scenes activity. In his court the United States was always the defendant, of course, but cases were varied.[2] They fell into these general categories: patents, Indian claims, transportation, government salaries (including military), requisitioned property, contracts, overtime pay, taxes, and "miscellaneous."

About 6 percent of the litigation in the court of claims involved suits over patent rights. Jones never liked to decide issues in which plaintiffs claimed that the government had infringed on their patents. Frequently the court had to estimate damages, after lengthy study of highly technical drawings, using federal statutes and judicial precedents. Jones tended toward the view that the government was not liable if the patent in question had been previously available to those skilled in whatever art was involved.[3] In his decisions regarding patent cases Jones usually went with the majority. One exception came when Wales Madden, speaking for the majority, interpreted

[2] See U.S. Court of Claims, *A Symposium: The United States Court of Claims*; U.S. Court of Claims, *Jurisdiction of the United States Court of Claims;* Saul R. Gomer, "Some Notes on Court of Claims Practice," *Government Contracts Review* 2 (April 1958):4–26; Clarence T. Kipps, Jr., "A Unique National Court: The United States Court of Claims," *American Bar Association Journal* 53 (November 1967): 1025–29; Marvin Jones, *Should Uncle Sam Pay—When and Why?*

[3] *Edward A. Juhl, Jr., Administrator of the Estate of Edward A. Juhl, Deceased* v. *United States*, 11 Ct. Cl. 587 (1950). Citation to a case refers to the beginning page of the opinion.

section 1498 of the United States Code to mean that a right of action for a patent does not apply to a federal employee if it occurs during his time of employment or service with the government. In a lone dissent Jones disagreed and argued that when four inventors included one government employee—which was the situation in the case before the court—the government should pay claims to the other three partners.[4]

Posing greater difficulties was litigation involving American Indians. Before 1946 the court of claims heard these cases as a result of special legislation. After that the court had the power to hear appeals from the Indian Claims Commission, and those cases had complex and conflicting histories. Jones doubted his ability to write a fair opinion in Indian litigation, but an examination of his decisions reveals adherence to the prevailing majority interpretation.

The high mortality rate of tribal claims stemmed from limitations in the Jurisdiction Act of 1928 and the narrow interpretation applied by the court of claims and the United States Supreme Court.[5] Jones held that recognition of Indian claims must be clear, explicit, and intentional and that, when they involved boundaries, the lines must be delineated accurately enough to allow reasonably correct calculations of acreage. Further, Jones believed that the Indian Claims Commission had jurisdiction over the review of judgments of the secretary of interior concerning Indians and that the responsibility of the court of claims ended when findings of the ICC were supported by substantial evidence.[6]

The transportation cases revealed Jones's down-to-earth understanding of complex matters. An example was *Union Pacific Railroad Company* v. *United States*. The suit concerned transportation rates and particularly whether jeeps were freight or passenger

[4] *Strategical Demolition Torpedo Company, Corporation* v. *United States*, 119 Ct. Cl. 291 (1951).

[5] James P. Gregory to author, May 16, 1973; Jerome A. Barron to author, June 28, 1973; Glen A. Wilkinson, "Indian Tribal Claims before the Court of Claims," in U.S. Court of Claims, *A Symposium*, pp. 551–528; "Systematic Discrimination in the Indian Claims Commission: The Burden of Proof in Redressing Historical Wrongs," *Iowa Law Review* 57 (June 1972): 1300–19.

[6] *Dissent in Minnesota Chippewa Tribe et al.* v. *United States*, 161 Ct. Cl. 258 (1963); *United States* v. *Seminole Nation*, 146 Ct. Cl. 171 (1959).

vehicles. The government labeled the jeep a cargo truck, but the plaintiff disagreed.

Jones gave the question his customary thorough but practical thought. He inquired about the origin of the jeep and its primary purpose. Was it a truck? He recalled, "I have seen my father haul everything from ploughshares to a crosscut saw in a buggy, but that hardly made the buggy a freight vehicle."[7]

He observed:

The army called it a truck, but that is not very persuasive, since the army called all wheeled vehicles trucks, including passenger cars, except the sedans. It was greatly used for hauling light equipment, especially in the combat area. But it was used all over France, North Africa and India, the South Pacific and everywhere the army went, . . . from the private to the top general, as a passenger car. It was not a streamlined luxury creation, but it was especially useful in rough terrain where the sedans, motorcycles, and other passenger cars could not go.[8]

Jones's decision that the jeep was a passenger vehicle won favorable reactions from Generals Omar Bradley and Dwight Eisenhower. Bradley wrote, "Having bounced over considerable portions of North Africa and Europe in one, I can assure you that your description of the jeep is most accurate and to the point."[9] Eisenhower said, "So far as my own war experience was concerned, the jeep was definitely 'passenger'—but sometimes I was plagued by the suspicion the lieutenants thought of the 'old man' as nothing but freight, composed mostly of brass."[10]

In transportation cases Jones looked carefully at government regulations and at mechanical operations. In a case brought by Bolin Drive-A-Way Company, Jones saw "no substantial difference in the result of having automatic as contrasted with mechanical engagement of the front axle when road conditions became abnormal, and disengagement when they became normal again."[11] Jones

[7] *Union Pacific Railroad Company* v. *United States*, 117 Ct. Cl. 534 (1950).

[8] Ibid.

[9] Omar N. Bradley to Marvin Jones, July 12, 1950, MJP. Unless otherwise noted, all interviews and correspondence citing Jones refer to Marvin Jones.

[10] Dwight D. Eisenhower to Jones, July 12, 1950, MJP.

[11] *Bolin Drive-a-Way Co., Corporation* v. *United States*, 151 Ct. Cl. 164 (1960).

used the following recollection from his childhood to explain why the plaintiff had not persuaded the court to the contrary:

The writer recalls that on his father's farm there were a good many rocks in one field. In using the cultivator in that field wooden pegs were placed in the shank so that when the plowshare or sweep hit the rock the peg would break and the plowpoint would drag back. It was then necessary to lift that part from the ground, restore the point to position, and insert another wooden peg. A short time thereafter someone in the manufacturing establishment with "a flash of genius" attached a strong spring which would hold the point in place, but when a rock was struck the point would automatically be drawn back and when the rock was passed the spring would pull it back into place. The fact that it was automatic did not change the end result. The same purpose was accomplished in a different fashion. . . . Likewise in the case at bar, we think the front axle not only could be but was engaged when abnormal road conditions developed, and was then disengaged when road conditions became normal again.[12]

Another kind of litigation decided in the court of claims was the congressional reference case, a dispute referred to the court by Congress for adjudication. Such a case usually came about through recognition by Congress that some individual patent rights failed to meet strict legal standards and yet had significant moral or equitable elements. The court was given responsibility for interpreting specific congressional acts.

Jones took the lead in dispute involving agricultural legislation. In 1941 the Calvert Distilling Company sued to recover funds paid the secretary of agriculture under voluntary marketing agreements originating from the Agricultural Adjustment Act of 1933. Under those terms each contracting distiller agreed to pay for all cereal grains used in the manufacture of liquor, to ensure parity for the producer. If the price paid by the distiller, plus processing and other taxes, sank below parity, the distiller was required to pay the difference.

Jones denied that the court of claims possessed jurisdiction in an opinion written for a unanimous court. He knew intimately congressional intent in regard to the AAA. Jones observed that under AAA legislation participants were barred from recovering administrative expenses. He concluded that Calvert

[12] Ibid.

undertakes to justify the alleged trust in behalf of itself on the ground that it got nothing out of the transaction—nothing out of the marketing agreement—and that it entered into the agreement purely because it wanted to be helpful and to contribute to the welfare of the farmers who were in desperate circumstances by virtue of economic conditions then prevailing. In other words, it claimed that insofar as those transactions are concerned it had become a purely philanthropic institution. Such a position is almost enough to stagger credulity.[13]

Jones went on to deny that the court of claims had jurisdiction, which may actually have been an indication that he failed to suppress his own prohibitionist tendencies.

As a judge Jones also faced the problem of government liability in connection with tax-exemption certificates provided by the Bankhead Cotton Act of 1934. The court's task was to decide whether the claims fell within congressional intent or were substantiated by judicial precedent. Eventually a divided court followed Jones's majority opinion in S. R. Brackin v. United States. Relying on Supreme Court decisions, Jones held that the act provided for a tax on the ginning of the *excess*, or surplus, production. The tax was to be collected only if the surplus had been marketed or moved into commerce.

Many lawyers believed that the Bankhead Act was unconstitutional, but Jones worked around this view when he wrote, "The Court does not think that the United States is legally obligated to pay the plaintiff out of the general fund of the treasury, for the plaintiff has paid no tax; he simply purchased tax-exemption certificates."[14] Jones conveniently failed to ascertain whether the plaintiff had an interest in the pool trust fund and whether the court might determine moral obligation.

Judge Whitaker differed from Jones. He called the Bankhead Act unconstitutional as evidenced from cases decided by the Fifth

---

[13] *Calvert Distilling Company* v. *United States*, 94 Ct. Cl. 517 (1941). Jones had been critical of alcohol legislation. He maintained a public image of abstinence, infrequently partook of alcoholic beverages, and regarded drinking as a personal weakness, seldom finishing more than one drink at a public gathering. He enjoyed cigars, and not until medical reports revealed its harmful effects on health did he abandon tobacco. See also Stanley J. Purzyck, "The Congressional Reference Case in the United States Court of Claims," *Catholic University of America Law Review* 10 (January 1961):35–43.

[14] *S. R. Brackin* v. *United States*, 96 Ct. Cl. 457 (1942).

Circuit Court of Appeals and the Court of Appeals for the District of Columbia. Whitaker said, "Whatever it cost a taxpayer to discharge his liability for the tax, I think he is entitled to recover."[15]

In another case brought before the court (*J. H. Crain v. United States*) Jones explained further his own idea about the workings of the Bankhead Act:

It is as if the manager of a show, the price of admission to which was sixty cents, handed a complimentary ticket to A. Not being in a position to use it, A sells it to B for 40 cents. The show is cancelled. Cash tickets are redeemed. B presents his ticket at the window and asks for a refund. The manager would probably say he received none of the funds in the first place. B was not compelled to buy a ticket. He was only required to buy a ticket if he went to the show.[16]

With obvious concern Jones elaborated:

We find no compulsion here. For generations the farmers have been bound down by surpluses with which they were powerless to deal. Glutted markets and ruinous prices were followed by waste and then scarcity with injury to both producer and consumer. Rotting surpluses followed by scarcity and want didn't make sense. . . .

A program was fashioned—crude in its beginnings, . . . to apportion the market, yoked to the demand or consumptive need. Linked to the program was a loan feature to carry a reserve supply to assure against shortage. . . . If a producer went along with his neighbors and used only his share of the market he was not taxed. If he tried to ride the sacrifices of the producers by intentionally marketing large excess volumes he was to be taxed. He was out of step and deserved to be taxed.[17]

Congress rarely refused to appropriate sums for judgments rendered by the court, but in one opinion (*Robert Morass Lovett et al. v. United States*) Jones wrote: "The authority of the Congress to make appropriations, within the framework of the Constitution, is plenary. The power to make appropriations carried with it the power to withhold or deny appropriations."[18] This right seemed to Jones "as fundamental as the Ten Commandments," and he maintained that as long as Congress acted within its authority the courts

---

[15] Ibid.
[16] *J. H. Crain and R. E. Lee Wilson, Jr., Trustees of Lee Wilson and Company, Business Trust v. United States*, 96 Ct. Cl. 443 (1942).
[17] Ibid.
[18] *Robert Morass Lovett et al. v. United States*, 104 Ct. Cl. 557 (1946).

had no right to pass judgment. Acting beyond authority was another matter. "No one has a right to be employed by the Government," Jones said, as an example, "but every citizen, whose rights have not been legally forfeited, is privileged to apply for any position within the Government and to have his application considered on its own merits."[19] Legislation restricting this was unconstitutional, in Jones's estimation.

"One of the chief glories of the Constitution," Jones added in his opinion, "is the fact that you cannot take the shirt from the back of a ragged street urchin without either securing the lad's consent or paying for the rags in the manner prescribed by law."[20] (The Lovett decision ran counter to prevailing public opinion—during another red scare. Later the Supreme Court upheld the court of claims verdict.)[21]

The most exhaustive statement of agrarian idealism that Jones the judge wrote came in *G. S. Kincaid* v. *United States*. The case involved a landowner who demanded that his tenants give him their share of benefits provided by the Agricultural Adjustment Act of 1938. Under those conditions, however, the government refused to pay the landowner, who then sued. In a unanimous opinion the court of claims denied the plaintiff's recovery. In the written decision Jones reviewed the agricultural situation of the 1930's:

> In 1932 agriculture was prostrate. Farmers were losing their homes all over the country by foreclosure. Farm prices were below the cost of production, and the purchasing power and declining prices had finally affected the industrial areas, so reducing the marketing outlets for the products of industry that losses were being sustained. Thus the entire economy was locked and sinking.
>
> One of the major steps in restoring the country was a program for agriculture which was to lead in the march back to equality for the citizens of this country and to a solid basis of national prosperity. While the original act was held invalid by the Supreme Court, the new act was based on the experience and knowledge gained from the operations and carried forward its philosophy and purposes. Both acts recognized the basic nature of the products of the land. The later act placed greater emphasis on the problems incident to the proper use of soil and water.

[19] Ibid.
[20] Ibid.
[21] *United States* v. *Lovett*, 328 U.S. 303 (1946); David Schwartz and Sidney B. Jacoby, *Government Litigation*, pp. 163–164.

Conservation was and is at all times so fundamental that its necessity has been recognized by practically all thinking people who are familiar with the subject. . . .

One can have little patience in these circumstances with anyone who tried to take an unfair advantage of his neighbor in transactions of this kind, and who indulged in practices the necessary tendency of which was to undermine the entire program. He cannot complain if he suffers the consequences of his own deliberate act. One could respect the attitude of those who refused to have anything to do with the program. Though they perhaps lacked understanding of its over-all purpose, they were nevertheless men of conviction. But for the man who accepted the program and assumed to do along, and yet who sought unfair advantage of his neighbors and fellow farmers, there cannot be much claim for generous action. He is entitled to just what the law gives him, only that and nothing more.[22]

A more important series of decisions concerned service-pay cases involving both civilian and military personnel. In an important decision, *Elchibegoff* v. *United States*, Jones wrote:

When all the facts of the case are taken into consideration it is difficult to find that there was a real compliance with the terms of the law and the rules of the United States Civil Service Commission. It is unfortunate that the matter was handled the way it was, because the Commission did finally determine that plaintiff was not suited to the work he was doing. After the date of the finding we think plaintiff's right to recover compensation was foreclosed, but the whole effort of the personnel officer of the Bureau of Economic Warfare indicated a determination to end the services before that finding without any real consideration for the rights of the plaintiff. In an effort to defend his action counsel for the defendant invokes the "letter that killeth" rather than "the spirit that giveth life."[23]

Legal scholars David Schwartz and Sidney Jacoby have noted that this decision marked the end of an era in which illegally discharged employees were not allowed to sue the government. Until then only persons on the federal payroll were able to bring court action. The case not only expanded the court's jurisdiction but also gave distressed employees the right to appeal unfair decisions.[24]

As a court of claims judge, Jones believed that awarding dam-

---

[22] *G. S. Kincaid* v. *United States*, 119 Ct. Cl. 257 (1951).
[23] *Ivan M. Elchibegoff* v. *United States*, 106 Ct. Cl. 541 (1946).
[24] David Schwartz and Sidney B. Jacoby, *Government Litigation*, pp. 220–221.

ages depended on provisions of the legislation concerned—whether damages were mandatory or merely directory. In *Wittner* v. *United States*, Jones held that procedure provisions of the Veterans' Preference Act of 1944 were mandatory.[25] In *Stringer* v. *United States* the court followed Jones's leadership when he wrote:

> The Congress is the policy-making branch of our government. It said plaintiff should have at least thirty days notice. The War Department gave him twenty-nine. Why? We have no doubt the official thought he was allowing exactly thirty days. But in his efforts to give not an ounce more than was necessary, he sliced the ham too thin. Then, too, the law requires the privilege of a personal appearance on appeal to the Civil Service Commission. This was not granted; and when it was belatedly allowed it was after a decision and in such a way as to say, "Oh, well, if we must listen to you, pay your own expenses, come to Washington and we'll hear you; but see how far you get."
>
> These are not little matters. They are of vast concern to the great array of veterans who at least are entitled to a good-faith compliance with the rights granted by a grateful people through their Congress. We cannot set the pattern of trimming away these rights.[26]

When the court considered domestic service-pay disputes, it encountered problems of overtime pay, survivors' benefits, pay incommensurate with responsibilities and slashes in the government work force.

An opportunity to resolve the question of overtime pay under provisions of the Federal Employees' Pay Act of 1945 came in cases involving reformatory-cottage employees who were in charge of women inmates at all hours of the day and night. In the Farley case Jones wrote:

> Try to imagine if you can, if anyone can, a reasonable creature in being after a regular 8-hour stint, which all the work the law allows in any one day, deciding, by choice, to spend two and one-half full nights of supposedly leisure time each week in charge of 20 people all of whom had committed offenses, some being narcotic violators, and being subject to call from inmates, and telephone calls from the officer of the day, ... to say nothing of administering to minor ailments and disturbances by babies, who were too young to read and respect the signs which said "Quiet, please," and the trying to classify it all as a simple condition of the right to work.

[25] *Loren H. Wittner* v. *United States*, 110 Ct. Cl. 231 (1948).
[26] *Rhea W. Stringer* v. *United States*, 117 Ct. Cl. 30 (1950).

It made no difference, Jones continued, if the plaintiff was single and made the reformatory cottage her place of residence; compensation must be granted employees for the extra time they worked.[27]

Jones also wrote majority opinions on survivor's benefits. Among his decisions was one allowing a deceased employee's wife to receive survivor's annuity benefits even though the employee had died before filing an application for those benefits. Jones said that, although the dead man had not taken sufficient precautions to meet the statute's terms, "the evidence of the deceased's intent and of the plaintiff's right is so overwhelming as to convince and satisfy anyone except a doubting Thomas."[28]

On complaints by federal employees that their responsibilities were greater than their civil-service levels, Jones wrote this opinion:

It is a well-settled principle of law that federal government employees are entitled only to the salaries of the position to which they are appointed regardless of the duties they actually perform. Appeals in this nature should be sent to the administrative officers. Persons seeking justice should thoroughly exhaust quasi-judicial remedies in their respective governmental agencies before taking the major step of bringing suit in a federal court.[29]

Another case required answering the question, May the government reduce its staff? When the Air Force laid off a number of civilian employees, the fired workers sued. Jones saw the right of employment in a different light. In "a growing nation in a rapidly changing world, where new inventions are being produced and new mysteries are being solved, it is inevitable that new Government agencies will be established and others enlarged," Jones said. "If at the same time the officials are not permitted to reduce or dismantle agencies that are no longer useful or whose work has been outgrown there will be grave danger of overlapping activities."[30] Unless those fired could prove arbitrary action, Jones concluded, the government remained within its rights to reduce the bureaucracy.

[27] *Cora C. Farley* v. *United States*, 131 Ct. Cl. 776 (1955).
[28] *Elsie C. Sonnabend* v. *United States*, 146 Ct. Cl. 622 (1959).
[29] *Arthur Price* v. *United States*, 112 Ct. Cl. 198 (1948); see also Newell W. Ellison, "The United States Court of Claims: Keeper of the Nation's Conscience for One Hundred Years," *George Washington Law Review* 24 (January 1956):251–266.
[30] *Peter E. Ray* v. *United States*, 144 Ct. Cl. 188 (1958).

A distantly related case concerned the right of an employee to recover suspended salary when the government had taken such action, forbidding a satisfactory investigation of the employee. Roberta Thomas, an American civil-service employee stationed in Germany, was forced to leave government service. She sued to recover pay withheld during her suspension. Jones compared Thomas' experiences with Jean Valjean in *Les Misérables* and decided in favor of the plaintiff. Jones wrote, "This Court represents the conscience of the Nation.... The law is not an end in itself. It is a means to an end. Its primary purpose is to reach the ends of justice between man and man and between the citizen and his government."[31]

The court faced a flood of difficult military claims after World War II and the Korean conflict. Jones's military decisions resulted in fewer landmark opinions than did his decisions in civilian cases, where more scholarly judges often overshadowed him. An exception was *Womer* v. *United States*. In that case there was conflicting testimony regarding the precise date of military disability. Jones decided for the government and limited the compensatory amount to the lesser figure. He said, "By limiting the judgment to the lesser of the two amounts a difficult determination is made certain."[32]

Military-retirement questions also posed some problems. Especially complex were two cases involving William G. Price, Jr., who had been a member of the National Guard since 1886. The court had to rule if actual service in the National Guard could be recognized for retirement purposes under the Retirement Equalization Act of 1948. Jones wrote, "It is difficult to maintain a stable, free country without a large measure of local control." He sympathized with Price "and the few others ... involved ... approaching the purple stage and tinted glow of the sundown." Jones concluded that Congress intended the 1948 act to apply to National Guard personnel, but Price had received a pension instead and no retirement pay. The following year Price sought recovery of full retirement pay while simultaneously retaining his pension. Jones, speaking for

---

[31] *Roberta I. Thomas* v. *United States*, 153 Ct. Cl. 399 (1961).
[32] *Porter Blake Womer* v. *United States*, 114 Ct. Cl. 415 (1949).

the majority, denied the claim. Price's pension payments said the court, were to be deducted from his retirement pay.[33]

An unusual problem regarding wartime transportation and Americans' affection for their pets came before the court in the case of *C. C. M. Pedersen v. United States.* The plaintiff, a State Department official, was entitled to a per diem for himself and his wife while delayed in port awaiting sailing. Mrs. Pedersen wanted the government to pay for her pets' transportation, and she refused to leave without them. Pedersen appealed. Full cost of the delay was $1,742, but the court awarded only $450 for Mrs. Pedersen's per diem.

Jones looked at the plaintiff's motivation and concern for animals in an unusual decision: "In our youth we always had dogs, mostly of the mongrel variety, but nevertheless dogs. We placed them just behind people, and when on rare occasions we fell out with any of our playmates, our hounds usually forged ahead." Jones then remarked, "We have very little respect and no affection for anyone who has not at some time in his life loved a dog.'" He concluded:

Mrs. Pedersen was certainly within her rights in refusing to travel without her pets. One can appreciate her unwillingness to leave them behind. On the other hand, she had no legal basis for charging the defendant $10 a day for the extra delay caused by her attitude, especially in a time of national peril, when family separations were the rule and not the exception, however appealing her sentiments may have been. We must apply the law and find it.[34]

The decision attracted attention, especially in the National Press Club. George Reedy, radio commentator and later press secretary for President Lyndon Johnson, wrote Jones a letter criticizing him for his favorable reference to dogs and signed the name of his Persian cat.[35]

[33] *William G. Price, Jr. v. United States,* 121 Ct. Cl. 664 (1951); *William G. Price, Jr. v. United States,* 123 Ct. Cl. 900 (1952).
[34] *C. C. M. Pedersen v. United States,* 115 Ct. Cl. 335 (1950).
[35] Toby Reedy to Jones, January 9, 1950, MJP. Jones responded to the "cat" by noting that, "while acknowledging my mistake, I can't correct it now without having both the cats and dogs after me. . . . But you may rest assured that when an opportunity comes again I shall pay adequate tribute to the felines and to you especially. You have been associating a little too much with

More serious were cases involving pay and allowances on the battlefield. A posthumous recipient of the Distinguished Service Cross, Gerald Stillman, a first lieutenant, had received a verbal assignment to command a battery. Such an order carried with it the rank of captain, but with bullets whizzing about, the promotion failed to meet strict interpretations of Article of War 119 (10 U.S.C. 1591). Stillman performed bravely but died in a Japanese prisoner-of-war camp. His heirs asked for his salary as captain. The adjutant general denied the request. The court of claims got the case.

Following precedent established by the Supreme Court in *United States v. Mitchell* (205 U.S. 161), Jones saw that the deceased man would have been shot on the spot if he had refused the command. Moreover, records had been destroyed in the war, and Jones rationalized that the defense rested its case on legalism. Jones ruled for Stillman's heirs and against the government.[36] Jones sent General of the Army Douglas MacArthur a copy of the decision. The chief judge was proud of it, and he sought public approval. MacArthur responded, "I have studied, read, and reviewed many judgments, but none gave me greater satisfaction than this one."[37]

This low-key publicity could coexist with Jones's quiet lifestyle. He lived out of the limelight, though he sought favorable publicity for his court. Each morning he walked from the University Club across Lafayette Square to the National Press Club, where he had breakfast, sometimes with his Texas friend Bascom Timmons. At the end of the day he returned to the club for a game of volleyball (which he played until past the age of sixty-five) and then had dinner with a number of friends like columnist Mary Haworth, an adviser to the lovelorn; Frank Dennis, assistant editor of the *Washington Post*; George Stimpson, author and Texas newspaperman; and Felix Cotton, of the International News Service.[38]

George Reedy and Bascom Timmons, but in spite of this my admiration for you continues at a high level." Timmons was one of Jones's closest newspaperman-confidants. Jones to Toby Reedy, January 9, 1950, MJP.

[36] *Charles N. Stillman, Administrator of the Estate of Gerald C. Stillman, Deceased v. United States*, 126 Ct. Cl. 750 (1953).

[37] Douglas MacArthur to Jones, December 10, 1953, MJP.

[38] Elizabeth Carpenter, "Judge Jones: Oasis of Calm," *American Statesman* (Austin), February 27, 1944.

Sometimes he relaxed by fishing or reading the Bible or the works of Tacitus, Marcus Aurelius, or Robert Ingersoll. For fun he read western novels.

As a judge, Jones practiced moralism and Christianity and injected both into his decisions. Perhaps that unfilled desire for the ministry was showing itself, or maybe it was a drive to make up for his shortcomings. In his search for truth as a judge he did not always see the legal issues that rose before a moral horizon.

Jones worshiped regularly at his office, at the First Methodist Church in Amarillo, and at Mount Vernon Place Methodist Church, in Washington. He gave liberally to Christian-identified causes. Like Henry Wallace, he had a deep faith, but he also knew that religious sentiments were seldom understood and even less often appreciated. Jones was first of all a politician.

As a politician Jones was as reluctant as the other judges on the court of claims to publicize an opinion delivered on a case involving three American alleged turncoats of the Korean War. The three soldiers, Otho Bell, William Cowart, and Lewis Griggs, were captured by the Communists in Korea. While in prison, they allegedly sympathized with their captors and participated in propaganda campaigns against the United States. At the end of the war they refused repatriation and in 1953 went to Communist China. The following year the United States Army formally discharged them, but in 1955 they returned home and brought suit to recover pay and allowances.

Five years later the court issued its ruling. No judge wanted to deliver the opinion. Rather than pass the buck, Jones wrote for a three-to-one majority that accepted the government's position: Because of acts of dishonor the men were guilty of a breach of contract of enlistment. Consequently they had abandoned their status as American soldiers and had forfeited all pay and allowances to which they might be otherwise entitled.[39]

The decision was favorably received in the press. Senator Sam Ervin of North Carolina wrote Jones a letter commending him for the excellent style and sound conclusions.[40]

---

[39] *Otho G. Bell, William A. Cowart, and Lewis W. Griggs* v. *United States*, 149 Ct. Cl. 248 (1960).

[40] Sam J. Ervin, Jr., to Jones, April 13, 1960, MJP; *Washington Post*, March 3, 1960.

Judge Madden dissented and refrained from the emotionalism of the "second red scare." He agreed that, under the conduct of the fundamental rights under the Constitution, "the Army... forfeited the pay already accrued to these plaintiffs, not by the process of trial and sentence... but by the crude and primitive method of refusing to give them their money."[41]

Later the Supreme Court reviewed the case and criticized Jones's decision. Justice Potter Stewart wrote:

> In the armed forces, as everywhere else, there are good men and rascals, courageous men and cowards, honest men and cheats. If a soldier's conduct fades below a specified level he is subject to discipline and his punishment may include the forfeiture of future but not of accrued pay. But a soldier who has not received such a punishment from a duly constituted courtmartial is entitled to the statutory pay and allowance of his grade and status, however ignoble a soldier he may be.[42]

Stewart thus rejected Jones's opinion that the plaintiffs could not recover back pay, and he pointed out that the alleged acts of dishonor upon which Jones substantiated his reasoning were emotional and irrelevant to the central issues.

Jones's search for a just result virtually always conformed to his own historical patterns. In cases before the court of claims he occasionally transcended precedents and government regulations to provide equity. In the case of the three soldiers however, his opinion brought him his sternest rebuke.

---

[41] *Otho G. Bell, William A. Cowart, and Lewis W. Griggs* v. *United States*, 149 Ct. Cl. 248 (1960).

[42] *Otho G. Bell et al,* v. *United States*, 366 U.S. 401 (1961).

15.

Property, Contracts, and Courthouse

Many property-requisition cases awaited Marvin Jones when he returned to the court of claims in 1945. He came to realize that private owners tended to inflate property values while government appraisers tended to underestimate them. Both parties, not surprisingly, relied on "expert" testimony but ignored fact when it was not helpful to them. Jones wrote on one occasion, "It is as natural for a human institution to look after its own interests as it is for the sparks to fly upward, but in order to justify recovery ... the plaintiff must show actual damages by virtue of breach of contract."[1]

During World War II the government fixed prices for airplane vibration-absorption devices at levels lower than estimates prepared by a maker of the devices, Lord Manufacturing Company. To meet wartime needs, the government took control of the plant. After the war the company sued for the difference between the 10.5 percent profit allowed by the government and the 68.5 percent profit returnable, the company claimed, in free-market operations.

Writing for the majority, Jones adhered to views already manifested in his role as war food administrator, observing that "the nation was in great peril—our national life being at stake." All Americans adjusted to these hardships:

Businessmen generally and even plaintiff's competitors were willingly accepting the 10 percent above cost for supplies and equipment needed in the war effort. . . . At such time it is unthinkable that a man would insist on profits of 50 to 100 percent and it is inconceivable that any court would allow such profits as just compensation. . . . the doctrine

---

[1] *Realty Associates, Inc., a Corporation* v. *United States*, 134 Ct. Cl. 167 (1956).

that prices may be based on what the traffic will bear has no place in our national economy at such a time.[2]

Jones reaffirmed that wartime price controls were reasonable in *St. Regis Paper Company* v. *United States*, a decision that also upheld exercise of power by the War Production Board. The reasonableness factor prohibited receiving damages for the "destruction of business" under the Tucker Act.[3]

The court also considered compensation for damage to property and equipment taken over on a rental basis by the government. For more than two years the United States government had used the facilities of Riverside Military Academy. The academy claimed damages of $166,715.41; the government countered with an offer of $15,366.67. Jones wrote for the majority that the plaintiff would be allowed a sum equal to the amount needed to restore the property to its takeover condition plus rent of $45,666.67. "Normally husky and healthy American boys, even though they come from the best families, which the plaintiff claims for its high-type school, are not primarily interested in using their spare time for playing croquet or growing roses," Jones wrote. "Growing boys do not immediately ... get over their tendency to play rough at times, if for no other purpose than to demonstrate that they are not sissies."[4] Jones refused to allow the new equipment, however, because that would have amounted to "a raid on the Treasury."

The property requisitions involved disputes over express or implied contracts between private parties and the federal government. Before creation of the court of claims individuals could hope to obtain satisfaction only from congressional appropriations decided largely on the principle of Anglo-American jurisprudence that the king can do no wrong. Any relief came as a gift from the government rather than as a right held by the citizen.

After establishment of the court the government moved toward the view that a citizen possessed the right to appeal a claim. Signi-

---

[2] *Lord Manufacturing Company* v. *United States*, 114 Ct. Cl. 119 (1949).

[3] *St. Regis Paper Company* v. *United States*, 110 Ct. Cl. 271 (1949). For a scholarly analysis of the Tucker Act, see David Schwartz and Sidney B. Jacoby, *Government Litigation*, pp. 125–198.

[4] *Riverside Military Academy, Inc., a Georgia Corporation* v. *United States*, 122 Ct. Cl. 756 (1952).

ficant developments came in 1950 and 1951 with Supreme Court decisions in *United States v. Moorman* and *United States v. Wunderlich*,[5] and two years later Congress recognized that the court of claims had been established on the philosophy of Article 3 of the United States Constitution.

Since then the court of claims has been acknowledged as a constitutional rather than a legislative court.[6] Legal scholars Maupin and Richie have observed:

> As a statement of strict law this is inaccurate: the Government, for instance, cannot be bound except by those with actual authority to contract for it. But if it is interpreted to mean that when the Court of Claims considers the equities of a case it does not attribute any special significance to the fact that one party is the Government, the dictum seems to be true.[7]

Jones himself moved toward the view "not only that the King can do wrong, but that he must answer for his wrong, in contract as in tort, just as his subjects do."[8]

The contract-claim dilemma faced by Jones's court centered around the proper relationship between administrative and judicial remedies. Although the court handled only 10 percent of all contract cases, contractual disputes accounted for more than 20 percent of the court's cases.[9] Claims judges base their opinions on the common law of contracts or on acts, precedents, and other criteria regarding fundamentals of consideration, bargain, and reliance. The chief judge, however, went a bit further. Jones dramatized common-law

---

[5] *United States v. Moorman*, 338 U.S. 457 (1950); *United States v. Wunderlich*, 342 U.S. 98 (1951). See Gilbert A. Cuneo and David V. Anthony, "Beyond Bianchi: The Impact of *Utah* and *Grace* on Judicial Review of Contract Appeals Boards' Decisions," in U.S. Court of Claims, *A Symposium: The United States Court of Claims*, pp. 602–630.

[6] See *Standard Rice Co. v. United States*, 101 Ct. Cl. 85 (1944), 323 U.S. 106 (1944); *Lyons v. United States*, 30 Ct. Cl. 352 (1895).

[7] Michael W. Maupin and Albert Richie II, "The Application of Common-Law Contract Principles in the Court of Claims: 1950 to Present," *Virginia Law Review* 49 (May 1963):850.

[8] Ibid., p. 851.

[9] Ibid., pp. 773–774; Francis M. Shea, "Statutory Jurisdiction of the Court of Claims: Past, Present and Future," *Federal Bar Journal* 29 (Summer 1970):160; Frank T. Peartree, "Statistical Analysis of the Court of Claims," in U.S. Court of Claims, *A Symposium*, p. 541.

concepts of fair play that were not present in the writings of other judges.

Court of claims contractual decisions may be considered to have come in two different eras since World War II. During the immediate postwar period claims resulted from extraordinary wartime legislation. After 1950 the court intensified its power of review.

One of Jones's first decisions concerned a defaulted construction contract. Jones maintained (for a three-to-two majority) that standard government contracts allowed an option of collecting liquidated damages or finishing the work and charging for the excess costs incurred in completing the agreement. The majority decision rejected a contention that the contractor's failure to finish the work on time was a continuing default until actual completion of the work.[10]

In another case the court considered the plight of a contractor who entered into a government contract but because of an unforeseen strike encountered increased labor costs. The central issue was government liability for higher costs. Following a precedent established by *United States* v. *Beuttas* (324 U.S. 768), Jones showed that it was not the contractor's fault that he was compelled to pay higher wages, but neither was it "the fault of the representatives of the Government who had the responsibility of handling the issues involved in this project." The plaintiff was not allowed extra compensation.[11]

In the post-1950 era the court of claims moved toward an unusual interpretation of offer and acceptance in contract cases. Traditionally a contract became valid when the acceptance was mailed. A question arose, however, when an agent of the United States mailed acceptance of an offer made by Rhode Island Tool Company. After the acceptance had been mailed but before it was delivered, the company discovered an error, notified the government, and withdrew its bid.

Jones characterized the common-law rule as like an oxcart

---

[10] *Maryland Casualty Company, a Corporation* v. *United States*, 93 Ct. Cl. 247 (1942).

[11] *George A. Fuller, a Corporation* v. *United States*, 105 Ct. Cl. 331 (1946).

operating in the age of the automobile. He decided that an offer could be withdrawn at any time before an acceptance had been received.[12]

Not all legal scholars agreed with Jones's interpretation. Maupin and Richie pointed out that the case ignored the fundamental problem of who would bear the burden of uncertainty during the contract's formation. They charged that the court allowed both offerer and offeree revocation rights, thus needlessly delaying compliance of a contract.[13]

In other cases the court was asked to decide whether the contract price should rise because of inflation. The alternative would be forcing the company to cut into its profit margin to complete the contract. Jones held businessmen liable for their lack of vision if the problem arose from their miscalculation or mistake. When government price freezes had occurred, however, Jones placed the liability on the government. In *Bateson-Stole, Inc.* v. *United States* he wrote:

> If placing a frozen ceiling on the wages which plaintiff was permitted to pay at the same time permitting the party instituting the freeze to pay higher wages on another tremendous project in the same neighborhood, which the officials must have known would absorb all the available labor in that area, is not interfering, then I have read the definitions in the law and secular lexicons to no purpose. I would allow plaintiff to recover at least the excess labor costs during the period of the freeze.[14]

Court decisions rendered by Jones during his last year of service followed a trend toward stringent limitations on government use of sovereign power. In a dissent in *Air Terminal Services, Inc.* v. *United States* he warned, "It is fitting to say, 'O, it is excellent to have a giant's strength'; but it is tyrannous to use it like a giant."[15]

On the other hand, Jones often ruled for the government. Unforeseen production difficulties and "acts of God" resulted in many

---

[12] *Rhode Island Tool Company* v. *United States*, 130 Ct. Cl. 698 (1955).

[13] Maupin and Ritchie, "The Application of Common Law Contract Principles in the Court of Claims: 1950 to Present," pp. 776–777.

[14] *Bateson-Stole, Inc.* v. *United States*, 145 Ct. Cl. 387 (1959).

[15] *Air Terminal Services, Inc.* v. *United States*, 165 Ct. Cl. 525 (1964); see also "Government Contracts: Implied Warranty Not to Alter Pre-Existing Conditions: Sovereign Immunity," *Cornell Law Review* 50 (Winter 1965): 316–321.

claims against the government. The court followed a general rule that the government could not be held liable for the producer's misfortunes unless specific government obligation could be found within the contract. This included even the "acts of God." The court of claims made an exception, however, in *Dillon v. United States.* The drought of 1942 caught the Vinita Hay Company of Oklahoma in an unenviable position. The company had promised to deliver hay, but grass shriveled in the sweltering heat of summer. Federal officials insisted on compliance with the contract, forcing the company to purchase hay at high prices in Nebraska. The company retaliated by suing the government for this amount plus damages.

In the decision Jones wrote:

> Anyone who has ever been in the fringe of the so-called Dust Bowl during the rare occasions on which these severe droughts sometimes prevail can realize the havoc that is wrought at such a time. The hot winds come and sweep with blistering trail across the prairies. The heavens become like brass and earth as iron.[16]

Jones added more "western talk," saying that it seemed that the hay company was an outlaw caught by a vigilante committee: when citizens "gave him the choice of whether he would be hung or shot, [he replied] that he could not develop any enthusiasm for either method."[17]

Jones allowed the plaintiff to recover for the Nebraska hay. He said: "In extraordinary cases where extreme hardship, unforeseen and not contemplated by either party, would necessarily result, a measure of relief may be granted if the unusual circumstances justify such action. This is the very essence of equity."[18]

During Jones's time as chief judge tax-refund suits formed the largest single category of litigation, comprising approximately 35 percent of the cases. The court of claims handled disputes alleging overpayment of taxes and refunds; the tax court handled liabilities assessed by the internal-revenue commissioner. Taxpayers exercised an option of taking their lawsuits into federal district courts or into the court of claims. Lawyers reviewed precedents and procedures to determine an individual client's best interest.

[16] *W. O. Dillon et al. v. United States,* 140 Ct. Cl. 508 (1957).
[17] Ibid.
[18] Ibid.

Property, Contracts, and Courthouse 249

As early as 1942, Jones was applying to these tax cases "the oft repeated principle that 'Men must turn square corners when they deal with the Government.' "[19] He displayed some bitterness in viewing the shams perpetrated on the United States government by taxpayers, and he believed that the government held a just claim to estate taxes.[20]

The issue of exempt corporations comprised most of Jones's tax cases. Under the Internal Revenue Code the government levied taxes on dues and initiation fees of various organizations. The evolution of his thought over the preceding six years was seen in 1948 in *Uptown Club of Manhattan v. United States*:

The test [for each case] is that if social features are a material purpose of the organization, it is a social club, subject to tax, but if such features are subordinate and incidental to the furtherance of a different predominant purpose, such as religion, the arts or business, it is not subject to tax.[21]

The court did not always follow Jones's reasoning. In a stormy controversial case by a three-to-two majority it decided that the federal government could tax the League of Women voters. The majority believed that influencing legislation was the league's main purpose and reason for being rather than engaging in research and voter education. Strongly dissenting, Jones countered with arguments that the league had enabled women to discharge capably duties that the right to vote had placed upon them.[22]

In the realm of judicial procedure Jones made a significant decision in *Kamen Soap Products Co. v. United States* (1953). The company alleged a claim for damages for breach of contract for sale and delivery of soap. The government counterclaimed fraud. When federal officials refused to release documents, the company had issued subpoenas *duces tecum*, which commanded the government to produce them. Government attorneys opposed the motion to issue the subpoenas.

[19] *Coca Cola Company v. United States*, 97 Ct. Cl. 241 (1942).
[20] *Saul B. Jacobs v. United States*, 131 Ct. Cl. 1 (1954).
[21] *Uptown Club of Manhattan v. United States*, 113 Ct. Cl. 422 (1948); see also *Seattle District No. 3 Mantle Club v. United States*, 98 Ct. Cl. 562 (1942).
[22] *League of Women Voters of the United States v. United States*, 148 Ct. Cl. 564 (1960).

Jones wrote that the court of claims must provide an orderly method for the disposition of claims against the government, as well as the waiver by Congress of sovereign immunity against suit. He added that, if Congress intended to exempt the government from the subpoena process for the production of documents, such intention must be clearly manifested in the statutes.[23] Reviewing the recent procedural history of the court of claims, W. Ney Evans, chairman of the court's Committee on Rules, wrote, "Kamen Soap was the first of four landmark decisions by the Court of Claims on the extent of its authority in the field of discovery and the nature of executive privilege within the field."[24]

Jones's judicial philosophy reflected neither profound nor original thought. In contrast to Learned Hand and Wales Madden, Jones remained an agrarian romantic—and a Methodist—after his appointment to the bench. He tried to balance law, congressional intent, and his own concept of equity, which was deeply rooted in his southwestern heritage. In contrast to Hugo Black, Jones refrained from judicial activism and consensus based upon established precedents written by others. His reasoning seemed obscure at times, but his decisions revealed a simple faith with greater appreciation for equity than for rules of procedure.

Jones usually compromised in claims disputes, protecting the government's pocketbook. He avoided legal jargon. He believed that judicial opinions should be read, understood, and even enjoyed by the general public. With clarity as his goal he reduced complex cases to their lowest common denominator, often to the dismay of more sophisticated, scholarly judges.[25]

Jerome Barron, of George Washington University, wrote of Jones:

The judge's philosophy was the philosophy of the enabling legislation of the court—to serve as the keeper of the nation's conscience. The judge always tried to fathom how Congress would react to a problem. He

---

[23] *Kamen Soap Products Company, Inc.* v. *United States*, 124 Ct. Cl. 519 (1953).

[24] W. Ney Evans, "Current Procedure in the Court of Claims," in U.S. Court of Claims, *A Symposium*, pp. 431–432.

[25] Wilson Cowen, interview with author, June 29, 1972; James Durfee, interview with author, June 29, 1972.

looked on the court as Congress' court. It was a unique, and I thought, entirely sound approach.[26]

Sanford Katz, of Boston College Law School, remarked:

While I think that some other judges on the court tended to be more impressed with one side or the other in the presentation of arguments, Judge Jones, was, I believe, fair and impartial. Even though he had served in the federal government as a Congressman for many years, he still had an open mind with regard to the government's responsibility. In other words, the government could be wrong in some cases.[27]

Alton Boyer, an attorney, wrote that "a legal scholar he [Jones] never held himself out to be—but if he had preferred that role instead of the Texas role, he had high abilities." Boyer said that it would be incorrect to suggest that Judge Jones paid legal technicalities "no heed, or was not as skilled in their manipulation as most. He did, however, have an ability easily to rise above them."[28]

But there was still another side to Marvin Jones: the attention he gave to administrative details, which took considerable time and thought. In the fifteen years after 1947, the year Jones assumed his role as chief judge of the court, he recorded some noteworthy administrative accomplishments. Before 1947 the court of claims had operated with an antiquated set of rules that led to conflicts with District of Columbia and other federal courts. Jones created a committee of judges to revise procedures. The result was modernized rules for the court.

Jones also helped reestablish the court of claims as a constitutional court. When he came as a judge, the court was classified as a congressional tribunal. Any change meant reversing a 1933 Supreme Court decision (in *Williams* v. *United States*) that the court of claims was an inferior court.[29] Within the court of claims the judges desired the independence that the Constitution guaranteed to fellow judges serving under Article 3. Constitutional court justices enjoyed life tenure or terms for good behavior. But in a court in

---

[26] Jerome A. Barron to author, June 28, 1973. See also "The Chief Judge's Cases Now Pending in the Supreme Court on Certiori" (1952–1967), MS, Marvin Jones Papers, hereafter cited as MJP.

[27] Sanford N. Katz to author, June 27, 1973.

[28] Alton Boyer to author, July 26, 1973; see also Ray S. Bolze to author, May 30, 1973.

[29] *Williams* v. *United States*, 289 U.S. 553 (1933).

which Uncle Sam paid, congressional retaliation over unfavorable decisions had frequently been claimed. That led Judge Sam Whitaker to advocate a return to constitutional status, while Marvin Jones wanted to preserve the court's congressional-reference jurisdiction; he wanted the court to have equality with other federal courts of appeal.

Using his close congressional ties with Sam Rayburn to best advantage, Jones succeeded in getting that accomplished. In an act of June 28, 1953, Congress affirmed the court as a constitutional body with jurisdiction throughout the nation. (Nine years later, in 1962, the Supreme Court, in *Glidden Company* v. *Zdanok*, would affirm the court's constitutional status but at the same time curtail congressional-reference jurisdiction. Justice John Harlan, with strong concurrence from Chief Justice Earl Warren, would conclude that the court of claims would cease rendering advisory opinions after it had disposed of cases in which substantial proceedings had already taken place.)[30]

In 1956, Jones helped win more prestige for the court of claims when Congress enacted legislation authorizing the chief justice of the United States to assign a judge from the court of claims temporarily as a circuit or district judge and to provide for service by a retired judge in any of these courts. The legislation also allowed the court of claims to present a budget estimate subject to approval of the Judicial Conference, in which the chief judge of the court of

---

[30] "Memorandum re H.R. 1070, 83d Cong., 1st sess., Relating to the United States Court of Claims," MJP; *Glidden Company* v. *Zdanok*, 370 U.S. 530 (1962); Wilson Cowen, chief judge, U.S. Court of Claims, interview with author, June 29, 1972; Frank T. Peartree, "Statistical Analysis of the Court of Claims," in U.S. Court of Claims, *A Symposium*, pp. 541–542; Stanley J. Purzyckik, "The Congressional Reference Case in the United States Court of Claims," *Catholic University of America Law Review* 10 (January 1961): 35–43; Edwin J. McDermott, "The Court of Claims: The Nation's Conscience," *American Bar Association Journal* 57 (June 1971):594–596. McDermott also notes that the legislative-reference issue did not end with the Glidden case. In 1966, Congress passed a law restoring the right of recovery denied claimants by the Glidden case. In Public Law 89–681 of October 15, 1966 (28 U.S.C., secs. 1492 and 2509), Congress established procedures for the chief commissioner of the court of claims to decide congressional-reference cases. In this unusual manner Congress hoped to preserve the constitutional status of the appeals court, as well as equity. Jerome A. Barron to author, December 18, 1974.

claims was permitted by the new law to participate.³¹ This placed the court at the appellate level.

Also in 1956, Jones helped get the court of claims out of its dilapidated facility and into a new building. Jones persuaded Texas Senator Lyndon B. Johnson and Representative Robert Jones of Alabama to introduce bills providing for the construction of a new courthouse on the present site. That gave George Stewart, architect of the Capitol, the opportunity to testify that "the character and arrangement of the United States Court of Claims building, originally designed, constructed, and occupied as the Corcoran Art Gallery, is not and never has been adaptable for efficient layout for use as a courthouse nor for the needs and requirements of the court." The building was also a firetrap.³²

Jones's desire to keep the court near the White House drew opposition from the Commission on Fine Arts and from the National Capital Planning Commission, which thought that the area should be reserved for the executive branch of government. City planners recommended a new courthouse near the Supreme Court. They were supported by Democratic Senators Wayne Morse of Oregon and Hubert Humphrey of Minnesota and Republican Senator John Sherman Cooper of Kentucky, plus citizens who feared that a new court of claims building would mean destruction of the historically significant Decatur Blair and Blair-Lee houses. While opponents talked, however, Jones's court and its personnel continued making plans for a new courthouse to be built on Lafayette Square.³³

In 1960 the pressure of public opinion and Mrs. John F. Kennedy forced Jones to compromise on the exterior design of the

---

³¹ Marvin Jones to William Langer, October 6, 1954, Jones to Emanuel Celler, May 9, 1955, MJP; U.S., Congress, House, Committee on the Judiciary, *Amend Title 28, United States Code, with Respect to Duties of Judges of the United States Court of Claims: Report 2349 to Accompany S. 977*, 84th Cong., 2d sess., June 13, 1956; 70 *U.S. Stat.* 487. Unless otherwise noted, all interviews and correspondence citing Jones refer to Marvin Jones.

³² U.S., Congress, Senate, Committee on Public Works, *Building for U.S. Court of Claims: Hearings, S. 3445*, 84th Cong., 2d sess., June 5–July 2, 1956, pp. 3–12, 15–17.

³³ Ibid.; "History Relating to the Purchase of the Old Corcoran Art Gallery for the Use of the United States Court of Claims," MS, March 29, 1960, MJP.

building and preserve the historical mood.³⁴ At the end of much bitter debate the court of claims moved into new quarters overlooking the square and the White House. Later, at the dedication of the building in 1967, Chief Justice Earl Warren observed:

> I have watched the construction of this building for almost five years and have realized, as the judges of the Court of Claims, that they needed and deserved a new home. That might be due somewhat to the propaganda of my friend, Marvin Jones, but . . . I am sure . . . that they were building a temple—a temple of justice. I know that Chief Judge Jones and his colleagues did.³⁵

Long-standing, tiring problems faded away. Marvin Jones's most difficult administrative chore had ended, and it signified the climax of his career as chief judge. The building stands as one of Jones's lasting contributions.³⁶

Three years before the dedication Jones had semiretired. On March 9, 1964, he had officially informed President Lyndon Johnson that he wanted to become a senior judge, coinciding with the retirement of his old friend Judge Sam Whitaker.³⁷ Jones did not think very highly of President John F. Kennedy and probably would have died in office rather than give the president the opportunity to appoint his successor. Jones respected Kennedy's successor, however.

Jones was eighty-two in 1964, mentally alert and in good health. He desired fewer responsibilities after fifty-four years in government service. President Johnson granted him the status of senior judge, an indication that Jones never intellectually or emotionally contemplated complete retirement.

---

³⁴ U.S., Congress, Senate, Committee on Public Works, *Public Buildings—1960: Hearings, S. 3279, S. 3280, and S. 3403*, 84th Cong., 2d sess., May 23, 1960; *Washington Star*, June 26, 1960, July 15, 1961; *Washington Post*, July 14, 1962.

³⁵ United States Court of Claims and United States Court of Customs and Patent Appeal, *Dedication of Court Building*, p. 18.

³⁶ Wilson Cowen, interview with author, June 29, 1972.

³⁷ Jones to Lyndon B. Johnson, March 9, 1964; Jones to Walter Jenkins, February 4, 1964, Lyndon B. Johnson Papers, Lyndon B. Johnson Library, Austin, Texas; Jones to Johnson, June 18, 1964, MJP.

16.

Bid Me Good Morning

Marvin Jones dreaded the approaching years, and he wondered if life was over. Since 1916 "life" for Jones had meant living in Washington, responsibility, a job. He concluded that he must stay active as long as his mind and body would permit. While he maintained his Washington residence at the University Club, he rented an apartment in Amarillo for extended visits.

His readjustment to Texas came slowly and with difficulty. He had been too long away from the state. He loved Texas, but in 1964 the prospects of removal from the Washington scene caused him to experience an intense year-long depression. He had a form of Potomac fever. Men who serve in all three branches of government, and even those who work in only one, thrive on being near the seat of power. Too, habits change slowly and painfully at eighty-two.[1]

Temporary relief came when President Johnson, with the support of House Agriculture Committee Chairman Bob Poage, named Jones to head the National Commission of Food Marketing. The commission resulted from a charge by the National Farmers' Union that price manipulations and chain-store practices lowered payments to farmers yet increased prices. To study the problem, Congress created the commission, consisting of fifteen members—five from the Senate, five from the House, and five from the private sector. The committee was to investigate and make its report and recommendations by July 1, 1966. Jones accepted the position enthusiastically. Each day he looked forward to these new responsi-

[1] Marvin Jones, interview with author, April 16, 1972. Unless otherwise noted, all interviews and correspondence citing Jones refer to Marvin Jones.

bilities. Again he felt a sense of belonging and of contribution.[2]

At the height of his joy Jones underwent a precautionary physical examination, and the dark clouds quickly returned. His doctors gave him an ultimatum. If he wanted to live, he must restrict strenuous activities. Jones wrote President Johnson:

> The position calls for someone of great stamina, as well as experience. My years of service in this field make the opportunity especially appealing to me, . . . but I feel that a younger man is needed—one who possesses the energies essential to this great task. If I began and could not finish it, it would make the situation worse instead of better.[3]

Limited service as a senior judge was the only answer. In April 1964, Chief Justice Earl Warren, who had often chatted with Jones at the University Club, had appointed Jones special master of the United States Supreme Court in a case that involved a boundary dispute between Louisiana and Mississippi, particularly the course of the Mississippi River at Deadman's Bend, a few miles above Natchez. Both states claimed title to oil land there worth millions of dollars.

Jones devoted himself to the case with his usual energy. He summoned witnesses, issued subpoenas, and reported findings. Later the Supreme Court upheld his analysis of the complex matter.[4]

After that, until 1970, Jones traveled to the sites of various United States courts of appeal—Fort Worth, Oklahoma City, Denver, Richmond, Los Angeles, and San Francisco—filling vacancies that arose because of illness or temporary absences. Regular members usually wrote the opinions, but senior judges like Jones shared their legal knowledge, and their votes were crucial to the outcome. Most sessions lasted less than two weeks, but one California trip for service with the Ninth Circuit Court of Appeals required a

---

[2] W. R. Poage to Friends (letter to constituents), May 8, 1964, Orville Freeman to Jones, July 8, 1964, MJP; U.S., Congress, Senate, Committee on Commerce, *Establishing a National Commission on Food Marketing*, 88th Cong., 2d sess., May 12, 1964, S. Rept. 1022; Jones to Lyndon Johnson, July 20, 1964, MJP.

[3] Jones to Johnson, September 18, 1964, MJP. Johnson accepted the resignation in September after the first meeting of the commission.

[4] Marvin Jones, *Report of Special Master, State of Louisiana v. State of Mississippi et al.*; Marvin Jones to author, May 5, 1972; Ray S. Bolze to author, May 30, 1973.

month. These assignments came in addition to the work of sitting as senior judge on the court of claims.[5]

After 1970, Jones's appearances became rarer, but pride would not let him resign. In a humane way the court remembered Jones for his past work and placed the present and the future in the hands of the Divine.

As senior judge, Jones added little to his judicial philosophy. He was guided by established precedents and procedures and by his sense of equity. He continued to favor fair play over a strict adherence to rules.[6] In affirming a decision of the tax court, Jones philosophized:

> Taxes are not a matter of machine-like logic. There is a human equation in taxation as in all the affairs of life. Taxes are levied on the successful individual to make temporary payments to the unsuccessful and his dependents even though they may all be individuals in good health.[7]

Jones's last significant opinion came in *Charles Dean Lesley* v. *State of Oklahoma* (407 F.2d 543 [1969]). Jones looked at "a youth of 19 years, largely unlettered, who had been a broomcorn cutter, who had never been in court, it being his first offense, a boy who had been reared in poverty, who faced a charge of robbery with firearms." The sheriff had told Lesley that he might receive the death penalty or a ninety-nine-year sentence if he did not plead guilty. Badly frightened, the boy, without an attorney, had pleaded guilty, and the court had assessed a forty-year prison sentence, whereas average sentences were only five years. After fourteen years Lesley was paroled; he then appealed for a pardon. This action raised the issue of the constitutionality of the original verdict.

Jones compared Lesley's plight with that of Jean Valjean in Victor Hugo's *Les Misérables*. After quoting from Hugo, Jones

---

[5] "Service of Senior Judge Marvin Jones with United States Courts of Appeals," undated MS, MJP.

[6] For some of Jones's more important circuit-court opinions see *Kent-Reese Enterprises, Inc.* v. *Hempy*, 378 F.2d 910 (1967), *General Warehouse, Two, Inc.* v. *United States*, 389 F.2d 1016 (1967); *Jack Harald Bowman et al.* v. *Curt G. Joa, Inc.*, 361 F.2d, 706; *Pacific Molasses Co.* v. *Federal Trade Commission*, 356 F.2d, 386 (1966).

[7] *John C. W. Dix and Caroline W. Dix* v. *Commissioner of Internal Revenue*, April 2, 1968, "Decision by Marvin Jones," MS, MJP.

commented that the book "was fiction. Here we are dealing with facts.... In law, as in life, all facts and circumstances must be examined before just conclusions are reached." Paying little attention to the plaintiff's character, Jones said that he wanted to emphasize that

> I believe in the enforcement of the law without which there can be no human rights. Law and Liberty are as intimately linked as the law of demand and supply. One cannot live without the other. But in this case, I am persuaded that the penalty for the crime has been fully paid and the purpose of the law has been fully accomplished.[8]

Having succesfully met these requirements, the majority overruled the district court's conviction.

Jones devoted more attention to a wide variety of interests. He suggested that Congress make annual sessions coincide with fiscal years of federal courts. He advised reforming the congressional committee system to distribute powers more widely. He made telephone calls to old friends and dined often with the Texas delegation. A stream of ideas flowed from Jones's pen as he attempted to hold his influence, but Congress ignored most of them. Despite his attempts to stay in the mainstream, he spent much time, by choice or chance, alone—but that was not unusual.

In semiretirement Jones continued to base many of his suggestions and actions on his religious beliefs. Unlike many such persons, however, he considered the world to be moving forward—with an occasional backslide. He participated in work of the Committee on the World Food Crisis and the American Freedom from Hunger Foundation. He believed that distribution of food remained the nation's number-one problem, and he based his interpretation on Genesis 1:29-30:

> And God said, Behold, I have given you every herb bearing seed, which is upon the face of all the earth, and every tree, in the which is the fruit of a tree yielding seed; to you it shall be for meat.
> And to every beast of the earth, and to every fowl of the air, and to every thing that creepeth upon the earth, wherein there is life, I have given every green herb for the meat: and it was so.

In newly discovered leisure time Jones increased his participa-

---

[8] *Charles Dean Lesley* v. *State of Oklahoma et al.*, 407 F.2d 543 (1969).

tion in International Christian Leadership, Inc. Of all his charities Cal Farley's Boys Ranch near Amarillo was his favorite. Jones was a close friend of Farley's, and he contributed financially and even visited the ranch frequently. There he talked with the boys and sought to inspire them to pursue knowledge and a deeper understanding of the Christian faith. Jones regarded this activity as more important than his contributions to the scholarship funds of Southwestern University, the University of Texas, and Texas A&M.[9]

In appreciation of his contributions to the court of claims, friends gathered there on October 22, 1968, for an unveiling of his portrait. Jones attended, too, accompanied by a sister. They heard prominent attorney Ashley Sellers, a former aide in the War Food Administration, eulogize Jones.

As a lifelong agrarian advocate, the talented Texan perfected laws, strengthened farm security, and used his southwestern agrarian philosophy with equity and a touch of romanticism. To his credit were the Agricultural Adjustment Act of 1933, the Farm Credit Administration Act, the Jones-Connally Cattle Act, the Soil Conservation and Domestic Allotment Act, the Bankhead-Jones Farm Tenancy Act, the Jones-Costigan Sugar Act, and the Agricultural Adjustment Act of 1938. Jones looked upon the breakthrough in soil, wind, and water conservation, along with section 32 of the amendments to the Agricultural Adjustment Act of 1935 as his major legislative achievements.

Jones's agrarian ideology originated with his family heritage on his parents' small farm in Texas. If he had enjoyed his experiences on the farm, he would not have quickly left it. Rather than remembering the experience of growing crops or raising cattle, Jones remembered only the hard, physical labor required. As he traveled from the farm to the legislature to the judiciary, absence from the land made his heart grow fonder. Similarly, once freed from the reins of the legislative plow, Jones became increasingly idealistic.

Was Marvin Jones a practical politician or an agrarian philosopher? His career as chairman of the House Agriculture Committee makes it plain that he was a practical politician; he knew politics as

---

[9] Jones to Louis H. Bean, May 24, 1968, Abraham Vereide to Marvin Jones, August 25, 1950, Cal Farley to Jones, August 25, 1950, Cal Farley to Jones, April 9, 1965, MJP.

the art of the possible with flexible legislative solutions interlaced with farm philosophy.

In a speech called "Land—Our Ultimate Security" Jones had listed the ten elements that comprised the farm program: soil conservation, interest rates, marketing agreements, rural electrification, commodity loans, uses of water, homes, price and income, agricultural research, and the stamp plan. The federal government should base agricultural policy on these elements to preserve the land and the agricultural way of life.[10]

Jones also added a warning to the USDA administrators that significant legislation came from the grass roots of America and that local and state governments were important. He saw that "this broad, big, varied country cannot be adequately served by rigid rules. The forms won't fit. What may be good for one community may be bad for another."[11] Arguing against a stratified society, he preached flexibility.

While Jones continually maintained that the nation rested on an agricultural foundation, he refrained from conceding that farm life was superior or that the agricultural-political process should favor small farmers. He believed that "country life is vital to itself and to the good life," and that urbanites needed education about agriculture's problems. He felt that "the city signifies distribution, but the farm signifies production of food which the city doesn't understand." He theorized that the better-educated large farmers were more effective producers and marketeers. They possessed the capital necessary to make modern farming innovations and thus received the principal advantages of agricultural legislation.[12]

Jones's life and thought manifested a heritage that had been shaped by American experiences from the late eighteenth century. Being of the westward movement, Jones shared somewhat the abstract doctrines that Henry Nash Smith isolated and structured in *Virgin Land*. Jones found solace in repeated references to the doctrine that

---

[10] Marvin Jones, "The Remarks of Marvin Jones," *Congressional Record* scrapbook, vol. 5 (76th Cong., 2d sess.), pp. 9132–37.

[11] Marvin Jones, "How Farm Policies Are Made," speech, USDA Graduate School Seminar, November 25, 1946, MS, MJP.

[12] Jones, telephone conversation with author, December 13, 1974.

agriculture is the only real source of wealth; that every man has a natural right to land; that labor expended in cultivating the earth confers a valid title to it; that the ownership of land, by making the farmer independent gives him social status and dignity; that constant contact with nature in the course of his labors makes him virtuous and happy; that America offers a unique example of a society embodying these traits; and as a general inference from all the propositions, that government should be dedicated to the interests of the freehold farmer.[13]

Here were the concepts of the myth of the garden that permeated the writings of Benjamin Franklin and Thomas Jefferson. Yet Jones realized that America was becoming an urban nation and that urban values would gradually emerge as the dominant ones.

Marvin Jones accepted and understood the realities of man's relationship with other men. They were far more meaningful to him than administrative procedures or judicial precedents. His restless, inquisitive mind enabled him to develop that rarity in recent American history, a broad agricultural philosophy. Moreover, because his approach to farm problems cut across commodity lines, he was able to work for consensus rather than commodity interests. He worked successfully to gain a broader-based support in Congress and among the American people for his cherished goals of farm credit and soil conservation. As a congressman he participated in the passage of more, significant legislation than that produced by any previous House agriculture chairman.[14] As war food administrator he ably handled delicate relationships with the chief executive as he achieved increased food production to meet wartime needs. As chief judge of the court of claims he made positive contributions in obtaining adequate facilities for the court and gaining recognition of the court as a member of the constitutional system, meanwhile setting judicial precedents of his own and flavoring his opinions with his own agricultural theories.

As the years passed, the figure of Marvin Jones, once proudly erect, bent slightly, then stooped. He leaned on a cane, but his eyes remained clear. His hair thinned and grayed. At last his once-eager interest faded. Then came pneumonia, a long convalescence, a fall,

[13] Henry Nash Smith, *Virgin Land: The American West as Symbol and Myth*, p. 141.
[14] Irvin May, Jr., "Marvin Jones: Agrarian and Politician," *Agricultural History* 51 (April 1977):421–440.

and injuries. He died at 7:00 P.M. on March 4, 1976, in the Panhandle.

Friends paused to remember and reflect. Jay Taylor, a prominent Amarillo rancher, observed that Jones understood the problems of the farmer and rancher better than anyone else in Washington.[15] Congressman George Mahon thought of Jones not as a legislator or a judge but as a great human being: "Not in my lifetime have I met a cleaner, finer, more decent and more compassionate man than Marvin Jones. He was one of God's noblemen."[16]

Thus ended the long life of a distinguished man who served the public, and served it well, for most of his adult life. As a student of his career, I seem to hear Marvin Jones saying from beyond the grave:

> Say not goodnight!
> But in some brighter clime,
> Bid me good morning.[17]

[15] *Amarillo Globe*, March 5, 1976.
[16] U.S. Court of Claims, *In Memoriam: Honorable Marvin Jones*, p. 9.
[17] Ibid., p. 13.

Bibliography

Primary materials are the most important sources for information regarding the career of Marvin Jones. The most valuable single source is the Marvin Jones Papers, which were in private hands in Jones's offices in Washington, D.C., and Amarillo, Texas, when I did much of my early research. Jones reprinted some of these documents in his books, and later he gave some materials to Texas Tech University and to Texas A&M University. Other valuable collections of materials are in the National Archives, in the United States Department of Agriculture Library, and in the papers of John Bankhead, James Byrnes, and Franklin D. Roosevelt. I have also kept extensive notes of telephone conversations. Government documents, oral-history interviews with Jones, and the recollections of his contemporaries, as well as his letters to me, contain important insights into his career and thought.

Manuscript Collections

Bankhead, John. Papers. Department of Archives and History, State of Alabama, Montgomery, Ala.
Bell, Jasper. Papers. Western Historical Manuscripts Collection, University of Missouri, Columbia, Mo.
Bradley, William S. Papers. In the possession of Mrs. William S. Bradley, Austin, Texas.
Bush Collection. Mary E. Bivens Memorial Library, Amarillo, Texas.
Byrnes, James F. Papers. Clemson University, Clemson, S.C.
Cannon, Clarence. Papers. Western Historical Manuscripts Collection, University of Missouri, Columbia, Mo.
Connally, Tom. Papers. Library of Congress, Manuscript Division, Washington, D.C.
Costigan, Edward P. Papers. University of Colorado Library, Boulder, Colo.
Guleke, James O. Papers. Nita Stewart Haley Memorial Library, Midland, Texas.

Hoover, Herbert. Papers. Herbert Hoover Presidential Library, West Branch, Iowa.
Johnson, Lyndon B. Papers. Lyndon B. Johnson Library, Austin, Texas.
Jones, Marvin. Papers. Irvin M. May Collection. Texas A&M University Archives, College Station, Texas.
———. Papers. Texas Technological University, Lubbock, Texas.
Morgenthau, Henry, Jr. Papers. Franklin D. Roosevelt Library, Hyde Park, N.Y.
National Archives. Washington, D.C. Record Groups 16, 233, 250.
O'Neal, Edward. Papers. State of Alabama, Department of Archives and History, Montgomery, Ala.
Peek, George N. Papers. University of Missouri, Western Historical Manuscripts Collection, Columbia, Mo.
Rayburn, Sam. Papers. Sam Rayburn Library, Bonham, Texas.
Roosevelt, Franklin D. Papers. Franklin D. Roosevelt Library, Hyde Park, N.Y.
Timmons, Bascom. Collection. Texas A&M University Archives, College Station, Texas.
Truman, Harry S. Papers. Harry S. Truman Library, Independence, Mo.
Wilson, Milburn L. Papers. Montana State University Library, Bozeman, Mont.

Government Documents

U.S., Congress. *Biographical Directory of the American Congress, 1774–1961*. Washington, D.C.: U.S. Government Printing Office, 1961.
———. *Congressional Record*. 65th Cong., 1st sess.–76th Cong., 3d sess., vols. 56–85, 1917–1940.
———. *Official Congressional Directory, 65th Congress, 1st Session*. Washington, D.C.: U.S. Government Printing Office, 1917.
———. *Official Congressional Directory, 66th Congress, 1st Session*. Washington, D.C.: U.S. Government Printing Office, 1919.
———. *Official Congressional Directory, 67th Congress, 2d Session*. Washington, D.C.: U.S. Government Printing Office, 1922.
———. *Official Congressional Directory, 72d Congress, 2d Session*. Washington, D.C.: U.S. Government Printing Office, 1932.
———. *Official Congressional Directory, 74th Congress, 1st Session*. Washington, D.C.: U.S. Government Printing Office, 1935.
———, House. *Unveiling of a Portrait of the Honorable Marvin Jones, Chief Judge, United States Court of Claims, and Former Chairman, House Committee on Agriculture*. Washington, D.C.: U.S. Government Printing Office, 1968.
———, House, Committee on Agriculture. *Agricultural Adjustment Act Amendments: Report to Accompany H.R. 8052*. 74th Cong., 1st

sess. Washington, D.C.: U.S. Government Printing Office, 1935.

———, House, Committee on Agriculture. *Agricultural Adjustment Act of 1937: Report to Accompany H.R. 8505.* 75th Cong., 2d sess. Washington, D.C.: U.S. Government Printing Office, 1937.

———, House, Committee on Agriculture. *Agricultural Credit: Emergency Farm Mortgage Act of 1933: Report to Accompany H.R. 4795.* 73d Cong., 1st sess. Washington, D.C.: U.S. Government Printing Office, 1933.

———, House, Committee on Agriculture. *Agricultural Products: McNary-Haugen Export Bill on H.R. 5563, Declaring Emergency in Respect to Certain Agricultural Commodities and to Promote Equality between Agricultural Commodities and Other Commodities: Hearings.* 68th Cong., 1st sess. Washington, D.C.: U.S. Government Printing Office, 1934.

———, House, Committee on Agriculture. *Agricultural Research: Hearings.* 74th Cong., 1st sess. Washington, D.C.: U.S. Government Printing Office, 1935.

———, House, Committee on Agriculture. *Agriculture: General Farm Legislation: Hearings.* 75th Cong., 1st. sess. Washington, D.C.: U.S. Government Printing Office, 1937.

———, House, Committee on Agriculture. *Bankhead Cotton Control Bill: Hearings*, 73d Cong., 2d sess. Washington, D.C.: U.S. Government Printing Office, 1934.

———, House, Committee on Agriculture. *Bankhead-Jones Farm Tenant Act: Conference Report to Accompany H.R. 7562.* 75th Cong., 1st sess. Washington, D.C.: U.S. Government Printing Office, 1937.

———, House, Committee on Agriculture. *Cotton Crop Reports, H.R. 14245: Hearings.* Washington, D.C.: U.S. Government Printing Office, 1926.

———, House, Committee on Agriculture. *Extending Bankhead-Jones Act to Puerto Rico: Report to Accompany H.R. 7908.* 75th Cong., 1st sess. Washington, D.C.: U.S. Government Printing Office, 1937.

———, House, Committee on Agriculture. *Farm Credit Act of 1933: Report to Accompany H.R. 5790.* 73d Cong., 1st sess. Washington, D.C.: U.S. Government Printing Office, 1933.

———, House, Committee on Agriculture. *Farm Credit Act of 1935: Hearings.* 74th Cong., 1st sess. Washington, D.C.: U.S. Government Printing Office, 1935.

———, House, Committee on Agriculture. *Farm Credit Bill of 1940: Report to Accompany H.R. 9843.* 76th Cong., 3d sess. Washington, D.C.: U.S. Government Printing Office, 1940.

———, House, Committee on Agriculture. *Farm Security Act of 1937: Report to Accompany H.R. 7562.* 75th Cong., 1st sess. Washington, D.C.: U.S. Government Printing Office, 1937.

———, House, Committee on Agriculture. *Farms: Amending Bankhead-Jones Farm Tenant Act: Hearings.* 76th Cong., 3d sess. Washington, D.C.: U.S. Government Printing Office, 1940.

———, House, Committee on Agriculture. *Farm Tenancy: Hearings.* 75th Cong., 1st sess. Washington, D.C.: U.S. Government Printing Office, 1937.

———, House, Committee on Agriculture. *Include Cattle as Basic Agricultural Commodity: Hearings.* 73d Cong., 2d sess. Washington, D.C.: U.S. Government Printing Office, 1934.

———, House, Committee on Agriculture. *McNary-Haugen Export Bill: Hearings on H.R. 5563.* 68th Cong., 1st sess. Washington, D.C.: U.S. Government Printing Office, 1924.

———, House, Committee on Agriculture. *Marketing of Farm Produce: Agricultural Adjustment Program: Hearings.* 72d. Cong., 2d sess. Washington, D.C.: U.S. Government Printing Office, 1932.

———, House, Committee on Agriculture. *Marketing of Farm Produce: Agricultural Relief: Hearings.* 69th Cong., 2d sess. Washington, D.C.: U.S. Government Printing Office, 1927.

———, House, Committee on Agriculture. *Marketing of Farm Produce: Agricultural Relief: Hearings.* 70th Cong., 1st sess. Washington, D.C.: U.S. Government Printing Office, 1928.

———, *House, Committee on Agriculture. Marketing of Farm Produce: Agricultural Relief: Hearings.* 71st Cong., 1st sess. Washington, D.C.: U.S. Government Printing Office, 1929.

———, House, Committee on Agriculture. *Marketing of Farm Produce: Swank Agricultural Bill: Hearings,* 72d Cong., 2d sess. Washington, D.C.: U.S. Government Printing Office, 1932.

———, House, Committee on Agriculture. *To Promote Farm Ownership by Amending Bankhead-Jones Farm Tenant Act to Provide for Government Insured Loans to Farmers: Hearings.* 76th Cong., 3d sess. Washington, D.C.: U.S. Government Printing Office, 1940.

———, House, Committee on Agriculture. *United Nations Conference on Food and Agriculture: Hearings.* 78th Cong., 1st sess. Washington, D.C.: U.S. Government Printing Office, 1943.

———, House, Committee on Expenditures in the Executive Departments. *Change the Name of the Department of Interior to the Department of Conservation and Public Works: Hearings.* 74th Cong., 1st sess. Washington, D.C.: U.S. Government Printing Office, 1935.

———, House, Committee on Public Lands. *Soil Erosion Program: Hearings.* 74th Cong., 1st sess. Washington, D.C.: U.S. Government Printing Office, 1935.

———, Joint Commission of Agricultural Inquiry. *Report.* Washington, D.C.: U.S. Government Printing Office, 1921–22.

———, Senate, Committee on Commerce. *Establishing a National Com-*

Bibliography

mission on *Food Marketing: Report 1022.* 88th Cong., 2d sess. Washington, D.C.: U.S. Government Printing Office, 1964.

———, Senate, Committee on Expenditures in Executive Departments. *Interior Department: To Change Name of Department of Interior and to Coordinate Certain Governmental Functions: Hearings.* 74th Cong., 1st sess. Washington, D.C.: U.S. Government Printing Office, 1935.

———, Senate, Committee on Public Works. *Public Buildings—1960: Hearings, S. 3279 and S. 3403.* 84th Cong., 2d sess. Washington, D.C.: U.S. Government Printing Office, 1960.

———, Senate, Committee on Public Works. *Building for the U.S. Court of Claims: Report 2739 to Accompany S. 3445.* 84th Cong., 2d sess. Washington, D.C.: U.S. Government Printing Office, 1956.

U.S. Bureau of the Budget. *The United States at War.* Washington, D.C.: U.S. Government Printing Office, 1946. Reprint. New York: Da Capo Press, Inc., 1972.

U.S. Court of Claims. *In Memoriam: Honorable Marvin Jones.* Washington, D.C.: U.S. Government Printing Office, 1976.

———. *Jurisdiction of the U.S. Court of Claims.* Washington, D.C.: U.S. Government Printing Office, 1970.

———. *The United States Court of Claims: Its Centennial.* Washington, D.C.: U.S. Government Printing Office, 1956.

——— and U.S. Court of Customs and Patent Appeal. *Dedication of Court Building.* St. Paul, Minn.: West Publishing Company, 1967.

U.S. Department of Agriculture. *Compilation of Soil Conservation and Domestic Allotment Act as Amended, Agricultural Adjustment Act of 1938, as Amended, Federal Crop Insurance Act as Amended, Sugar Act of 1937, Appropriation Items Relating Thereto, and Miscellaneous Laws.* Washington, D.C.: U.S. Government Printing Office, 1940.

———. *Yearbook of Agriculture,* 1940. Washington, D.C.: U.S. Government Printing Office, 1940.

U.S. War Food Administration. *Final Report of the War Food Administrator: 1945.* Washington, D.C.: U.S. Government Printing Office, 1945.

Court Cases

Air Terminal Services, Inc. v. *United States.* 165 Ct. Cl. 525 (1964).

American Institute for Economic Research v. *United States.* 157 Ct. Cl. 548 (1962).

Anne C. Sheeles v. *United States.* 118 Ct. Cl. 362 (1951).

Arthur Price v. *United States.* 112 Ct. Cl. 198 (1948).

Atchison, Topeka, and Santa Fe Railway Company v. *United States.* 121 Ct. Cl. 467 (1952).

Baltimore Steam Packet Company v. *United States.* 112 Ct. Cl. 448 (1948).
Barnard-Curtis Company v. *United States.* 157 Ct. Cl. 103 (1962).
Bateson-Stole, Inc. v. *United States.* 145 Ct. Cl. 387 (1959).
Bolin-Drive-a-Way Company, a Corporation v. *United States.* 151 Ct. Cl. 164 (1960).
Branch Banking and Trust Company et al. v. *United States.* 115 Ct. Cl. 341 (1950).
Calvert Distilling Company v. *United States.* 94 Ct. Cl. 517 (1941).
C. C. M. Pedersen v. *United States.* 115 Ct. Cl. 335 (1950).
Cecil W. Armstrong et al. v. *United States.* 152 Ct. Cl. 731 (1961).
Charles Dean Lesley v. *State of Oklahoma et al.* 407 F2d 543 (1969).
Charles N. Stillman, Administrator of the Estate of Gerald C. Stillman, Deceased v. *United States.* 126 Ct. Cl. 750 (1953).
Christopher S. Long v. *United States.* 93 Ct. Cl. 544 (1941).
Coca Cola Company v. *United States.* 97 Ct. Cl. 241 (1942).
Cora C. Farley v. *United States.* 131 Ct. Cl. 776 (1955).
David M. Miller v. *United States.* 135 Ct. Cl. 1 (1956).
Edward A. Juhl, Jr., Administrator of the Estate of Edward A. Juhl, Deceased v. *United States,* 116 Ct. Cl. 587 (1950).
Elsie C. Sonnabend v. *United States.* 146 Ct. Cl. 622 (1959).
Forest of Dean Iron Ore Company v. *United States.* 106 Ct. Cl. 250 (1946).
Frank Wilifred Williams and Raymond Steve Harvey, Individually and Doing Business as Ogeechee Auto Wrecking Company v. *United States.* 111 Ct. Cl. 356 (1948).
General Warehouse, Two, Inc. v. *United States.* 389 F2d 1016 (1967).
George A. Fuller, a Corporation v. *United States.* 105 Ct. Cl. 331 (1946).
Glidden Company v. *Zdanko.* 370 U.S. 530 (1962).
G. S. Kincaid v. *United States.* 119 Ct. Cl. 257 (1951).
Helen H. England et al. v. *United States.* 133 Ct. Cl. 768 (1956).
Horace Heidt Foundation v. *United States.* 145 Ct. Cl. 322 (1959).
Ivan M. Elchibegoff v. *United States.* 106 Ct. Cl. 541 (1946).
J. H. Crain and R. E. Lee Wilson, Jr., Trustees of Lee Wilson and Company, a Business Trust v. *United States.* 96 Ct. Cl. 443 (1942).
J. H. Crain and R. E. Lee Wilson, Jr., Trustees of Lee Wilson and Company, a Business Trust v. *United States.* 114 Ct. Cl. 94 (1948).
J. J. Kelley Company v. *United States.* 107 Ct. Cl. 594 (1947).
Joe A. Dewsbury v. *United States.* 137 Ct. Cl. 1(1956).
John Lloyd Smelcer v. *United States.* 130 Ct. Cl. 510 (1955).
Kamen Soap Products Company, Inc. v. *United States.* 124 Ct. Cl. 519 (1953).
Kent-Reese Enterprises, Inc. v. *Hempy.* 378 F.2d 910 (1967).
League of Women Voters of the United States v. *United States.* 148 Ct. Cl. 564 (1960).

Bibliography 269

Lord Manufacturing Company v. *United States*. 114 Ct. Cl. 119 (1949).
Loren H. Wittner v. *United States*. 110 Ct. Cl. 231 (1948).
Loyal Band of Creek Indians et al. v. *United States*. 118 Ct. Cl. 373 (1951).
Lyons v. *United States*. 30 Ct. Cl. 352 (1895).
Maryland Casualty Company v. *United States*. 135 Ct. Cl. 428 (1956).
Merchants Club v. *United States*. 106 Ct. Cl. 562 (1946).
Myer Schneiderman et al. v. *United States*. 117 Ct. Cl. 715 (1950).
Nolan Brothers, Inc. v. *United States*. 98 Ct. Cl. 41 (1942).
Osage Nation v. *United States*. 119 Ct. Cl. 592 (1951).
Otho G. Bell, William A. Cowart, Lewis W. Griggs v. *United States*. 149 Ct. Cl. 248 (1960).
Otho G. Bell et al. v. *United States*. 366 U.S. 401 (1961).
Perley W. Smith v. *United States*. 145 Ct. Cl. 104 (1959).
Perry McGlore v. *United States*. 96 Ct. Cl. 507 (1942).
Peter E. Ray v. *United States*. 144 Ct. Cl. 188 (1958).
Phillips Pipe Line Corp. v. *United States*. 94 Ct. Cl. 462 (1941).
Porter Blake Womer v. *United States*. 114 Ct. Cl. 415 (1949).
Prieke and Sons, Company of Illinois, a Corporation v. *United States*. 106 Ct. Cl. 789 (1946).
Realty Associates, Inc., a Corporation v. *United States*. 134 Ct. Cl. 167 (1956).
Rhea W. Stringer v. *United States*. 117 Ct. Cl. 30 (1950).
Rhode Island Tool Company v. *United States*. 130 Ct. Cl. 698 (1955).
Riverside Military Academy, Inc., a Georgia Corporation v. *United States*. 122 Ct. Cl. 756 (1952).
Roberta I. Thomas v. *United States*. 153 Ct. Cl. 399 (1961).
Robert L. Guyler v. *United States*. 161 Ct. Cl. 159 (1963).
Robert Morass Lovett et al. v. *United States*. 104 Ct. Cl. 557 (1946).
Russell H. Williams et al. v. *United States*. 130 Ct. Cl. 435 (1955).
St. Regis Paper Company v. *United States*. 110 Ct. Cl. 271 (1949).
Samuel Furman v. *United States*. 135 Ct. Cl. 546 (1952).
Saul B. Jacobs v. *United States*. 131 Ct. Cl. 1 (1954).
Scripture Press Foundation v. *United States*. 152 Ct. Cl. 463 (1961).
Seattle District No. 3 Mantel Club v. *United States*. 98 Ct. Cl. 562 (1942).
Sico Foundation v. *United States*. 155 Ct. Cl. 554 (1961).
S. R. Brackin v. *United States*. 96 Ct. Cl. 457 (1942).
Standard Rice Company v. *United States*. 101 Ct. Cl. 85 (1944).
Strategical Demolition Company, a Corporation v. *United States*. 119 Ct. Cl. 291 (1951).
Swiss Federal Railway and Confederation of Switzerland v. *United States*. 125 Ct. Cl. 444 (1953).
Tennessee Soap Company v. *United States*. 130 Ct. Cl. 154 (1954).
Trailerships, Inc. v. *United States*. 106 Ct. Cl. 215 (1946).
Union Pacific Railway Company v. *United States*. 117 Ct. Cl. 534 (1950).

United States v. *Lovett.* 328 U.S. 303 (1946).
United States v. *Moorman.* 338 U.S. 457 (1950).
United States v. *Seminole Nation.* 146 Ct. Cl. 171 (1959).
United States v. *Wunderlich.* 342 U.S. 98 (1951).
Uptown Club of Manhattan v. *United States.* 113 Ct. Cl. 422 (1948).
Wah Chang Corporation v. *United States.* 151 Ct. Cl. 41 (1960).
Whitman Publishing Company, a Corporation v. *United States.* 106 Ct. Cl. 689 (1946).
William E. Nash v. *United States.* 141 Ct. Cl. 135 (1958).
William Ody Washington v. *United States.* 137 Ct. Cl. 344 (1957).
William S. Price, Jr. v. *United States.* 121 Ct. Cl. 644 (1951).
William S. Price, Jr. v. *United States.* 123 Ct. Cl. 900 (1952).
W. O. Dillon et al. v. *United States.* 140 Ct. Cl. 508 (1957).

Books

Abernathy, Thomas P. *The Formative Period in Alabama, 1815–1828.* 2d ed. University, Ala.: University of Alabama Press, 1965.

———. *From Frontier to Plantation in Tennessee: A Study in Frontier Democracy.* University, Ala.: University of Alabama Press, 1932.

Albertson, Dean. *Roosevelt's Farmer: Claude R. Wickard in the New Deal.* New York: Columbia University Press, 1955.

American Freedom from Hunger Foundation. *World Food Congress.* Washington, D.C.: American Freedom From Hunger Foundation, 1963.

Arnett, Alex Mathews. *Claude Kitchin and the Wilson War Policies.* Boston: Little, Brown, and Co., 1937.

Auxier, George W. *Industrial Mobilization for War.* Vol. 1. New York: Greenwood Press, 1969.

Baker, Benjamin. *Wartime Food Procurement and Production.* New York: Columbia University Press, King's Crown Press, 1951.

Baker, Gladys L., et al. *Century of Service: The First 100 Years of the United States Department of Agriculture.* Washington, D.C.: U.S. Government Printing Office, 1963.

Baldwin, Sidney. *Poverty and Politics: The Rise and Decline of the Farm Security Administration.* Chapel Hill: University of North Carolina Press, 1968.

Barkley, Alben W. *That Reminds Me.* Garden City, N.Y.: Doubleday and Co., 1954.

Barnhart, John D. *Valley of Democracy.* Bloomington: Indiana University Press, 1953.

Benedict, Murray R. *Can We Solve the Farm Problem?* New York: Twentieth Century Fund, 1955.

———. *Farm Policies of the United States, 1790–1950.* New York: Twentieth Century Fund, 1953.

Bibliography

Bernstein, Barton J., ed. *Towards a New Past*. New York: Random House, 1967.
Billington, Ray Allen. *Westward Expansion: A History of the American Frontier*. 2d ed. New York: Macmillan Co., 1960.
Black, John D. *Agricultural Reform in the United States*. New York: McGraw Hill Book Co., 1929.
———. *Food Enough*. Lancaster, Pa.: Jacques Cattel Press, 1943.
Blackorby, Edward C. *Prairie Rebel: The Public Life of William Lemke*. Lincoln: University of Nebraska Press, 1963.
Blaisdell, Donald C. *Government and Agriculture*. New York: Farrar and Rinehart, 1940.
Blum, John M., ed. *From the Morgenthau Diaries: Years of Crisis, 1928–1938*. Boston: Houghton-Mifflin Co., 1959.
Braeman, John; Brammer, Robert H.; and Walters, Everett, eds. *Change and Continuity in Twentieth-Century America*. Columbus, Ohio State University Press, 1964.
Brown, Nugent E. *B Hall, Texas*. San Antonio, Texas: Naylor Co., 1938.
Brown, Ray Hyer. *Robert Stewart Hyer: The Man I Knew*. Salado, Texas: Anson Jones Press, 1957.
Burns, James MacGregor. *Roosevelt: The Lion and the Fox*. New York: Harcourt, Brace, and World, 1956.
Byrnes, James F. *Speaking Frankly*. New York: Harper and Brothers, 1947.
Campbell, Christiana McFadyen. *The Farm Bureau and the New Deal*. Urbana: University of Illinois Press, 1962.
Cantor, Louis. *A Prologue to the Protest Movement*. Durham, N.C.: Duke University Press, 1969.
Chandler, A. C., and Thames, A. B. *Colonial Virginia*. Richmond, Va.: Times-Dispatch Co., 1907.
Chandler, Lester V. *America's Greatest Depression, 1929–1941*. New York: Harper and Row, 1970.
Clyde, Paul H. *The Far East*. 3d ed. Englewood Cliffs, N.J.: Prentice-Hall, 1958.
Cochran, John H. *Dallas County: A Record of Its Pioneers and Progress*. Dallas: Andrew S. Mathis Service Publishing Co., 1928.
Conkin, Paul K. *Tomorrow a New World: The New Deal Community Program*. Ithaca, N.Y.: Cornell University Press, 1959.
Conner, Seymour V. *The Peters Colony of Texas: A History and Biographical Sketches of the Early Settlers*. Austin: Texas State Historical Association, 1959.
Conrad, David. *The Forgotten Farmers*. Urbana: University of Illinois Press, 1965.
Dale, Edward Everett. *The Cross Timbers: Memories of a North Texas Boyhood*. Austin: University of Texas Press, 1966.

Davis, Joseph Stancliffe. *The Farm Export Debenture Plan.* Stanford, Calif.: Stanford University Food Research Institute, Miscellaneous Publication 54, 1929.
Dulles, Foster Rhea. *The American Red Cross: A History.* New York: Harper and Brothers, 1950.
Dykeman, Wilma, and Stokely, James. *Seeds of Southern Change: The Life of Will Alexander.* Chicago: University of Chicago Press, 1962.
Eby, Frederick. *Education in Texas: Source Materials.* Austin: University of Texas, 1918.
Ellis, Edward R. *A Nation in Torment: The Great Depression.* New York: Capricorn Books, 1971.
Evins, Joe L. *Understanding Congress.* New York: Clarkson N. Porter, 1963.
Fite, Gilbert C. *American Agriculture and Farm Policy Since 1900.* New York: Macmillan Co., 1960.
―――. *The Farmers' Frontier, 1865-1900.* New York: Holt, Rinehart and Winston, 1966.
―――. *George N. Peek and the Fight for Farm Parity.* Norman: University of Oklahoma Press, 1954.
―――. *Peter Norbeck: Prairie Statesman.* Columbia: University of Missouri Press, 1948.
Folmsbee, Stanley J.; Corlew, Robert E.; and Mitchell, Enoch L. *Tennessee: A Short History.* Knoxville: University of Tennessee Press, 1969.
Freidel, Frank. *Franklin D. Roosevelt: The Triumph.* Boston: Little, Brown and Co., 1956.
Gee, Mary Gaston. *The Ancestry and Descendants of Anzi Williford Gaston II of Spartenburg County, South Carolina.* Charlottesville, Va.: By Mrs. Wilson Gee, 1944.
Genung, A. B. *The Agricultural Depression Following World War I and Its Political Consequences.* Ithaca, N.Y.: Northeast Farm Foundation, 1954.
Gold, Bela. *Wartime Economic Planning in Agriculture.* New York: Columbia University Press, 1949.
Gray, L. C. *A History of Agriculture in the Southern United States to 1860.* 2 vols. Gloucester, Mass.: Peter Smith, 1958.
Green, Donald E. *Land of the Underground Rain.* Austin: University of Texas Press, 1973.
Greer, James K. *Grand Prairie.* Dallas: Tardy-Publishing Company, 1935.
Griswold, A. Whitney. *Farming and Democracy.* New York: Harcourt, Brace and Co., 1948.
Hanna, Charles A. *The Scotch-Irish or the Scot in North Britain, North Ireland and North America.* Vol 2. Baltimore, Md.: Genealogical Publishing Co., 1968.

Hart, Freeman H. *The Valley of Virginia in the American Revolution, 1763–1789.* Chapel Hill: University of North Carolina Press, 1942.

Hicks, John D. *The Republican Ascendancy, 1921–1933.* New York: Harper and Row, 1960.

Hofstadter, Richard. *The American Political Tradition and the Men Who Made It.* New York: Alfred A. Knopf, 1948.

Hoover, Herbert. *Addresses upon the American Road, 1933–1938.* New York: Charles Scribner's Sons, 1938.

Hubbard, Preston J. *Origins of the TVA: The Muscle Shoals Controversy, 1920–1932.* New York: W. W. Norton and Co., 1968.

Ickes, Harold L. *The Secret Diary of Harold L. Ickes.* Vol. 1. *The First Thousand Days, 1933–1936.* New York: Simon and Schuster, 1953.

Jones, C. N. *Early Days in Cooke County, 1848–1873.* Gainesville, Texas: C. N. Jones, 1936.

Jones, Marvin. *How War Food Saved American Lives.* Washington, D.C.: National Capitol Press, n.d.

———. *Marvin Jones Memoirs.* Edited by Joseph M. Ray. El Paso: Texas Western Press, 1973.

———. *Report of the Special Master: State of Louisiana v. State of Mississippi et al.* Washington, D.C.: Byron S. Adams Press, 1965.

———. *Should Uncle Sam Pay—When and Why?* Washington, D.C.: Printed by the author, 1963.

———. *The Tariff Bill, July 13, 1921.* Washington, D.C.: U.S. Government Printing Office, 1921.

———. *Vocational Retraining of Disabled Soldiers.* Washington, D.C.: U.S. Government Printing Office, 1918.

Jones Family, The: Texas Pioneers. N.P.: Jones Historical Committee, 1950 (in the possession of Herbert K. Jones and Franklin P. Jones, Lubbock, Texas).

Kelley, Alfred H., and Harbison, Winfred A. *The American Constitution: Its Origins and Development.* 3d ed. New York: W. W. Norton and Company, 1963.

Key, Della Tyler. *In the Cattle Country: History of Potter County, 1887–1966,* 2d ed. Quanah-Wichita-Falls, Texas: Nortex Offset Publications, 1972.

Kile, Orville Meaton. *The Farm Bureau through Three Decades.* Baltimore, Md.: Waverly Press, 1948.

Knoblauch, H. C.; Law, E. M.; and Meyer, W. P. *State Agricultural Experiment Stations: A History of Research Policy and Procedure.* Washington, D.C.: U.S. Government Printing Office, 1962.

Lathrop, Barnes F. *Migration into East Texas, 1835–1860: A Study from the United States Census.* Austin: Texas State Historical Association, 1949.

Leuchtenberg, William E. *Franklin D. Roosevelt and the New Deal.* New York: Harper and Row, 1963.

Link, Arthur S. *Wilson the Diplomatist*. Baltimore: Johns Hopkins Press, 1957.

———. *Woodrow Wilson and the Progressive Era, 1910–1917*. New York: Harper and Brothers, 1954.

Livermore, Seward W. *Politics Adjourned: Woodrow Wilson and the War Congress*. Middletown, Conn.: Wesleyan University Press, 1966.

Lowitt, Richard. *George W. Norris: The Persistence of a Progressive, 1919–1933*. Urbana: University of Illinois Press, 1971.

McCoy, Donald R. *Calvin Coolidge: The Quiet President*. New York: Macmillan Co., 1967.

———. *Landon of Kansas*. Lincoln: University of Nebraska Press, 1966.

McGovern, George, ed. *Agricultural Thought in the Twentieth Century*. Indianapolis: Bobbs-Merrill Co., 1967.

Martin, Addie, ed. *Valley View Centennial, 1872–1972*. Valley View, Texas: Valley View Centennial Committee, 1972.

Mason, Alpheus T. *Harlan Fiske Stone: Pillar of the Law*. New York: Viking Press, 1956.

Matasow, Allen J. *Farm Politics and Policies in the Truman Years*. Cambridge, Mass.: Harvard University Press, 1967.

Meriwether, Robert L. *The Expansion of South Carolina, 1729–1765*. Kingsport, Tenn.: Southern Publishers, 1940.

Moley, Raymond. *After Seven Years*. New York: Harper and Brothers, 1939.

———. *The First New Deal*. New York: Harcourt, Brace, and World, 1966.

Morgan, Robert J. *Governing Soil Conservation*. Baltimore: Johns Hop- Press, 1965.

Murray, Robert K. *The Harding Era: Warren G. Harding and His Administration*. Minneapolis: University of Minnesota Press, 1969.

———. *The Politics of Normalcy: Governmental Theory and Practice in the Harding-Coolidge Era*. New York: W. W. Norton and Co., 1973.

Nixon, Edgar B. *Franklin Roosevelt and Conservation, 1911–1945*. Vol. 1. Hyde Park, N.Y.: General Services Administration, 1957.

Nourse, Edwin G.; Davis, Joseph S.; and Black, John D. *Three Years of the Agricultural Adjustment Administration*. Washington, D.C.: Brookings Institution, 1937.

Ord, Paul, ed. *They Followed the Rails: In Retrospect: A History of Childress County*. Childress, Texas: Childress Reporter, 1970.

Paddock, Buckley B., ed. *Fort Worth and the Texas Northwest*. Vol. 4 of *History of Texas*. Chicago: Lewis Publishing Co., 1922.

Peek, George N., and Johnson, Hugh. *Equality for Agriculture*. Moline, Ill.: Moline Plow Co., 1922.

―――, with Crowther, Samuel. *Why Quit Our Own.* New York: D. Van Norstrand Co., 1936.
Perkins, Van L. *Crisis in Agriculture: The Agricultural Adjustment Administration and the New Deal, 1933.* Berkeley and Los Angeles: University of California Press, 1969.
Richards, Henry I. *Cotton and the AAA.* Washington, D.C.: Brookings Institution, 1936.
Richardson, Rupert Norval. *The Frontier of Northwest Texas, 1846–1876: Advance and Defense by the Pioneer Settlers of the Cross Timbers.* Glendale, Calif.: Arthur H. Clark, Co., 1963.
Romasco, Albert U. *The Poverty of Abundance: Hoover, the Nation, the Depression.* New York: Oxford University Press, 1965.
Roosevelt Agricultural Committee. *Agriculture in the 1936 Presidential Election.* Chicago: Cutchfield and Company, 1936.
Rosenman, Samuel, comp. *The Public Papers of Franklin D. Roosevelt.* 13 vols. New York: Random House, 1938–1950.
Rowley, William D. *M. L. Wilson and the Campaign for the Domestic Allotment.* Lincoln: University of Nebraska Press, 1960.
Saloutos, Theodore, and Hicks, John D. *Twentieth-Century Populism: Agricultural Discontent in the Middle West, 1900–1939.* Lincoln: University of Nebraska Press, 1951.
Schapsmeier, Edward L., and Schapsmeier, Frederick H. *Henry A. Wallace of Iowa: The Agrarian Years, 1910–1940.* Ames: Iowa State University Press, 1968.
Schlebecker, John T. *Cattle Raising on the Plains, 1900–1961.* Lincoln: University of Nebraska Press, 1963.
Schlesinger, Arthur M., Jr. *The Age of Roosevelt: The Coming of the New Deal.* Boston: Houghton-Mifflin Co., 1958.
Schwartz, David, and Jacoby, Sidney B. *Government Litigation.* Fairfax, Va.: Coiner Publications, 1963.
Shideler, James H. *Farm Crisis, 1919–1923.* Berkeley and Los Angeles: University of California Press, 1957.
Smith, A. Morton. *The First 100 Years in Cooke County.* San Antonio, Texas: Naylor Co., 1955.
Smith, Daniel M. *The Great Departure: The United States and World War I: 1914–1920.* New York: John Wiley and Sons, 1965.
Smith, Frank E. *Congressman from Mississippi.* New York: Capricorn Books, 1964.
Smith, Henry Nash. *Virgin Land: The American West as Symbol and Myth.* New York: Vintage Books, 1957.
Southwestern University. *Bulletins of Southwestern University.* June, 1904. Kansas City, Mo.: Hudson-Kimberly Publishing Co., 1904.
―――. *The Sou'Wester.* Vol. 2. Buffalo, New York: Hausauer-Jones Printing Co., 1905.

Spillman, William J. *Balancing the Farm Output.* New York: Orange-Judd Publishing Co., 1927.
Stanley, F. *The Texas Panhandle: From Cattlemen to Feed Lots.* Borger, Texas: Jim Hess Printers, 1971.
Sternsher, Bernard. *Rexford Tugwell and the New Deal.* New Brunswick, New Jersey: Rutgers University Press, 1964.
Tacheron, Donald G., and Udall, Morris K., eds. *The Job of the Congressman.* Indianapolis: Bobbs-Merrill Co., 1966.
Thompson, Victor A. *The Regulatory Process in OPA Rationing.* New York: Columbia University Press, King's Crown Press, 1950.
Timmons, Bascom M. *Garner of Texas: A Personal History.* New York: Harper and Brothers, 1948.
Tindall, George B. *The Emergence of the New South, 1913–1945.* Vol. 10 of *A History of the South*, edited by Wendell H. Stephenson and E. Merten Coulter. Baton Rouge: Louisiana State University Press and University of Texas, Littlefield Fund for Southern History, 1967.
United Nations Conference on Food and Agriculture. *Final Act and Section Reports.* Washington, D.C.: U.S. Government Printing Office, 1943.
―――. *Yearbook of the United Nations, 1946–1947.* Lake Success, N.Y.: United Nations, Department of Public Information, 1947.
United States Court of Claims. *A Symposium: The United States Court of Claims.* Oberlin, Ohio: Oberlin Printing Co., 1967.
Wade, Homer Dale. *Establishment of Texas Technical College, 1916–1923.* Lubbock: Texas Tech Press, 1956.
Warren, Harris Gaylord. *Herbert Hoover and the Great Depression.* Norton Library Edition. New York: W. W. Norton and Co., 1967.
Warwick, Mrs. Clyde W. *The Randall County Story.* Hereford, Texas: Pioneer Book Publishers, 1969.
Webb, Walter Prescott. *The Great Plains.* New York: Ginn and Company, 1931.
―――, and Carroll, H. Bailey. *The Handbook of Texas.* Vol. 2. Austin: Texas State Historical Association, 1952.
Wilcox, Walter. *The Farmer in the Second World War.* Ames: Iowa State College Press, 1947.
Wright, Louis B. *The Cultural Life of the American Colonies, 1607–1763.* New York: Harper and Row, 1957.
Zinn, Howard, ed. *New Deal Thought.* Indianapolis: Bobbs-Merrill Co., 1966.

Articles

Alexander, Will. "Overcrowded Farms." In U.S. Department of Agriculture. *Yearbook of Agriculture, 1940.* Washington, D.C.: U.S. Government Printing Office, 1940.

Bibliography

Allen, Lee N. "The Democratic Presidential Primary Election of Texas of 1924 in Texas." *Southwestern Historical Quarterly* 61 (April 1958): 474–493.

Anderson, Clifford B. "The Metamorphosis of American Agrarian Idealism in the 1920's and 1930's." *Agricultural History* 35 (October 1961): 182–188.

Banfield, Edward C. "Ten Years of the Farm Tenant Purchase Program." *Journal of Farm Economics* 31 (August 1949): 469–486.

Blythe, Stuart O. "The Seventieth Congress." *Country Gentleman* 55 (December, 1927): 5, 123, 126.

Case, H. C. M. "Farm Debt Adjustment During the Early 1930's." *Agricultural History* 34 (October 1960): 173–181.

Christensen, Alice M. "Agricultural Pressure and Governmental Response in the United States, 1919–1929." *Agricultural History* 11 (January 1937): 33–42.

Davis, Joseph S. "The Export Debenture Plan for Aid to Agriculture." *Quarterly Journal of Economics* 53 (February 1929): 250–277.

Diamond, Solomond. "Washington Notes." *Commercial Law Journal* 64 (July 1959): 205–210.

Ellison, Newell W. "The United States Court of Claims: Keeper of the Nation's Conscience for One Hundred Years." *George Washington Law Review* 24 (January 1956): 251–266.

"The Farm Bloc—A Peril or a Hope?" *Literary Digest* 71 (December 24, 1921): 10–11.

Fish, S. E. "Judges, Juries, and Law." In *Amarillo*, compiled by Clara T. Hammond. Amarillo, Texas: George Autry, 1971.

Fite, Gilbert C. "The Agricultural Issue in the Presidential Campaign of 1928." *Mississippi Valley Historical Review* 37 (March 1951): 653–684.

Gamer, Saul R. "Some Notes on Court of Claims Practice." *Government Contracts Review* 2 (April 1958): 4–26.

"Governmental Contracts: Implied Warranty Not to Alter Pre-Existing Conditions: Sovereign Immunity." *Cornell Law Review* 50 (Winter 1956): 316–321.

Grantham, Dewey, W., Jr. "Texas Congressional Leaders and the New Freedom, 1913–1917." *Southwestern Historical Quarterly* 53 (July 1949): 35–48.

Gregory, Clifford V. "The American Farm Bureau Federation and the AAA." *Annals of the American Academy of Political and Social Science* 179 (May 1935): 152–157.

Haley, J. Evetts. "Cow Business and Monkey Business," *Saturday Evening Post* 207 (December 18, 1934): 26–29.

Hall, Tom G. "Wilson and the Food Crisis: Agricultural Price Control During World War I." *Agricultural History* 47 (January 1973): 25–46.

Hamilton, C. Horace. "Break the Backbone of the Tenant System." *Rural America* 12 (October 1934): 3–5.
———. "Texas Farm Tenure Activities." *Journal of Land and Public Utility Economics* 14 (August 1938): 330–333.
Heacock, Walter J. "William B. Bankhead and the New Deal." *Journal of Southern History* 21 (August 1955): 347–359.
Hill, Robert J. "The Topography and Geology of the Cross Timbers and Surrounding Regions in Northern Texas." *American Journal of Science* 33 (1887): 291–303.
Johnson, E. C. "Agricultural Credit." In U.S. Department of Agriculture. *Yearbook of Agriculture, 1940.* Washington, D.C.: U.S. Government Printing Office, 1940.
Johnson, William R. "National Farm Organizations and the Reshaping of Agricultural Policy in 1932." *Agricultural History* 37 (January 1963): 35–42.
Jones, Charles O. "Representation in Congress: The Case of the House Agricultural Committee." *American Political Science Review* 55 (June 1961): 358–367.
Jones, Marvin. "Honorable Marvin E. [sic] Jones Explains Proposed Farm Program." *Cotton Digest* 10 (October 16, 1937): 514–515.
Kipps, Clarence T., Jr. "A Unique National Court: The United States Court of Claims." *American Bar Association Journal* 53 (November 1967): 1025–29.
Lang, Herbert H. "Fort Worth's Role in the Origins of the Helium Industry." *West Texas Historical Association Year Book* 47 (1971): 127–145.
Link, Arthur S. "The Federal Reserve Policy and the Agricultural Depression of 1920–21." *Agricultural History* 20 (1946): 166–175.
———. "The Wilson Movement in Texas, 1910–1912." *Southwestern Historical Quarterly* 48 (October 1944): 169–185.
Maddox, James S. "The Bankhead-Jones Farm Tenant Act." *Law and Contemporary Problems* 4 (October 1937): 434–455.
Maris, Paul V. "Farm Tenancy." In U.S. Department of Agriculture, *Yearbook of Agriculture, 1940.* Washington, D.C.: U.S. Government Printing Office, 1940.
Marquis, J. Clyde. "How the Congress Handles Farm Needs." *Country Gentleman* 84 (July 5, 1919): 17, 34.
———. "The Railroad Question in Congress." *Country Gentleman* 84 (November 8, 1919): 18, 58.
———. "Who's Who in the New Congress." *Country Gentleman* 86 (April 9, 1921): 18.
Maupin, Michael W., and Richie, Albert, II. "The Application of Common-Law Contract Principles in the Court of Claims: 1950 to Present." *Virginia Law Review* 49 (May 1963): 850.

Bibliography 279

May, Irvin, Jr. "Marvin Jones: Agrarian and Politician." *Agricultural History* 51 (April 1977): 421–440.

———. "Marvin Jones: Representative of and for the Panhandle." *West Texas Historical Association Year Book* 52 (1976): 91–104.

———. "Peter Molyneaux and the New Deal," *Southwestern Historical Quarterly* 73 (January 1970): 309–325.

———. "Welfare and Ranchers: The Emergency Cattle Purchase Program and Emergency Work Relief Program in Texas, 1934–1935." *West Texas Historical Association Year Book* 47 (1971): 3–19.

Moody, M. L. "A Course of Study for Rural Schools." *Texas School Journal* 20 (September 1902): 81–84.

Morgenthau, Henry, Jr. "The Morgenthau Diaries: The Paradox of Poverty and Plenty." *Colliers* 120 (October 25, 1947).

Murphy, Paul. "The New Deal Agricultural Problem and the Constitution." *Agricultural History* 29 (October 1955): 160–169.

"Nation-Wide Problems of Farm Tenancy." *Congressional Digest* 16 (February 1937): 37–64.

O'Brien, Patrick. "A Re-Examination of the Senate Farm Bloc, 1921–1933." *Agricultural History* 67 (July 1973): 248–263.

Owsley, Harriet Chappell. "The Morton B. Howell Papers." *Tennessee Historical Quarterly* 25 (Fall 1966): 287–309.

Patenaude, Lionel V. "The Texas Congressional Delegation." *Texana* 11 (Winter 1971): 3–16.

Preston, Howard H., and Bennett, Victor W. "Agricultural Credit Legislation of 1933." *Journal of Political Economy* 42 (February 1934): 6–33.

Purzyck, Stanley J. "The Congressional Preference Case in the United States Court of Claims." *Catholic University of America Law Review* 10 (January 1961): 35–43.

Rasmussen, Wayne D., and Baker, Gladys. "A Short History of Price Support and Adjustment Legislation and Programs for Agriculture, 1933–1965." *Agricultural Economic Research* 18 (July 1966): 69–78.

Rogers, Tommy W. "Origin and Destination of Tennessee Migrants, 1850–1860." *Tennessee Historical Quarterly* 27 (Summer 1968): 118–122.

Saloutos, Theodore. "New Deal Agricultural Policy: An Evaluation." *Journal of American History* 61 (September 1974): 394–416.

Scott, Thomas A. "The Impact of Tennessee's Migrating Sons." *Tennessee Historical Quarterly* 27 (Summer 1968): 123–141.

Shea, Francis M. "Statutory Jurisdiction of the Court of Claims: Past, Present, and Future." *Federal Bar Journal* 29 (Summer 1970): 160.

Slichter, Gertrude Almy. "Franklin D. Roosevelt and the Farm Policy,

1929–1932." *Mississippi Valley Historical Review* 43 (September 1956): 238–258.

"Systematic Discrimination in the Indian Claims Commission: The Burden of Proof in Redressing Historical Wrongs." *Iowa Law Review* 57 (June 1972): 1300–19.

Tugwell, Rexford. "Some Aspects of New Deal Farm Policy: The Resettlement Idea." *Agricultural History* 33 (October 1959): 159–163.

Newspapers

Amarillo (Texas) *Evening Post*. 1924.
Amarillo (Texas) *Globe*. File on Marvin Jones.
Amarillo (Texas) *News*. File on Marvin Jones.
Canyon (Texas) *News*. 1906–1910, 1927–1955.
Chicago Sun. 1944.
Clarksville (Texas) *Standard*. May 17, 1856.
Claude (Texas) *News*. 1920.
Columbus (Nebr.) *Daily Telegram*. 1925–1936.
Commercial and Financial Chronicle. 1922–1928.
Dalhart (Texas) *Texan*. 1933–1935.
Dallas (Texas) *Morning News*. 1916–1976.
Fort Worth (Texas) *Star Telegram*. 1931.
Gainesville (Texas) *Register*. 1917.
Houston (Texas) *Chronicle*. 1933.
Kiplinger Agricultural Letter. Washington, D.C. 1930–1945.
Lawton (Okla.) *Daily Constitution*. 1916.
Lockney (Texas) *Beacon*. 1919.
Motley County (Texas) *News*. 1934–1938.
New York World. 1925.
New York Times. 1916–1976.
Pampa (Texas) *Daily News*. 1936.
Panhandle (Texas) *Herald*. 1919.
Quanah (Texas) *Tribune*. 1917.
Spearman (Texas) *Reporter*. 1927.
Tulia (Texas) *Herald*. 1974.
Washington (D.C.) *Post*. 1916–1976.
Washington (D.C.) *Star*. 1962.

Unpublished Materials

Barnett, Elva Marshall. "Paul Whitfield Horn, 1870–1932." Master's thesis, Texas Technological College, 1938.

Christensen, Alice M. "Agricultural Pressure and Governmental Response in the United States." Ph.D. dissertation, University of California, 1937.

Dawkins, Mrs. E. F. "The Texas Democratic Primary Election of 1910." Master's thesis, Texas Technological College, 1948.

Ferrell, Henry Clifton, Jr. "Claude A. Swanson of Virginia." Ph.D. dissertation, University of Virginia, 1964.
Floyd, Fred. "A History of the Dust Bowl." Ph.D. dissertation, University of Oklahoma, 1950.
Harvey, Nyla. "Social and Economic History of Borger, Texas." MS. Panhandle-Plains Historical Museum, Canyon, Texas.
"He Lives, He Lives." Mimeographed. Overton, Texas: First Methodist Church, 1973.
Jones, Ralph Wood. "A History of Southwestern University." Ph.D. dissertation, University of Texas, 1960.
Pearson, John E. "Cotton Policies and the Economic Welfare of Cotton Producers." Ph.D. dissertation, Indiana University, 1956.
Willborn, Glen DeWitt. "A History of Southwestern University, Georgetown, Texas." Master's thesis, Southwestern University, 1928.

Interviews

Anderson, Clinton. Interview with author, August 10, 1972.
Bledsoe, Samuel. Interview with Dean Albertson, 1954. Columbia Oral History Project.
Bresnahan, Pauline. Interview with author, July 6, 1972.
Cowen, Wilson. Interview with author, June 29, 1972.
Davis, Chester C. Interviews with Dean Albertson, 1952, 1953. Columbia Oral History Project.
Deschler, Lewis. Interview with author, October 15, 1971.
Durfee, James R. Interview with author, June 29, 1972.
Dykes, Jeff. Interview with author, August 8, 1972.
Evans, Rudolf M. Interviews with Dean Albertson, 1952, 1953. Columbia Oral History Project.
Haley, J. Evetts. Interview with author, May 21, 1973.
Hardeman, D. B. Interview with author, August 17, 1972.
Hays, Brooks. Interview with author, June 6, 1973.
Hill, Carl, Jr. Interview with author, May 21, 1973.
Hutson, John B. Interview with Dean Albertson, 1952. Columbia Oral History Project.
Johnson, Mrs. Lyndon B. Interview with author, June 6, 1974.
Jones, Herbert King, and Jones, Franklin Pierce. Interviews with author, May 24, May 25, 1973.
Jones, Marvin. Interviews with author, March 22, 1971, August 12, 1971, October 15, 1971, June 23, 1972, July 20, 1972, June 5, 1973, June 11, 1973, January 14, 1974.
———. Interview with David Murrah, August 1, 1972. Texas Tech University, Southwest Collection.
———. Interview with Dean Albertson, 1952. Columbia Oral History Project.

———. Interview with Elizabeth Kaderli, March 22, 1969. Lyndon B. Johnson Library, Austin, Texas.
———. Interview with James S. Ward, October 11, 1967.
———. Interview with Jerry Hess, 1970. Harry S. Truman Library.
Mahon, George. Interview with author, October 15, 1971.
Mills, Wilbur. Interview with author, August 17, 1972.
Nichols, Jimmy. Interview with author, August 11, 1973.
Patman, Wright. Interview with author, October 16, 1971.
Pepper, Claude. Interview with author, May 16, 1972.
Poage, W. R. Interviews with author, October 15, 1971, August 8, 1972.
Porter, Paul. Interview with author, June 15, 1973.
Ramspeck, Robert. Interview with author, August 11, 1972.
Rasmussen, Wayne. Interview with author, August 16, 1972.
Shanks, Graham. Telephone conversation with author, August 14, 1972.
Simms, Johnnie. Telephone conversation with author, June 14, 1973.
Spann, Mrs. John M. (Altravene Clark). Interview with author, March 23, 1973.
Sparkman, John. Interview with author, August 11, 1972.
Sutton, William. Interview with author, May 23, 1973.
Taber, Louis. Interview with Dean Albertson, 1956. Columbia Oral History Project.
Timmons, Bascom M. Interview with author, 1973.
Umphres, Hugh L. Interview with author, May 23, 1973.
Van Huss, Lotes. Interview with author, July 14, 1972.
Ward, James S. Interviews with author, August 10, 1972, August 16, 1972.
Ware, Tolbert. Interview with author, May 23, 1973.
Wright, Jim. Interview with author, August 11, 1972.

Index

Agricultural Adjustment Act of 1933, 102–107, 118, 120, 126, 139–141, 231, 234, 259
Agricultural Adjustment Act of 1938, 164–168, 170, 174, 259
Agricultural Adjustment Administration, 111, 116–117, 120–121, 182, 215
Agricultural Adjustment Amendments Act (1935), 135–139, 259
Agricultural Conference of 1922, 66
agricultural credit, 56, 59–60, 101–102, 104–108, 122–123
agricultural imports, 52–53; Aswell on, 56; of coconut milk, 56; of sugar, 121–122
Agricultural Marketing Act (1929), 76, 82
agricultural research, 74; appropriations for, 56, 116–117, 133; in cotton, 76, 164, 167–168; Jones's proposals for, 135, 161–162
agriculture: after New Deal, 175; and Congress, 48; and cotton surpluses, 75; depression in, 55; and domestic allotment, 89–91, 95–97, 142, 188; during WW I, 35, 40; during WW II, 192, 194–197, 213–222 passim, 226, 248; and Export Debenture Plan, 52, 58–78, 83–84, 89, 91–92, 137, 142; farm bloc and, 50, 52–53; FDR and, 92–94; finance for, 47, 53–55, 59–60, 82, 84–86, 101–113 passim, 122–123, 129, 152, 158–159, 162, 166, 176–177, 188 (see also farm finance; New Deal, banking and); Landon on, 148–149; lobbyists for, 50; McNary-Haugenism and, 58, 60, 64, 66–73, 83, 137; New Deal and (see New Deal, agricultural conditions during, agricultural legislation of); under Harding, 47; under Hoover, 82, 91, 93–94; westward expansion of, 3–4, 6, 7–8; world markets for, 74, 89, 175
Air Terminal Services, Inc. v. *United States*, 247
A.L.A. Schechter Poultry Corporation v. *United States*, 138
Alexander, Will W., 127, 129, 156
Amarillo, Texas, 18–19, 30, 132, 181
American Bankers Association, 178
American Cotton Shippers Association, 175
American Farm Bureau Federation, 89, 135, 160, 162, 174–175, 178
American Federation of Labor, 192
American Freedom from Hunger Foundation, 258
American National Livestock Association, 115, 178
Anderson, Sydney, 55
Andreson, August, 137, 165, 186, 206
Appleby, Paul, 127, 156, 183–184, 200, 202, 215
Aswell, James, 51, 56, 79

Bailey, Joseph Weldon, 9, 18
Baldwin, C. B. ("Beanie"), 213, 215

283

Baldwin, Sidney, 132, 154
Bankhead, John Hollis II, 117–121, 135, 137, 140, 175–176; and Farmers Home Act, 153–154; and tenancy legislation, 129–130, 151–158
Bankhead, William Brockman, 117, 124, 163, 165, 184
Bankhead Cotton Control Act, 117–120, 137, 141–142, 232–233
Bankhead-Jones Farm Tenancy Act, 151–158, 259
Bank Holiday of 1933, 102
bankruptcy, 10, 47. See also New Deal, banking and
barley, 116
Barrett, Leonidas C., 19–21, 24
Barron, Jerome, 250
Bateson-Stole, Inc. v. *United States*, 247
Beam, Harry, 100–101
Bell, J. Ross, 72
Bell, Otho, 241
Benedict, Murray, 106, 108
Bennett, Hugh, 132–134
Benson, Ezra Taft, 207
Berger, Victor, 44
Bilbo, Theodore, 168
Bishop, Ed, 180
Bishop, Henry, 21
Bivins, Julian, 114, 123
Black, A. G., 178
Black, Eugene, 30, 33
Black, Hugo, 250
Black, John D., 90
Black, Sam, 16
Boileau, Gerald, 100–101, 165
Bolin Drive-a-Way Co., Corporation v. *United States*, 230–231
Bowles, Chester, 217
Box, John, 74
Boyd, Bart, 215
Boyer, Alton, 251
Bradley, Frederick, 203
Bradley, Omar, 230
Bradley, William S., 147
Brand, Charles, 58
Bravo Ranch, 21
Brenckman, Fred, 207
Briggs, Clay, 74

Briscoe, Dolph, Sr., 114
Brock, J. E., 115
Brown, R. W., 151
Browning, James N., 21
Buchanan, James P. ("Buck"), 74, 134, 137–139, 142, 181
Byrnes, James: activities of, 199, 217, 222; characteristics of, 204, 225; and Jones, 183, 195, 225, 227; and Office of Economic Stabilization, 191–192, 194; and War Food Administration, 193, 197, 203, 225
Byrns, Joseph W., 125, 143, 159

C.C.M. Pedersen v. *United States*, 239
Cade, James, 77
Cal Farley's Boys Ranch, 259
Calvert Distilling Company v. *United States*, 231–232
Cannon, Clarence, 177, 196
Capper-Haugen bill, 68
Capper-Volstead Cooperative Marketing Act, 56
Carden, Cap R., 100–101
Carey, Robert D., 68, 115
Carr, Mary, 14
Carraway, Hattie, 71
cattle, 8, 35, 44; during WW II, 195, 211, 216–217; Export Debenture Plan and, 69–70, 137; Jones-Connally Act and, 113–117, 259; McNary-Haugenism and, 66–67, 70, 137; New Deal and, 101, 107, 113–117, 259; tubercular, 116–117; under Hoover, 94
Cellar, Emanuel, 88
Charles Dean Lesley v. *State of Oklahoma*, 257–258
Charles N. Stillman, Administrator of the Estate of Gerald C. Stillman, Deceased v. *United States*, 240
Christopherson, Charles, 66
Civilian Conservation Corps, 182
Clarendon College, 14
Clark, Champ, 30–31, 34, 48
Clark, John D., 100, 107
Clayton, W. L., 200

Index

Cobbin, Leroy, 227
Collier, James W. ("Billy"), 84
Committee on Farm Tenancy, 151, 153–155
Committee on World Food Crisis, 258
Commodity Credit Corporation, 161, 209–210, 212, 215, 221
congressional election: of 1916, 23–28; of 1918, 40; of 1934, 124; of 1936, 144–146; of 1938, 171; of 1940, 179–181
congressional reference cases, 231–235
Conkin, Paul, 99
Connally, Thomas Terry, 74, 92, 114–115
Conner, Arthur B., 133, 167
contract cases, 244–248
Colley, Harold D., 206
Coolidge, Calvin, 47, 54, 58–61, 63, 68–69, 71
Cooper, John Sherman, 253
Cora C. Farley v. *United States*, 236–237
corn, 4, 8, 12, 124; bloc, 50, 66; during WW II, 218; Export Debenture Plan and, 69; McNary-Haugenism and, 66; New Deal and, 123; tariff and, 52
Costigan, Edward, 121
Cotton, Felix, 240
cotton, 4, 8, 14–15, 35, 89; after New Deal, 174–176; and Bankhead Cotton Control Act, 232–233; bloc, 50; crop insurance for, 167; and domestic allotment, 95; during WW I, 37; Export Debenture Plan and, 69, 73; exports of, 175; FDR on, 93; Federal Farm Board and, 86, 88–89; Jones on, 50, 74–76, 96, 164, 167–170, 175–176; McNary-Haugenism and, 66–67; and New Deal, 101, 106–107, 110, 117–120, 123–124, 137–138, 141–142, 164, 167–170, 172, 175–176, 232–233; new markets for, 74; new uses for, 75–76; and Philippine independence, 65; reports about, 74–

76; research on, 167–170
crop insurance, 167–174
Cowart, William, 241
Cowen, Wilson, 208
Cox, Edward, 186
Crudgington, Jonathan W., 40
Cummings, Fred, 101, 140
Custer City, Texas, 7

dairy products: coconut milk competes with, 63–65; during WW II, 210–211; McNary-Haugenism and, 67; and New Deal, 101, 115–116
Dalhart, Texas, 182
damages, concept of, 236, 244
Davis, Chester: and agricultural legislation, 66, 90, 137–140, 178; and War Food Administration, 193–194, 196, 198–199, 203–204, 206–207, 210
Democratic party, 10; and Al Smith, 72–73; campaigns of, 27, 62–63, 123–124, 146–150, 183–185; conflict in, 61–63, 83; and farm vote, 57, 58, 123–124, 146–147; and Harding scandals, 57; Jones on principles of, 130–131 n.7; and Wilson's health, 46–47
Dempsey Act, 133
Dennis, Frank, 240
Dent, Hubert, 34
Deschler, Lewis, 32
Dirksen, Everett, 143
Disney, Wesley, 182
domestic allotment, 89–91, 95–97, 142, 188
Doughton, Robert, 159
Doxey, Wall, 100–101, 107, 119, 143, 163, 186
drought, 12, 111–115, 17, 123, 132, 148, 248
Duck Creek (Garland), Texas, 8
Duncan, Richard, 124
Dust Bowl, 111–115, 117, 128, 132–133

East Texas Chamber of Commerce, 164, 168
Eighteenth Congressional District,

41, 144; impact of New Deal on, 181–183
Eisenhower, Dwight D., 230
Elchibegoff v. *United States*, 235
Ellendar, Allen, 175
Ellerd, Reuben, 22, 24, 28
Elm Grove School, 13–15
Emergency Agricultural Credits Act, 53
Emergency Farm Mortgage Act (1933), 106–108
emergency tariff, 52
Ervin, Sam, 241
Esch-Cummins Act, 45
Evans, Rudolph ("Spike"), 205
Evans, Silliman, 92
Evans, W. Ney, 250
ever-normal granary, 160–162, 165–166
Executive Order 6084 (1933), 101–102, 104, 107
Export Debenture Plan, 52, 58–78, 83–84, 89, 91–92, 137, 142
Ezekiel, Mordecai, 95, 102

farm blocs, 50, 53
farm cooperatives, 56, 59
Farm Credit Act, 102, 107–108, 259
Farm Credit Administration, 130, 178; establishment of, 101, 104; expansion of, 128; and farm mortgages, 113–114; loans of, 182; and tenant program, 153
farmers, 4, 9; Jones and, 99, 230–231, 233; on New Deal cotton program, 117–119, 146, 164; on tariff, 60; world markets' impact on, 56, 74. See also agriculture; New Deal, agricultural conditions during; tenancy
Farmers' National Grain Corporation, 160
Farmers' Union, 89, 160, 178, 192, 207, 255
farm finance: after New Deal, 174; banking and, 101–102, 104–108, 129, 178; Commodity Credit Corporation and, 161, 209–210, 212, 221; Coolidge on, 59–60; during the 1920's, 47, 53–55; Farm Credit Administration and, 101–102, 104, 107–108, 113–114, 128–129, 153, 175, 178, 182; FDR on, 158; Federal Farm Mortgage Corporation and, 113–114, 178; Jones on, 84–86, 95, 101–102, 104–109, 112–114, 122–123, 128, 129, 152–154, 158–159, 162, 164, 166, 176–177, 188, 260; legislation regarding, 116, 122–123, 153–154, 166; National Agricultural Conference of 1935 and, 135–136; Miller on, 145; problems of, under Hoover, 82, 91–92; tenancy and, 128–132, 140, 151–158, 177–178, 259
farm labor deferments, 213, 221–222
Farm Loan Act of 1916, 53, 129
Farm Security Administration, 155, 213, 215
Federal Crop Insurance Corporation, 166
Federal Emergency Relief Administration, 109, 112
Federal Farm Board, 82, 86–87, 91
Federal Farm Mortgage Corporation, 113–114, 178
Federal Surplus Commodities Corporation, 139, 166
Federal Surplus Relief Corporation, 116
Ferguson, Homer, 203
Ferris, Scott, 29
Finnell, H. H., 135
Fish, Hamilton, Jr., 87, 143, 186–187
Fite, Gilbert C., 65
Flannagan, John, 100–101, 160–161, 163
Fletcher, Duncan U., 107
flax, 116, 118
food distribution, 35; during WW II, 194–195, 197, 200, 203, 210 (*see also* U.N. Conference on Food and Agriculture); and domestic allotment, 95; effect of tariffs on, 60; federal government and, 87; Jones on, 69–70, 84, 88, 205, 258; New

Index 287

Deal and (*see* New Deal, agricultural legislation of, relief legislation of); Office of Economic Stabilization and, 191, 197; Red Cross and, 86; world markets and, 89
food production, 35; effect of tariff on, 60; FDR on, 93; Jones on, 69, 205–206, 210–212, 214–222; New Deal and (*see* New Deal, agricultural legislation of); in WW II, 192, 194, 196, 200. *See also* U.N. Conference on Food and Agriculture
Ford, Henry, 54
Fordney-McCumber Tariff, 53, 59–60, 67, 69
foreign trade, 53, 55–56, 90, 103, 175–176
Frank, Jerome, 127
Frazier-Lemke Bankruptcy Bill, 122
freight rates, 30, 40, 44, 55; after New Deal, 174; Coolidge on, 59; Jones on, 95, 161, 166; and President's Farm Commission, 68
fruits and vegetables, 4, 8, 11; during WW II, 211, 216–218, 222
Fuller, Claude, 124
Fulmer, Hampton, 80; and Emergency Farm Mortgage Act, 107; position of, on House Agriculture Committee, 100–101, 102–103, 179; praises Jones, 186; protests Louisiana research station, 169; and relief legislation, 88; and tenancy issue, 155–156
Future Trading Act: 53

Gainesville, Texas, 8–9, 38
Gard, Warren, 43
Garner, John Nance, 79, 98; as Jones's sponsor, 30–31, 33, 48–49, 94; on Farm Credit Administration, 104; offers Jones position on veterans' committee, 67–68; opposes Rainey-Norbeck bill, 91; political aspirations of, 92; and Red River bridge, 38
Garrett, Daniel, 74
Garrett, Finis, 67

Gaston, James (great-grandfather), 6
Gaston, Mary (great-grandmother), 6
Gaston, Sarah (Mrs. John Hawkins, grandmother), 6
Gilchrist, Fred, 101
Gillett, Frederick H., 48, 54, 61
Glass, Carter, 46
Glidden Company v. *Zdanok,* 252
Glover, David D., 100
Gooding Bill (1922), 66
Goss, Albert, 178
government employee reduction cases, 237
Gray, Chester, 161
Gregory, Clifford V., 127, 184
Griggs, Lewis, 241
G. S. Kincaid v. *United States,* 234–235
Guleke, James O., 23, 27
Guyer, Ulysses S., 186

Hamilton, Alexander, 71, 99
Hamilton, C. Horace, 157
Hancock, Fran, 213, 215
Hand, Learned, 250
Harding, Warren G., 46–47, 53, 56–57
Hardy, Rufus, 42
Harlan, John, 252
Harrison, Pat, 48, 121
Hatch, Carl, 182
Haugen, Gilbert, 49–51, 58, 79, 81, 100
Hawk, Wilbur, 111
Hawkins, John (grandfather), 6, 7
Haworth, Mary, 240
Hearne, Clayton, 15, 18
Hege, James, Jr., 4
Hege, William, 4
Hill, Grover, 114, 123, 195, 205, 208, 215
Hirth, W. W., 66
hogs, 8; domestic allotment and, 95; during WW II, 197, 216; Export Debenture Plan and, 69; FDR on aid for, 93; McNary-Haugenism and, 66–67
Home Owners' Loan Corporation, 109, 181

288　INDEX

Hoover, Herbert, 91, 109; failures of, 93; favors food-management controls, 192; named war food administrator, 36; nominated for president, 72; opposes Export Debenture Plan, 73, 83; and relief measures, 77, 84
Hope, Clifford: and Emergency Farm Mortgage Act, 107; opposes controls, 161; position of, on Agriculture Committee, 100–101; praises Jones, 186; supports farm loans, 142; on Wallace, 104
Hope–Norbeck bill, 90
Hopkins, Harry, 112, 198, 205
Houston, David, 35, 37
Howard, Edgar, 68
Hudgens, Roy W., 213
Hudspeth, Elmer, 74
Humphrey, Hubert, 253
Hutson, Jack, 209–210, 215–216, 221
Hyde, Arthur, 83, 85–86

Ickes, Harold, 112, 133–134
import/export controls: Export Debenture Plan and, 52, 58–78, 83–84, 89, 91–92, 137, 142; McNary-Haugenism and, 58, 60, 64, 66–73, 83, 137; New Deal and, 121
Indian claims cases, 191, 229
Intermediate Credit Act, 56
Interstate Commerce Commission, 45, 173
Isbell, Fletcher, 10

Jackson, Burris, 164, 167
Jackson, Robert, 223, 227
Jacoby, Sidney, 235
Jay, John, 227
Jefferson, Thomas, 130–131, 188, 261
J. H. Crain v. United States, 233
Johnson, Hiram, 61
Johnson, Hugh S., 58, 65, 112
Johnson, Luther, 158, 168
Johnson, Lyndon B., 239, 253–254
Joint Committee of Agriculture Inquiry, 55
Jones, Dora Maud (sister), 12
Jones, Franklin King (brother), 23

Jones, Herbert (brother), 9
Jones, Horace (father), 6, 8–11, 54
Jones, John Marvin: agrarian philosophy of, xv, 3, 13–14, 37, 69–70, 88, 96, 99–100, 130–131, 152, 156, 171, 185, 202, 224–225, 259–261; birth of, 8; character of, xiv, 3–4, 13, 16–17, 29, 124, 190, 200–201, 232, 240–241, 250, 255, 258–259; death of, 261–262; dines with FDR, 223; early influences on, 9–13, 16–17; education of, 13–17; farming of, 14–15, 54; genealogy of, 4; legal practice of, 18–22, 30; military service of, 40–41; on National Commission of Food Marketing, 255–256; religious beliefs of, xiv, 9–11, 20–21, 241, 258
in U.S. House: and Agricultural Adjustment Act of 1933, 102–107, 126; and Agricultural Adjustment Amendments Act of 1935, 136–138; and Agricultural Conference of 1922, 66; agricultural views of, 49, 69–70, 83–84, 88, 91, 95–96, 99–100, 105, 109, 127–128, 130, 151–152, 156, 160, 260; attitude of, toward relief and welfare, 108–109, 112–113, 128; attitude of, toward Supreme Court, 159; attitude of, toward WW I, 33; and Bankhead Cotton Control Act, 117–120; changes stand on Muscle Shoals, 54–55; as chairman of Agriculture Committee, 79–91, 93–97; congressional perspective of, 187–188, 261; as congressman, 37–38, 49–51, 57, 80–82, 96–97, 102–103, 108–109, 119, 130–131, 163–164, 171, 174, 177; constituent relations of, 11, 123, 140, 164, 181–183, 206; on Coolidge, 60–61, 68, 71; and cotton, 50, 74–76, 164, 167–170, 175–176; critical of Houston, 37; and Farm Credit Act, 107–108; and Farm Credit Administration, 101–102, 104, 175; and farm finance, 85–86, 101–102, 104–109, 112–113, 122–123, 129, 152, 158–

159, 162, 164, 166, 176–177, 188; and Farm Research Act, 135; and Farm Security bill, 155; and Farmers' Home bill, 153–154; and federal laboratories, 167–170; on Harding's agricultural legislation, 53–56; on Haugen, 51; and House reforms, 45, 258; and H. R. 13991, 94–97; influences on career of, 30–31; and Joint Committee of Agriculture Inquiry, 55; and Jones-Connally Act, 113–117; last congressional speeches of, 185–186, 260; and Lever Food and Fuel Control Act, 36–37; and New Deal, 99–100, 127–128, 187–188 (see also New Deal, agricultural legislation of); opposes McNary-Haugenism, 67–74; as political campaigner, 23–29, 60–63, 72–73, 77, 144–146, 171, 179–181, 183–185; and price controls, 36–37, 89, 166; and protective tariff, 51–53, 67, 69, 136; relationship of, with farm blocs, 50; relationship of, with FDR, 92, 97, 103, 158–159, 161–162, 164–165, 171–173, 179–181; and second AAA, 164–168; and section 32, 120, 136–138, 162, 175; and soil conservation, 132–135, 161, 174, 191; and Soil Conservation and Domestic Allotment Act, 142–144; and sugar, 20–22; supports Wilson, 37, 39; and tenancy legislation, 129–131, 140, 151–158, 160–164, 174, 177
in War Food Administration: administrative policies of, 208–209, 218; agricultural policies of, 196–199, 204–206, 210–212, 215–216, 218–222, 226; appointed war food administrator, 204–207; characteristics of, 212–214, 224–226, 261; and Food Fights for Freedom, 211–212; and Office of Economic Stabilization, 195–204; and Office of War Mobilization, 204; and production goals, 210–211, 214, 218–222; relationship of, with Congress, 195–197, 212, 221–223; and victory gardens, 215–216
—in U.S. Court of Claims: administration of, 251–254; appointed chief judge, 227; appointed to, 179, 189; on battlefield pay cases, 240; on concept of damages, 236, 238, 244; on congressional reference cases, 231, 235; on constitutional court issue, 245, 251–253; on contract cases, 244–248; and court building, 253–254; and federal judiciary, 126, 172, 205, 224; on government reduction cases, 237; on Indian claims, 191, 229; judicial characteristics of, 190, 227–228, 248, 250–251, 261; judicial procedure of, 249–250; on Korean War military claims, 238, 241–242; legal philosophy of, 190, 235, 237, 241–243, 249–250, 257–258; on military retirement cases, 238; on overtime-pay cases, 236–237; on patent rights, 228–229; on property-requisition cases, 243–244; on survivor-benefit cases, 237; as senior judge, 255–262; on tax-refund suits, 248–249; on transportation cases, 229–231, 239

Jones, Metze (sister), 61
Jones, Nola Anna (sister), 12
Jones, Robert Delbert (brother), 8–9, 14, 16, 23
Jones, Robert Degge (grandfather), 4, 7–8
Jones, Robert Emmett, Jr., 253
Jones, Theodocia Hawkins (mother), 6, 8–11
Jones Act (1928), 75–76
Jones-Connally Act, 113–117, 259
Jones-Costigan Act, 120–122, 141, 259
judicial procedure, 249–250

Kamen Soap Products Co. v. *United States*, 249
Katz, Sanford, 251
Kelchner, Warren, 201
Kendrick, John B., 44, 56
Kennedy, John F., 254

INDEX

Kennedy, Mrs. John F., 253
Kerr-Smith Tobacco Act, 141–142
Ketcham, John, 69–71, 100
Ketcham-Jones bills, 71
Kincheloe, David, 64
King, Martha Eliza (Mrs. Robert Degge Jones, grandmother), 4
Kirkendall, Richard, 100
Kitchin, Claude, 34, 37
Kleberg, Richard, 100–101, 113, 116, 164, 187, 206
Knox, Frank, 198
Ku Klux Klan, 61–62

LaFollette Amendment (1934), 116–117
LaGuardia, Fiorello H., 86, 88
Lackey, J. H., 40
Ladd-Sinclair bill, 66
land-grant colleges and universities: and agricultural experiment stations, 68; and agricultural research, 58, 74–76, 116–117, 126, 133, 135, 161–162, 164, 167, 260; and cotton research, 167–170; and Farm Research Act, 135; research of, during 1920's, 55–56
Landon, Alfred M., 146–150
Lanham, Fritz G., 74, 79
Larsen, William, 100
Lawton, Oklahoma, 29
League of Nations, 41, 46
League of Women Voters, 249
Lee, Fred, 90, 94, 102
Lee, Larry W., 15–16
Lemke, William, 122
Les Misèrables, 238, 257
Lever, Asbury, 35
Lever Food and Fuel Control Act, 35–36
Lincoln, Murray, 200
Little, Edward, 66
Lodge, Henry Cabot, Sr., 61
Luce, Robert, 85–86
Ludlow, Louis, 87

McAdoo, William Gibbs, 61
MacArthur, Douglas, 240
McCarthy, Leighton, 223

McCormack, John, 84, 186
McCormick, Vance, 29
McCoy, Donald, 59
McDonald, J. E., 89, 164
McDuffie, John, 124
McGill, George, 160
McGill, Ralph, 213
McKinley-Adkins bill, 69–70
McKeown, Thomas D., 122
McLaughlin, Charles, 124
McNary, Charles, 58, 89, 107, 142
McNary-Haugenism, 58, 60, 64, 66–73, 83, 137
Madden, Wales, 228, 241, 250
Mahon, George, 262
Mansfield, Joseph J., 74, 79
Massachusetts Retail Grocers' Association, 218
Matasow, Allan, 218
Maupin, Michael W., 245, 247
Maverick, Maury, 187
Mayfield, Earle B., 74
meat packing: and black market, 195; and rationing, 216–219; regulation of, 52, 53; support for, 101
Miami, Texas, 14–15
military retirement cases, 238–239
milk, 63–65. *See also* dairy products
Miller, Clarence, 17
Miller, Ernest ("Dusty"), 19, 180
Miller, John, 145
Mitchell, William D., 71
Moffett, "Cotton George," 167
Mondell, Frank, 56
Moore, Walton, 67
Morgan, Gerald, 106, 162
Morgenthau, Henry, Jr., 94, 101, 104, 107–108, 139, 209
Morse, Wayne, 253
Murray, Reid, 206
Muscle Shoals, 54
Myers, William I., 94, 101–102, 104, 107, 140, 207

National Agricultural Conference (1935), 135–136
National Co-operative Council, 160–161
National Grange, 69–70, 89, 160–162

Index

National Industrial Recovery Act, 109, 133
National Recovery Administration, 112, 138
Nelson, Donald M., 192
Nelson, O. H., 21
Nelson, William, 100
New Deal: agricultural appropriations during, 137–139, 141, 162, 174–175; agricultural conditions during, 102, 110–115, 117–133 passim, 137–140, 157, 162–168 passim, 174–175, 234–235; agricultural legislation of, 101–110, 112–123, 128–139, 140–144, 151–158, 160–168, 170, 174, 234, 259; agricultural origins of, 94–97; banking and, 101–102, 104–109, 113–114, 122–123, 129; legal difficulties of, 138–142, 159–160, 163, 231–232; relief legislation of, 108–109, 112–114, 116–117, 121, 126–128, 137–139, 151–158, 166–167, 174–175, 182; and tenancy, 128–132, 140, 144, 151–158, 259
New Uses for Cotton Committee, 76
Newton, Walter, 44
Non-Partisan League, 59
Norbeck-Burtness bill, 60
Norris, George, 66, 147
Norris-Simpson amendment (1933), 106
Norris-Sinclair bill, 59

O'Brien, John, 106, 162
Office of Civilian Defense, 211
Office of Economic Stabilization, 191–192, 194–195, 204, 220
Office of Price Administration, 192, 195, 210–211, 215–217, 223
Office of Public Administration, 192, 195, 210–211, 216–217, 223
Office of War Information, 211
Office of War Mobilization, 204
O'Neal, Edward, 135, 175, 207
Otho G. Bell, William A. Cowart and Lewis W. Griggs v. *United States,* 241–242
overtime-pay cases, 236–237

Packers and Stockyards Act, 53, 59, 104
Palmer, Arthur W., 75
Pampa, Texas, 109
Panhandle Livestock Association, 115
parity: domestic allotment and, 89–91, 95–97, 142, 188; during New Deal (*see* New Deal, agricultural legislation of); during WW II, 196, 213, 220; Export Debenture Plan and, 52, 58–78, 83–84, 89, 91–92, 137, 142; McNary-Haugenism and, 58–60, 64, 66–73, 83, 137; Thomas-Swank bill and, 89
Parkinson, W. W., 146
Parran, Thomas, 200
patent rights cases, 228–229
Patman, Wright, 166
Patton, James G., 207
Patton, Nat, 164
peanuts, 116
Peek, George N., 58, 65–66, 90, 102, 137–138
Peery, Charles, 152
Perkins, Milo, 204
Philippine independence, 58, 63–65
Pickard, Edwart T., 75
Poage, W. R., 164, 255
Poe, Clarence, 127
Polk, James G., 100
Pope, James, 160
Pope, Joe, 23
Pope-McGill bill, 160, 166
Porter, Paul, 147–148, 210
Potato Act, 142
potatoes, 142, 167, 195, 218, 222
poultry, 211, 218, 222
Prescott, William, 22, 28
presidential election: of 1916, 24, 29–30; of 1920, 47–48; of 1924, 60–63; of 1928, 72; of 1932, 92–93; of 1936, 146–150; of 1940, 179, 183–185
President's Farm Commission (1925), 68
Pressman, Lee, 127, 140
price controls: during WW I, 35–37; during WW II, 195, 197, 198–199, 204, 210, 215; Jones on, 35–37, 53,

89, 166; Office of Economic Stabilization and, 191–192
price fixing, 35, 53
price supports: for cotton, 75; domestic allotment and, 89–91, 95–97, 142, 188; during New Deal (see New Deal, agricultural legislation of); during WW II, 212, 213, 216; Export Debenture Plan and, 52, 58–78, 83–84, 89, 91–92, 137, 142; Jones and, 175–176; McNary-Haugenism and, 58, 60, 64, 66–73, 83, 137; Thomas-Swank bill and, 89; War Finance Corporation and, 66; War Food Administration and, 216
production ceilings, 210
Progressive Party, 62–63
Prohibition, 40, 42–43, 46, 58
Purnell, Fred, 100

railroads, 44–45
Rainey, Homer, 105, 122–123, 125
Rainey-Norbeck bill, 90
Rankin, John, 124
rationing, 217, 219, 222
Rayburn, Sam: chairs Commerce Committee, 79; characteristics of, 81, 187; and Flannagan bill, 163; opposes McNary-Haugenism, 74; position of, on congressional reference jurisdiction, 252; relationship of, with Jones, 16, 30, 33, 38, 159, 183, 184; seeks to become Democratic floor leader, 124 n.21; supports Texas cotton laboratory, 168
Reconstruction Finance Corporation, 84–86, 210
religion, 4, 6, 21–22, 144, 241, 247–248; and food distribution, 258
Red Cross, 86
Red Scare (WW I), 44
Reed, Stanley, 139–140
Reedy, George, 239
relief and welfare: for drought and flood victims, 112; federal crop insurance as, 167; Hopkins and, 112; Jones and, 87–88, 108, 112, 128, 191, 258; La Follette amendment and, 116–117; section 32 funds for 139; surpluses and, 86–89, 116, 139, 176
Rhode Island Tool Company v. *United States,* 246
rice, 69, 101, 222
Richie, Albert, II, 245, 247
Robert Morass Lovett et al v. *United States,* 233–234
Roberta I. Thomas v. *United States,* 238
Roberts, Owen, 140–141, 227
Roberts, W. S., 14
Robinson, Joseph, 121, 138
Rogers, Ross, 179
Roosevelt, Franklin D., 101, 128, 171, 179–180; and agricultural legislation, 106–107, 108, 118, 122, 140–141, 164–168; agricultural views of, 92–93; characteristics of, 82; death of, 224; designates drought and flood relief, 112; endorses Muscle Shoals, 55; and Farm Credit Administration, 175; and farm finance, 114, 123, 158–159; health of, 223; inauguration of, 98–99; opposes section 32, 139; opposes Texas cotton laboratory, 169; position of, on tenancy, 128, 140, 148, 151, 161–163, 173, 177; relationship of, with Jones, 92, 97, 103, 158–159, 161–162, 164–165, 171–173, 179–181, 194, 201–207, 209, 223–224; and soil conservation, 133–134, 173; and sugar, 120–122; and Supreme Court, 159–160; and U.N. Conference on Food and Agriculture, 200–203; and War Food Administration, 192–194, 197–198, 203, 204–206, 209–210, 220
Roosevelt Agriculture Committee (1936), 147–150
Russell, Richard, 206
rye, 116

St. Regis Paper Company v. *United States,* 244

Index 293

Sanborn, Henry B., 21
Sanders, Morgan, 74
Schain, Josephine, 200
Schrieber, Hollis, 80–81
Schwartz, David, 235
Scott, Joe C., 213
section 32, 120, 136–138, 141, 162, 174–175, 196, 259
Sellers, Ashley, 208, 259
service-pay cases, 235–242
Settle, William H., 147
sheep, 66, 107, 115
Sheppard, Morris, 30, 74
Smith, Al, 61, 72–73, 77
Smith, Earl, 90
Smith, Ellison D. ("Cotton Ed"), 95, 142, 160; and Agricultural Adjustment Act of 1932, 106–107; and Agricultural Adjustment Act of 1938, 162, 166; as chairman of Senate Agriculture and Forestry Committee, 106–107, 116, 119, 162, 166; characteristics of, 82, 95, 101; cotton policies of, 175–176; and Jones-Connally Act, 116
Smith, Henry Nash, 260
Smoot-Hawley Tariff, 77
Snyder, John, 111, 123
socialism, 44, 46, 53, 86, 99, 128, 143
soil conservation, 72, 173, 175; after New Deal, 174; during WW II, 197, 203; FDR on, 128; Jones on, 95, 113, 133–135, 161–162, 174, 176, 181–182, 188, 191, 234–235, 260; Landon on, 149; legislation regarding, 142–144, 160–161, 163, 166, 174, 234, 259; research regarding, 132–133, 135, 182; Soil Conservation Service and, 133, 215
Soil Conservation and Domestic Allotment Act, 142–144, 160, 163, 174, 234, 259
Soil Conservation Service, 133, 215
sorghum, 8, 116
Southwestern University, 15–16, 259
soybeans, 218
Spann, Altravene Clark, 80–81, 147

Spillman, William J., 90
S. R. Brackin v. United States, 232–233
Stafford, William, 86
State of Texas v. Mrs. Edna Henson, 20–21
Steagall, Henry B., 105, 219
Stephens, John Hall, 21–22, 24, 27–29
Stewart, Charles L., 68
Stewart, George, 253
Stewart, Potter, 242
Stimpson, George, 240
Stimson, Henry, 198
Stinnett, A. S., 23
Stringer v. United States, 236
sugar, 52; New Deal programs and, 101, 121–122, 141, 222
Sumners, Hatton, 49, 74, 122, 159
surpluses, 163; of cotton, 74–75; Export Debenture Plan and, 72–73; FDR on, 93; and government distribution, 87–88; H.R. 13991 and, 95; McDonald on, 89; Jones on, 69, 95; New Deal programs and (*see* New Deal, agricultural conditions during, agricultural legislation of); under Harding, 47, 50, 56, 65; under Hoover, 82; and Red Cross distribution, 86; and world markets, 89
survivor's benefits cases, 237

Taber, John, 142
Taber, Louis, 69–70
Taft, Robert A., 179
tariffs, 52, 60, 73; effects of, 77; Jones on, 60, 67, 69–70, 141, 149; McNary-Haugenism and, 65; President's Farm Commission and, 68
Taylor, Jay, 114, 123–124, 205, 262
tax-refund suits, 248–249, 257
Teapot Dome, 57
tenancy, 173; during New Deal, 127–130, 132, 144, 157–158, 160–164; legislation regarding, 128–132, 151–158, 259
Tennessee Valley Authority, 108

Texas Agricultural Experiment Station, 75, 133
Texas A&M University, 135, 167, 169, 259
Texas and Southwestern Cattle Raisers' Association, 114–115
Texas Farm Bureau Cotton Association, 74
Thirteenth Congressional District, 22
Thomas, John William Elmer, 107
Thomas, Seth, 138
Thomas amendment, 106–107
Thomas-Swank bill, 89
Thomason, Ewing, 187, 206
Thompson, Ernest A., 23
Timmons, Bascom, 23, 38, 44, 83, 240
Tincher, Jasper Napoleon ("Poly"), 68
tobacco, 4, 37; crop insurance for, 167; domestic allotment and, 95; during WW II, 218; FDR on, 93; Kerr-Smith Tobacco Act and, 141; New Deal programs and, 101, 141
Tobey, Charles, 118–119, 143
Tolley, Howard, 142
Torn, Elmore, 168
Townsend Plan, 145–146
transportation, 182, 229–231, 239. *See also* freight rates
Treadway, Allen, 136
Treaty of Versailles, 41
Truman, Harry, 224, 227
Tucker Act, 244
Tugwell, Rexford, 94, 127, 151
Tulia, Texas, 38
Turkey Trot Ranch, 19
Turner, Thomas F., 23

Ulmstead, William, 213
U.N. Conference on Food and Agriculture (1943), 200–203, 210, 222
Underwood, Mell G., 124
Underwood, R. E., 23
U. S. Court of Claims: battlefield pay cases of, 240; on concept of damages, 236, 238, 244; characteristics of, 189; constitutional court issues of, 245, 251–253; contract cases of, 244–248; court building of, 253–254; and federal judiciary, 126, 172, 205, 224; government reduction cases of, 237; Indian claims cases of, 191, 229; Jones's administration of, 251–254; Jones appointed to, 179, 189; Jones appointed chief judge of, 227; judicial procedure of, 249–250; Korean military claims cases of, 238, 241–242; Madden's contributions to, 228, 241, 250; military retirement cases of, 238; origins of, 245, 251–253; overtime-pay cases of, 236–237; patent rights cases of, 228–229; property-requisition cases of, 243–244; survivor-benefit cases of, 237; tax-refund cases of, 248–249; transportation cases of, 229–231, 239
U.S. Department of Agriculture, 55–56, 89, 133, 155, 191, 195
U.S. Department of Interior, 133–134
U.S. House Agricultural Appropriations Committee, 176–177
U.S. House Agriculture Committee, 173–178; and Agricultural Conference of 1937, 160; Aswell on, 56; characteristics of, 173–178; composition of, 79–80, 100–101, 155 n.6, 173; considers Federal Farm Mortgage Corporation, 113; and cotton bloc, 50; and domestic allotment, 95–96, 143–144; during Hundred Days, 100–108; and Export Debenture Plan, 70–71; and food distribution, 85–88; Haugen and, 49–51; Jones and, 49, 79–80, 173–174, 176–178, 210–211; legislation of, 35–36, 89, 102–107, 113–119, 121–122, 137–139, 160, 162, 164–166; and McNary-Haugenism, 60, 66–67; and Muscle Shoals, 54; and NRA, 138; production goals of, 210–211; and section 32, 137–139; and soil conservation, 134, 143–144; and tenancy, 132, 144, 151–158, 174, 186–187; under

Hoover, 73–91, 93–97; and U.N. Conference on Food and Agriculture, 203
U.S. House Banking and Currency Committee, 85–86, 105, 209–212
U.S. House Committee on Committees, 49
U.S. House Committee on Expenditures in the Executive Departments, 134
U.S. House Committee on Expositions and Roads, 31
U.S. House Foreign Affairs Committee, 39
U.S. House Indian Affairs Committee, 22
U.S. House Industrial Arts Committee, 31
U.S. House Insular Affairs Committee, 31
U.S. House Interstate and Foreign Commerce Committee, 43
U.S. House Judiciary Committee, 49, 159
U.S. House Military Affairs Committee, 34, 54
U.S. House Reform in the Civil Service Committee, 31
U.S. House Rules Committee, 143, 156
U.S. House Special Committee on Post-War Economic Policy and Planning, 219
U.S. House Ways and Means Committee, 30–31, 48, 105
U.S. Senate Agriculture and Forestry Committee, 106–108, 116, 119, 121, 164; during second AAA, 164–168; and tenancy issue, 130
U.S. Senate Finance Committee, 121
U.S. Supreme Court, 103, 126, 138, 234
United States v. *Beuttas*, 246
United States v. *Butler*, 139, 159
United States v. *Mitchell*, 240
United States v. *Moorman*, 245
United States v. *Wunderlich*, 245
U.S. Treasury, 103

University of Texas School of Law, 16–17, 259
Uptown Club of Manhattan v. *United States*, 249

Valley View, Texas, 8
Van Huss, Lotus, 80–81
Vandenberg, Arthur, 121
veterans, 40, 43, 67
veterans' benefits, 43
victory gardens, 215
Vinson, Fred, 204, 210, 215, 220
Virgin Land, 260–261
vocational training, 40

Wagner, Robert F., 107
Wallace, Henry Agard, 94; and AAA, 140; agricultural policies of, 142, 175–176, 178, 196; and agricultural legislation, 90, 102, 107, 114–116, 119–120, 154; characteristics of, 148, 215, 241; and drought relief, 112; and NRA, 138; and research laboratories, 168–169; and tenancy, 160–164; as vice-presidential candidate, 183–185; and soil conservation, 134–135
Wallace, Henry C., 58
Walton, T. O., 135, 167, 207
War Advertising Council, 211
Ward, James, 225
war debts, 42
Ware, Charles, 15, 18, 23
Ware, Richard, 15, 18
War Finance Corporation, 53, 66
War Food Administration, 195, 197–199; administrative policies of, 208–209, 218; agricultural policies of, 210–226 passim; Davis and, 203–205; during WW I, 36; during WW II, 192–194; and Food Fights for Freedom, 211–212; and food spoilage, 223; Jones as head of, 204–207, 212–214, 224–226, 261; and Office of Economic Stabilization, 195–204; and Office of War Mobilization, 204; and price supports, 216; and production goals, 210–211, 214, 218–222; relation-

ship of, with Congress, 212, 221–223; reorganization of, 215; Truman on, 224; and victory gardens, 215–216
War Labor Board, 191–192
War Mobilization Board, 217
War Production Board, 192
Warren, Earl, 252, 254, 256
Warren, Lindsay, 159
Weideman, Carl, 105
Westbrook, Lawrence, 151
Whaley, Richard, 190, 195, 227
wheat, 4, 8, 12, 14, 96, 124; bloc, 50, 88; domestic allotment and, 95; during New Deal, 101, 110, 123; during WW I, 35; during WW II, 218; Export Debenture Plan and, 69, 73; FDR on, 93; Federal Farm Board and, 86–89; legislation regarding, 36, 60, 174–175; McNary-Haugenism and, 66–67
Wheeler, Katherine, 80
Whitaker, Samuel, 232–233, 254
Wichard, Claude, 192–196, 206, 223
Wigglesworth, Richard, 138
Wilcox, Walter, 182, 214

Williams v. *United States,* 251
Williams, Guinn, 79
Wilson, Milburn L., 94–95, 127
Wilson, Woodrow, 23–24, 29–30, 32–33, 36–37, 39–40, 46
Wittner v. *United States,* 236
W. O. Dillon v. *United States,* 248
woman suffrage, 40, 42–44, 46
Womer v. *United States,* 238
wool, 52, 66
Works Progress Administration, 182
World War I, 24, 32–35, 38–41
World War II: agricultural problems during, 195, 197, 213–214, 220–221, 223; consumption during, 211; Food Fights for Freedom campaign in, 211–212; food strategy during, 194–195, 199–200, 216, 218–222
World War Veterans' Committee, 67
Worley, Eugene, 206
Wurzbach, Henry, 74
Wyoming Stock Growers' Association, 115

Young, James, 35–36, 49
Youngblood, Bonney, 75

www.ingramcontent.com/pod-product-compliance
Lightning Source LLC
Chambersburg PA
CBHW030304080526
44584CB00012B/438